HISTORIC PHOTOS OF
ORANGE COUNTY

TEXT AND CAPTIONS BY LESLIE ANNE STONE

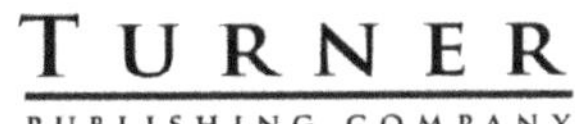

Another idyllic day dawns on Newport Harbor for these early morning anglers in 1960. Newport's 15 miles of beaches receive 10 million visitors a year, making the area one of Southern California's top tourist destinations. It's also a popular setting for television shows. In the 1960s scenes from *Gilligan's Island* were filmed in Newport Beach, and more recently, series based in the area have included *The OC* and *Arrested Development.*

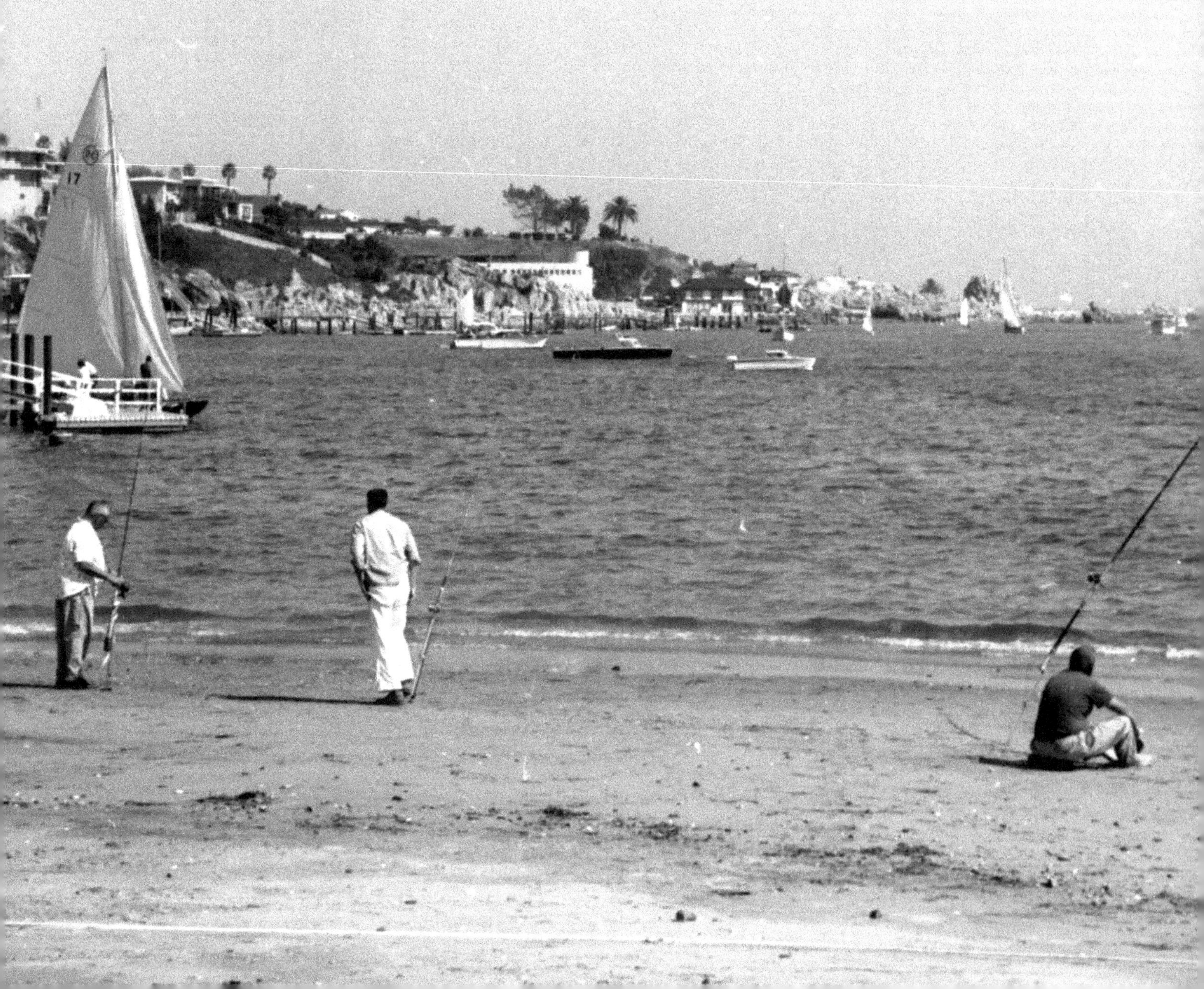

HISTORIC PHOTOS OF
ORANGE COUNTY

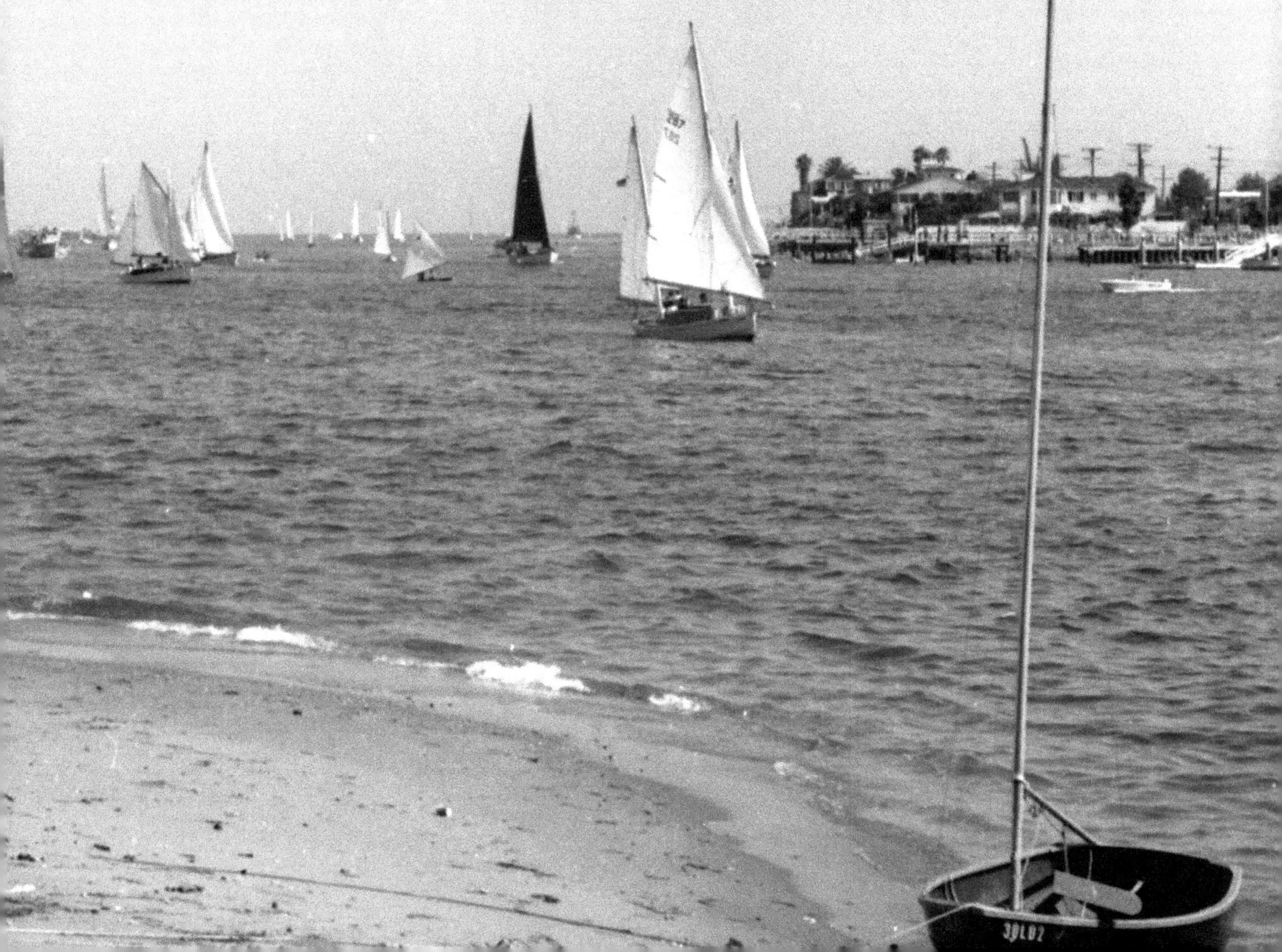

Turner Publishing Company
www.turnerpublishing.com

Historic Photos of Orange County

Library of Congress Control Number: 2008904903

ISBN-13: 978-1-59652-487-3

Printed in the United States of America

ISBN 978-1-68442-029-2 (hc)

Contents

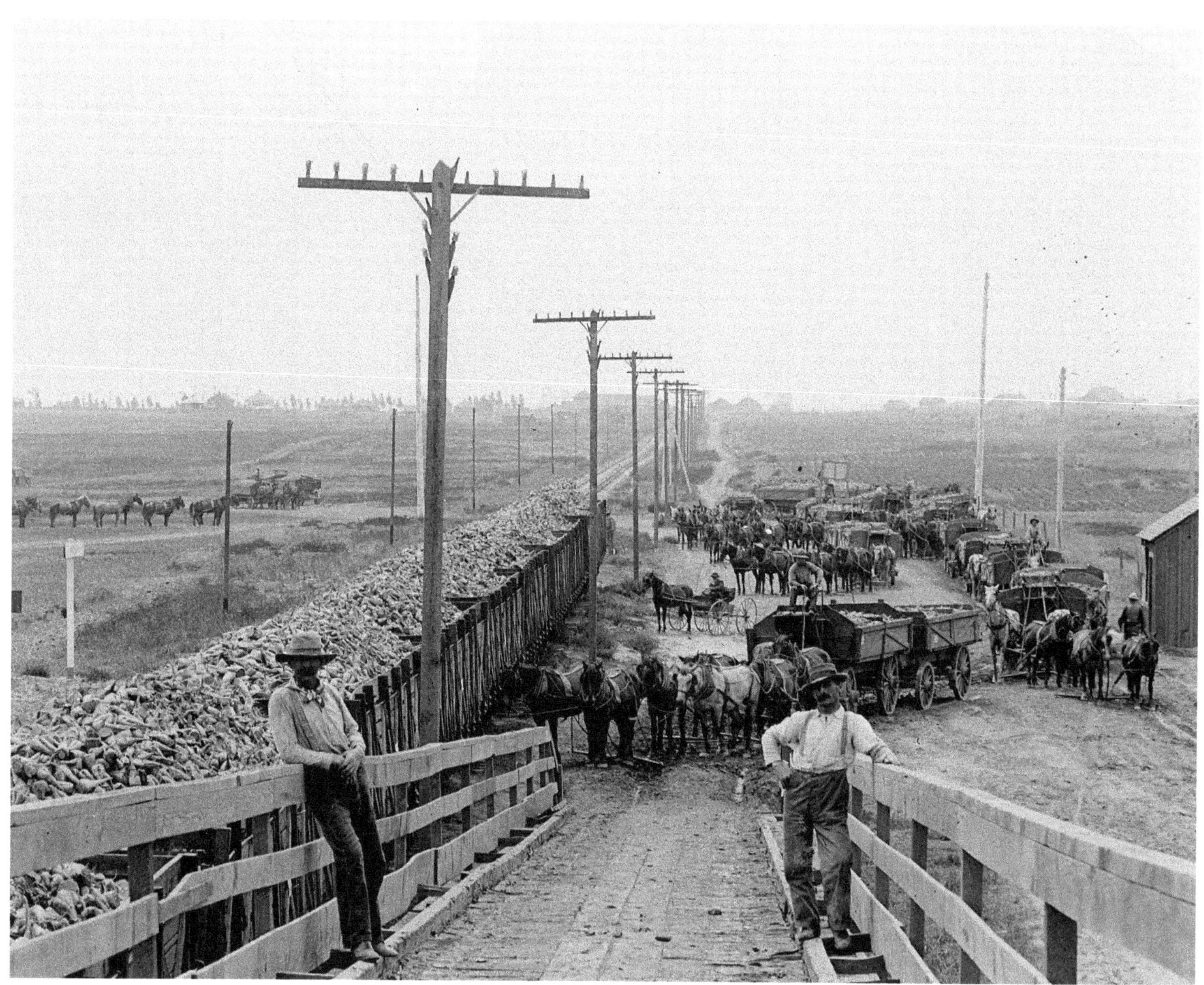

The sugar beet industry flourished in Orange County in the late 1800s. From all over the county, horse-drawn wagonloads of the tan-colored roots were carted to designated railroad collection points, where they were hauled up beet ramps such as this one and dumped into railroad cars for transport to sugar refineries. Sugar beet production declined sharply after the 1920s when curly top, a disease spread by the beet leafhopper, decimated crops.

Acknowledgments

This volume, *Historic Photos of Orange County,* is the result of the cooperation and efforts of many individuals, organizations, and corporations. It is with great thanks that we acknowledge the valuable contribution of the following for their generous support:

First American Corporation
Japanese American National Museum
Orange County Archives
Sherman Library

We would also like to thank the following individuals for valuable contributions and assistance in making this work possible:

Charles Beal, Sons of Union Veterans of the Civil War
Phil Brigandi, Orange County Archives
Dean Dixon, Buena Park Historical Society
Chris Jepson, Orange County Archives
Irma Morales, Orange Public Library, El Modena Branch

Preface

Orange County has thousands of historic photographs that reside in archives, both locally and nationally. This book began with the observation that, while those photographs are of great interest to many, they are not easily accessible. During a time when Orange County is looking ahead and evaluating its future course, many people are asking, "How do we treat the past?" These decisions affect every aspect of the region—architecture, public spaces, commerce, infrastructure—and these, in turn, affect the way that people live their lives. This book seeks to provide easy access to a valuable, objective look into the history of Orange County.

The power of photographs is that they are less subjective than words in their treatment of history. Although the photographer can make decisions regarding subject matter and how to capture and present it, photographs do not provide the breadth of interpretation that text does. For this reason, they offer an original, untainted perspective that allows the viewer to interpret and observe.

This project represents countless hours of review and research. The researchers and writer have reviewed thousands of photographs in numerous archives. We greatly appreciate the generous assistance of the individuals and organizations listed in the acknowledgments of this work, without whom this project could not have been completed.

The goal in publishing this work is to provide broader access to this set of extraordinary photographs that seek to inspire, provide perspective, and evoke insight that might assist people who are responsible for determining Orange County's future. In addition, the book seeks to preserve the past with adequate respect and reverence.

With the exception of touching up imperfections caused by the damage of time and cropping where necessary, no other changes have been made. The focus and clarity of many images is limited to the technology and the ability of the photographer at the time they were taken.

The work is divided into eras. Beginning with some of the earliest known photographs of Orange County, the first section records photographs through the end of the nineteenth century. The second section spans the turn of the century through World War I. Section Three moves from the 1920s through World War II. The last section covers the postwar years to the late 1960s.

In each of these sections we have made an effort to capture various aspects of life through our selection of photographs. People, commerce, transportation, infrastructure, religious institutions, and educational institutions have been included to provide a broad perspective.

We encourage readers to reflect as they go walking in Orange County, strolling through its cities, its parks, and along its beaches. It is the publisher's hope that in utilizing this work, longtime residents will learn something new and that new residents will gain a perspective on where Orange County has been, so that each can contribute to its future.

—Todd Bottorff, Publisher

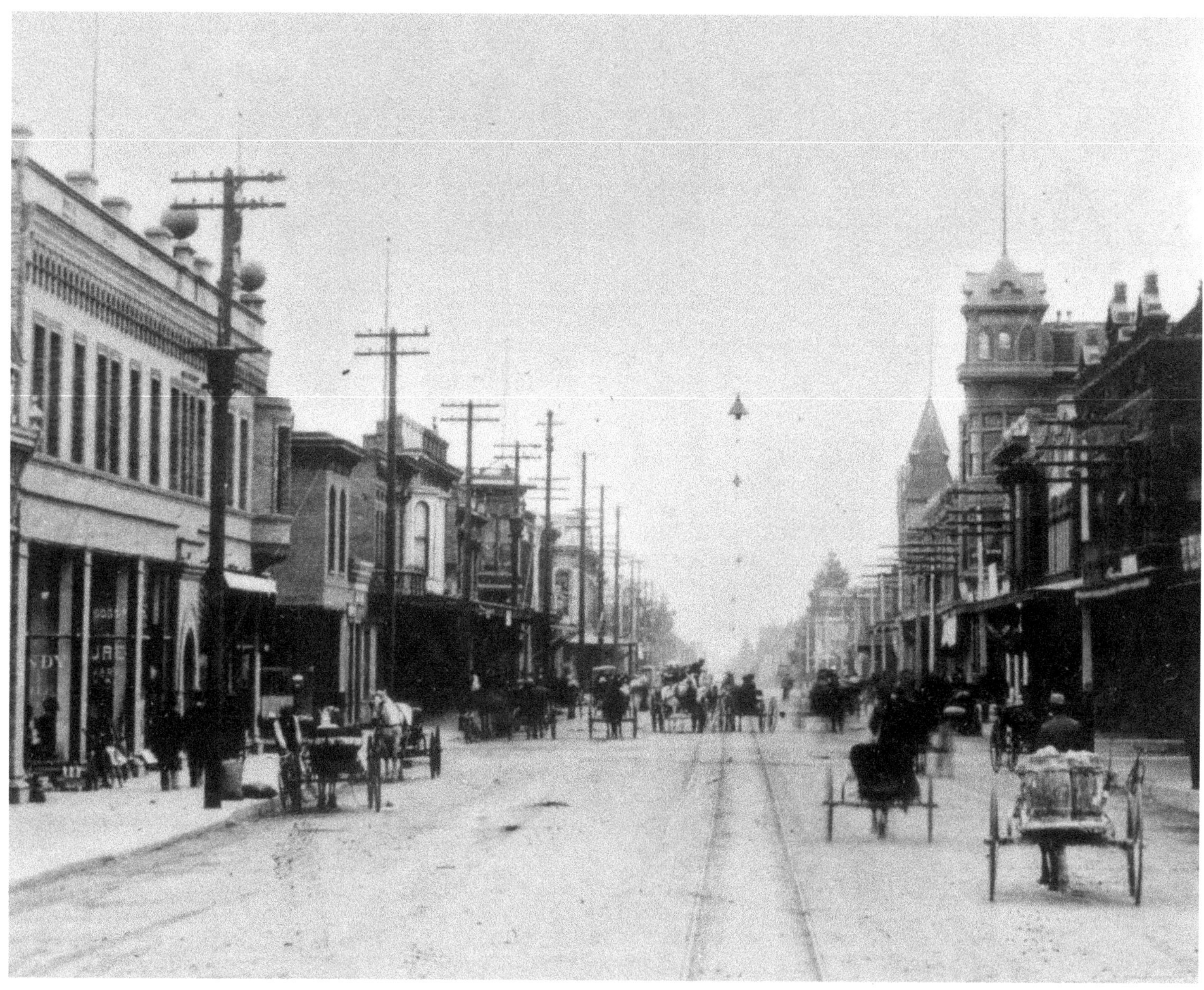

The town of Santa Ana was laid out in 1869 by William Spurgeon, a 40-year-old adventurer from Kentucky who chose the site for its close proximity to the more established areas of Anaheim, Tustin, and Orange. Less than 20 years later, at the time this photo was taken, Santa Ana was a thriving community with a population of 3,600 and a central business district composed of two-story brick buildings that conveyed stability and permanence.

Changing Beauty and Ceaseless Fruition

(1870–1899)

The written history of Orange County starts with Father Junipero Serra and the founding of the San Juan Capistrano Mission in 1776, but in truth, a complex civilization thrived here long before the arrival of the Spanish. Whether Serra was a saint who converted the savages to a civilized Christian life, or a despot who enslaved and abused a compliant people is still open to interpretation, but by the time the mission system ended in 1833, California's Native American population had been reduced by nearly three-fourths.

Mexico assumed control of California in 1822 and secularized the missions ten years later. The Great Stone Church at San Juan Capistrano weathered away to picturesque ruins. Thus began the rancho period in which all of Southern California was controlled by a few wealthy dons. Rancho Santiago de Santa Ana, the only Spanish land grant that lay entirely within the boundaries of present-day Orange County, was owned by the families of Jose Antonio Yorba and Juan Peralta.

The Land Act of 1851 provided the legal impetus to break up the ranchos, but climatic change did the real work. A month of continuous rain in the winter of 1861-2 was following by two years of severe drought. Any cattle that hadn't already drowned the previous year starved to death on the dusty plains. The first American pioneers arrived at a propitious time: with little competition left from ranchers, the county's transition to agriculture was relatively smooth.

Early settlers to the region arrived seeking fertile farmland; they found that virtually anything would grow in the sandy soil. Anaheim was founded by German vintners and was later a major producer of chiles. Westminster was reclaimed from the marshes for celery fields. Raisin production was centered in the city of Orange and some of the first citrus orchards laid out in Placentia. Beans, sugar beets, avocados, lemons, apricots, peaches, and walnuts all prospered in the temperate climate.

In the late 1800s the new settlements in the southeast corner of Los Angeles County grew steadily. Enterprising, adventurous men with names like Spurgeon, Talbert, Whitaker, Chapman, and Glassell tamed the wilderness and built promising new economic centers. Anaheim was the first city to incorporate, in 1870, followed by Santa Ana and the city of Orange in 1886 and 1888. With financial success came the desire for autonomy, and the county of Orange split off from Los Angeles in 1889. Santa Ana was elected the new county seat.

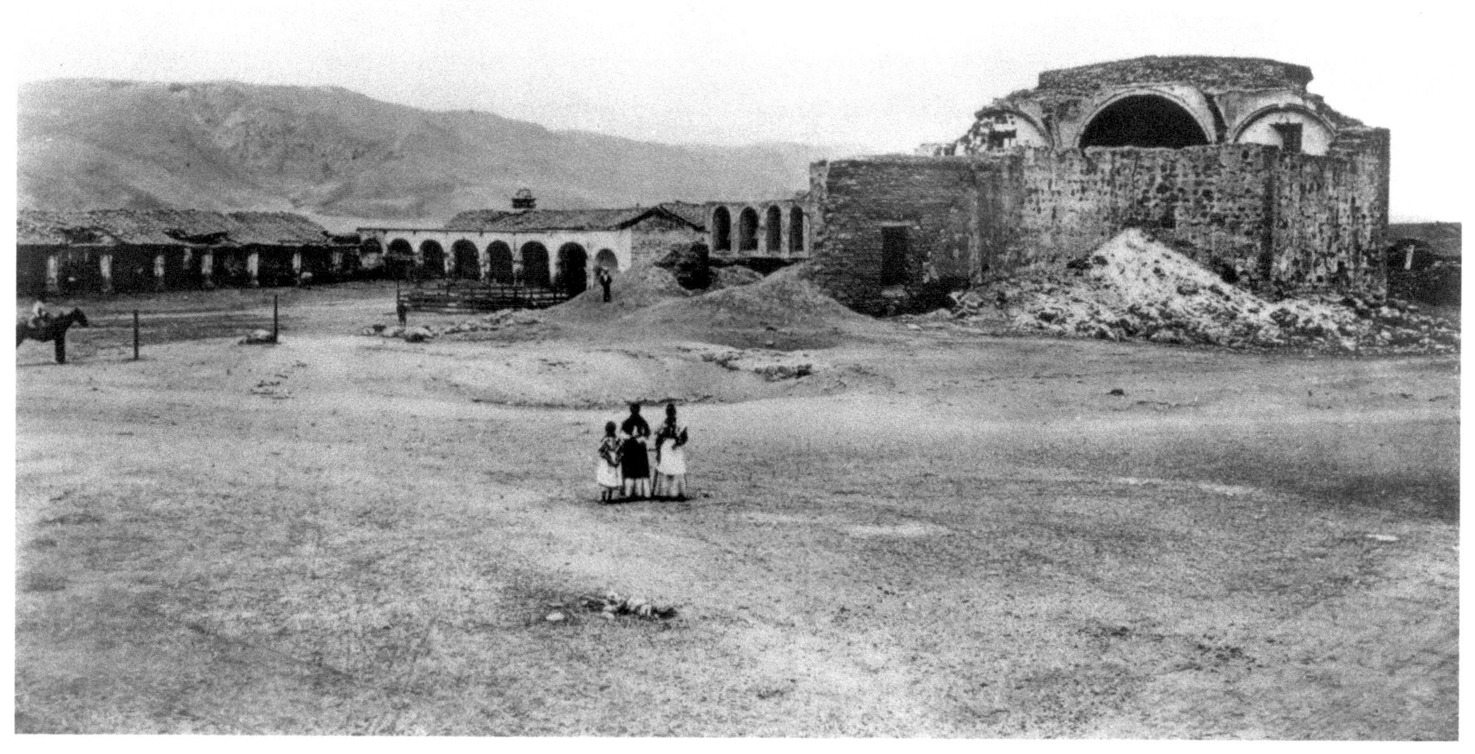

Once the jewel of the California missions, San Juan Capistrano lay in ruins by 1876, the date of this photograph. The Great Stone Church, at right, functioned as a chapel for only six years before a massive earthquake leveled it in 1812, tragically killing 40 Native Americans worshipping inside. After nearly a century of intermittent restoration efforts, the mission today is an international tourist destination.

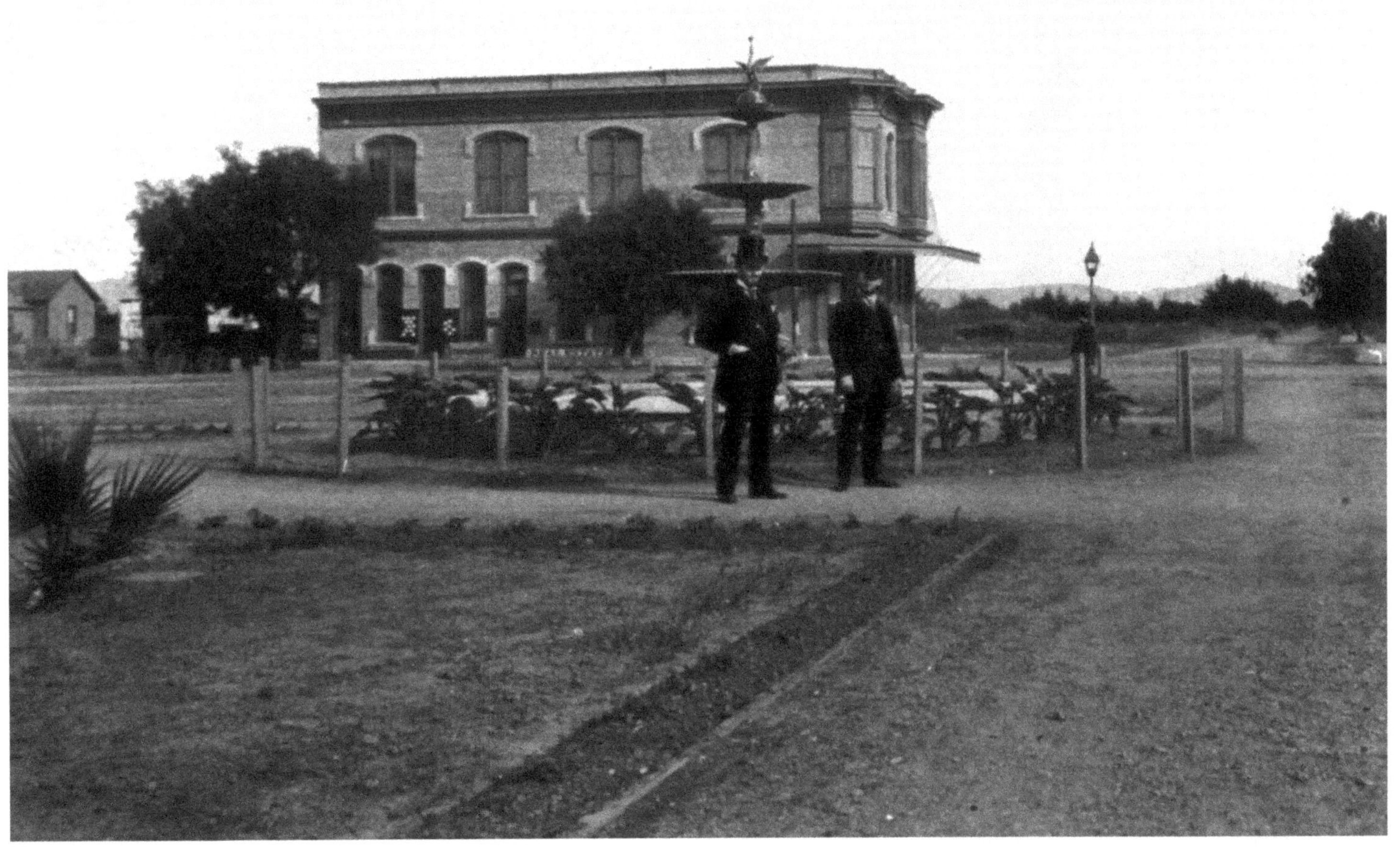

In 1871, Alfred Chapman and Andrew Glassell, both Los Angeles–area lawyers, founded the city of Orange (called Richland at the time) on land received in payment for legal work. The area was surveyed into 25-by-50-foot lots platted around an oval park. This 1887 photograph captures these humble beginnings. The lone building is the Bank of Orange, and it has been suggested that the two dapper gents in front of the fountain are Chapman and Glassell.

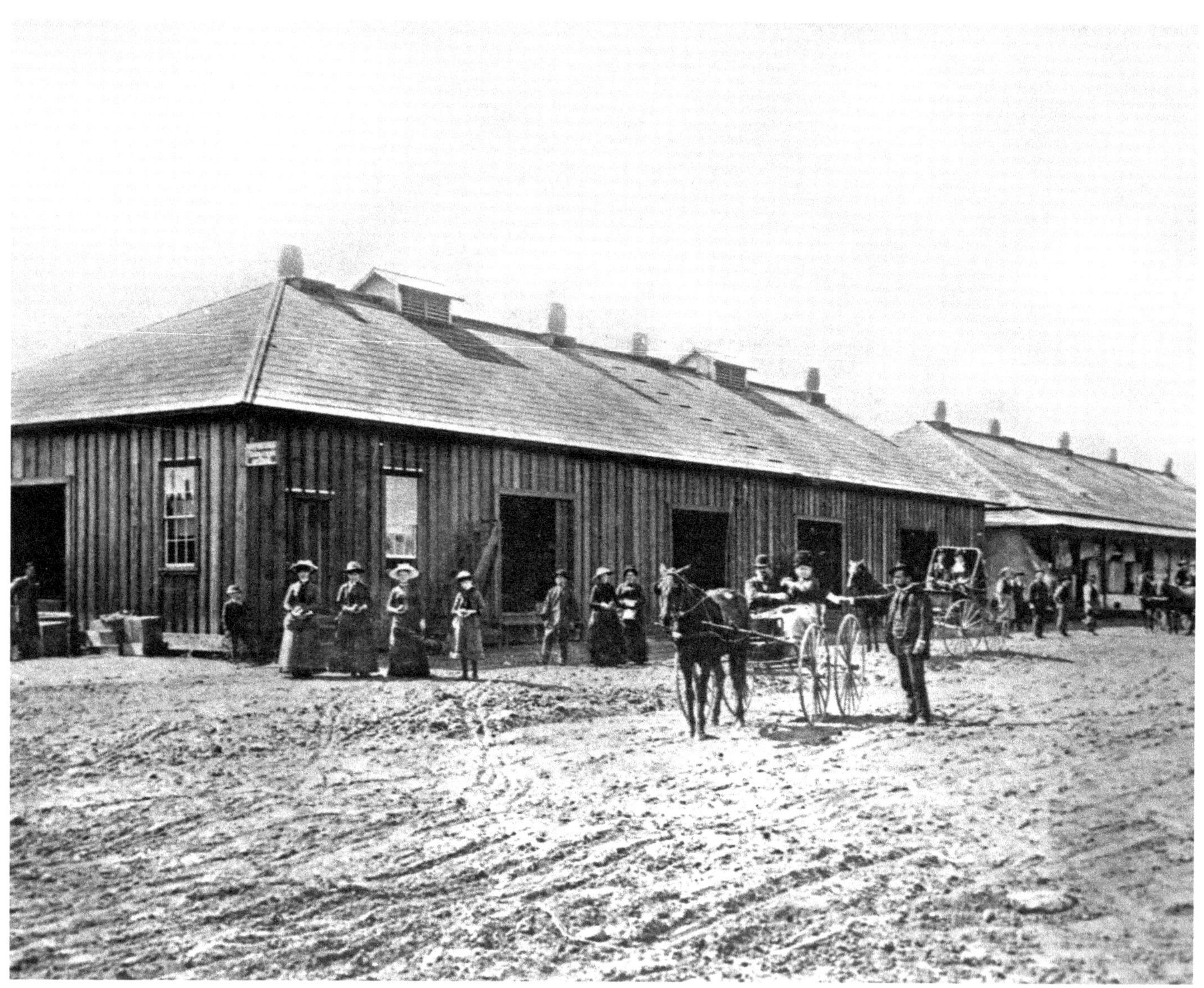

The McPherson Brothers came to the Orange County region in 1872 and set out the area's first raisin vineyard on 220 acres near the present-day city of Orange. In its peak years the company produced 90,000 boxes of raisins annually. The McPherson packinghouses, located at the corner of McPherson Road and Chapman Avenue, are shown here in 1886, the year their entire crop, and that of all the area's grape growers, was wiped out by disease.

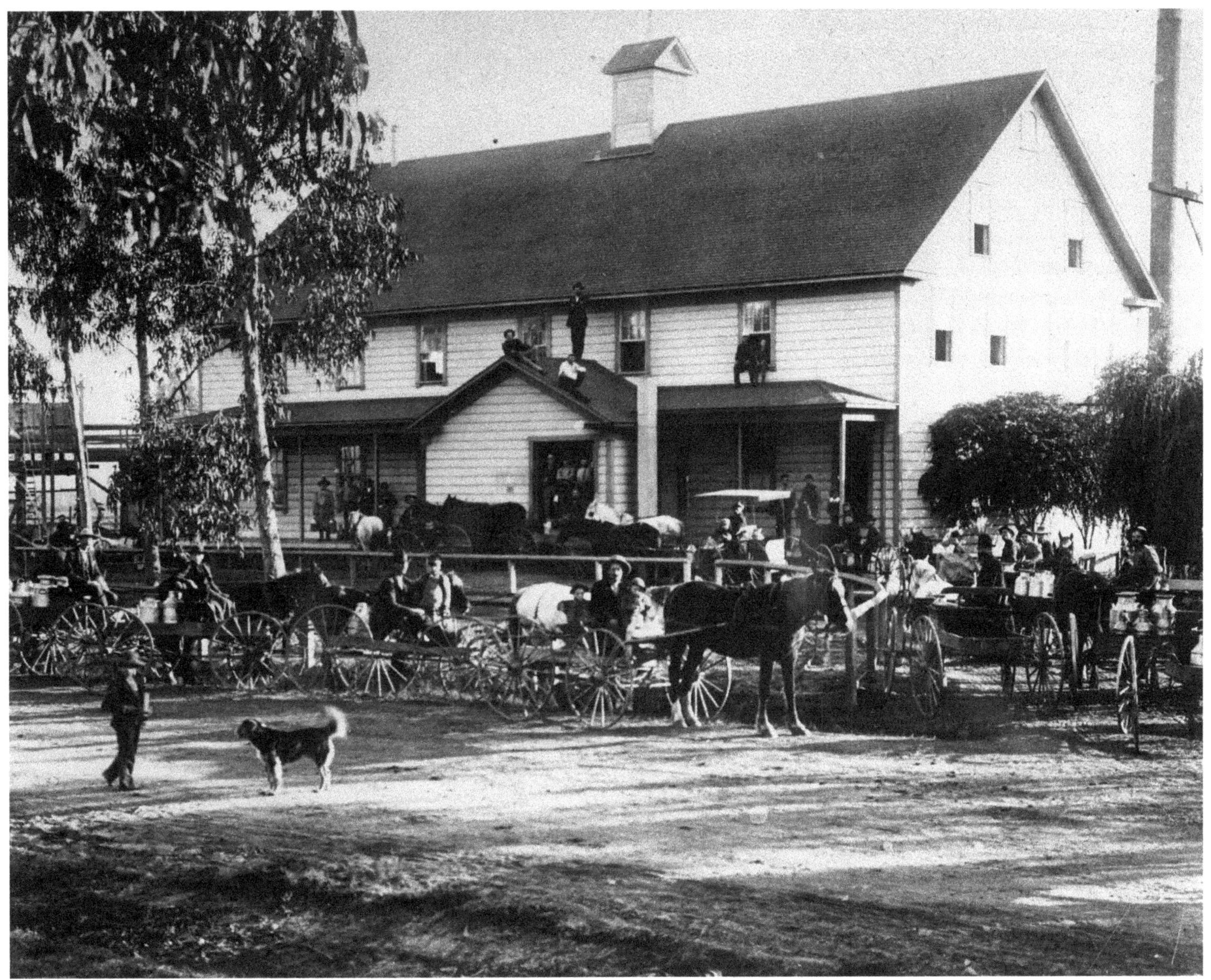

Buena Park's Pacific Creamery Company, the first evaporated-milk cannery in California, opened in 1889, the same year that Orange County split off from Los Angeles County. The company's "Lily California Sterilized Cream" won gold medals at the Buffalo Pan-American Exposition of 1901 and the Paris Exposition of 1903, and in large part sustained the local economy for many years. The building was torn down in 1955 to make way for a freeway.

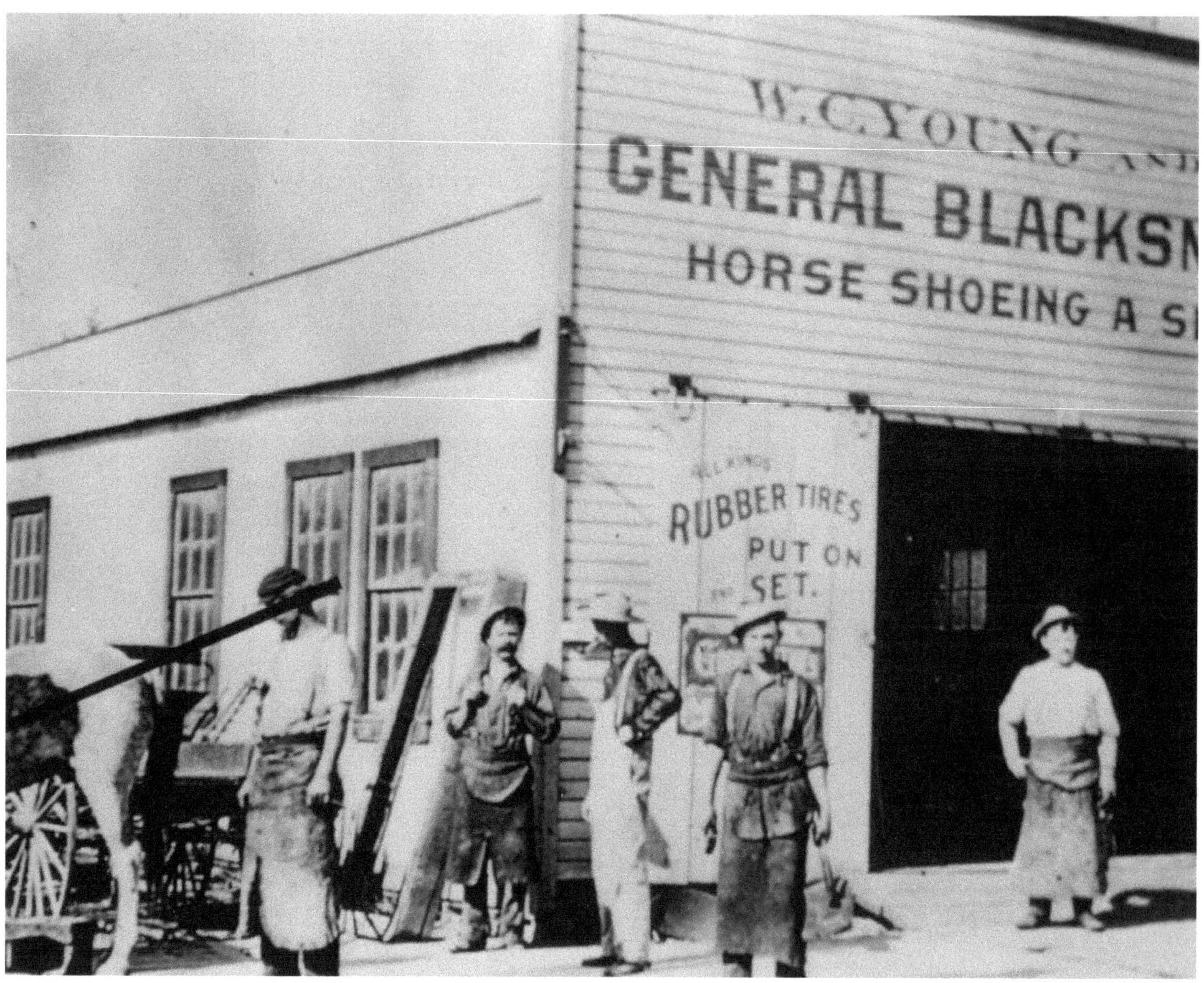

Horses naturally played a crucial role in the development of pioneer towns. An 1887 map of downtown Santa Ana reveals 13 establishments devoted to the maintenance of horses and wagons, including livery stables, haylofts, feedlots, and blacksmiths. W. C. Young and Company General Blacksmithing was located at the corner of North Sycamore and West Fifth Street. Mr. Young, a full-time blacksmith, also served as fire chief for 16 years.

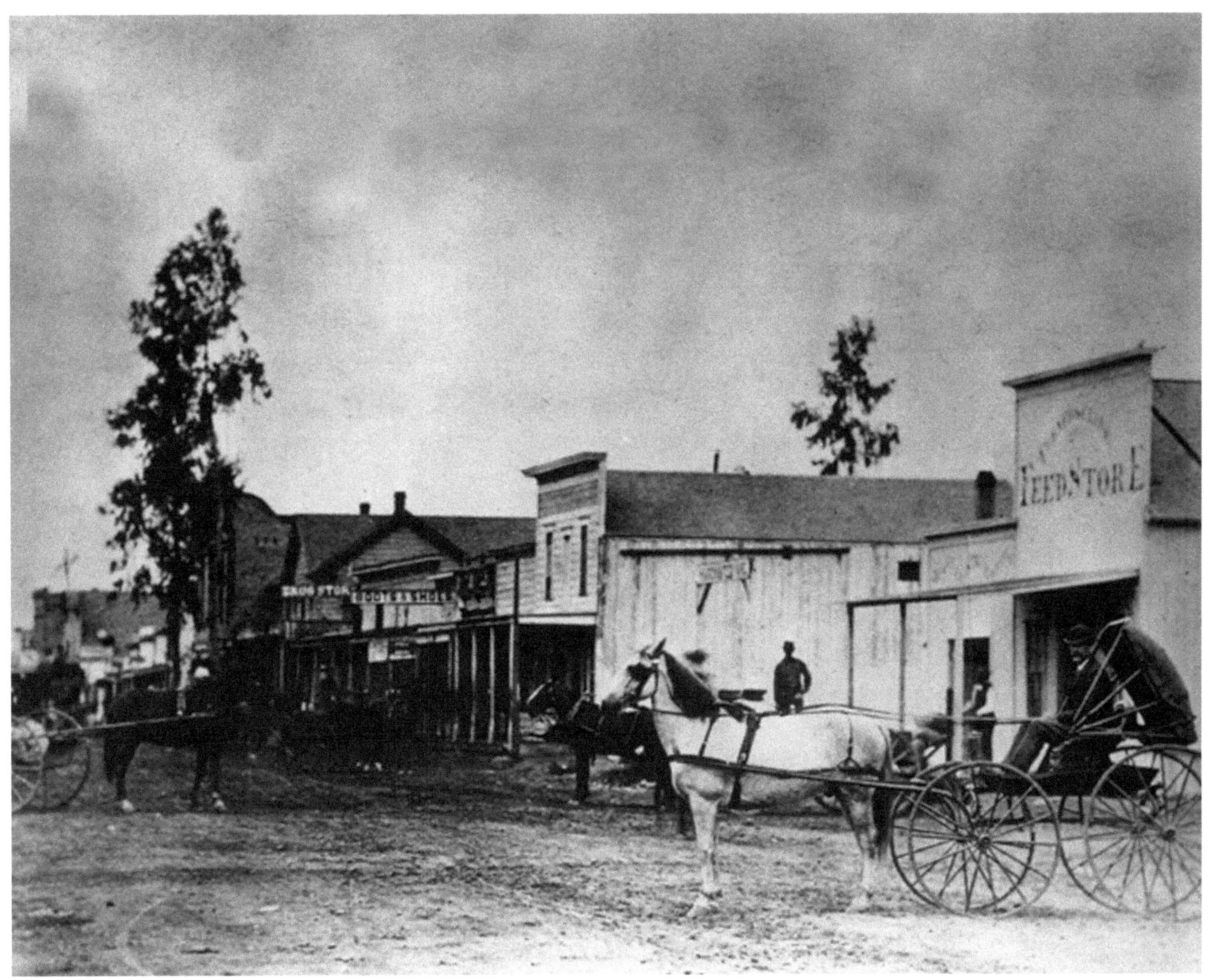

Mr. C. E. French sits in his buggy at Fourth and Main in Santa Ana in this 1890s-era photograph. The earliest settlers to the area that would become Santa Ana arrived from the Midwest in the mid-1860s, finding waist-high mustard grass, cactus, and not much else. Lumber was scarce and had to be shipped from Northern California to Anaheim Landing (now Seal Beach Naval Station). Early businesses such as these were simple, unpainted board and batten structures.

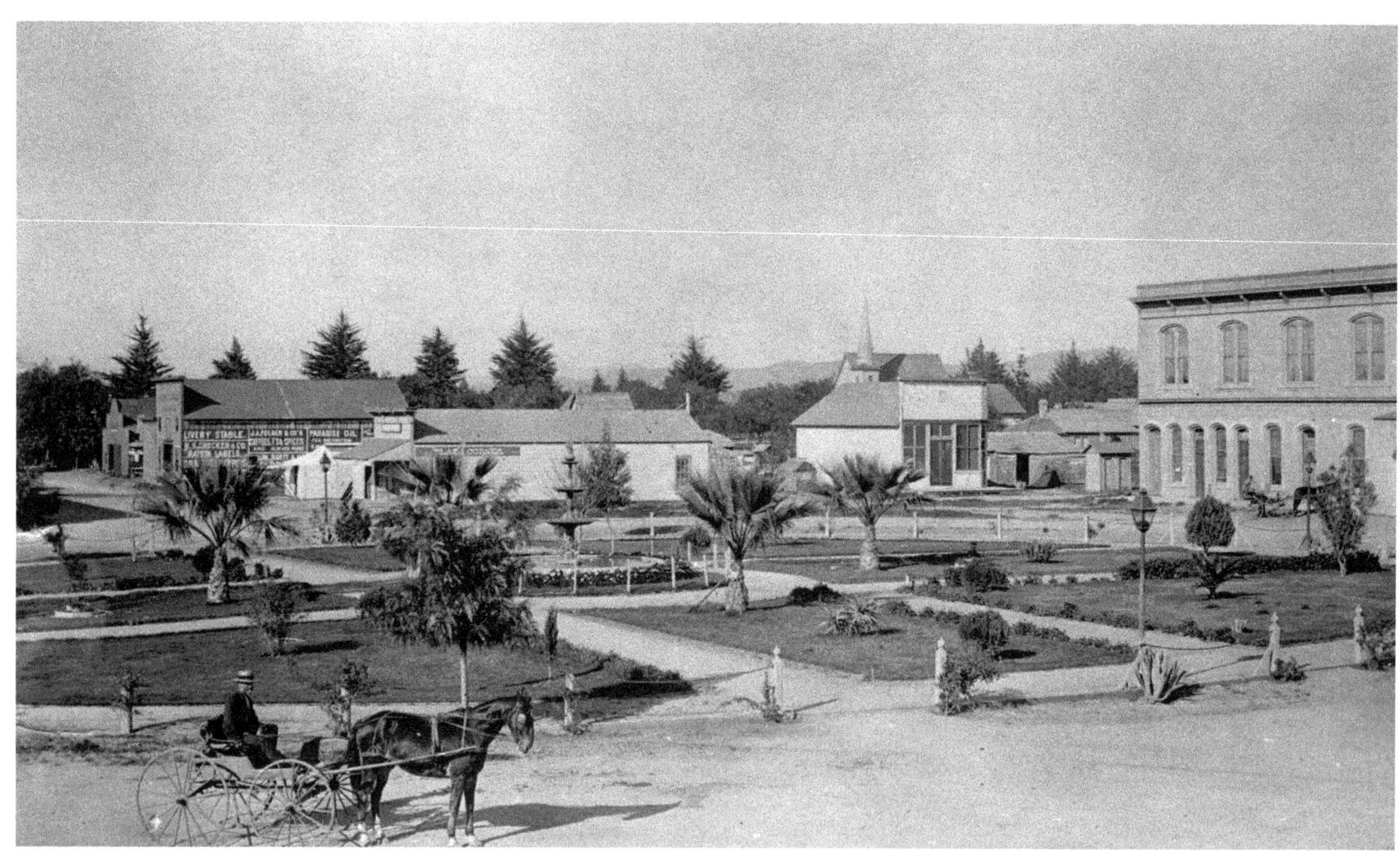

Orange city founder Captain Glassell was no doubt influenced by the City Beautiful movement of the late nineteenth century in planning a city where all businesses would face the scenic central Plaza. Though many of the lots ringing the Plaza were still vacant in 1898, the year of this photo, a three-tiered fountain had been installed, and streetlights, sidewalks, fence posts, and the rudiments of landscaping are all evident.

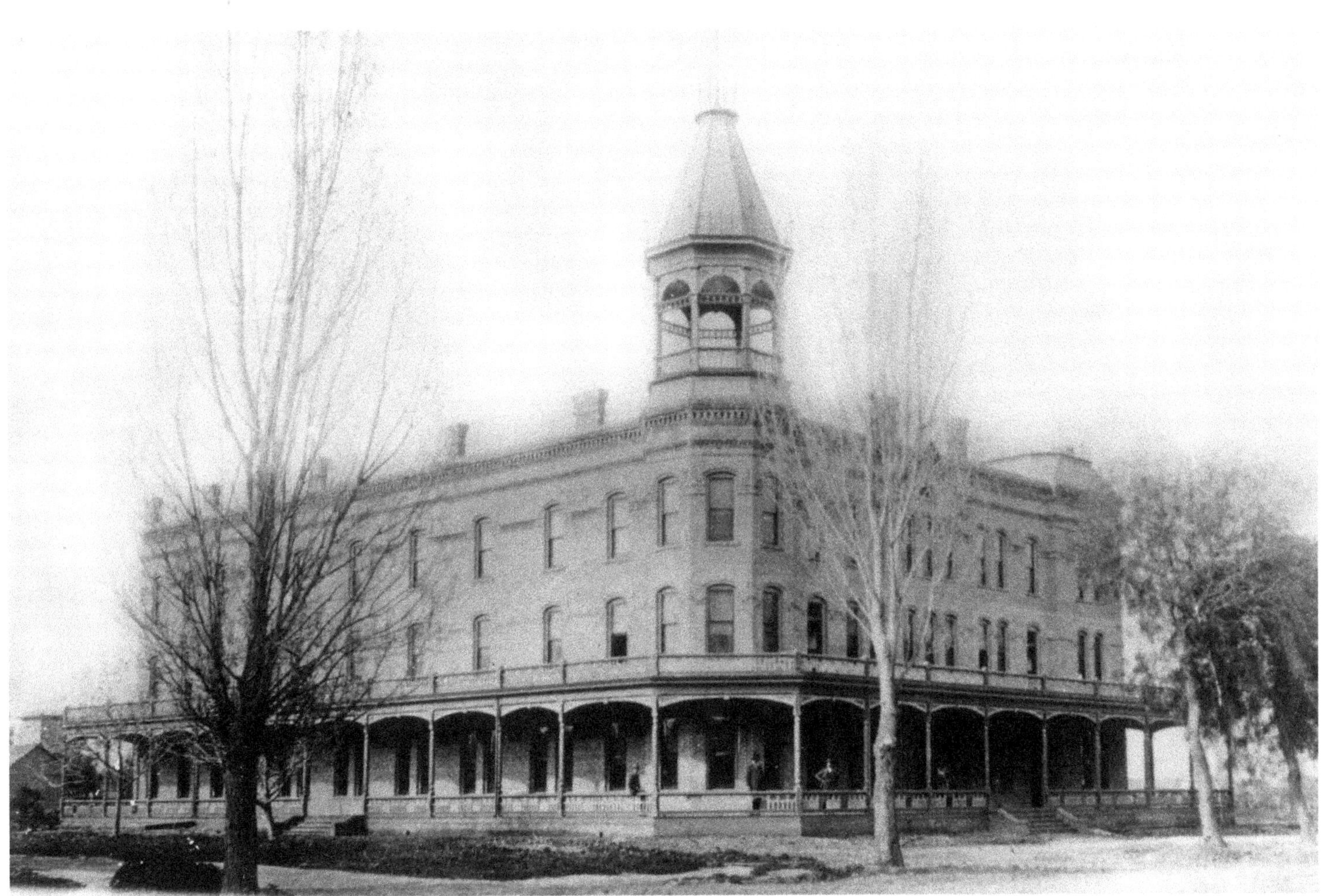

The Rochester Hotel, which once stood at 310 West Chapman in Orange, was one of three hotels built during the boom of the 1880s to lure tourists and investors to town. Despite promotion on contemporary postcards as "the best hotel between Los Angeles and San Diego," the Rochester was never successful, and over the years the building served many alternate uses, including briefly housing the county's first college. It was razed in 1931.

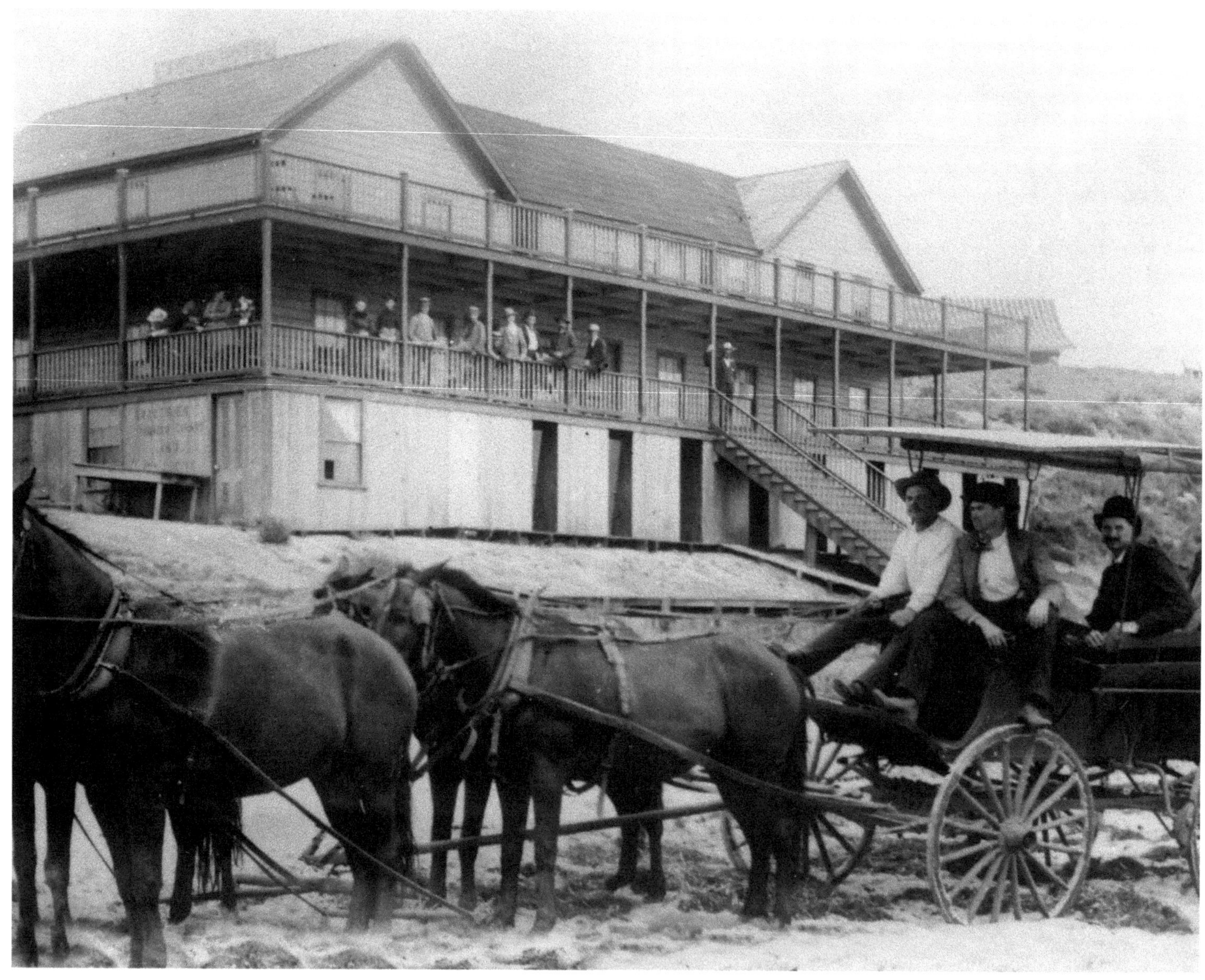

Laguna Beach's Yoch Hotel, pictured in 1889, the year of its establishment, was built by Henry Goff and purchased by Laguna Beach postmaster Joseph Yoch for $600. By the standards of the time, the Yoch Hotel was enormous, with 32 rooms and two bathrooms. In an area where lumber was scarce, the Yoch's formidable bulk was achieved through the rather unconventional method of joining sections of another defunct hotel to the core structure.

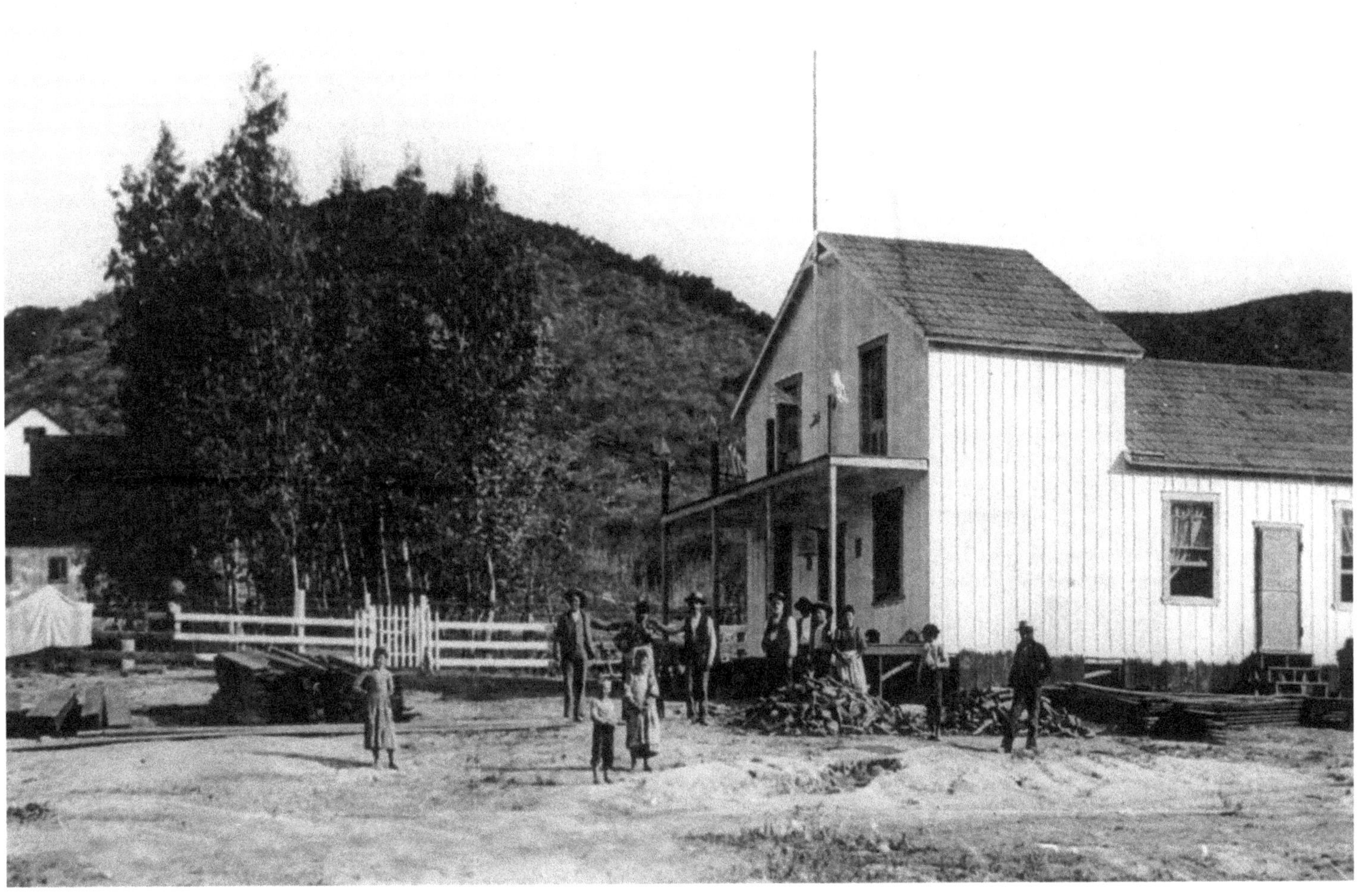

In the early decades of the twentieth century, Orange County would have three hot-springs resorts. San Juan Hot Springs, shown here in 1890, was located in a scenic canyon 12 miles east of San Juan Capistrano. A successful resort operated there from 1883 to 1936, promising to cure everything from rheumatism to melancholia with its 122-degree mineral waters. The resort was reopened in 1980 but fell victim to freeway expansion just 12 years later.

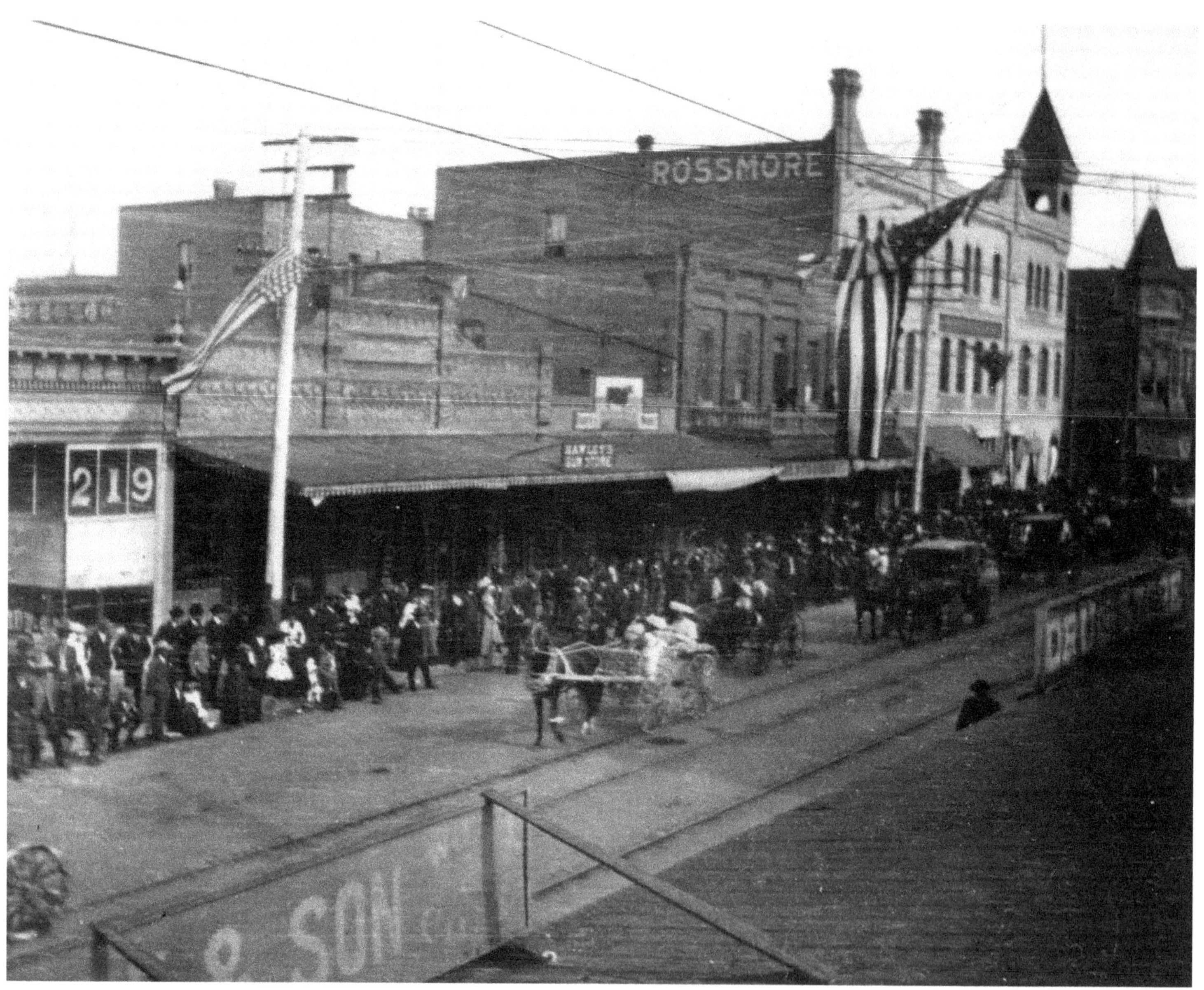

Starting as far back as the 1870s, the residents of Santa Ana have marked every holiday or celebration with bands, floats, horses, circus animals, children, and special interest groups taking to the streets to see and be seen. Before the advent of television, computer games, and amusement park rides, small-town residents had to invent their own entertainment. In this 1890s-era photo, parade participants in their Sunday best wave to the Fourth Street crowd.

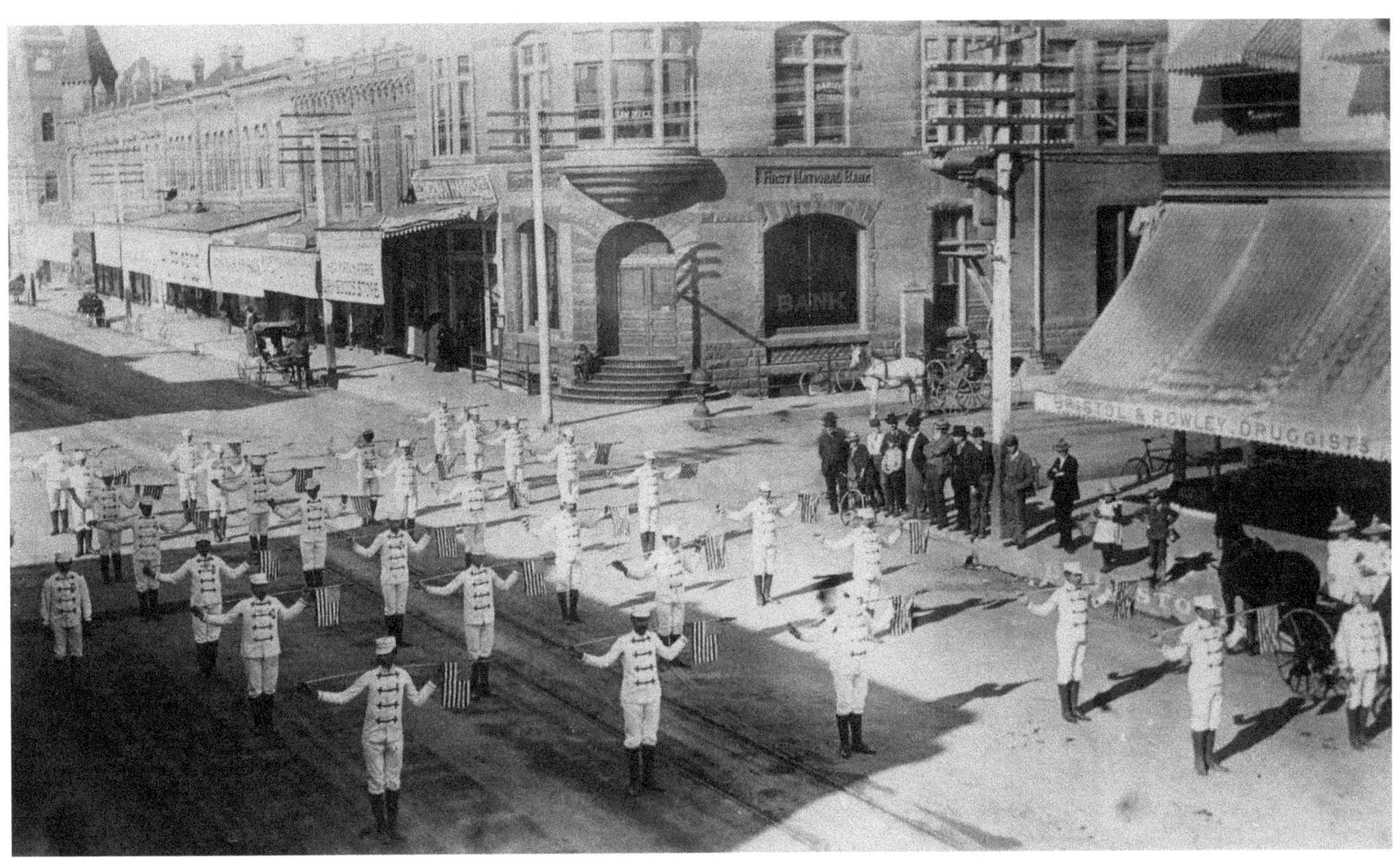

A drill team marches down Santa Ana's Fourth Street past the First National Bank. The three-story brick building, crowned with a corner tower, was built at a cost of $45,000 at the height of the late-1880s land boom. Other substantial brick buildings built in Santa Ana's downtown area during the same period include the elegant 75-room Brunswick Hotel, as well as many fine Victorian homes, such as the famed Howe-Waffle House.

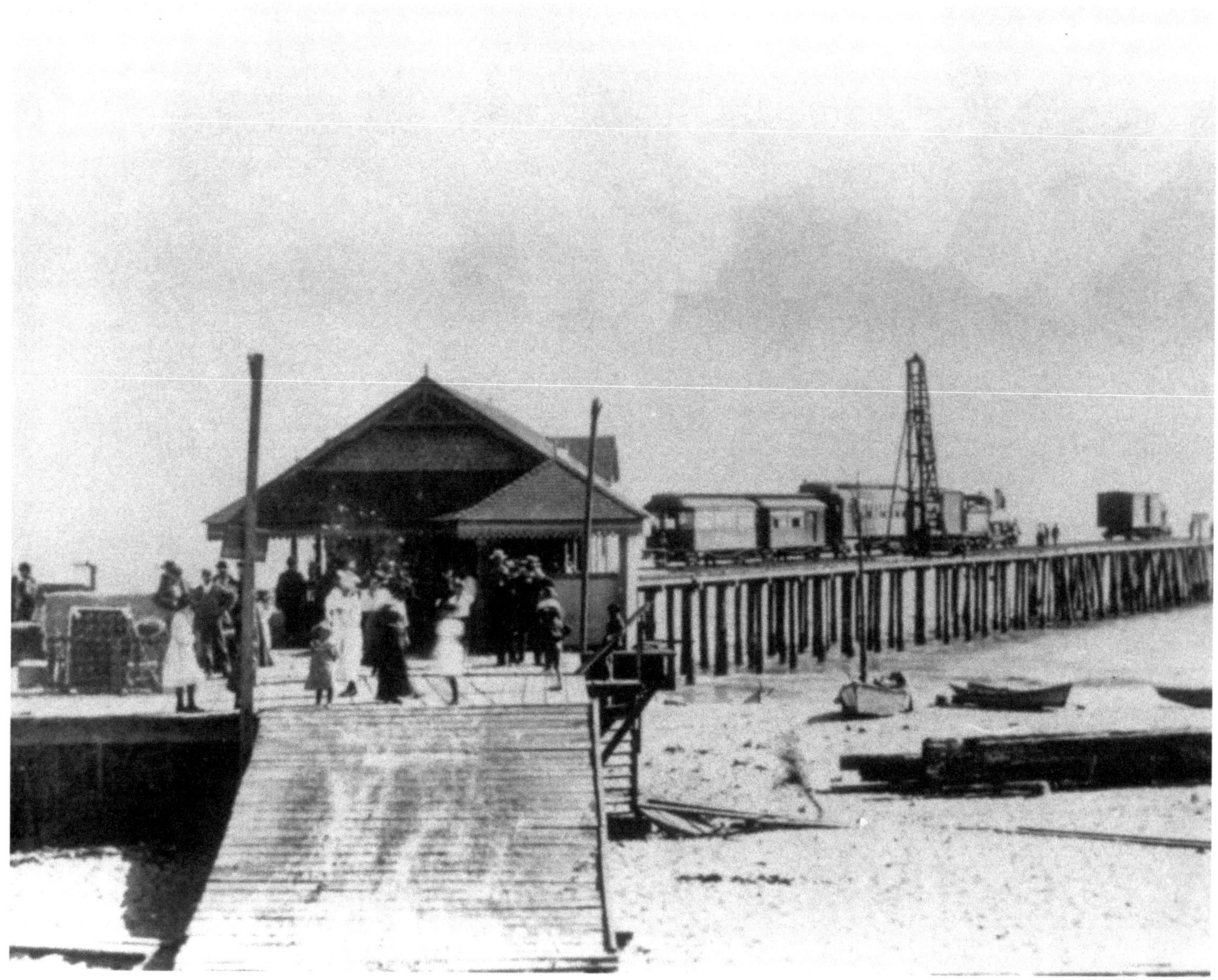

In 1891 the McFadden Wharf, named for its builders James and Robert McFadden, was completed on a sandy spur of land that would one day become known as Newport Beach, ushering in a decade of success as a shipping port for the fledgling city. The following year the Santa Fe and Newport Railroad extended its tracks to the end of the pier, connecting Newport Beach to Santa Ana.

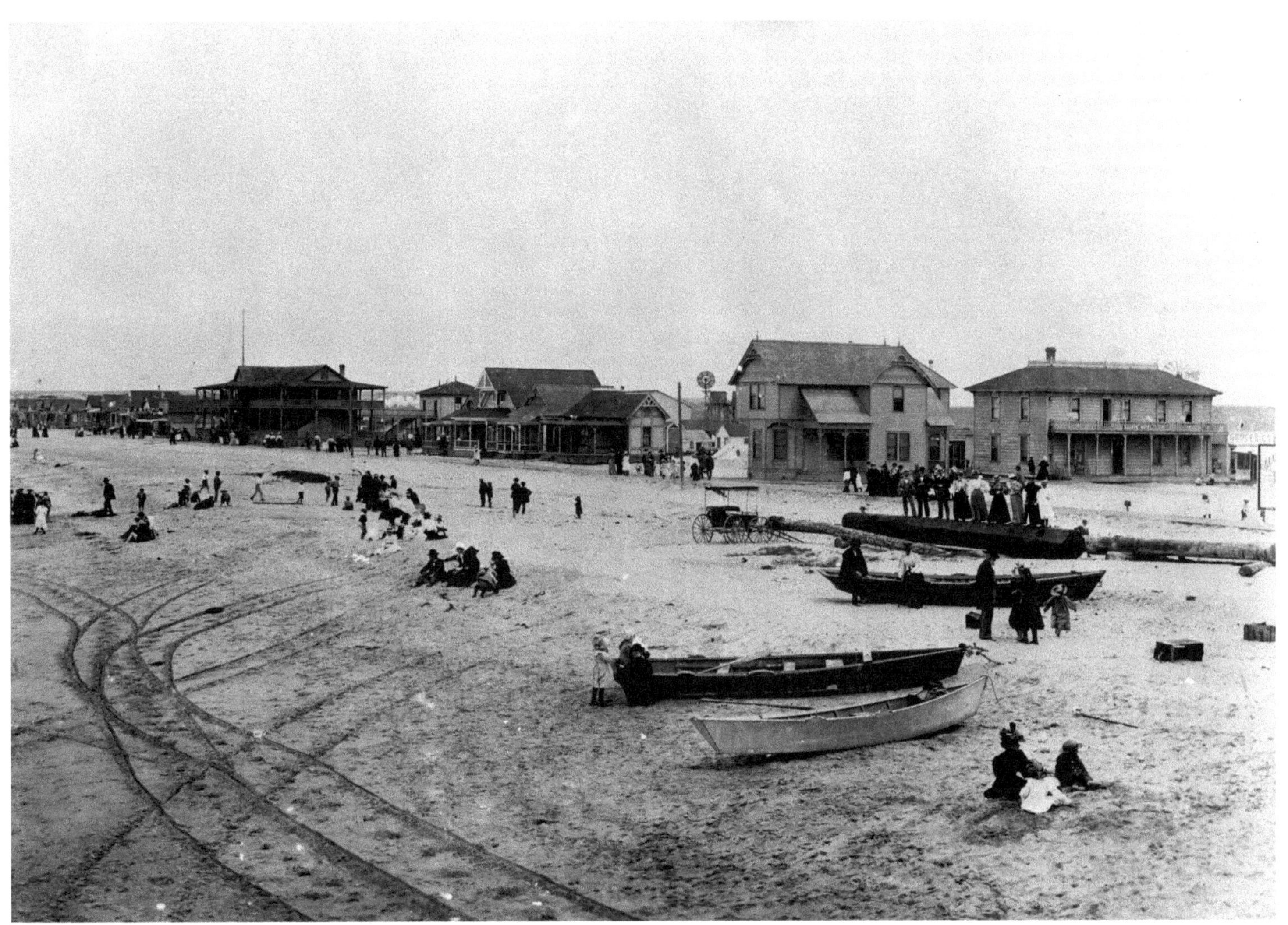

Shown here in 1895, the tiny village of Newport Beach seems to have sprouted from the sand. Sharp's Hotel, the two-story wood structure at right, was brought to town in pieces—dismantled at its previous location south of San Juan Capistrano and reassembled on the beach. The building served 18 years as a boarding house for wharf workers and became famous for its fish dinners. It burned to the ground in 1910.

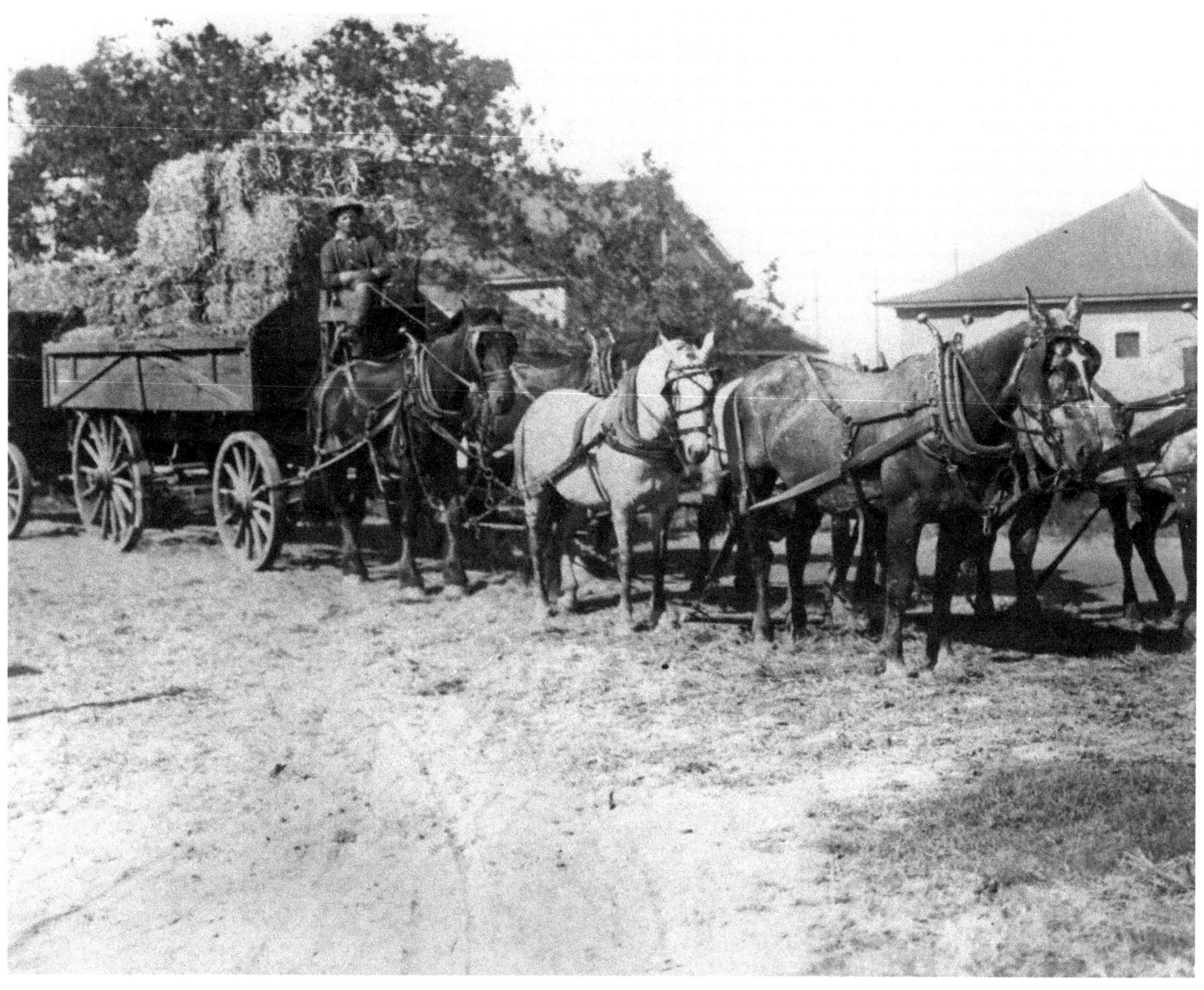

This 1890s photograph shows a team of horses hauling hay at the Talbert farm. James T. Talbert arrived in the area that would become Fountain Valley in 1896 and purchased 322.5 acres of swampland. Construction of the Talbert Drainage District reclaimed the swampland for agricultural use, and the area was soon known for bean and beet production. Talbert's three sons—Sam, Tom, and Henry—became involved in farming also, and in real estate.

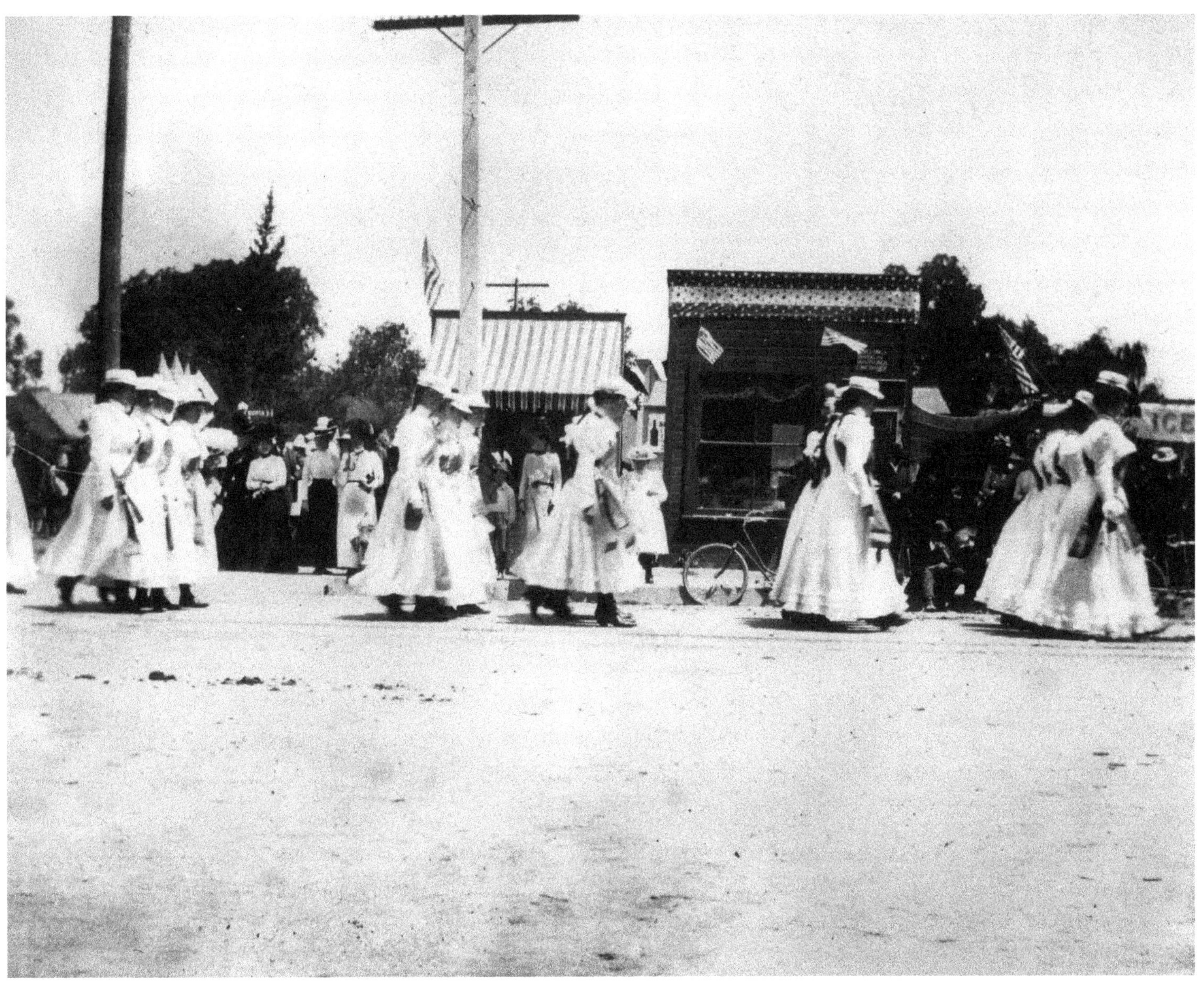

An unidentified women's group marches down Fourth Street in a turn-of-the-century Santa Ana parade. Orange County has a rich tradition of unique community parades. Dana Point and San Juan Capistrano mark the annual whale and swallow migrations, respectively, with their March parades. La Habra's Corn Festival celebrates the September harvest. And, of course, Disneyland presents its renowned high-tech parade of Disney characters nightly in Anaheim.

This photo, ca. 1890, shows the Talbott and Smith shop, located at 120 E. Fourth Street, on the southwest corner of Bush and Fourth in Santa Ana. Mr. E. B. Smith is second from the left. Talbott and Smith was a typical redbrick general store of the era selling everything from groceries and "crockery" to brooms, wicker baskets, metal pails, and sewing needles.

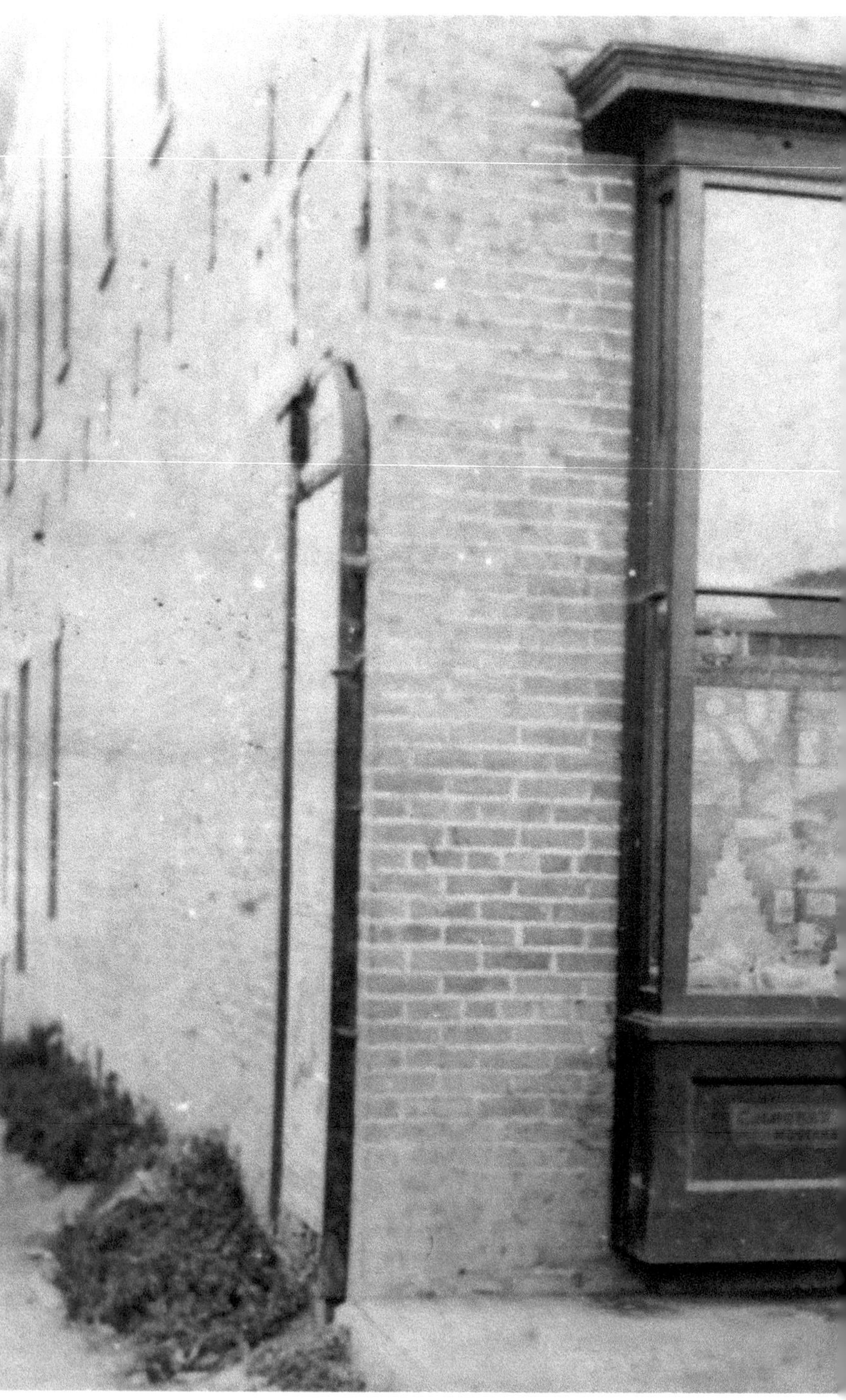

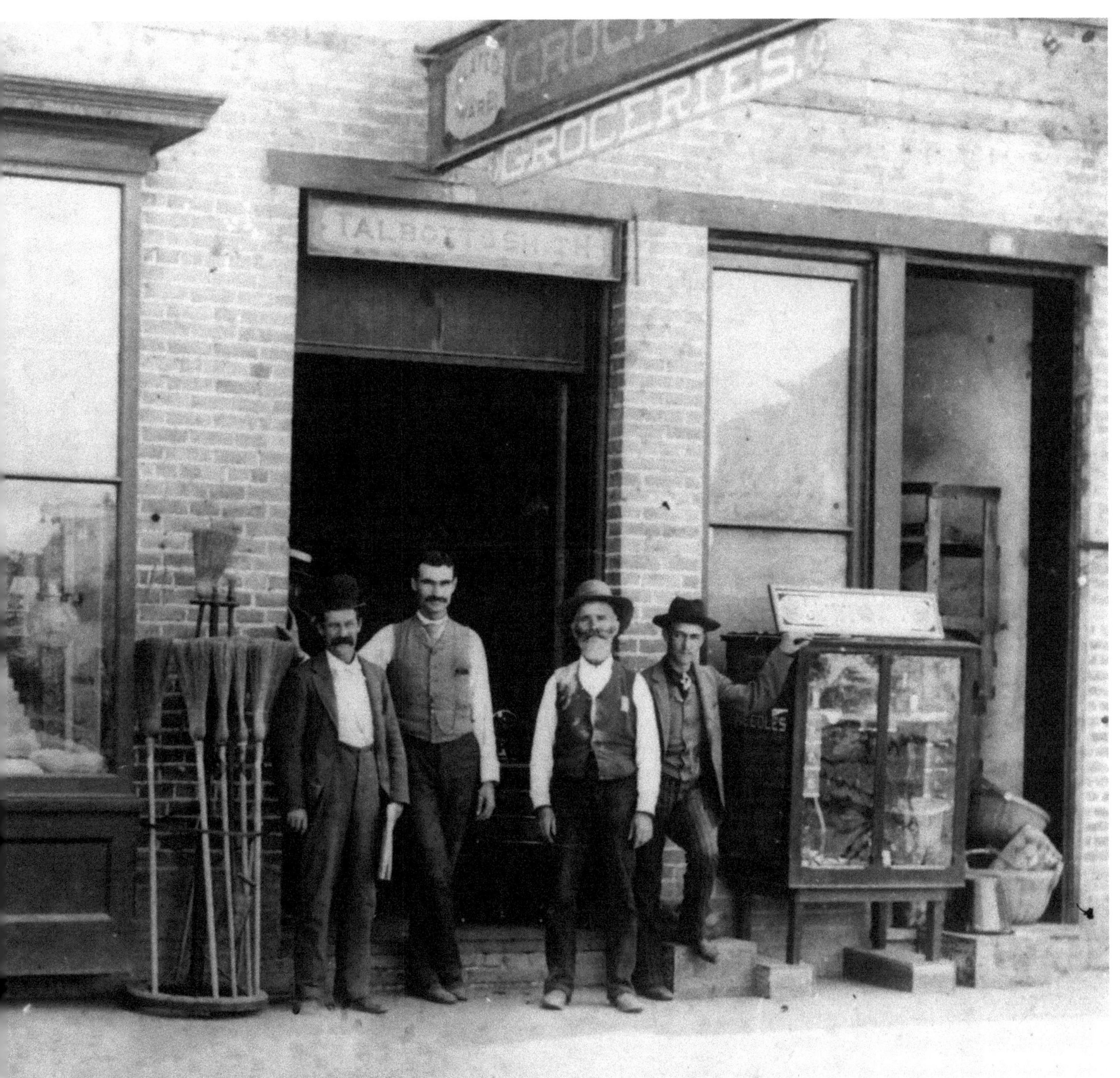
GROCERIES

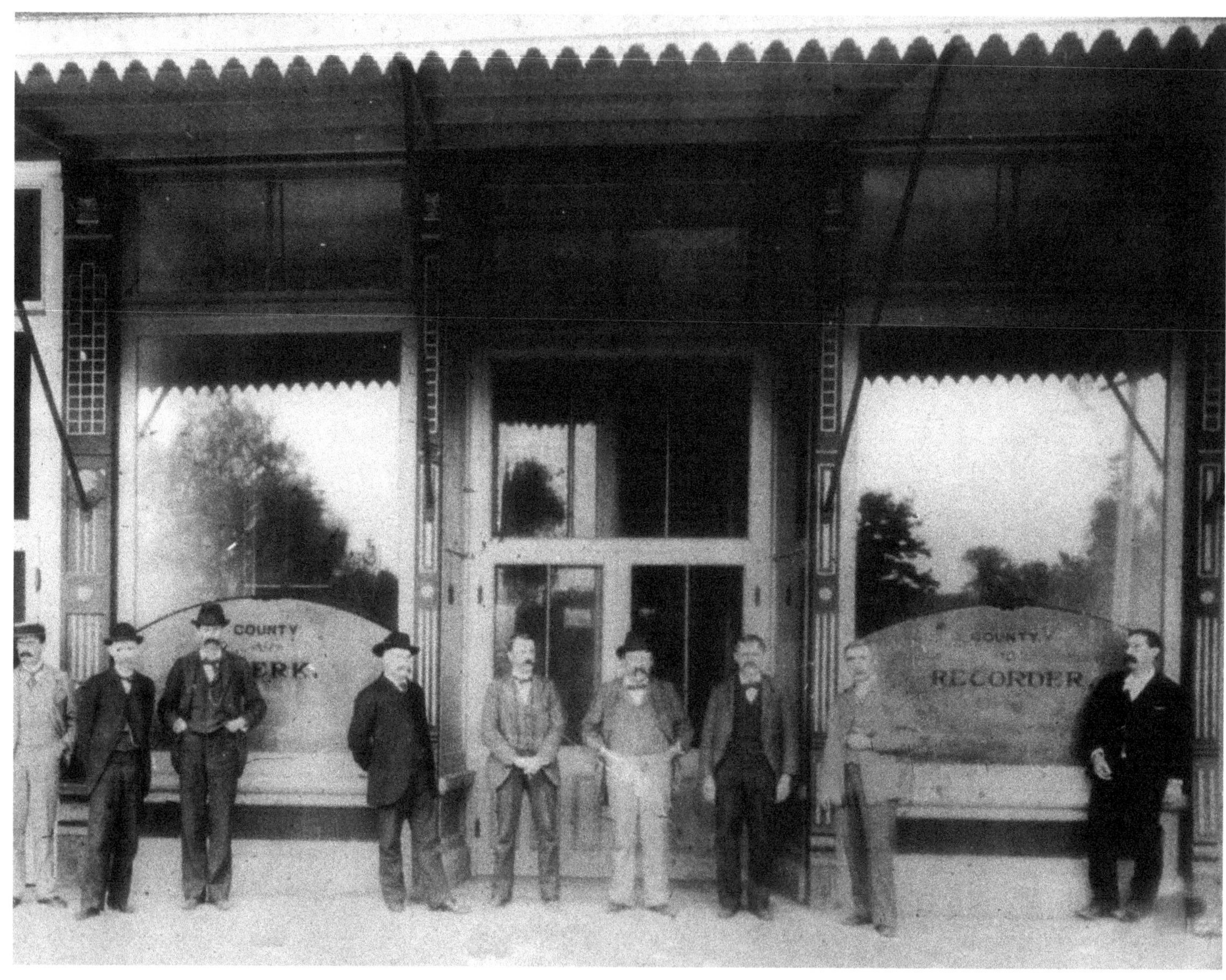

With the growth of the cities in the southeastern part of what was then Los Angeles County, it became apparent that a smaller county should be formed with a more accessible county seat. Orange County split off in 1889, with Santa Ana as the new county seat. Santa Ana quickly stepped up to fill the role, establishing offices for the county assessor, tax collector, school superintendent, clerk, and recorder in the Congdon Building by 1895.

The Biggest Little County in the West

(1900–1919)

The arrival of the Southern Pacific and Santa Fe railroads to Orange County in the late 1800s had launched the land boom of 1887-8. Promotional brochures and leaflets promulgated the wonders of the county to prospective investors in flowery language, each realtor seeking to outdo the next in hyperbole. Santa Ana was "chief among ten thousand, or the one altogether lovely!" Tustin was described as the place where "the Angel of Peace to Earth first descended . . . where Beauty reposes." El Modena residents boasted they lived in the Italy of the New World, and promoters of Anaheim claimed their air could relieve "asthma and catarrhal and inflammatory phthisis."

The boom busted by the turn of the century, however, about the same time that many initially successful Orange County crops began to succumb to disease and predation by insects, making the cultivation of new crops and industries a priority. To that end Santa Ana launched the first annual Parade of Products in 1906, in which every community in Orange County was invited to design a float showcasing their agricultural products. The city of Orange followed suit a few years later with the first International Street Fair, featuring prized chickens and sideshow attractions.

While a triumvirate of inland cities—Santa Ana, Orange, and Anaheim—was largely responsible for the formation of the new county and for shepherding it into the modern age, it was the coastal communities of Newport Beach, Huntington Beach, and Laguna Beach that established Orange County's reputation as a tourist destination. By the turn of the century beachside resorts had developed, with bathhouses, hotels, and even amusement rides and games to accommodate the Victorian vogue for "bathing." Newport and Huntington incorporated in 1906 and 1909, and Laguna would become a city in 1927. By that time the 1920s would be at full roar, and the Orange County beach communities would be favored by Hollywood royalty.

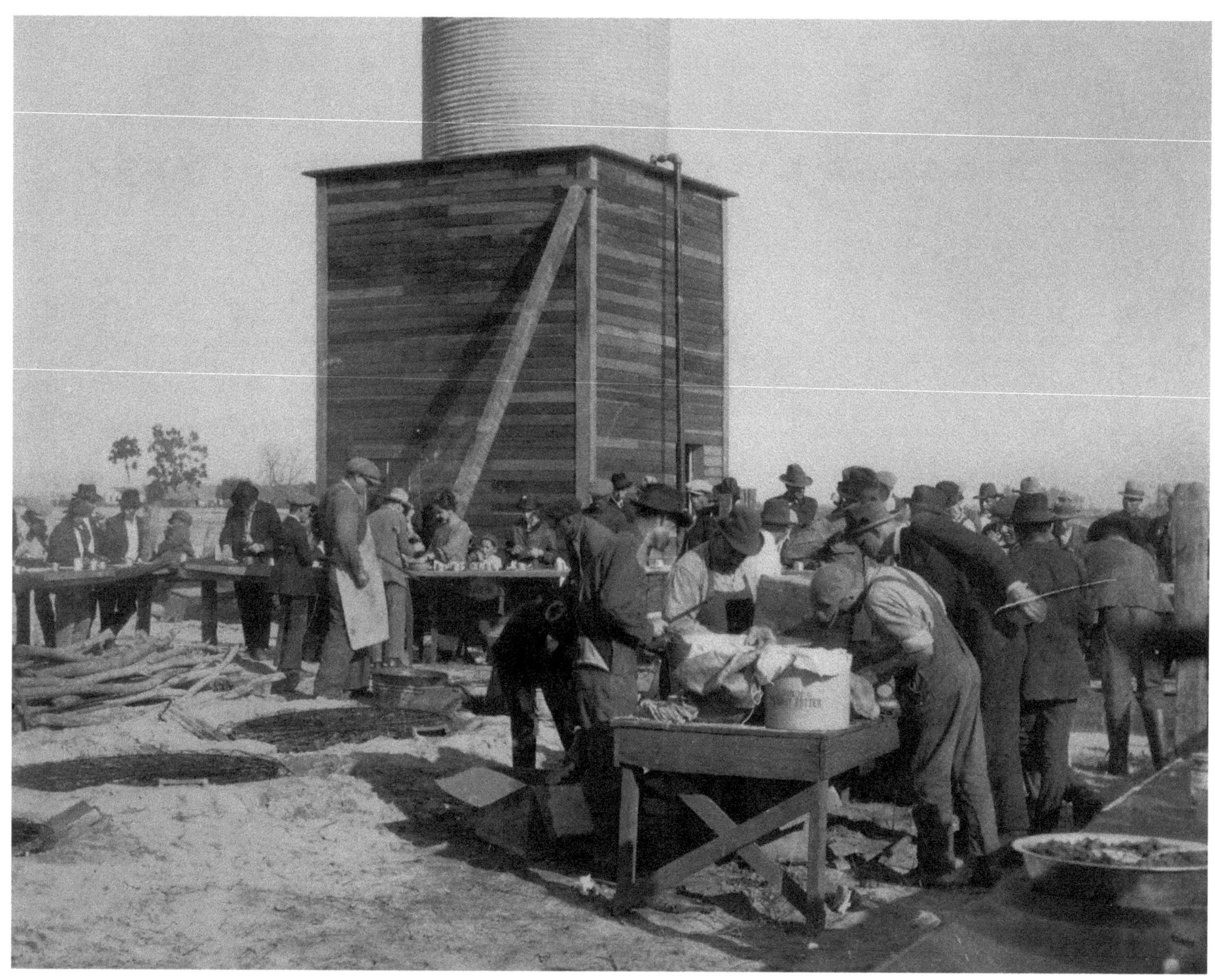

During the late-1880s land boom, real estate agents attracted prospective investors to remote Orange County with rosy hyperbole and fun-filled outings that included bands, entertainment, and a picnic lunch. Here guests at Henry Talbert's ranch are fed a barbecue meal in an attempt to loosen their wallets. A vat of what appears to be baked beans sits on the table at right.

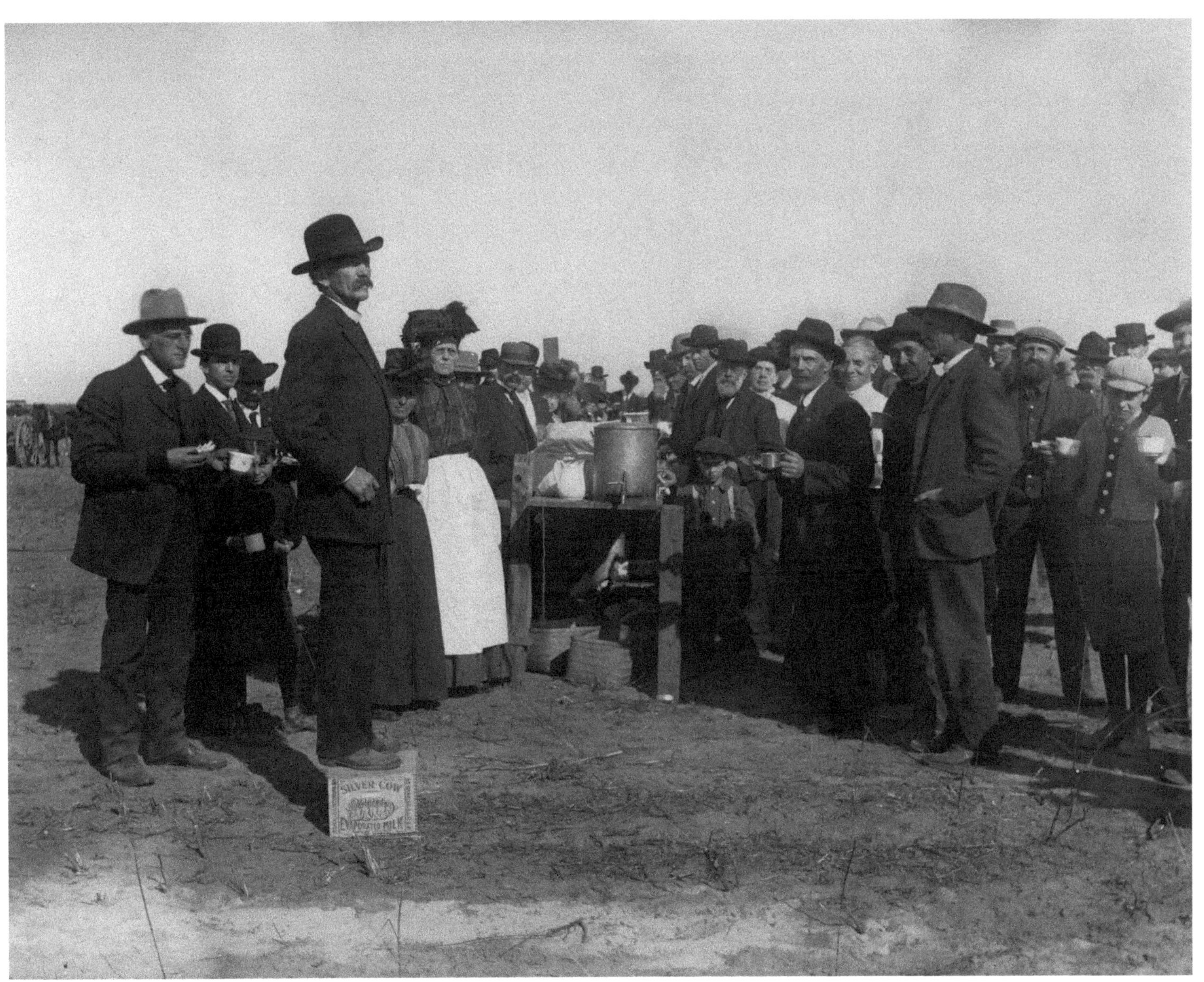

A prosperous-looking farmer (a member of the Talbert family, perhaps?) stands on a crate of Silver Cow evaporated milk and addresses a rapt audience. Their stomachs full, they sip their coffee and dream about the bright future that could—and did—await those who purchased land in fertile, temperate Orange County.

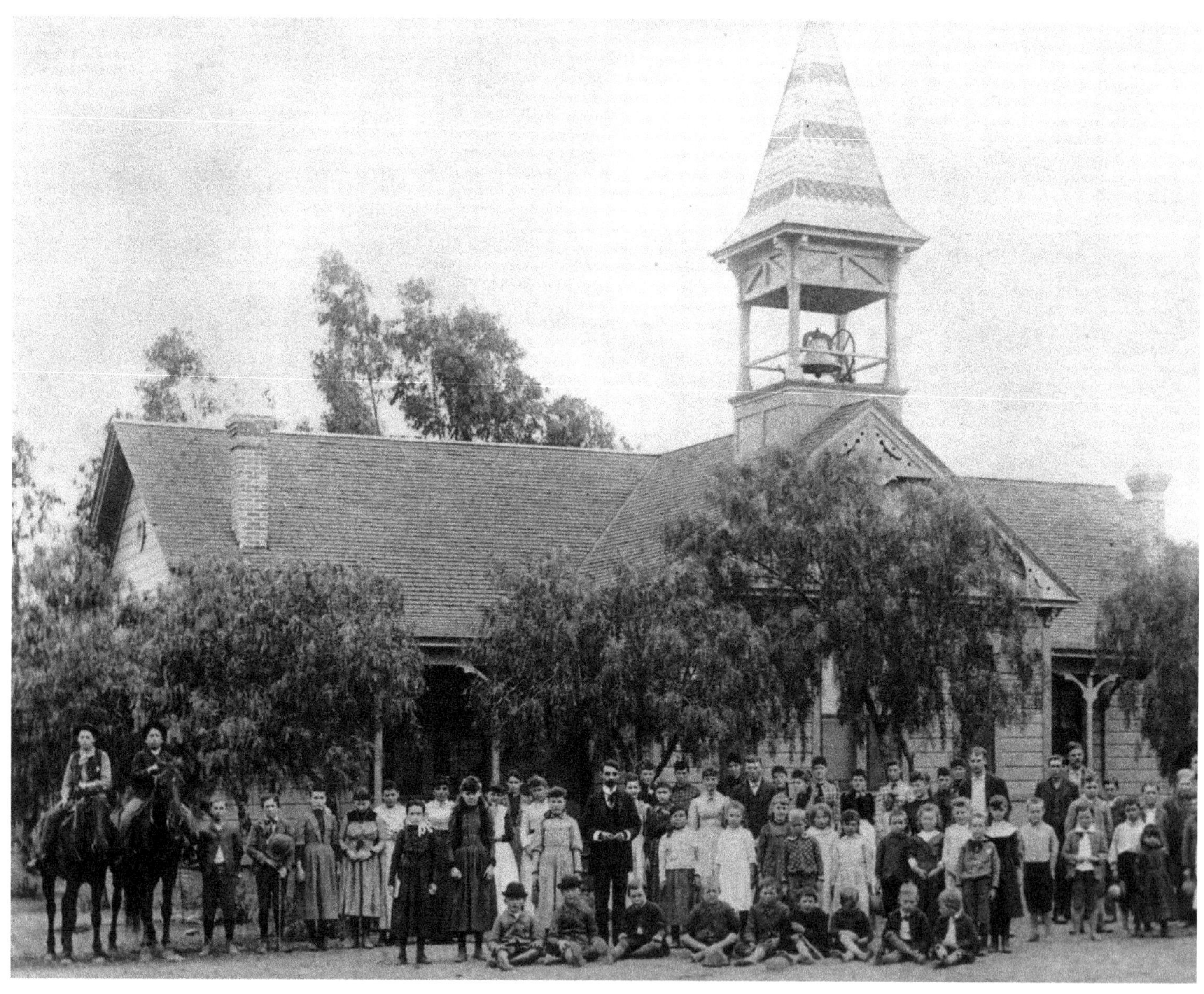

Mountain View School, so named for the scenic hills surrounding it, opened in 1881 and is seen here about a decade later. The community it served was also known then as Mountain View, but was incorporated as Villa Park in 1962 to avoid annexation by the city of Orange. Villa Park, whose motto is the "Hidden Jewel," is today Orange County's smallest city in terms of population, an exclusive enclave completely surrounded by Orange.

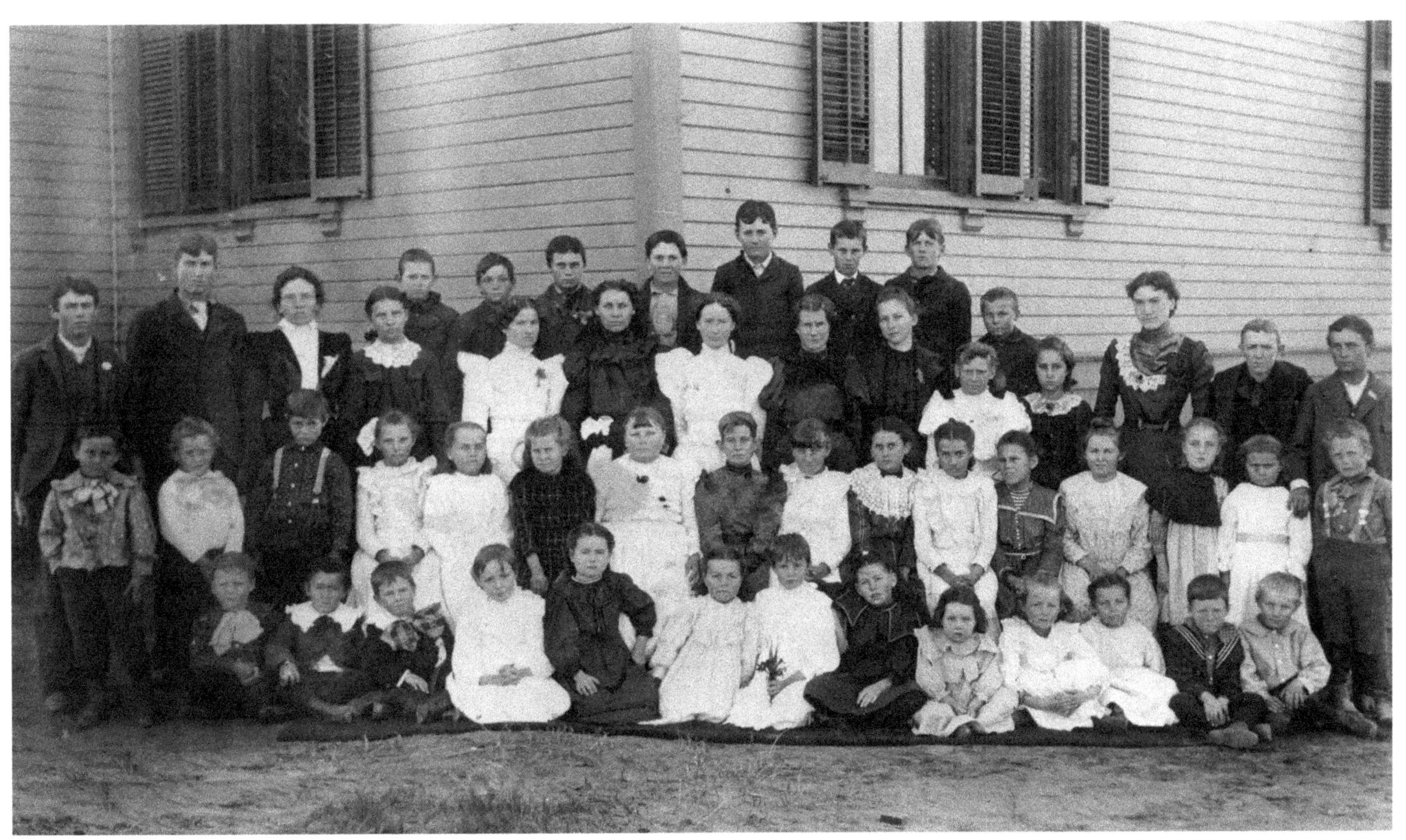

Buena Park's first schoolhouse was built in 1892 and opened with 23 students. By 1898, when this photo was taken, attendance had more than doubled, with fully 10 percent of the student body composed of various members of the Moody family, after whom a city street was later named. County records valued the property at $3,950 and listed 226 books in the school library. Buena Park today is served by seven different school districts.

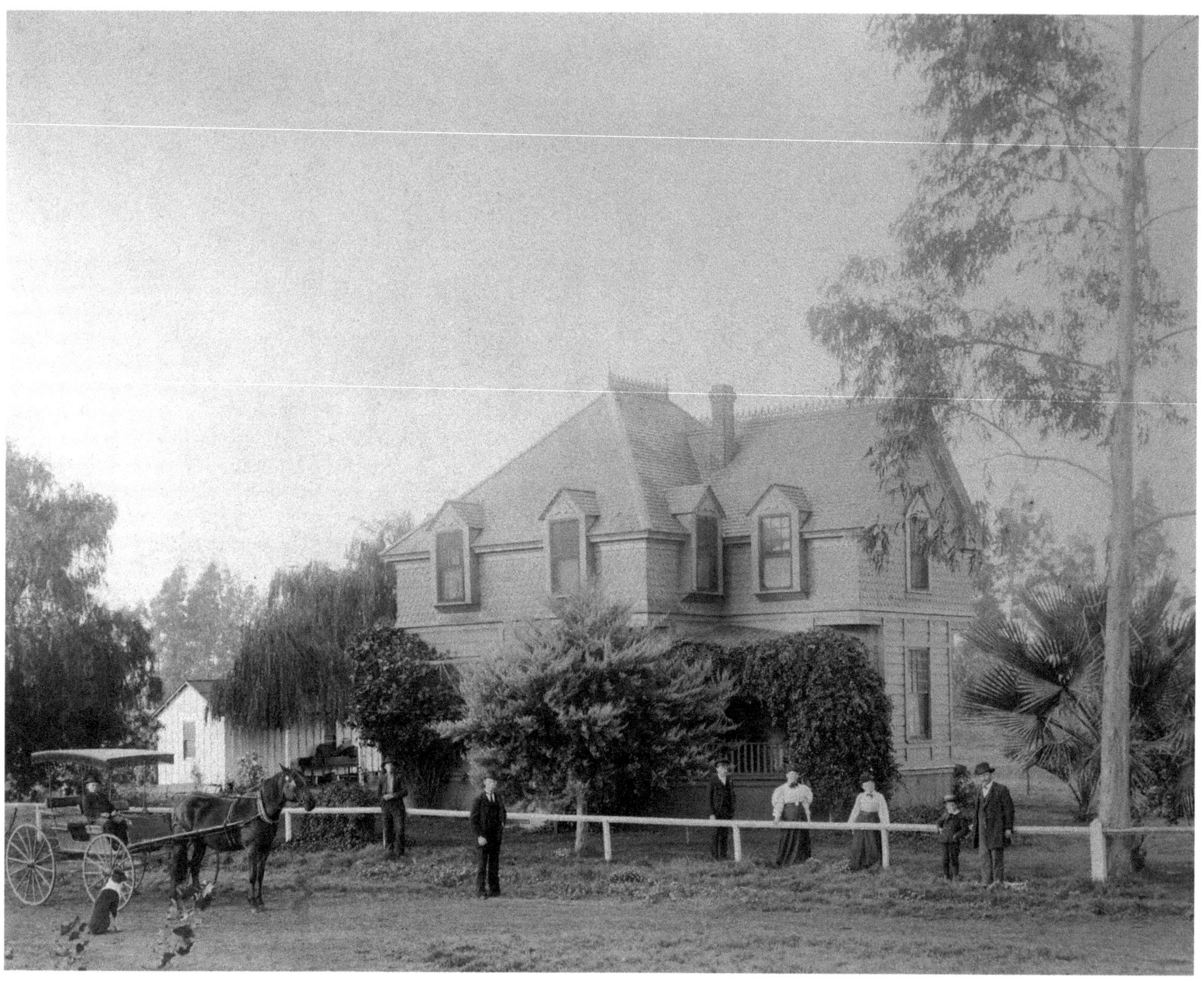

The first standing house in the area that would become Buena Park was a squatter's shack that appeared in a remote corner of Rancho Los Coyotes around 1884. By 1896, the year of this photograph, many fine homes such as this one belonging to the Reis family had been constructed.

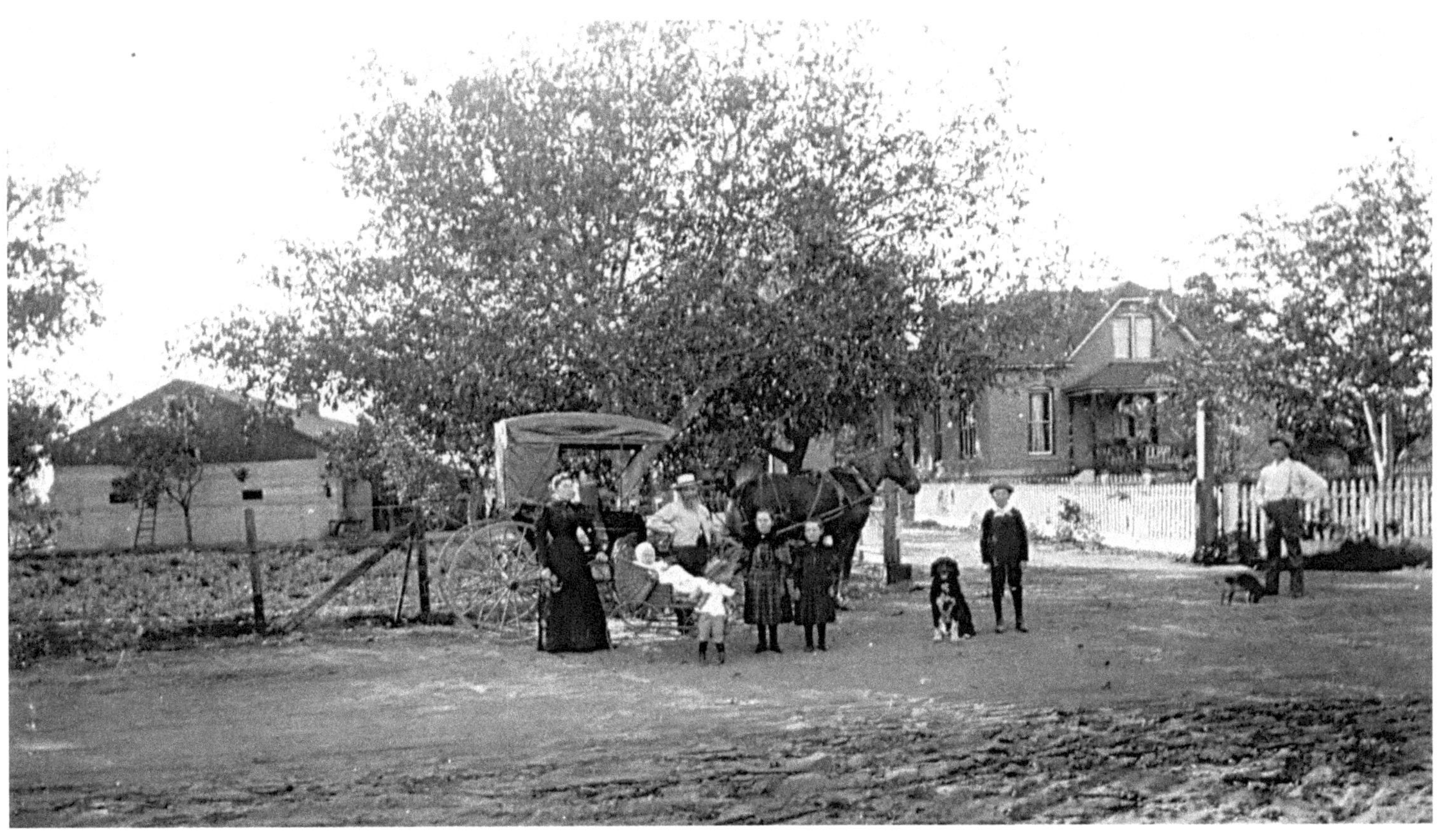

Although winemaking in Orange County was centered in Anaheim, Joseph Young maintained a successful vineyard in the city of Orange from 1876 to 1910. The Young home and vineyard, shown here in 1895, was located on Fairhaven Avenue. In 1886 disease devastated the area's vines, putting most local vintners out of business. By the early part of the twentieth century, grapes were no longer a viable commercial crop in Southern California.

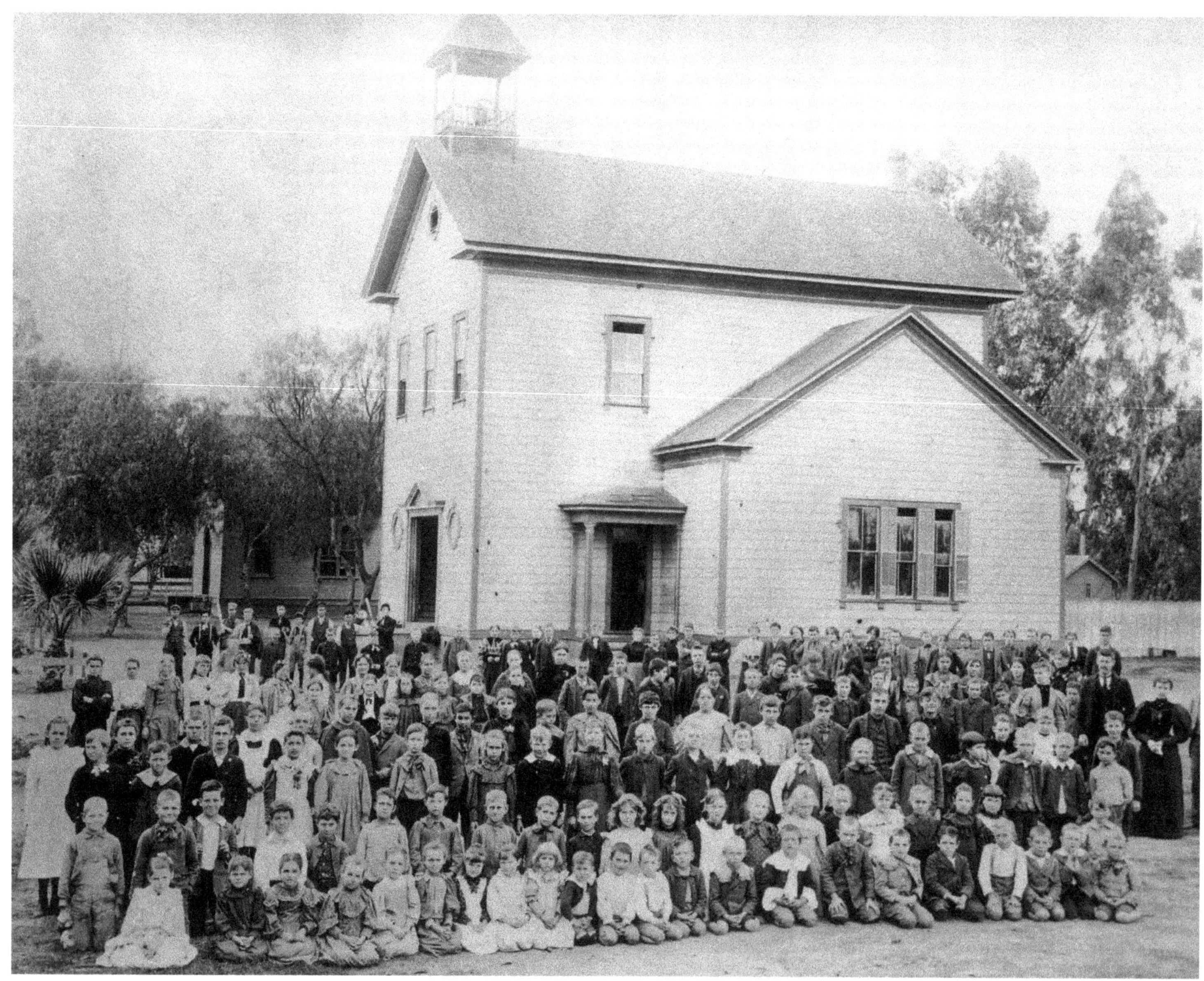

The Garden Grove school district organized in 1874. Shown here in 1897 is the entire student body posing in front of the schoolhouse. The children in the back row at left appear to be holding baseball equipment. Garden Grove remained a small rural crossroads between Anaheim and Santa Ana until the arrival of the railroad in 1905. Today the city is famed for Robert Schuller's Crystal Cathedral and has significant Vietnamese and Korean populations.

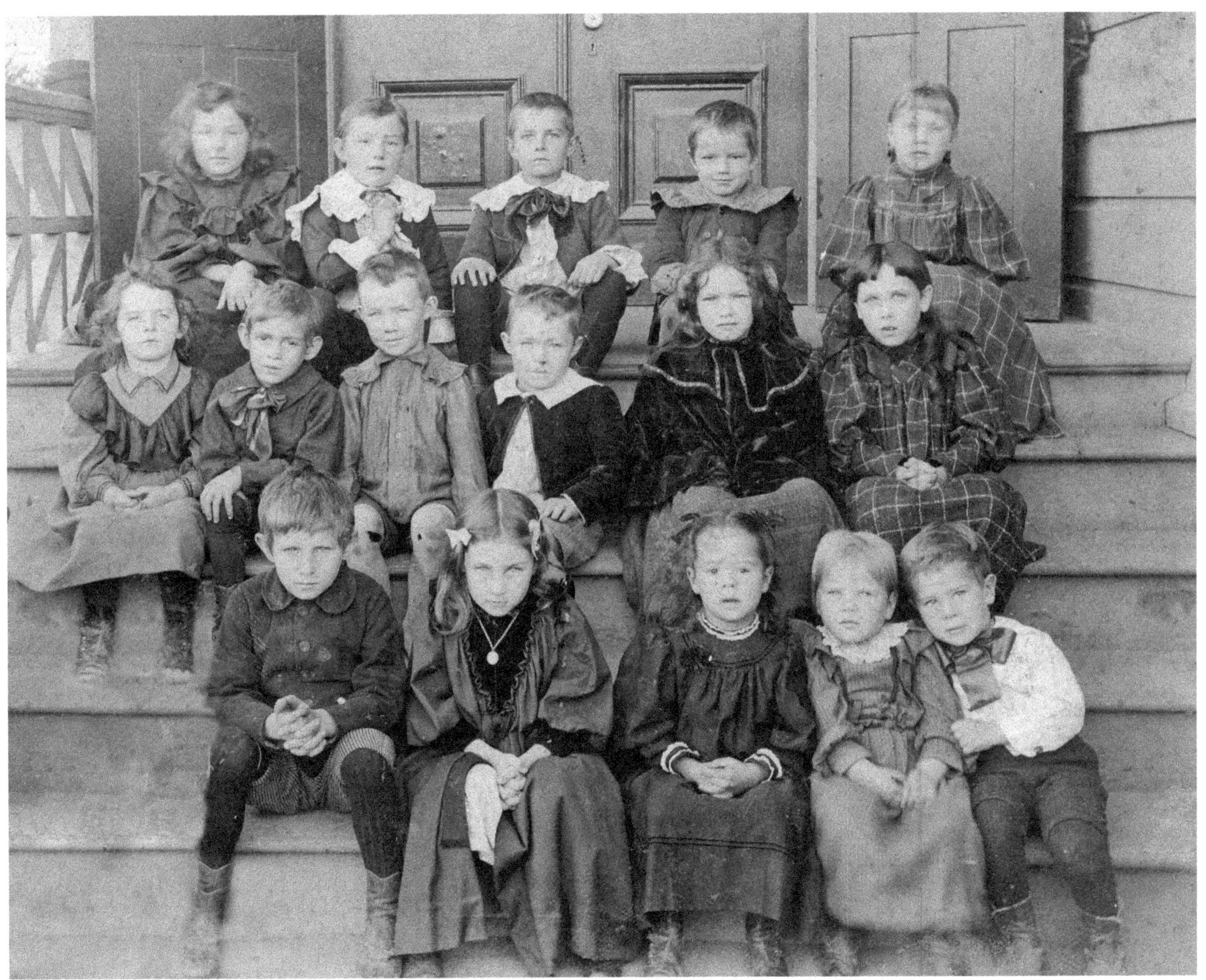

In 1898, the year this photograph was taken, there were six churches in the city of Orange, representing the Methodist, Presbyterian, Lutheran, Baptist, and Episcopal faiths. Shown here are the youngest members of First Christian Church, established in 1883 at the corner of Chapman and Grand. In 1961 the church moved to a new building on Walnut Avenue, where it still stands.

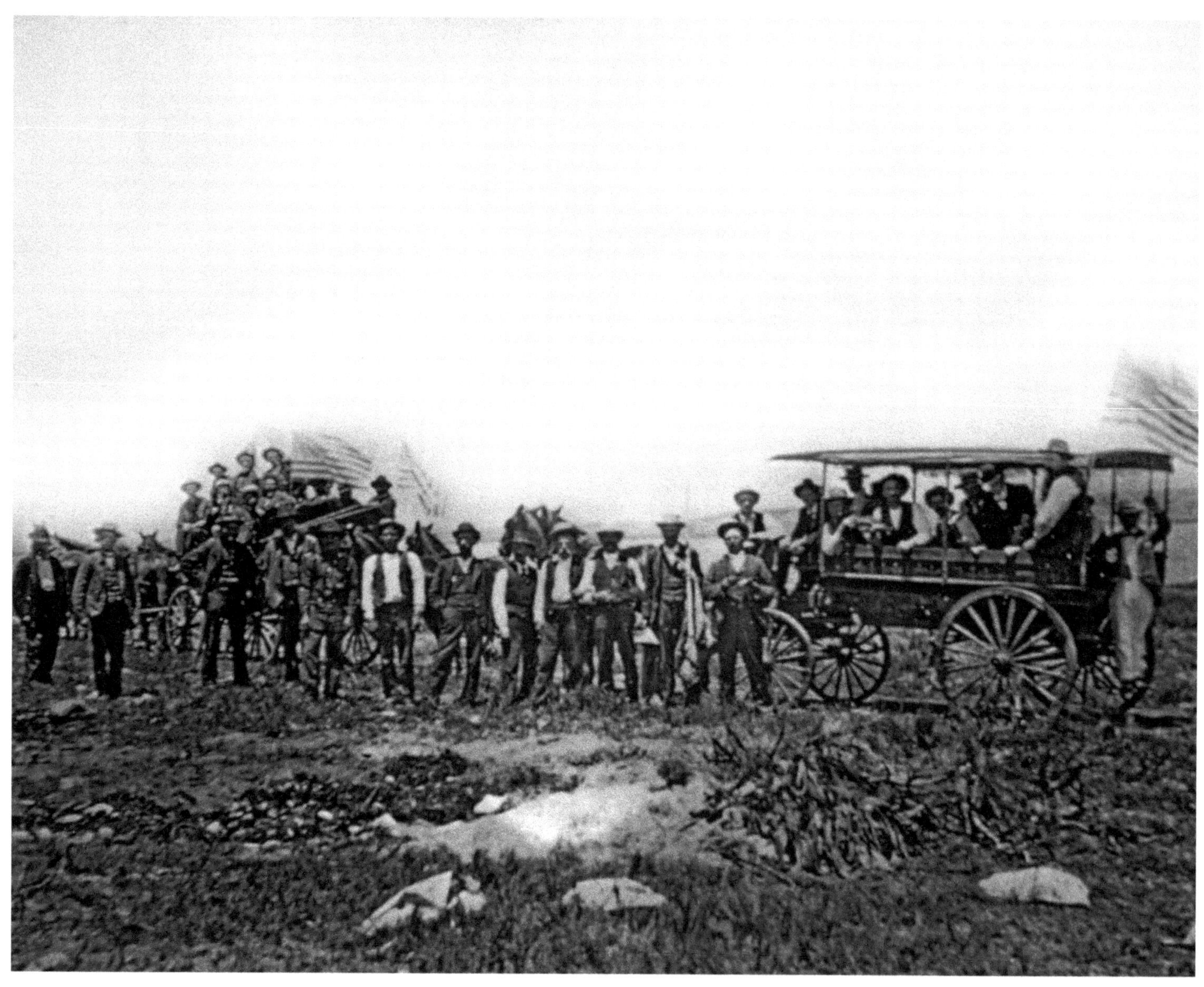

Their gloomy demeanors notwithstanding, the motto of the Boston and Narragansett Fishing Club of Santa Ana was "to have as good a time as possible as often as possible." This photo was taken at Abbott's Landing, just west of today's Balboa Pavilion, in the summer of 1899. Abbott's Landing was named for Edward J. Abbott, a prominent early resident who planted the first trees there.

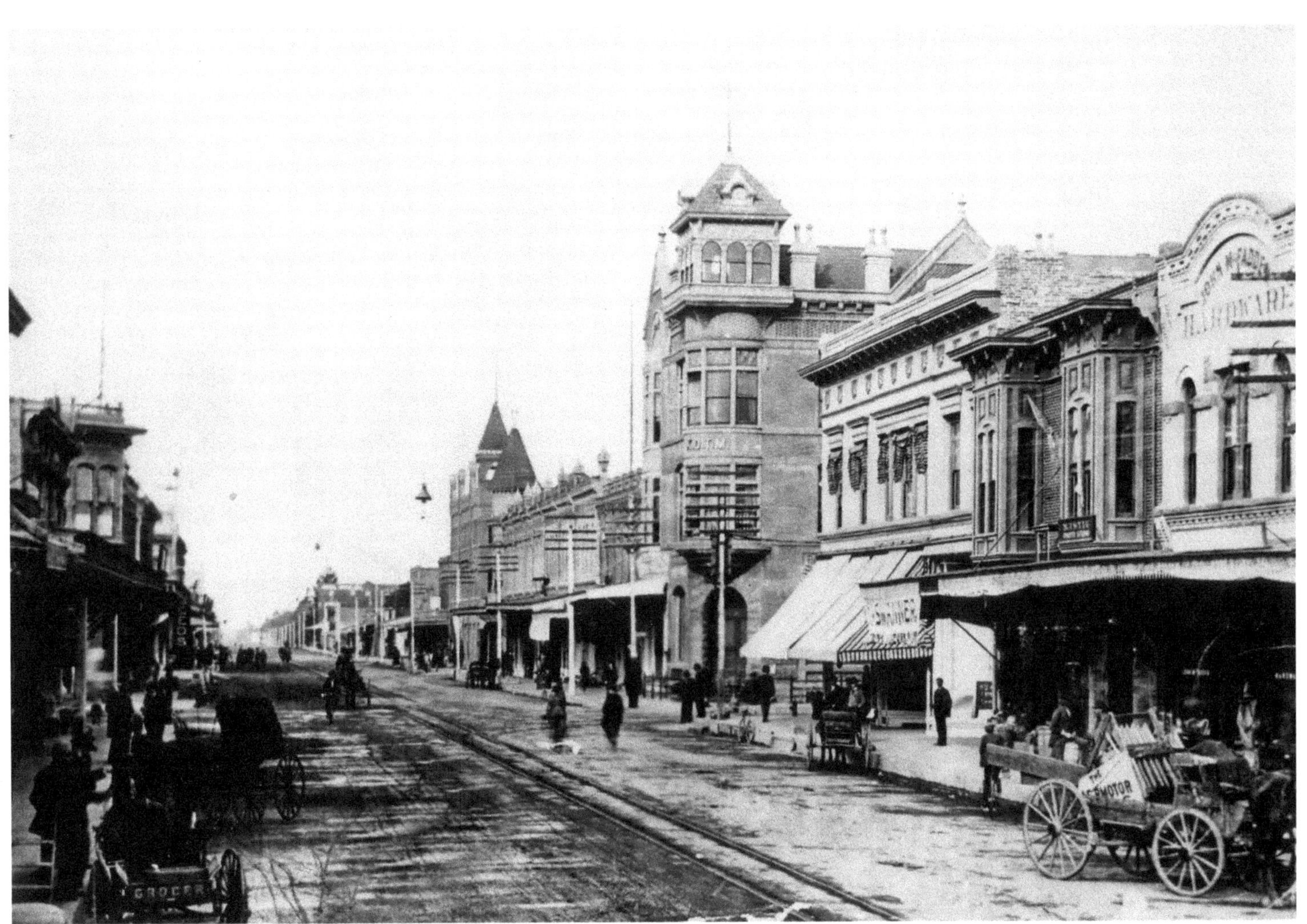

This photograph was taken looking west on Fourth Street from Bush in Santa Ana, ca. 1900. At far right is McFadden's Hardware, opened in 1879 by John McFadden. McFadden was one of four brothers who settled in Orange County in the 1870s and played significant roles in the development of Santa Ana and Newport Beach. His brothers James and Robert built the McFadden Wharf that ushered in Newport's decade as a shipping port.

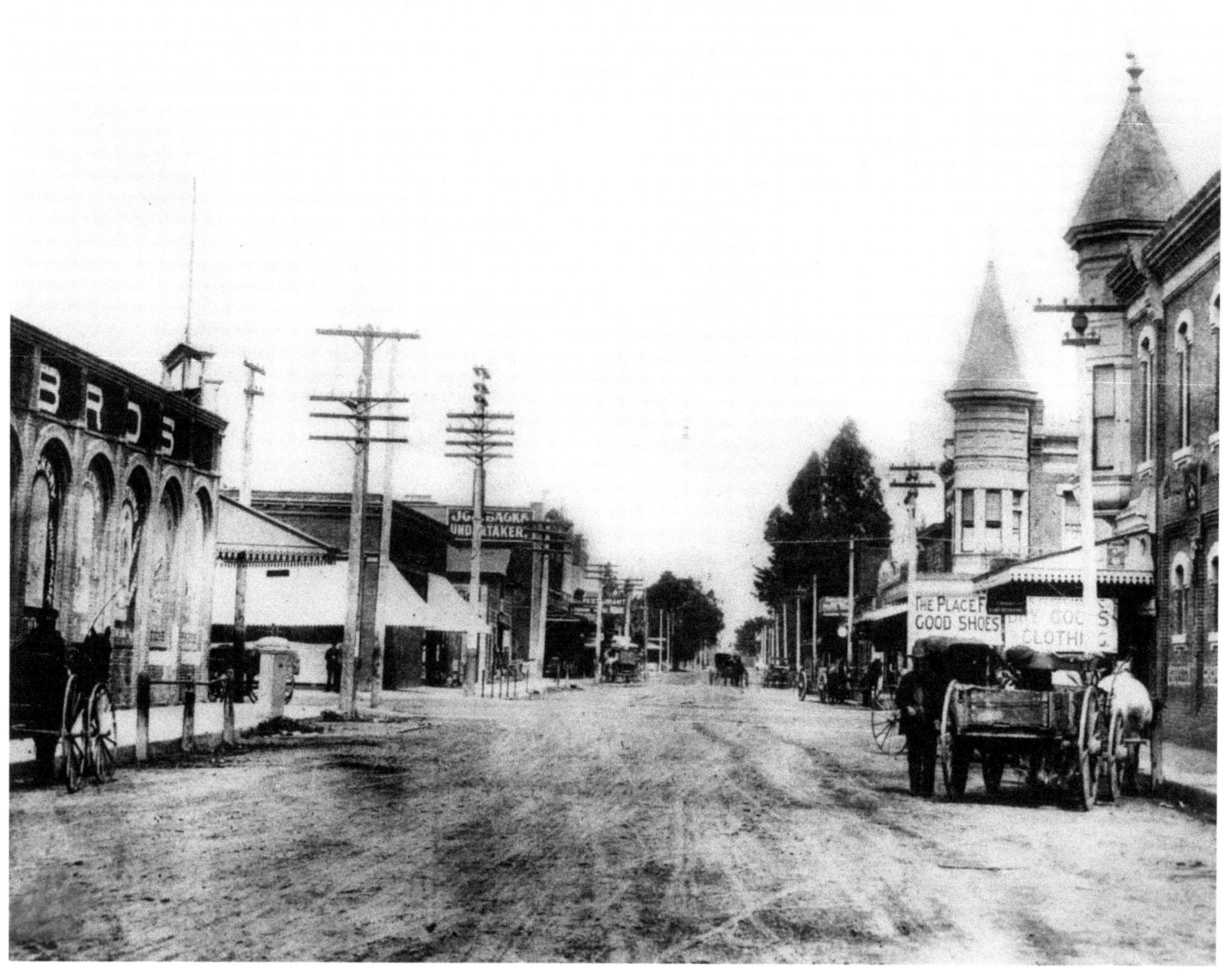

The unique turrets of the Federman Building are seen at right in this turn-of-the-century photograph of downtown Anaheim. In 1870 Anaheim became the first Orange County city to incorporate, but it lost the bid for county seat in 1889 to rapidly growing Santa Ana. Anaheim would not regain its preeminence in the county until 1955 with the opening of Disneyland, which quickly turned the city into a worldwide tourist destination.

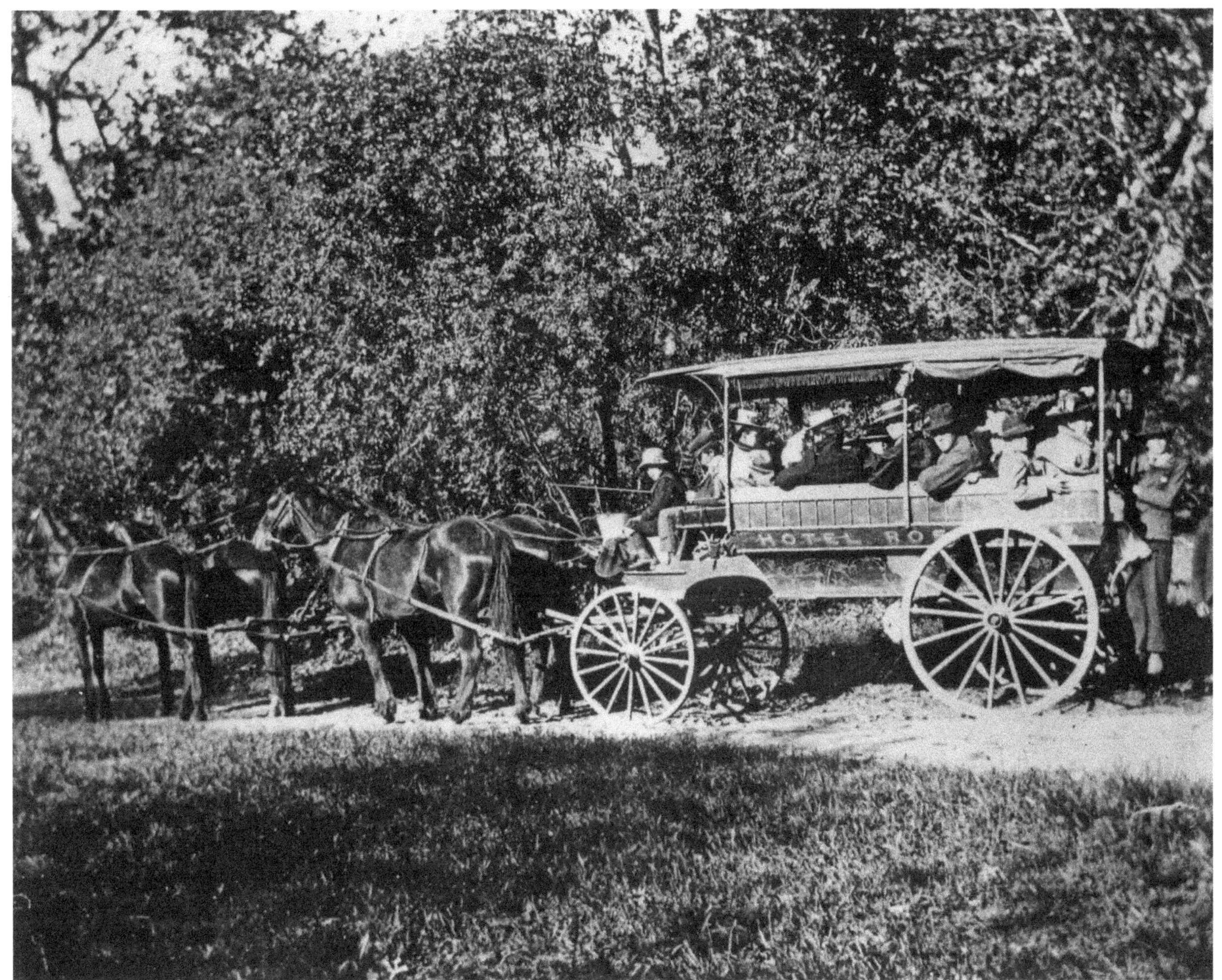

The elegantly appointed Rossmore Hotel was the height of luxury when it opened in 1887 at 406 North Sycamore in Santa Ana, even going so far as to provide its guests with the nineteenth-century equivalent of a shuttle bus. The "Tally Ho" bus, shown here ca. 1900, was a horse-drawn stagecoach that ran between the hotel and Irvine Park—a popular recreational site then and now, and OC's first park.

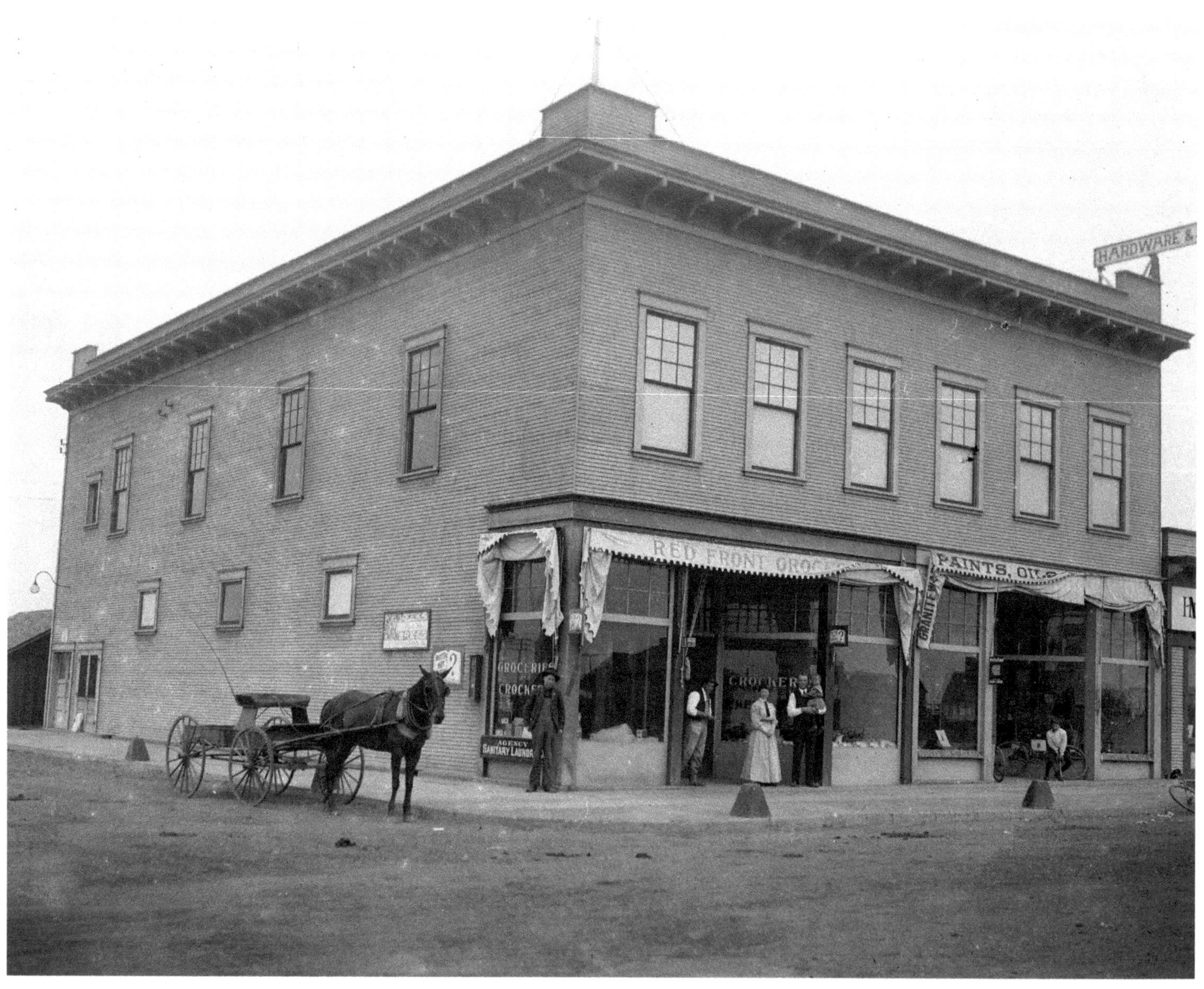

The land that would one day become Huntington Beach was purchased in 1901 by the West Coast Land and Water Company syndicate, which hoped to turn the area into a resort called "Pacific City," the West Coast equivalent of Atlantic City. This commercial building on Main Street housed Stewart Meeting Hall on the top floor and a combination grocery and hardware store on the lower level to service the needs of the hoped-for influx of settlers.

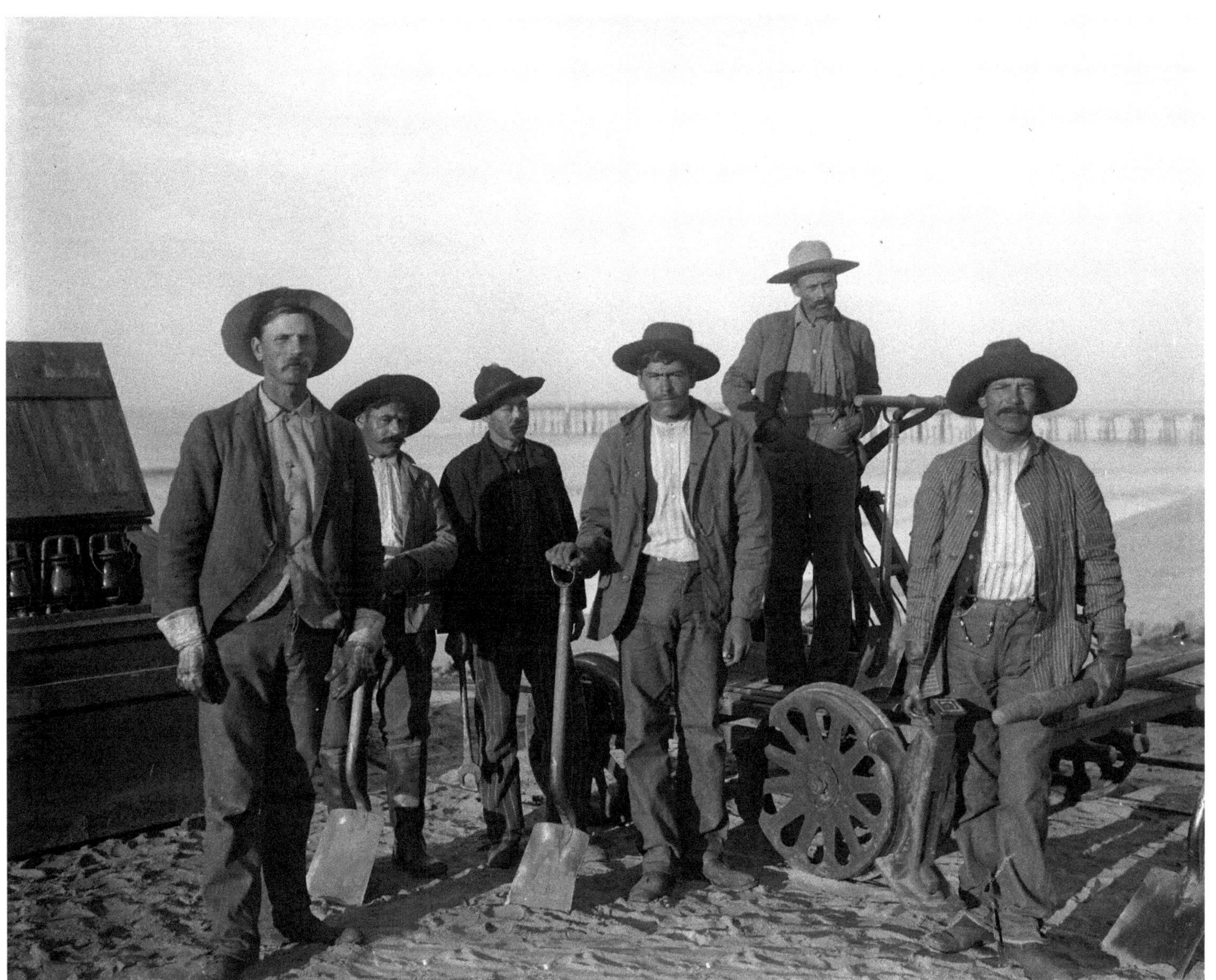

Huntington Beach at one point was served by three different railroad lines, providing plenty of employment opportunities for crews such as this, hired to lay and maintain tracks. The hard-working crew poses on a handcar with the Huntington Pier just visible behind them in this photo from the early 1900s. The wooden box at left stores red warning lanterns that were hung around job sites, serving much the same function as traffic cones today.

One of Santa Ana's most popular events around the turn of the century was the Fourth of July celebration. As part of the festivities of 1900, Emil Markburg was attempting a spectacular feat—dangling below a hot air balloon basket, attached only by a strap held between his teeth—when he fell to his death 500 feet below in front of a crowd of horrified spectators.

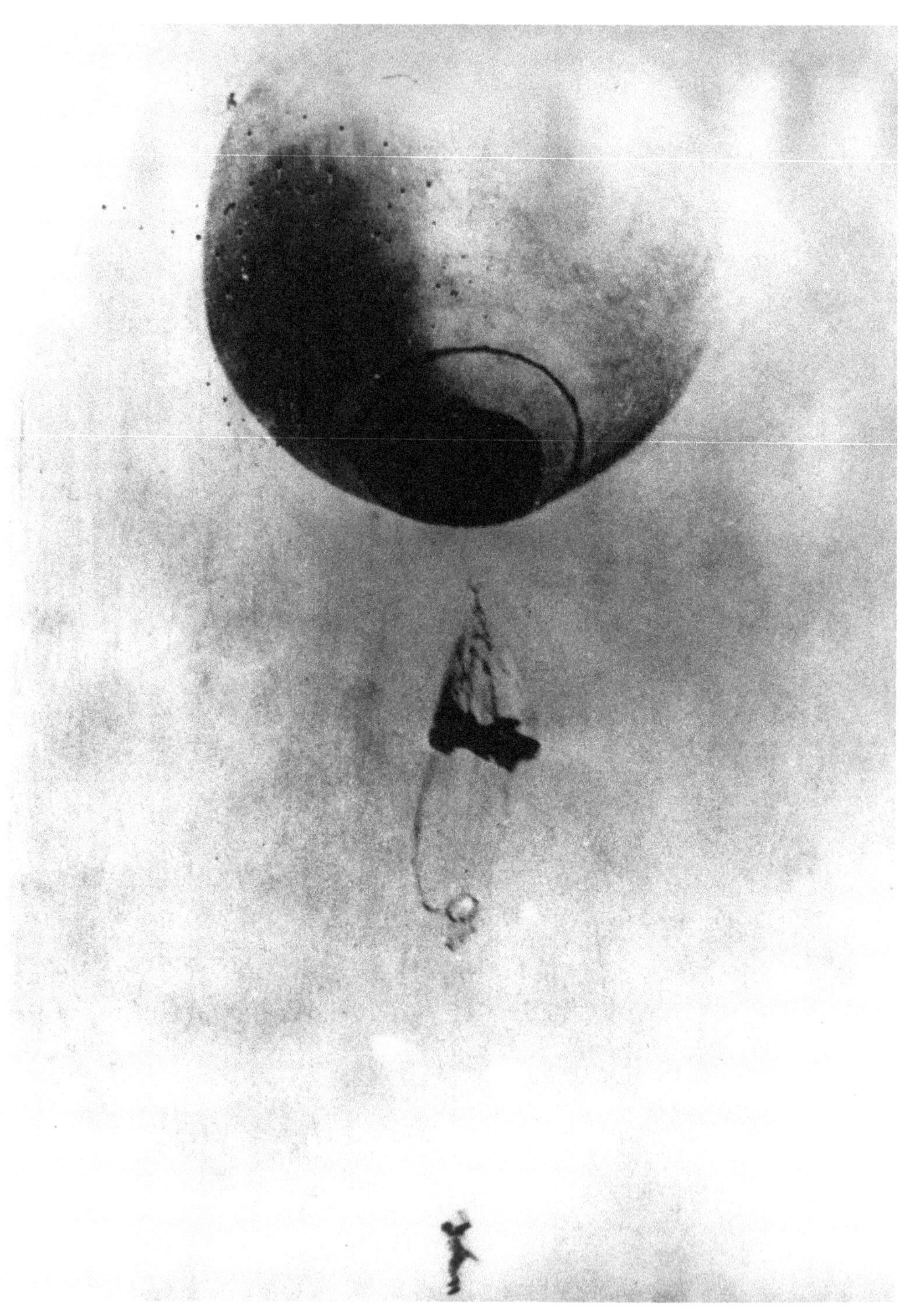

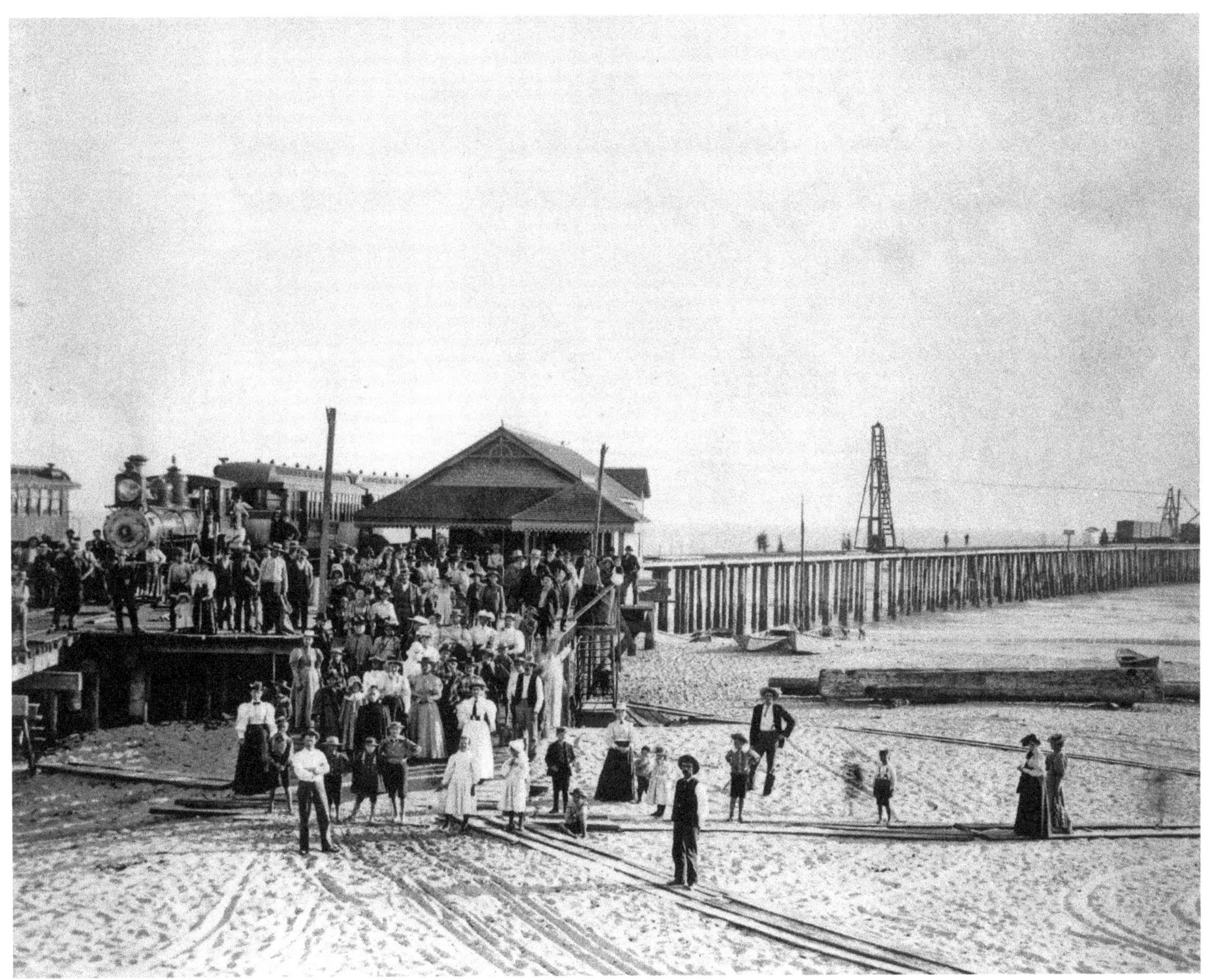

Passenger service from Santa Ana to Newport Beach on the Santa Fe Railroad started in 1891. The 11-mile route took 12 minutes—a fraction of the time it would take to drive the same distance today. The arrival of the train at McFadden Wharf was cause for much excitement; the whole town would flock to the station to see who had arrived and to get the latest news.

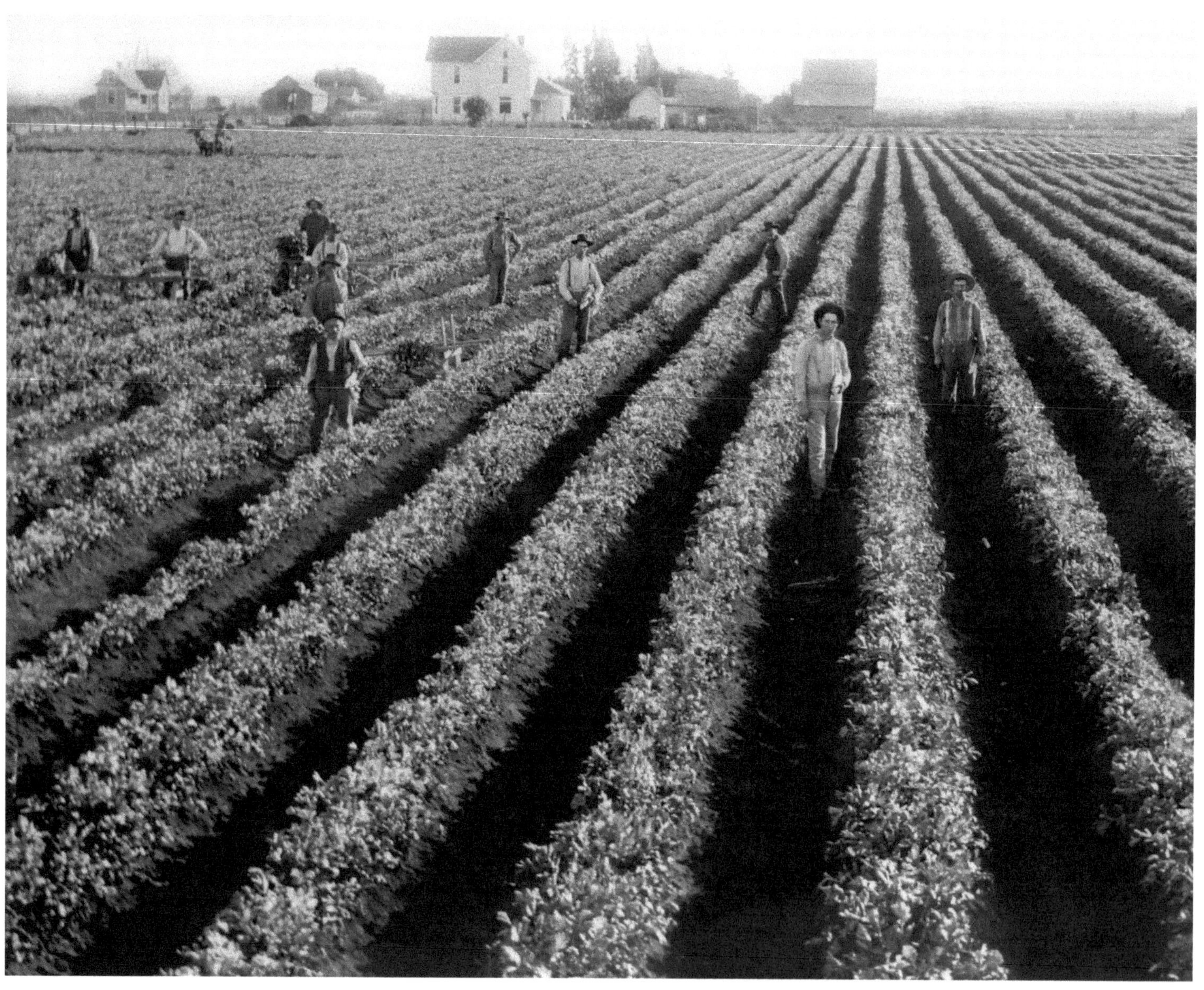

Founded in 1870 as a temperance colony, Westminster briefly experienced success as a center of celery production, despite repeated harassment of its many Chinese farm workers, and the marshy conditions that necessitated outfitting the horses with "peat shoes" to keep them from sinking into the mud. Disease wiped out the crops in the early 1900s, not long after the time of this photo. Westminster today is known as Little Saigon, due to its large population of Vietnamese Americans.

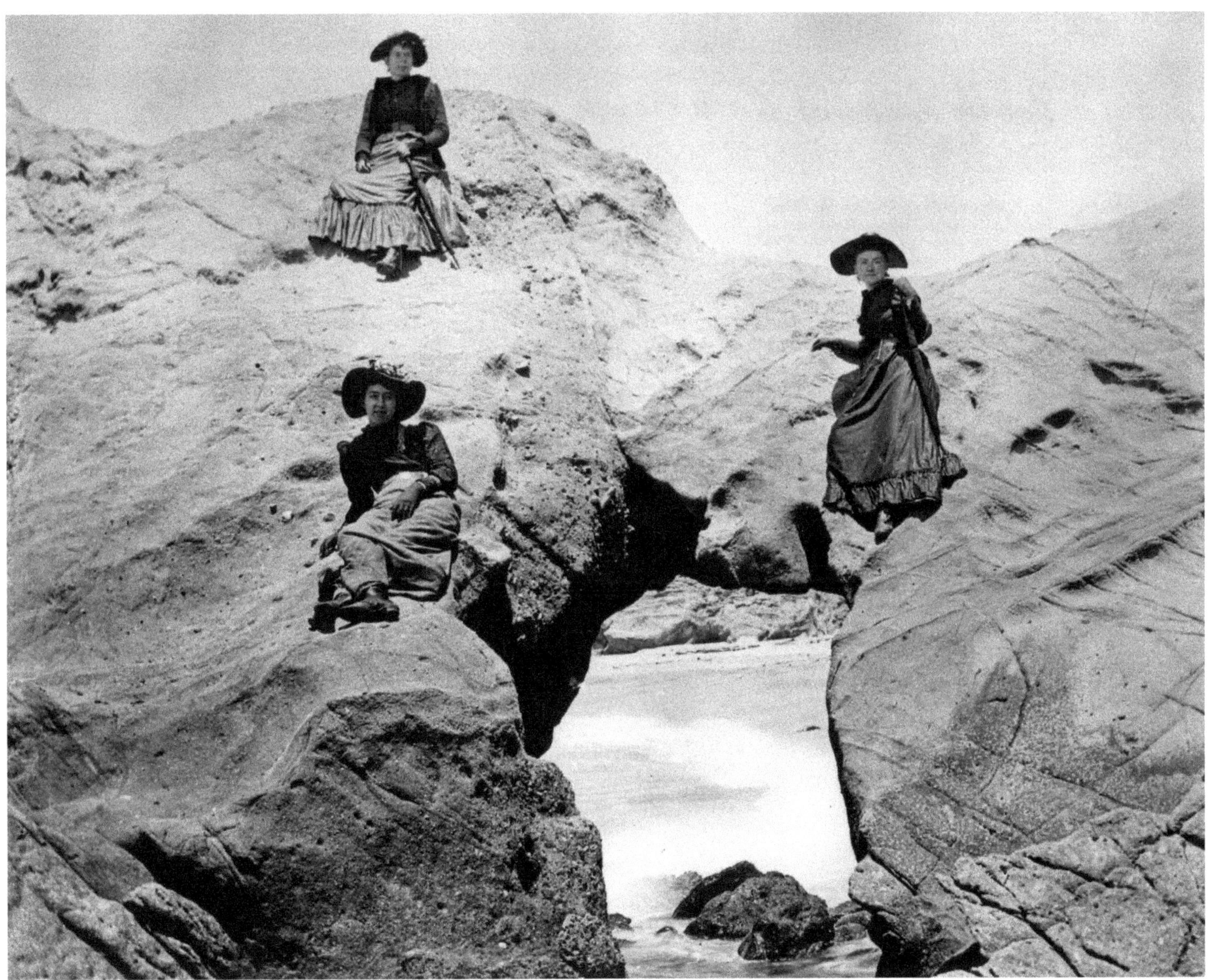

Around 1900, three women pose by the opening of one of the three natural rock formations that give Three Arch Bay its name. The rugged topography of this scenic beach just south of Laguna has proved the muse of many. It was here that Errol Flynn fought off pirates in the swashbuckling 1935 film *Captain Blood,* and that Hollywood luminaries like Edith Head, Fredric March, and Sterling Holloway made their homes.

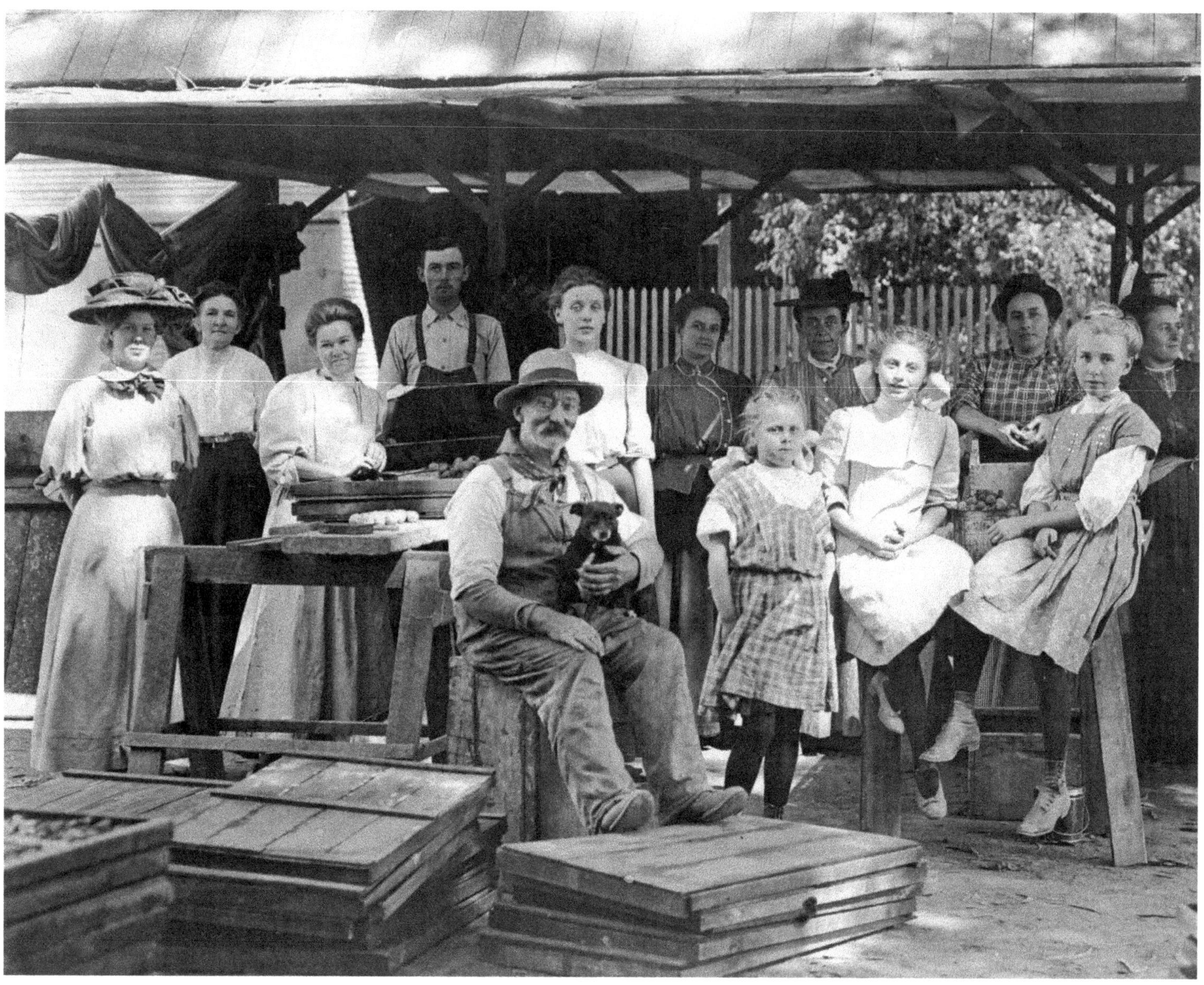

Dried apricots were a profitable business for the two decades leading up to World War I. Most harvesting was done by locals—often girls and boys on summer break from school—working in temporary apricot-picking camps under improvised awnings at the side of the road. Boys did the picking and girls did the halving, a rather unpleasant task involving sharp knives and hands drenched in sticky juice.

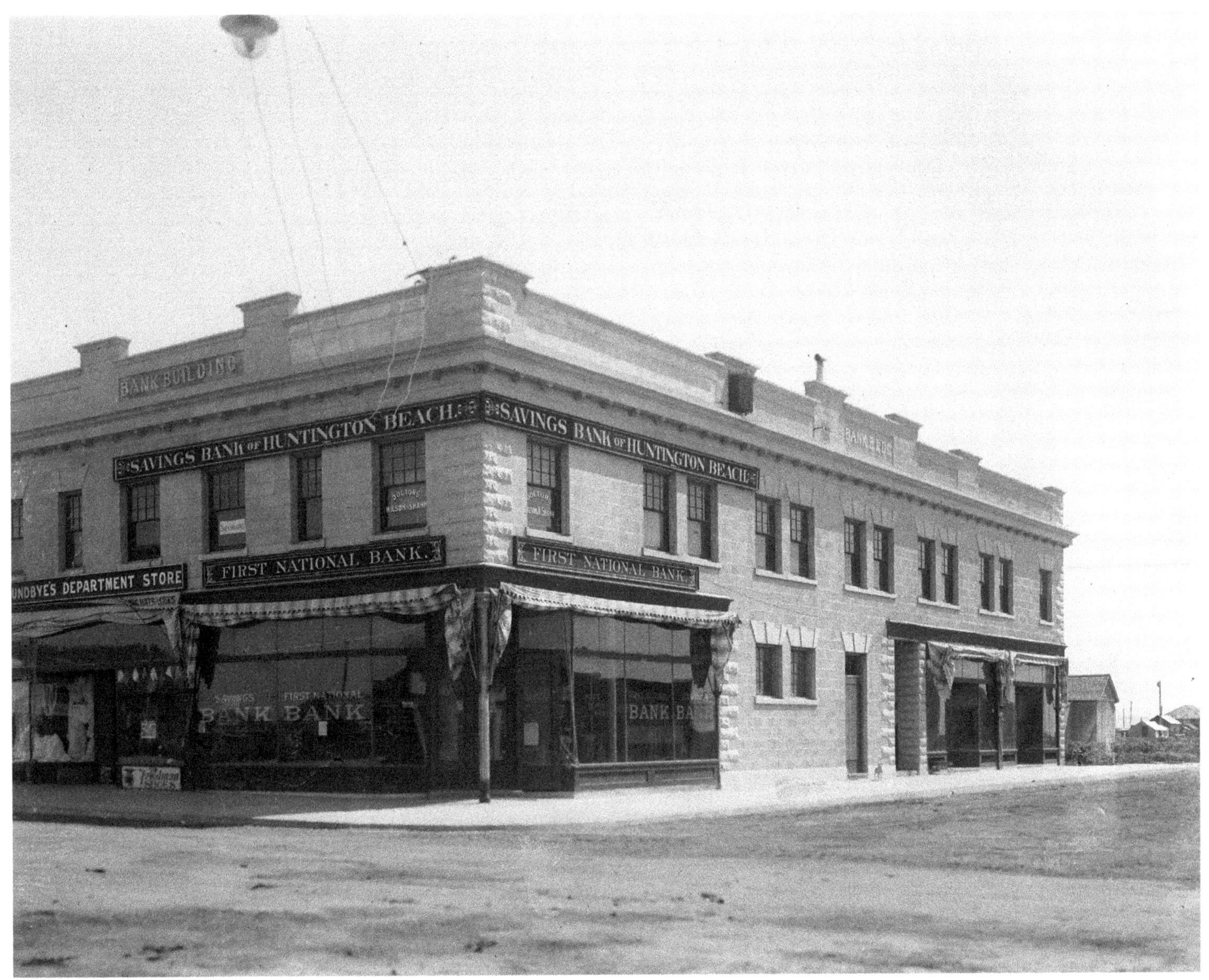

Pacific Beach was renamed Huntington Beach in 1903 in honor of Henry Huntington, who built the town's first pier and extended a line of his Pacific Electric Railway to it. The resulting land boom caused the price of lots to skyrocket from $200 an acre to $3,000, and a commercial center quickly developed on the high bluff overlooking the ocean. Shown here is the First National Bank building on Main Street.

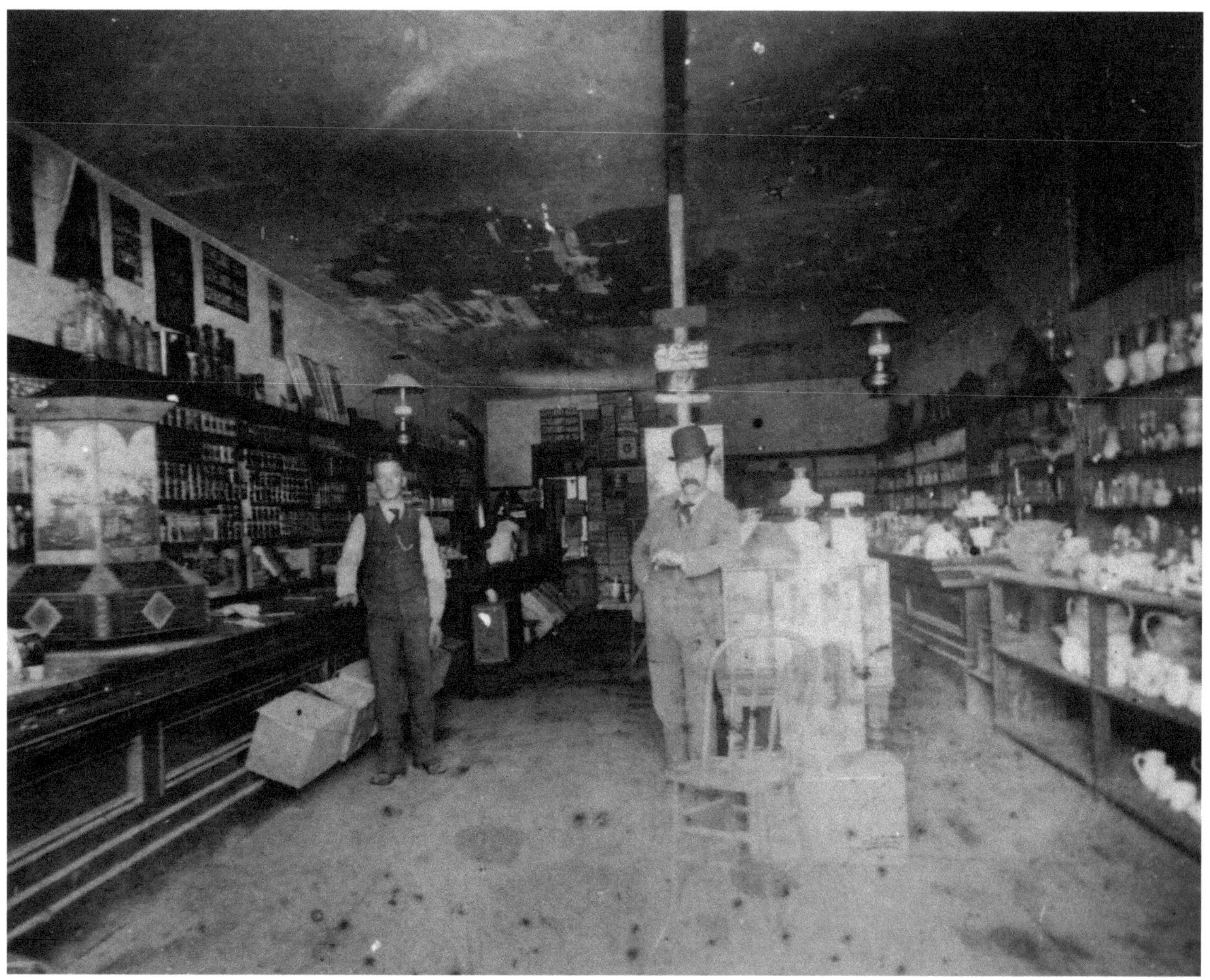

The John Martin store, located near the southwest corner of Bush and Fourth streets, was typical of downtown Santa Ana businesses in 1900. Deep and narrow, this general store was sandwiched between two other similarly confined, windowless spaces. Though the facades of the buildings that housed these business establishments were impressively ornate, with decorative brickwork and cornices, the interiors tended to have low ceilings and be dimly lit with gas lamps.

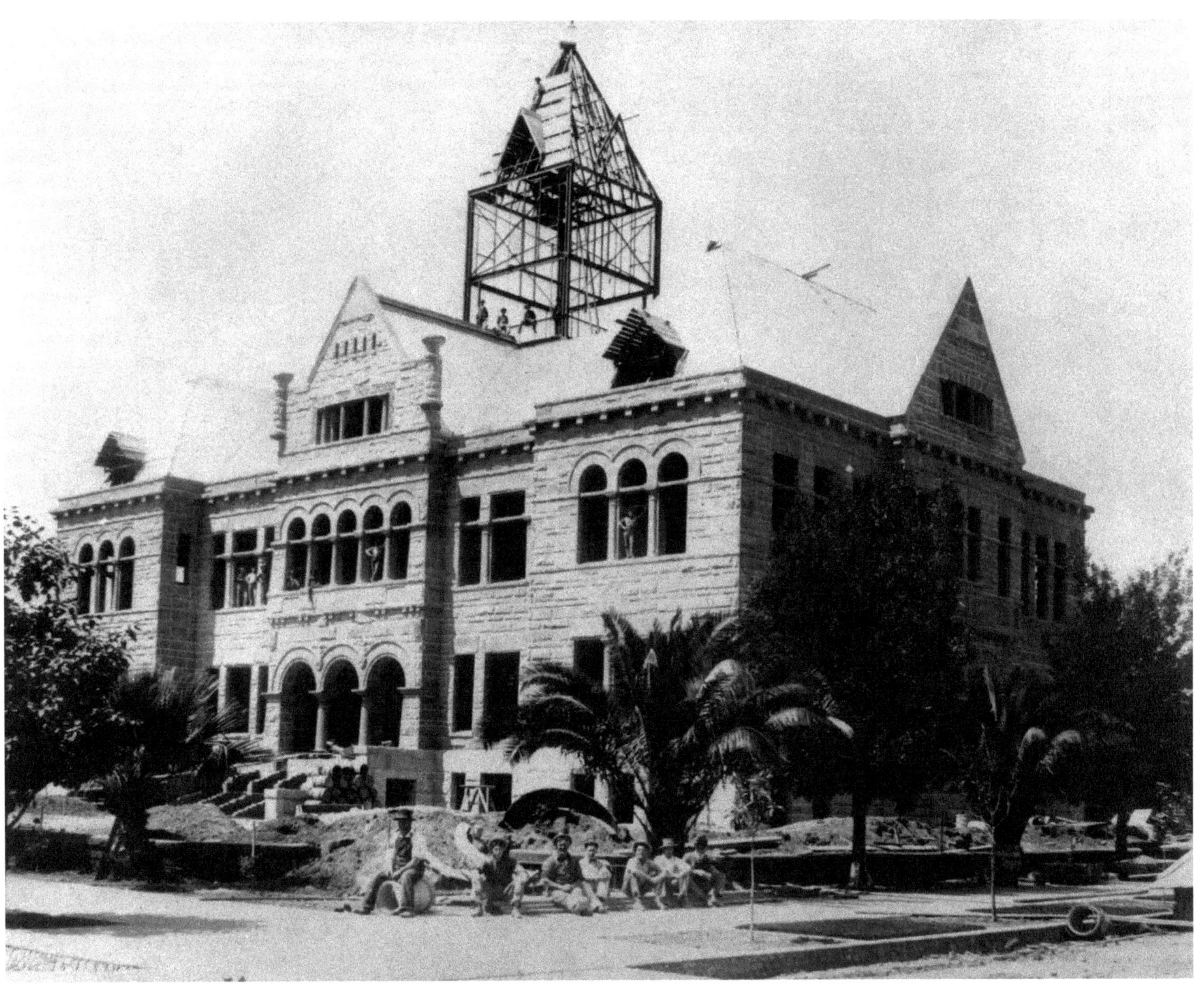

Shown nearing completion in this 1901 photograph, the Santa Ana County Courthouse was designed by noted L.A. architect and former superintendent of buildings C. L. Strange. Constructed of sandstone and granite, the building had a price tag of $117,000 and replaced an earlier courthouse immediately adjacent to the site. This California historic landmark currently houses primarily educational displays and archives.

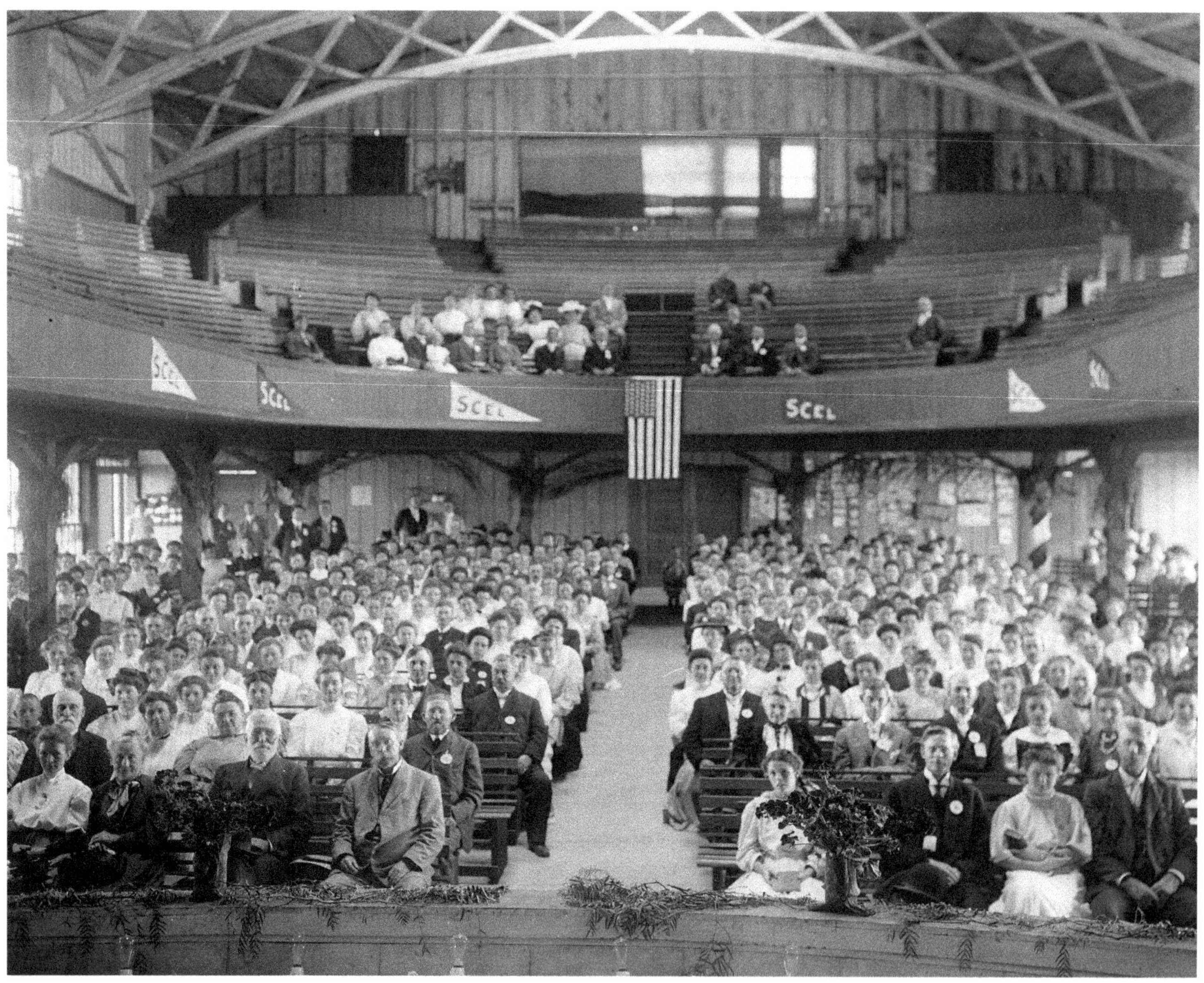

By 1904 the Pacific Electric Railroad had arrived in Huntington Beach, connecting the city to Long Beach and the rest of Los Angeles County, and city boosters were eager to attract tourists. Soon they lured the Methodist convention away from Long Beach by donating a large campsite and building a 3,000-seat auditorium for them. In this photo the auditorium is hosting a meeting of the Epworth League, a Methodist youth organization.

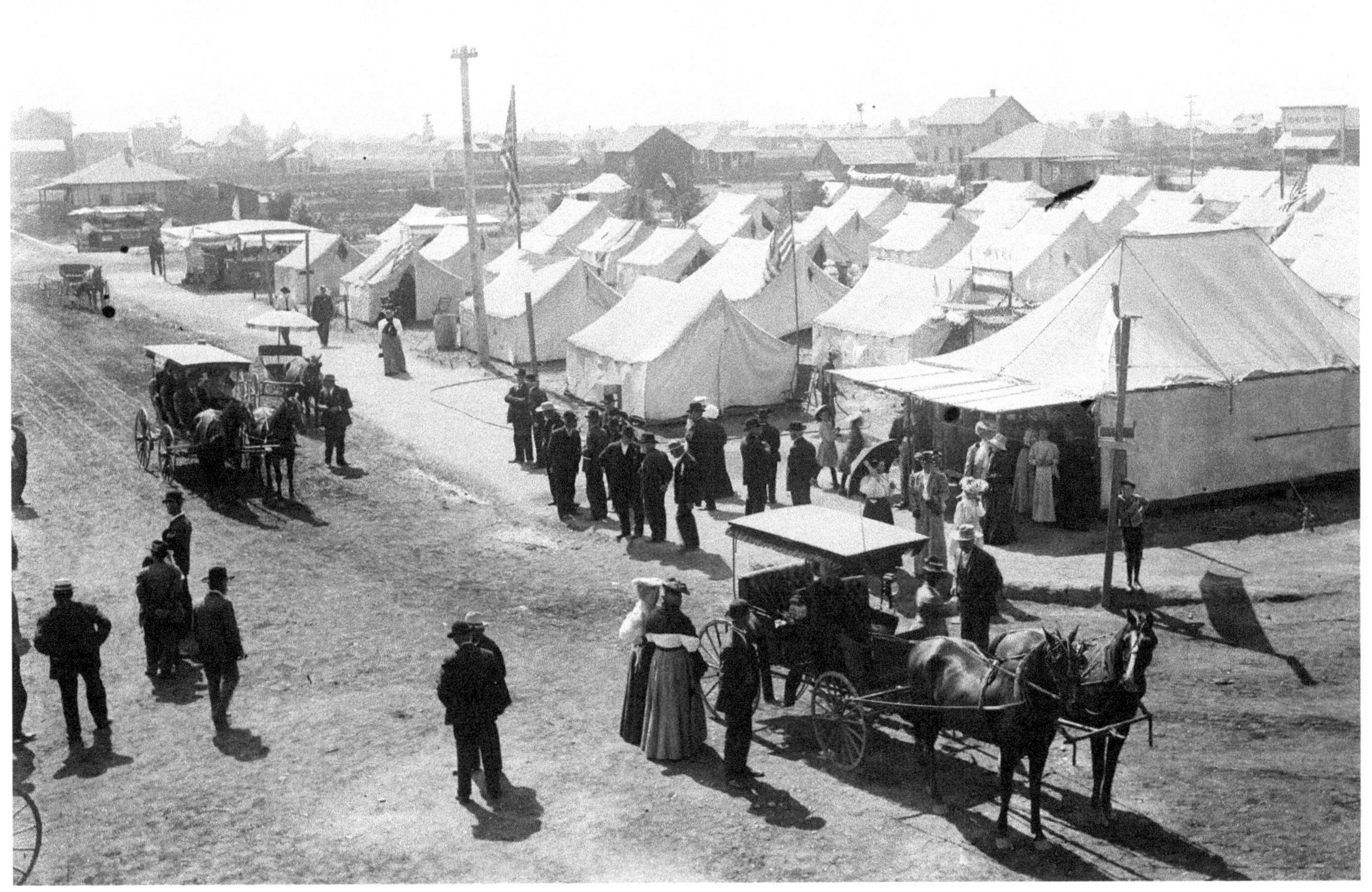

Between 1905 and 1920, the open land in front of the Methodist Tabernacle Auditorium in Huntington Beach became a sea of tents in the summer months, hosting at various times Grand Army of the Republic encampments, Methodist revivals, and Socialist meetings. This photograph likely shows a group of Methodists gathered to attend an Epworth League convention.

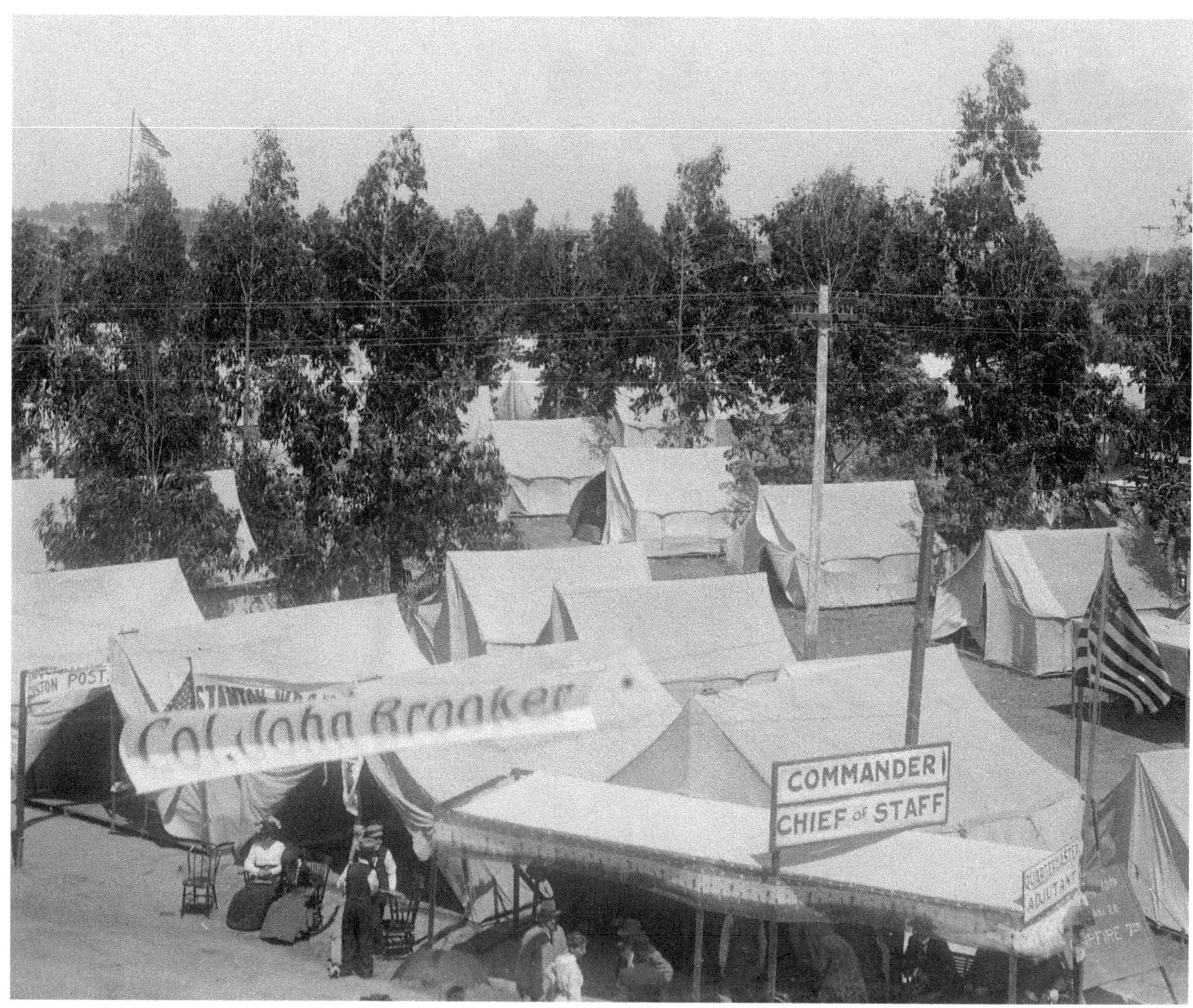

The Grand Army of the Republic (GAR), established in 1866, was one of the first organized interest groups in American politics, formed to lobby for pension legislation. The group also held regular encampments, such as this 1911 regional gathering in Huntington Beach, an event named in honor of Colonel John Brooker, veteran of the Battles of the Wilderness and Spotsylvania. Colonel Brooker died in 1909 and was buried in nearby Artesia Cemetery.

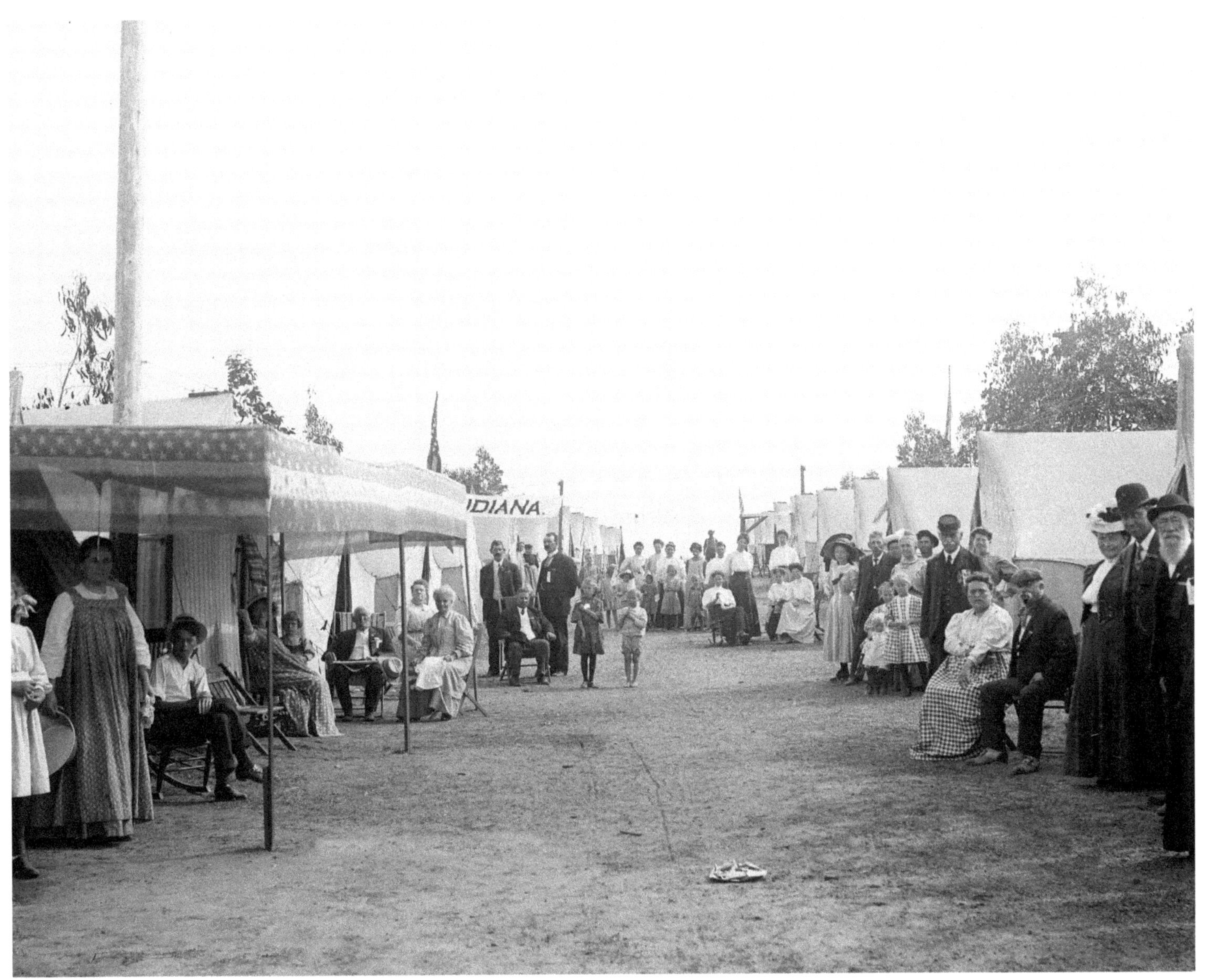

A gathering of men, women, and children convenes at Huntington Beach's Tent City. The group may have been attending a Methodist revival, or may have been members of one of the many women's auxiliary organizations generated by the Grand Army of the Republic, such as the National Woman's Relief Corps, Ladies of the GAR, or Daughters of Union Veterans of the Civil War.

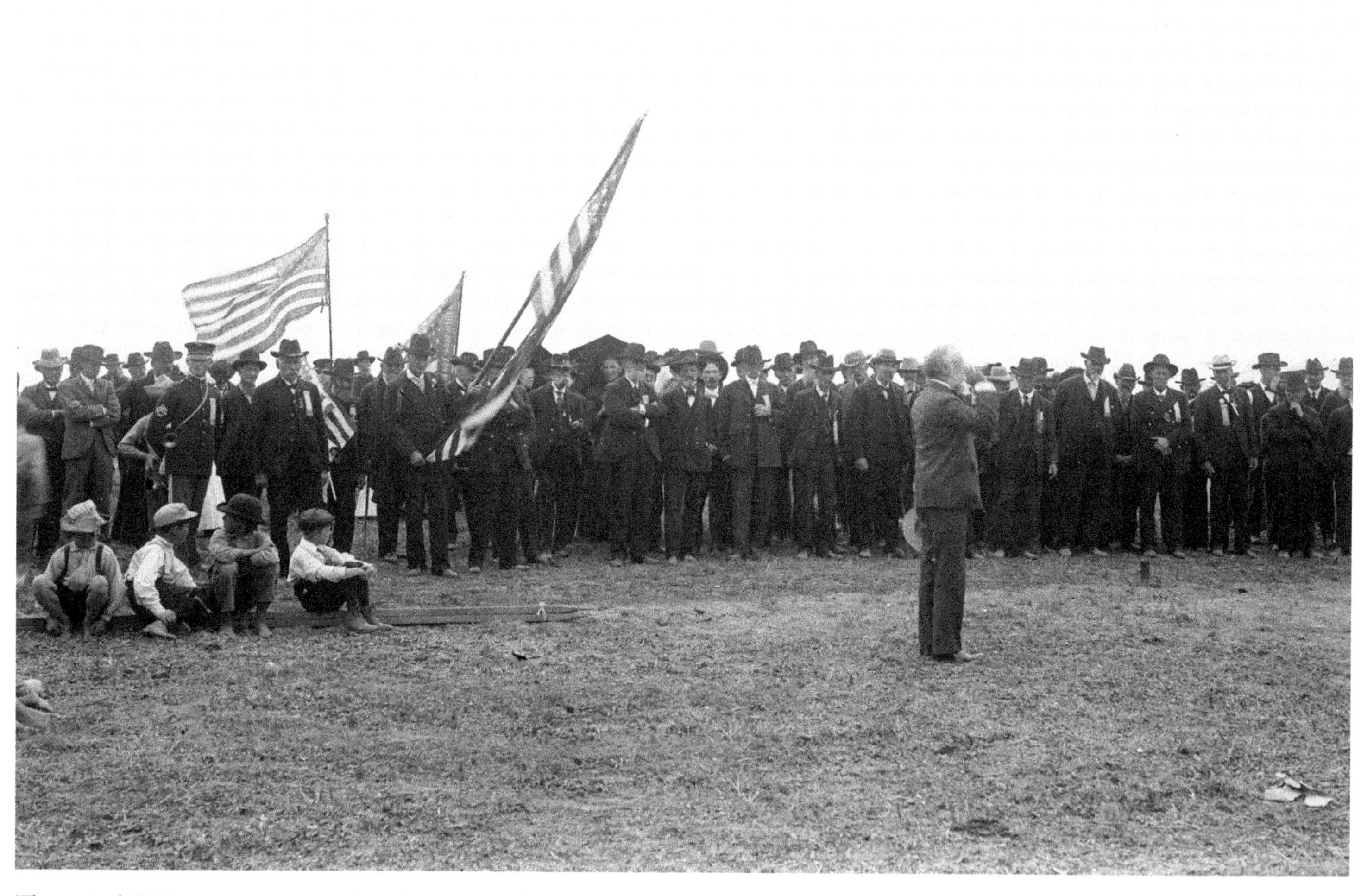

The typical GAR encampment, such as this 1905 gathering, was a chance for Civil War veterans to reminisce about battle experiences, remember fallen comrades, and raise funds for monuments and other worthy causes. But it was also a time of great pomp and pageantry, featuring the posting of the colors, parades, grand patriotic vocal and instrumental concerts, awards ceremonies, formal banquets, fife and drum corps, and speeches by dignitaries.

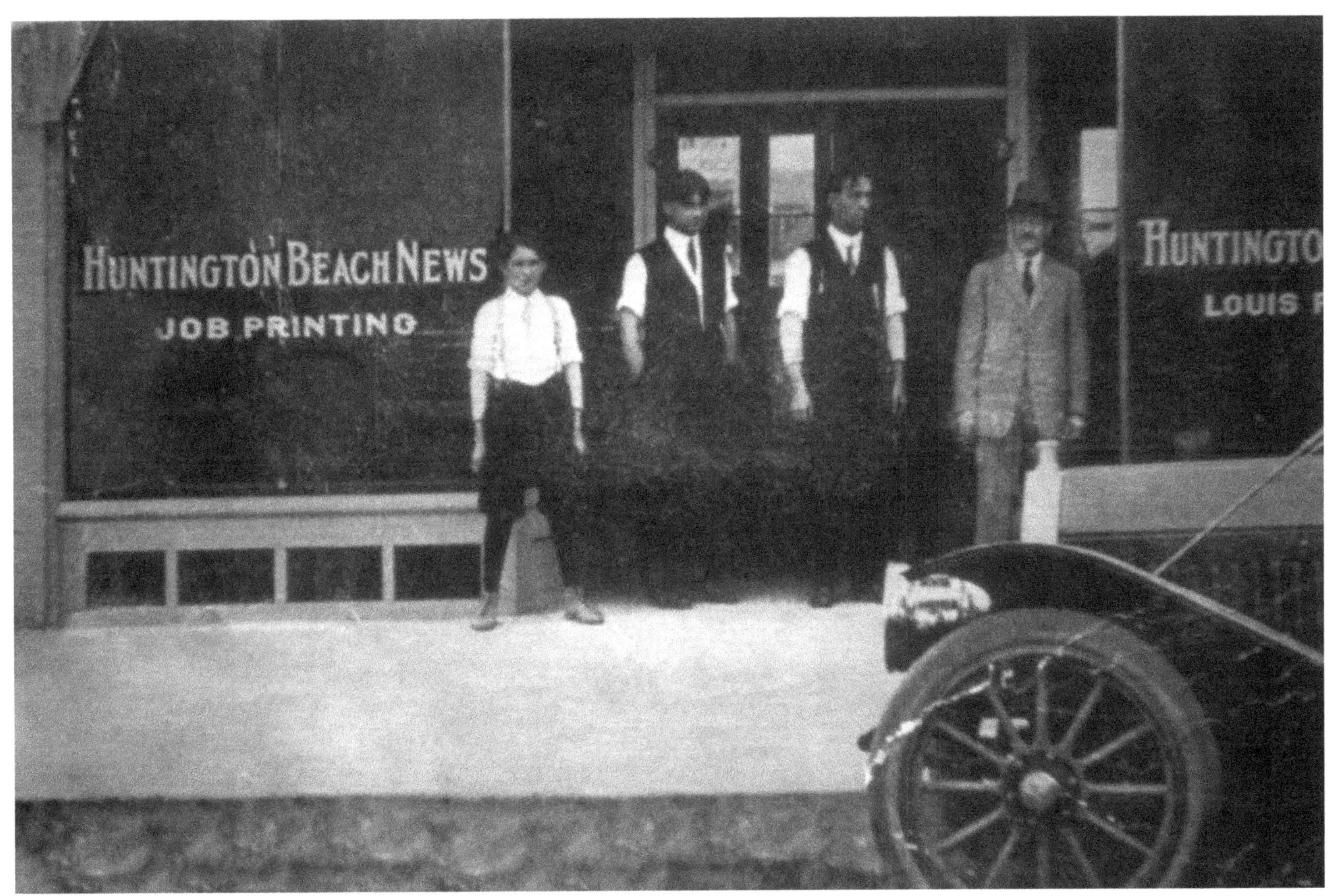

Huntington Beach News was founded in 1905 and occupied the building adjacent to Stewart Hall. In a county where newspapers tended to change names, go on hiatus, or merge with other papers at an alarming rate, *Huntington Beach News* was remarkably long-lived, surviving in print form for nearly a century. The paper was at one point owned by actor Jack Kelly, better known as Bart Maverick of the *Maverick* television series. Since 1996 the *Huntington Beach News* has been available online only.

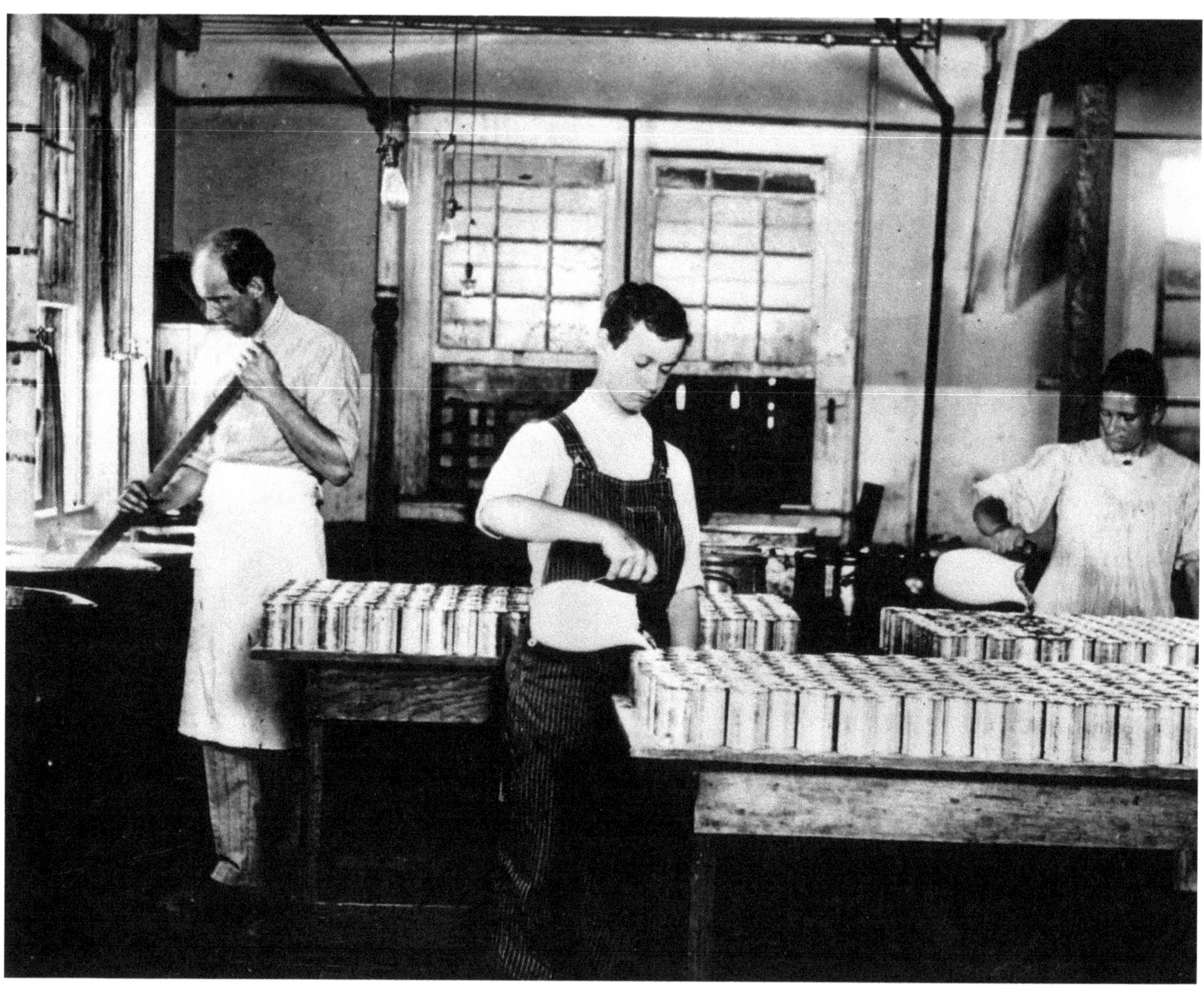

Santa Ana resident Elizabeth Taylor started the J. E. Taylor Canning Company in the kitchen of her Fourth Street home in 1892 as a way to establish her sons in business. By 1901 the family had built a small factory and was shipping 100 tons of peaches and apricots all over the United States, Europe, and the Pacific Islands. The original house and offices still stand, the office retaining its tin ceiling and varnished wainscot.

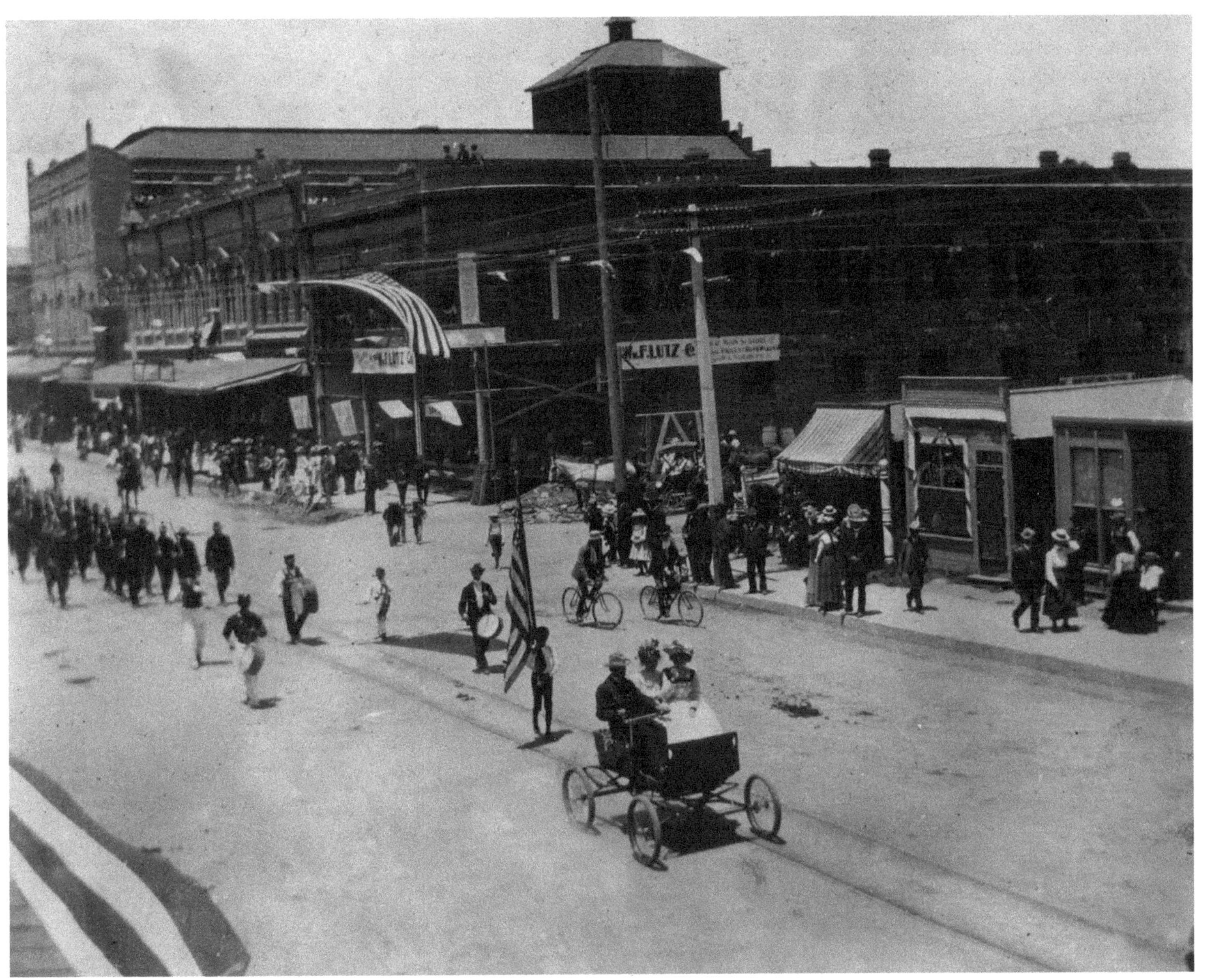

The completion of the Pacific Electric Railway line from Los Angeles to Santa Ana cemented the city's status as a major player and was celebrated in 1906 by the first annual Parade of Products. The inaugural event included 33 horse-drawn floats, each promoting a different Orange County agricultural product, such as honey, celery, and poultry. The event also included, as shown here, a contingent of veterans of the Spanish-American war.

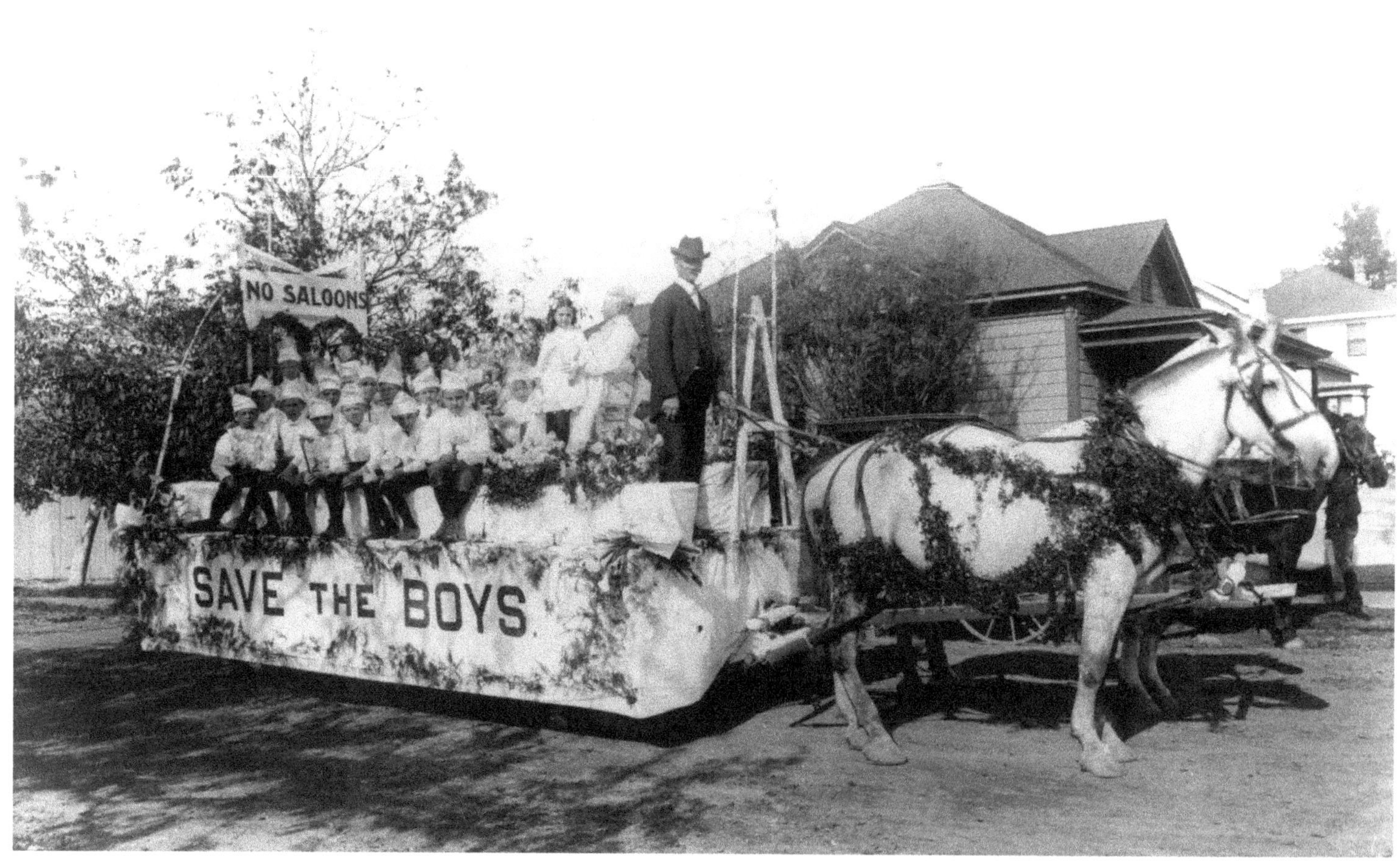

The Los Angeles chapter of the Women's Christian Temperance Union had established the tradition of sponsoring a float in the Pasadena Rose Parade, and the chapter to the south in Orange County saw an opportunity to follow suit with the Parade of Products. A dozen prepubescent teetotalers rode along on the white float with the WCTU members who promulgated their abstinence agenda by chanting "Never! Never! Never! Santa Ana free forever!"

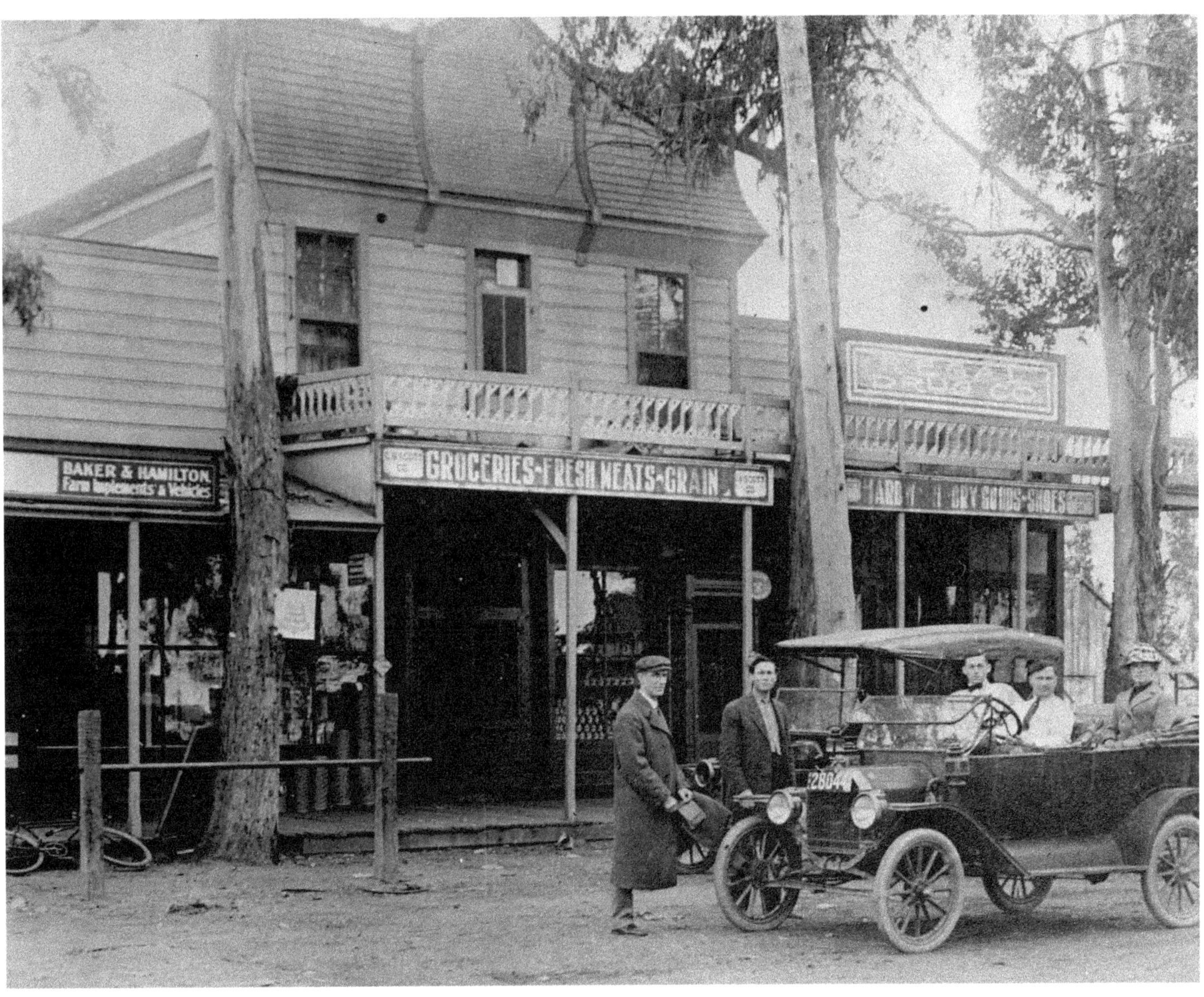

This general store, built by town founder James Whitaker on Grand Avenue, was Buena Park's first business. By the early 1900s it had been sold to his nephew J. Harry Whitaker, who served as the town's first postmaster. Grand Avenue was at that time the widest street in the state of California, lined with majestic eucalyptus trees. Grand Avenue is now Beach Boulevard, a major eight-lane thoroughfare, and the trees, sadly, are no more.

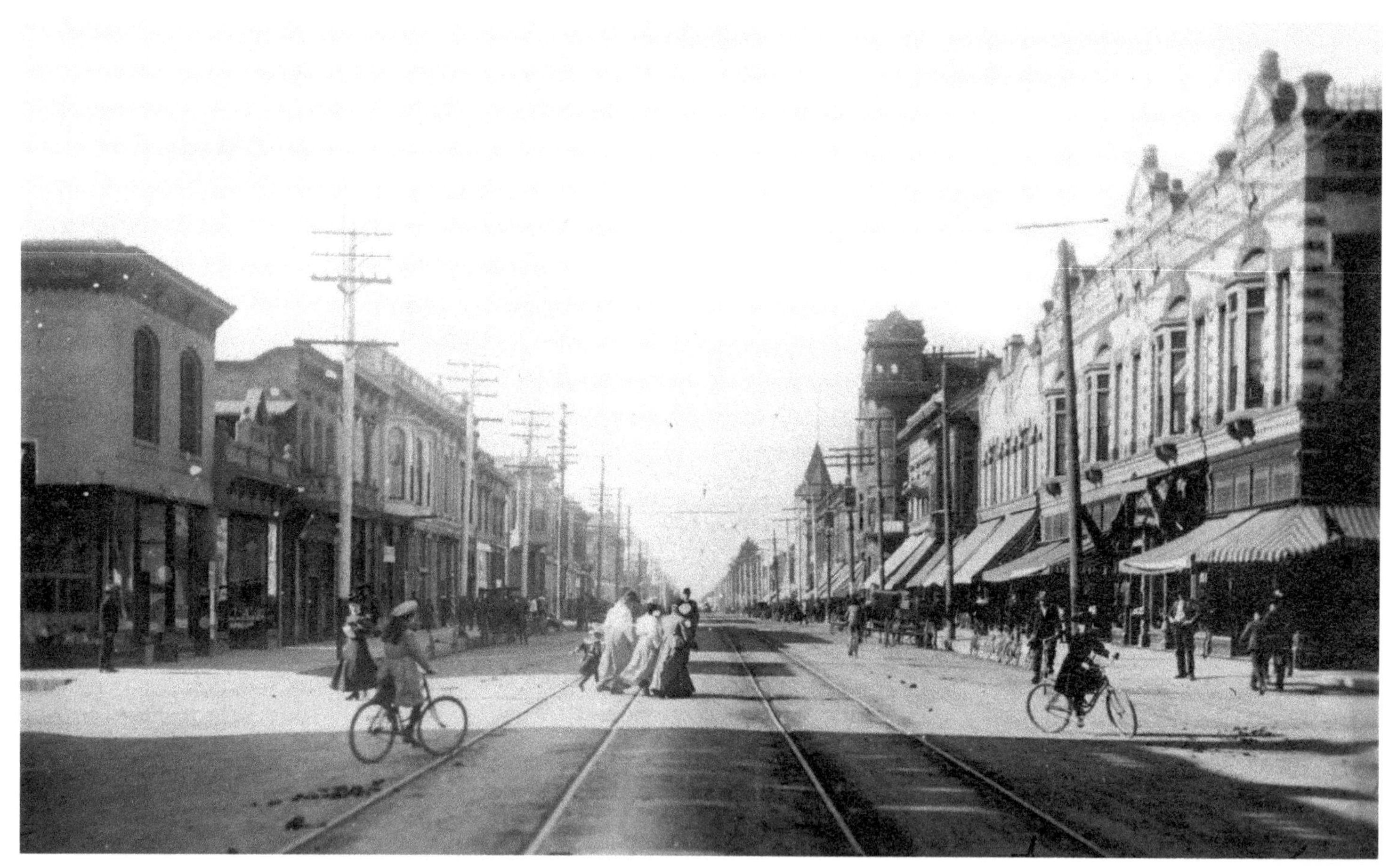

Two young Santa Ana ladies ride their bicycles across the recently installed railroad tracks on Fourth Street in this 1907 view. Shortly after the city incorporated in 1886, the newly elected board of trustees set to work establishing law and order within the city limits. Among the laws enacted was one prohibiting the riding of bicycles on sidewalks by anyone over the age of ten.

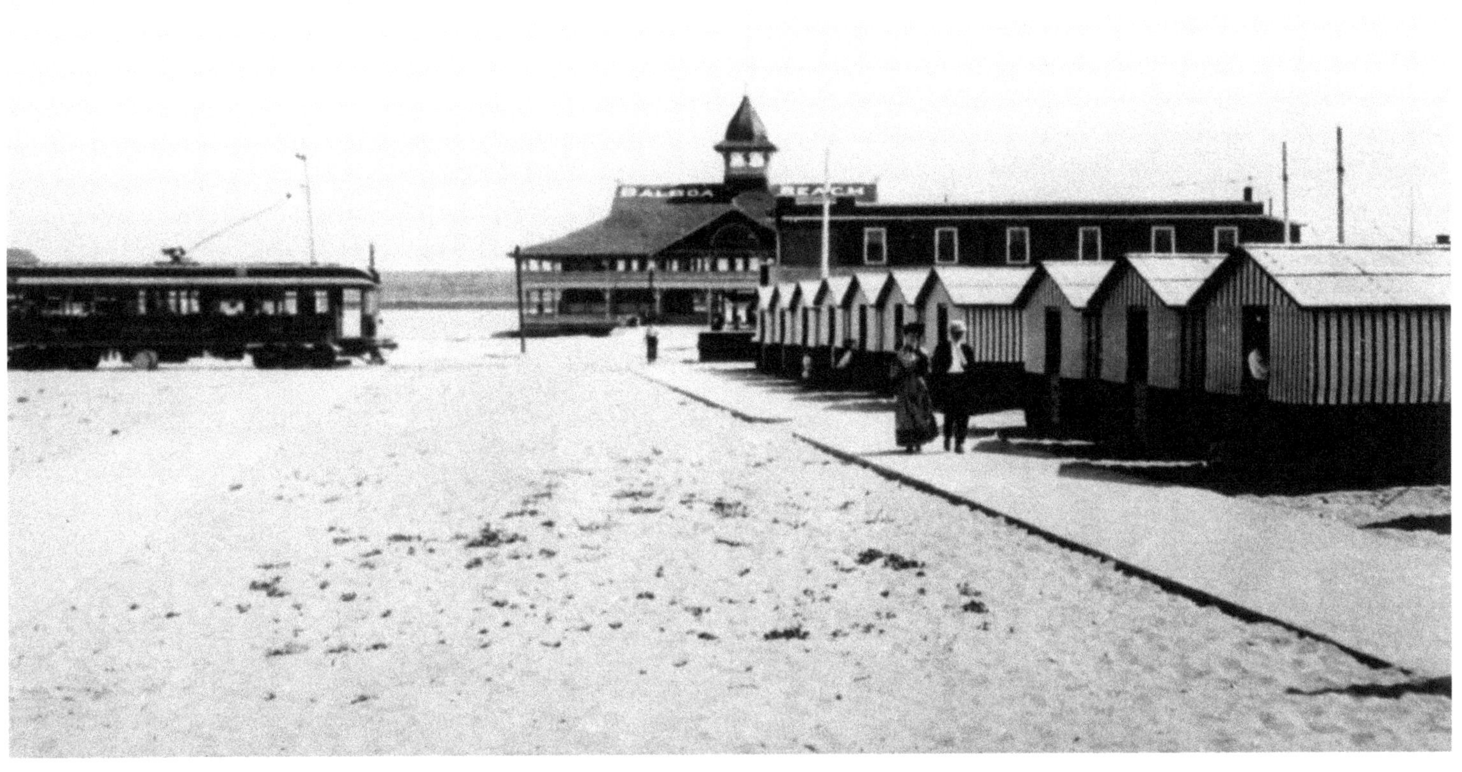

The opening of Balboa Pavilion on July 4, 1906, in Newport Beach was designed to coincide with the arrival of the Pacific Electric Railway Red Car line extension that made it possible for visitors from the Los Angeles area to access the formerly remote site. This 1910 photo shows the line of beach tent cottages that sprang up seemingly overnight to accommodate the massive influx of visitors.

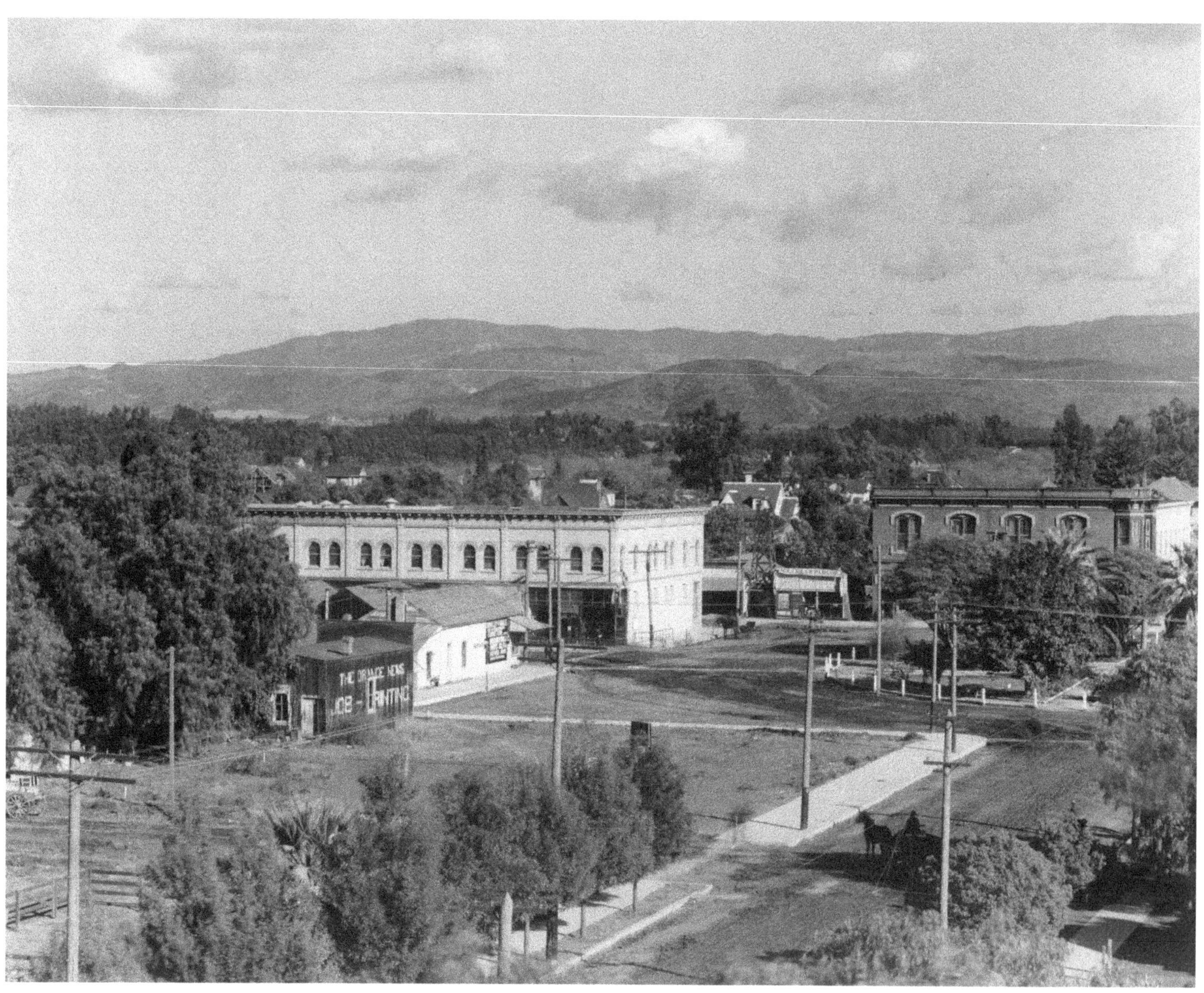

In 1907 the rustic offices of the *Orange News*, at far left, were dwarfed by the far grander edifices of the Edwards Block, at center, and the Bank of Orange, at right. These monumental structures, so seemingly out of place against the rural landscape, reflected the architectural ideals of the 1893 Chicago World's Fair, which would influence city planning for decades to come.

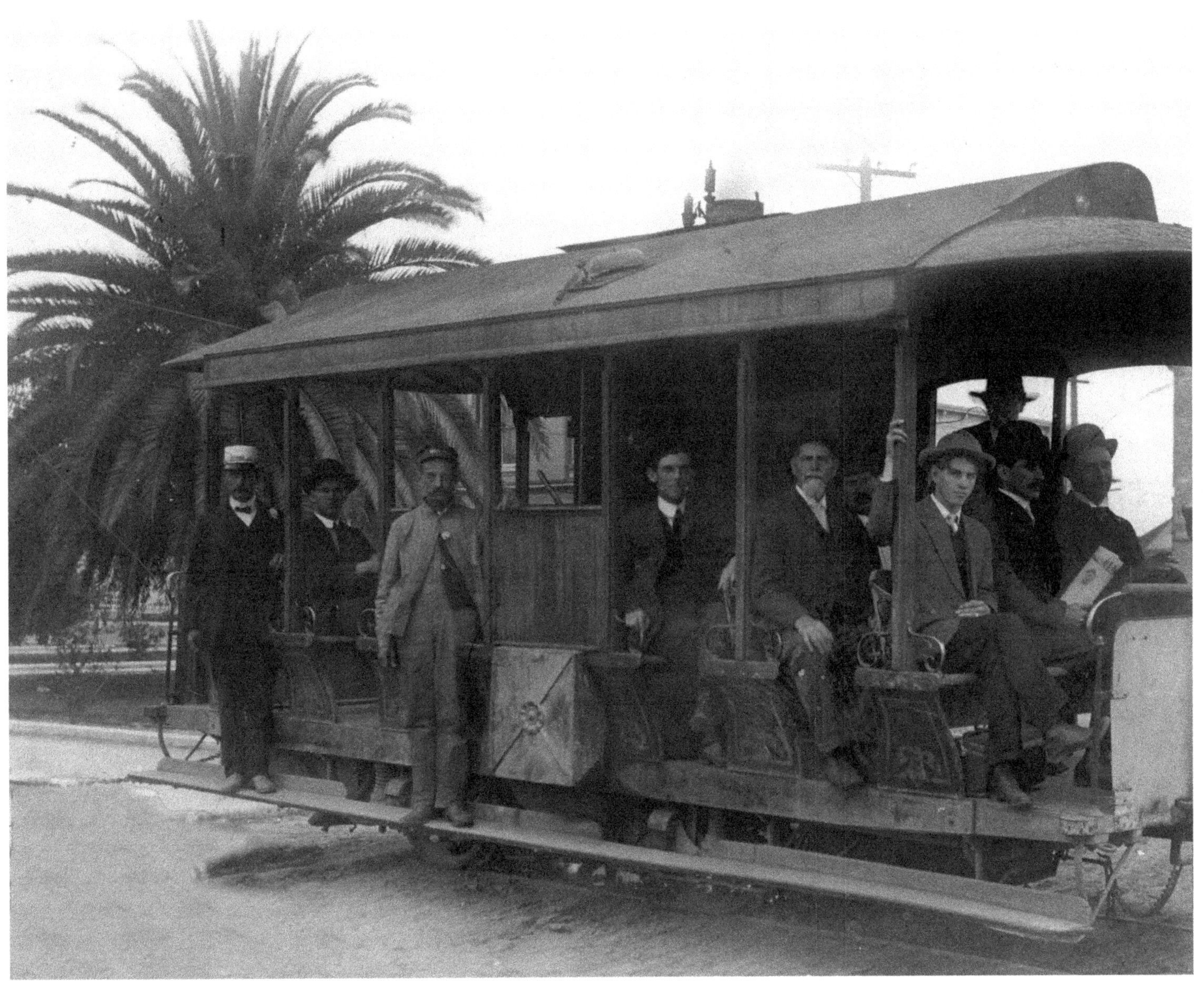

Far from being odorless, smokeless, and noiseless, as promoted, the Dummy was an oil-burning, steam-driven motorcar that spooked horses, belched sticky black smoke, and moved at a languorous pace. Conceived by the Tolle brothers (Ed Tolle is standing at the rear of the car in this 1907 photograph), the Dummy, or "Peanut Roaster," ran on narrow gauge railroad tracks between Santa Ana and Orange for almost 20 years.

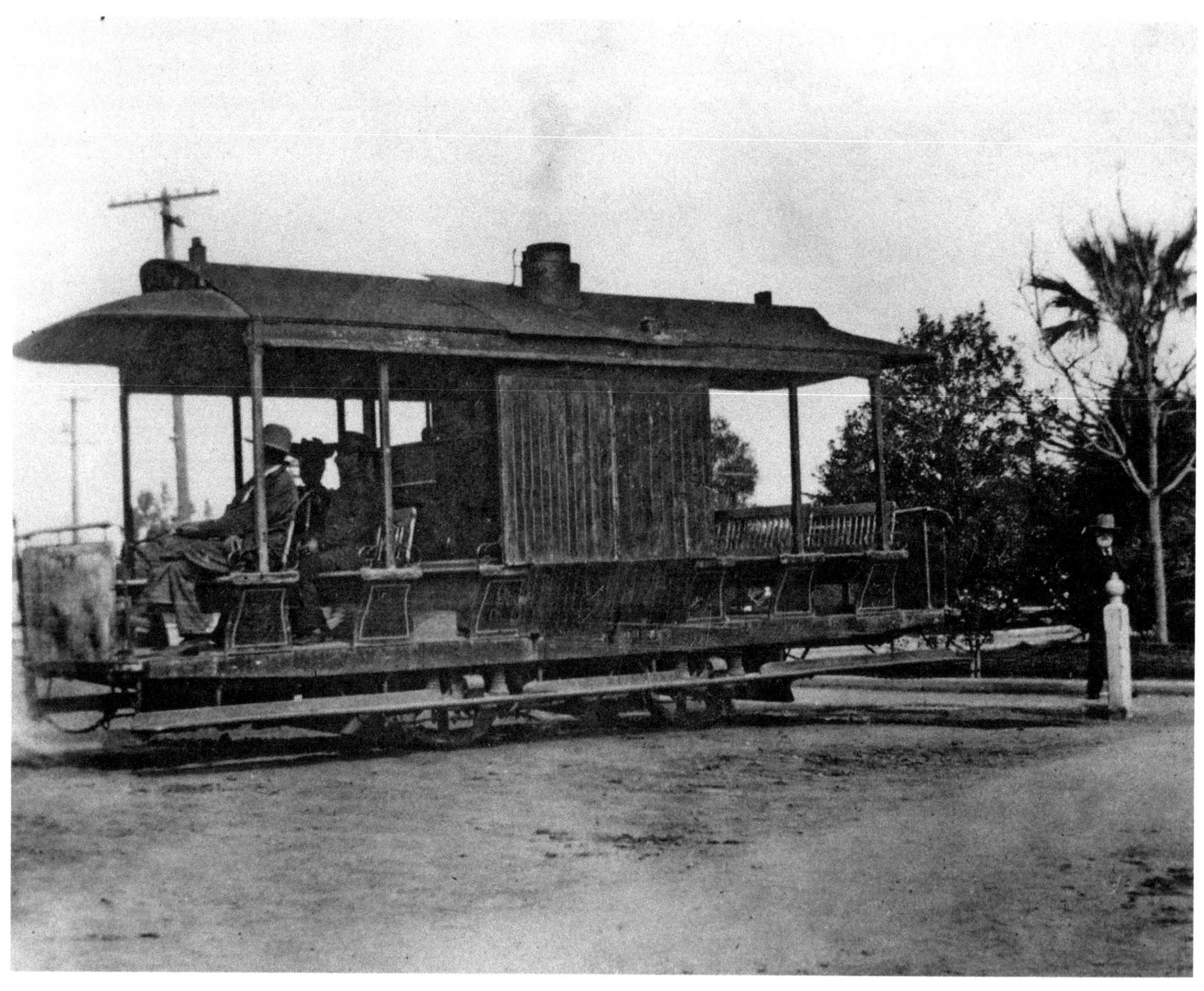

The Orange Dummy, seen here from the other side, was 20 feet long and carried up to 24 passengers at speeds of eight miles an hour. The Dummy was essentially a stopgap measure between the outmoded horsecar lines of the Santa Ana, Orange and Tustin Street Railway Company, and the completion of the Pacific Electric Red Car line from Los Angeles to Santa Ana in 1906.

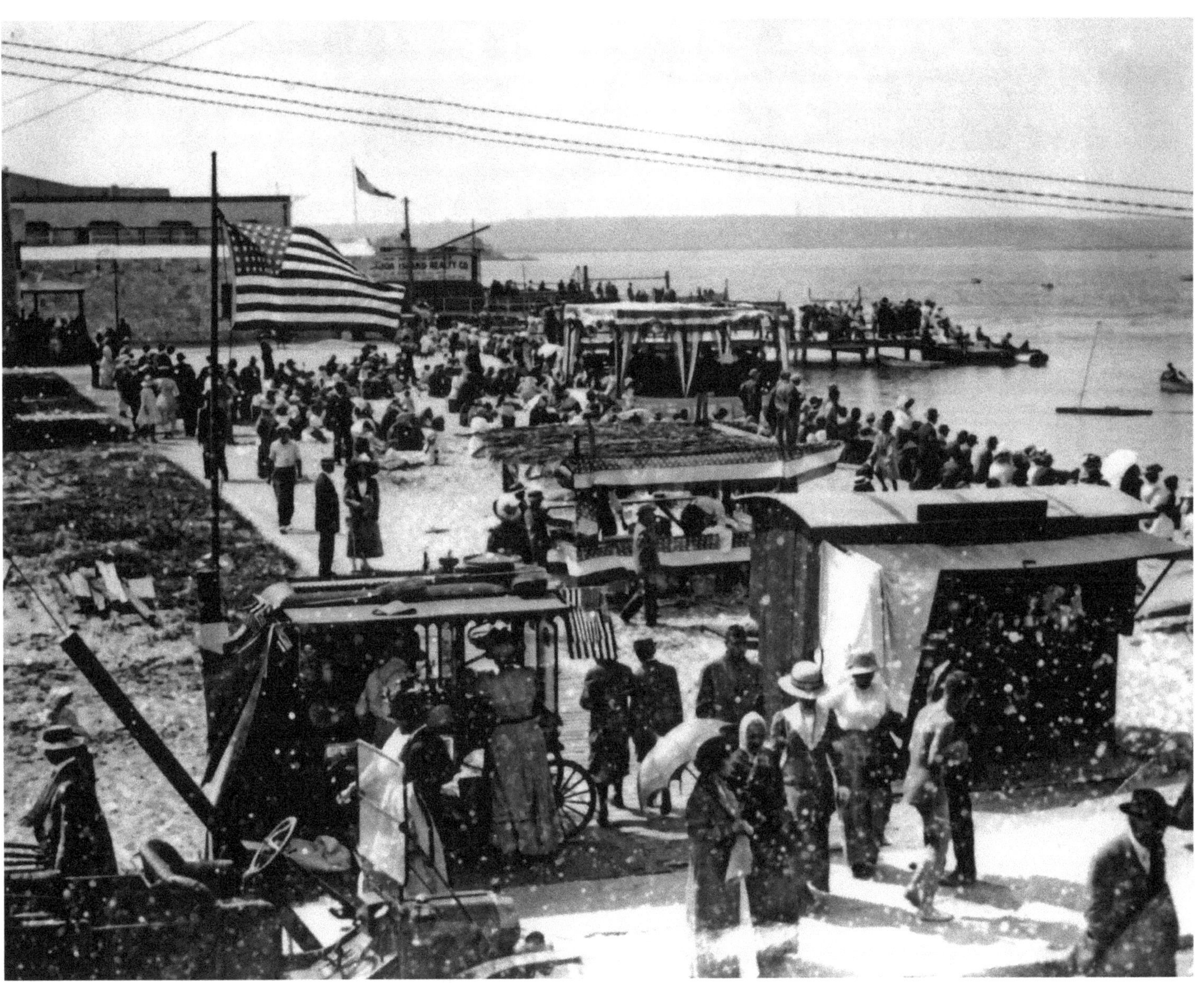

This early twentieth century photo depicts an outing on Balboa. The bunting and flags would seem to indicate an Independence Day celebration. Particularly noteworthy is the large flag at left, which appears to have 42 stars. The U.S. flag jumped from 38 stars to 43 in 1890 with the concurrent admission to the Union of five states, so this flag was not official. Laws governing standardization of the American flag were not passed until 1912.

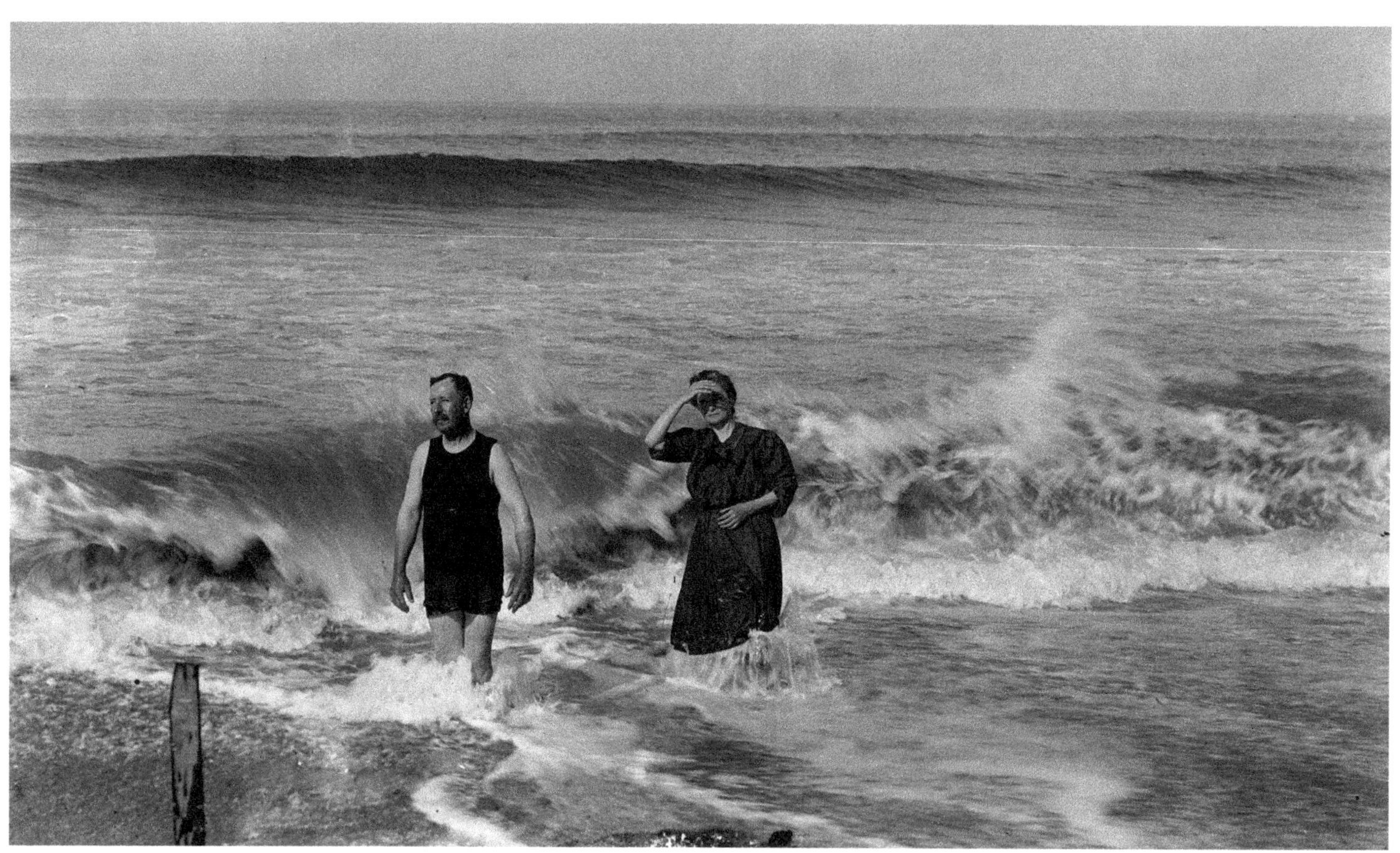

A fun-loving couple models the latest in lightweight wool bathing attire while frolicking in the waves at Huntington Beach in 1908. Huntington Beach boasts eight miles of wide, uninterrupted beachfront, the largest stretch on the West Coast, and is internationally known for surfing. In 2006 the city's Conference and Visitors Bureau trademarked the expression "Surf City USA," which led to legal battles with beachwear retailers in the city of Santa Cruz.

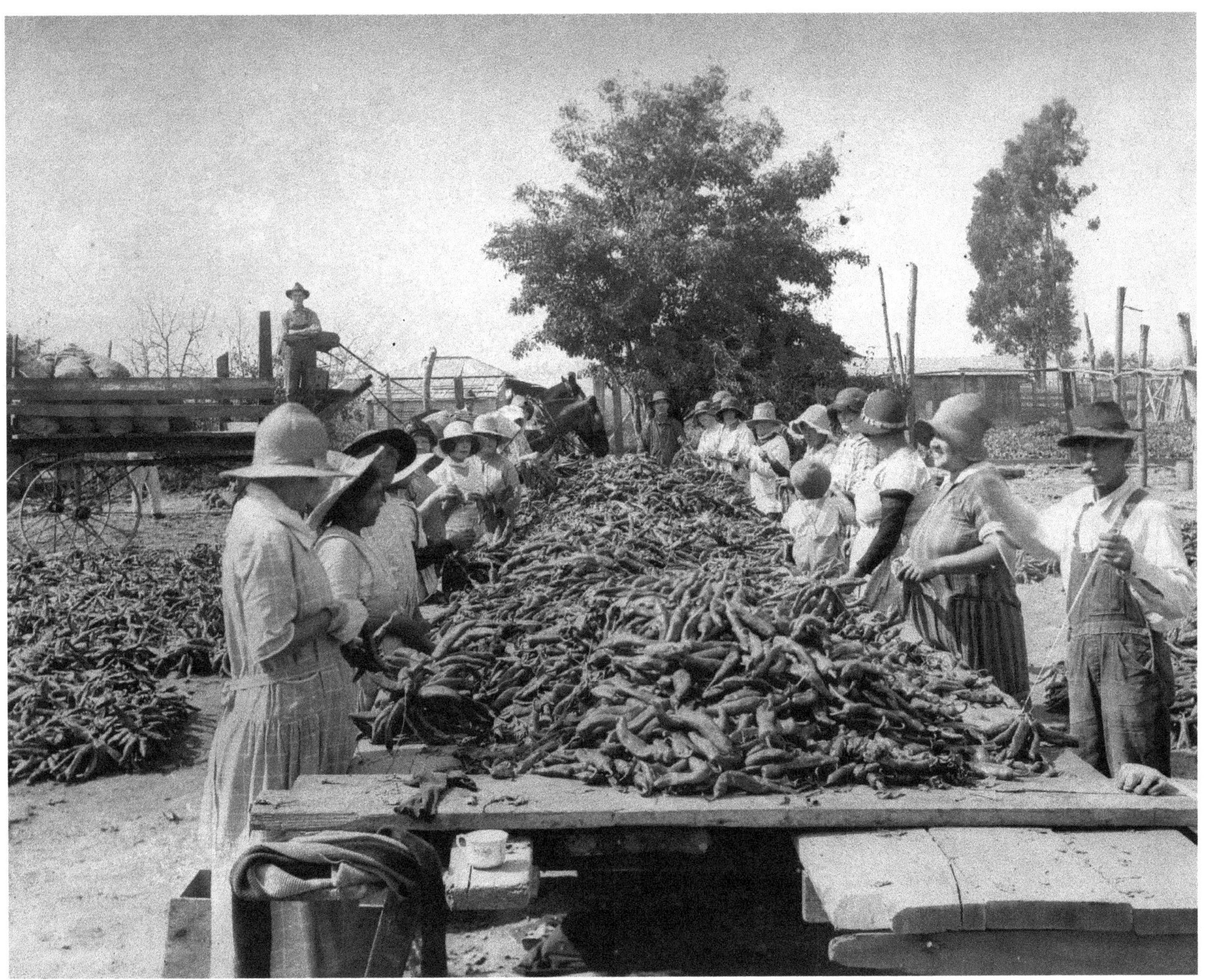

The sandy soil and temperate climate of Orange County proved amenable for the growing of a wide variety of crops. Chili pepper production started around 1890 near Anaheim and was so successful that Orange County was soon providing all of the chilis grown in California. Mexican chilis and Anaheim chilis were two particularly popular varieties. Unfortunately, as with so many other early crops, the industry was destroyed by a parasite, in this case, the chili weevil.

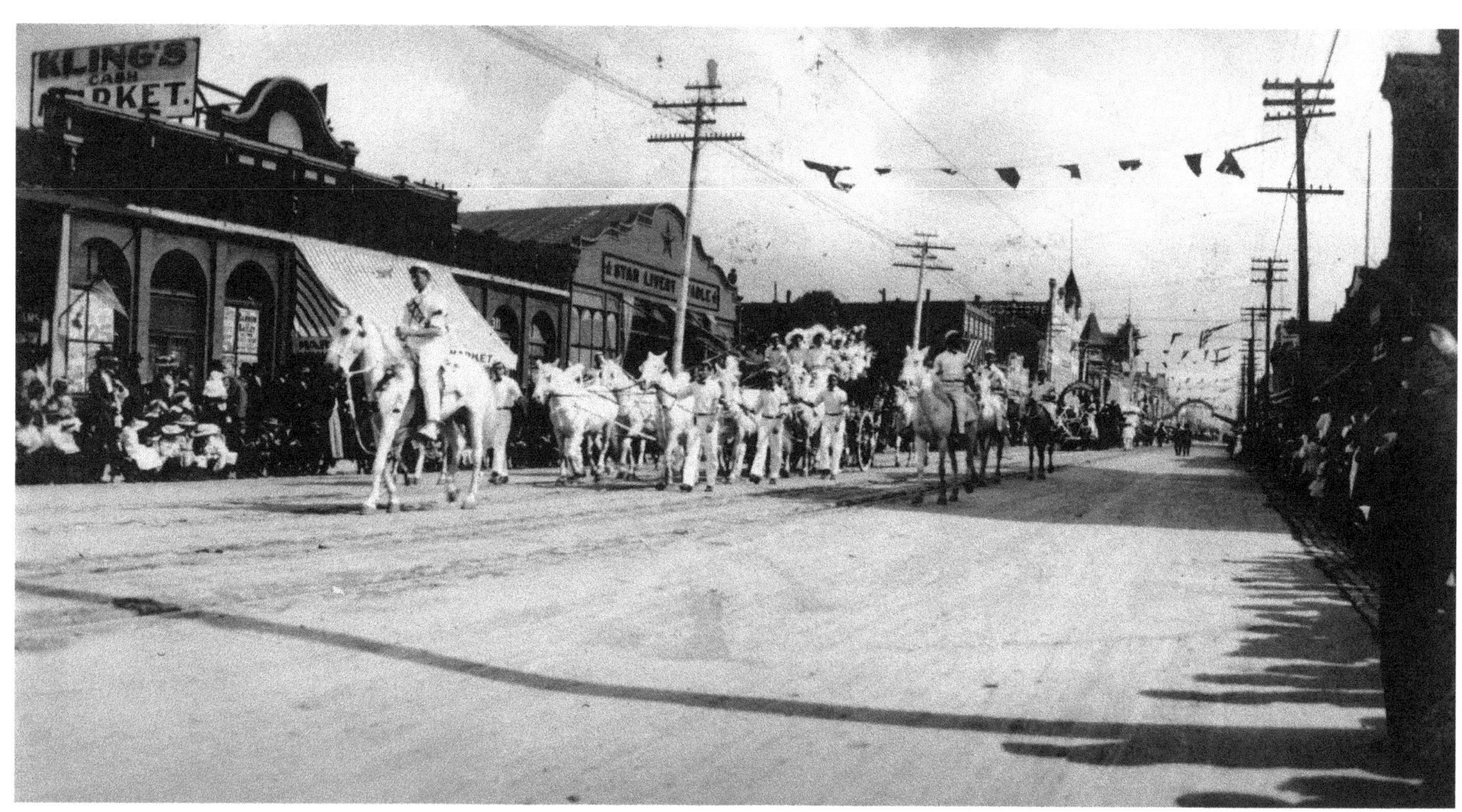

In 1908 the enrollment of Orange Union High School was only about a hundred students, so it would appear that a large percentage of the student body participated in the school's entry in Santa Ana's third annual Parade of Products, shown here. OUHS, established in 1903, was the fourth high school in the county. Prior to its formation, Orange Elementary School graduates had to travel to Santa Ana for higher education.

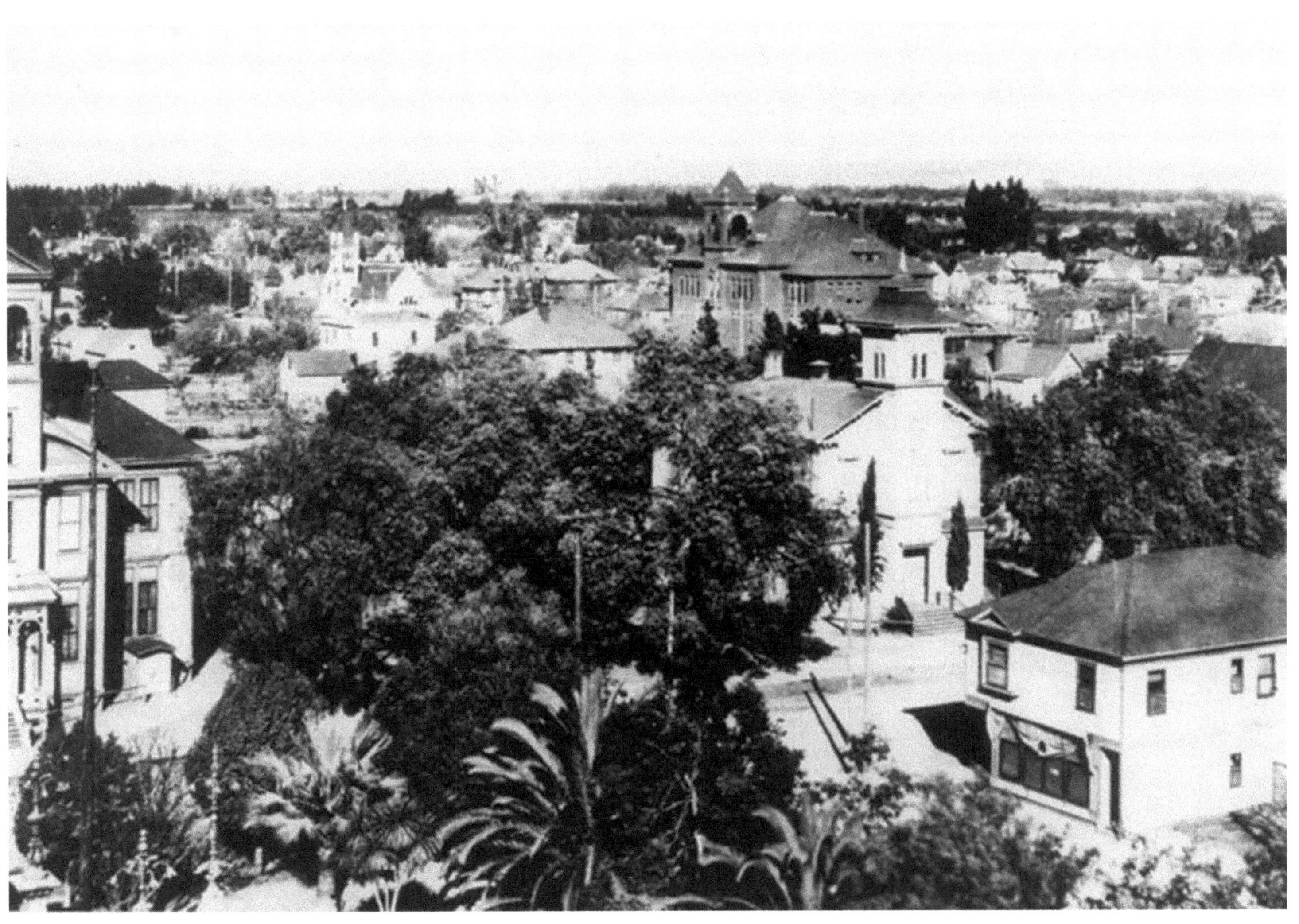

This 1910 bird's-eye view of Santa Ana, taken just 24 years after incorporation, shows a highly developed commercial area and many large-scale, two- and three-story Victorian homes. Off in the distance can be seen the Richardson Romanesque–style County Courthouse, crowned with its distinctive cupola. The cupola would fall victim to the Long Beach earthquake of 1933, giving the courthouse of today a much different silhouette.

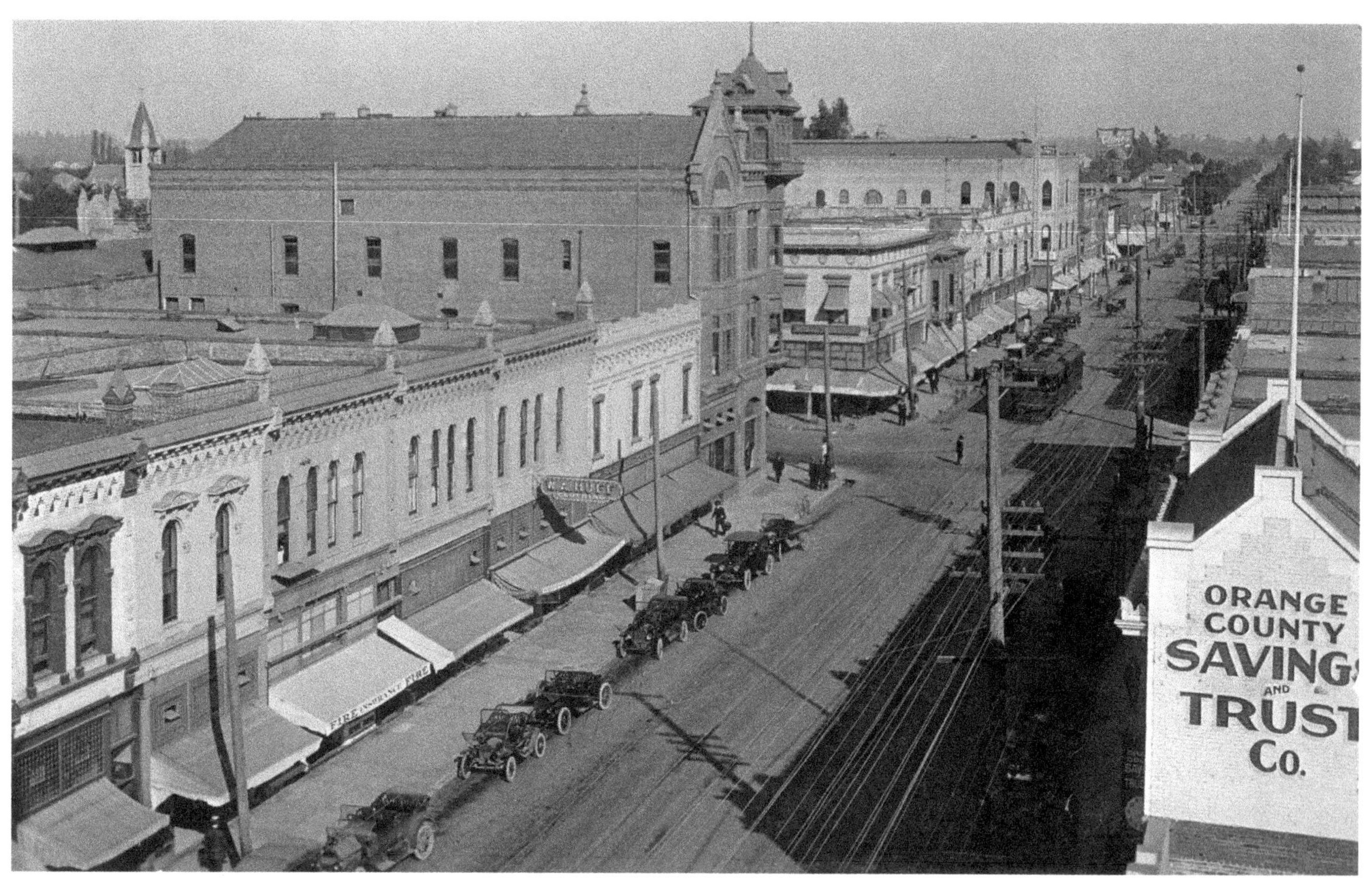

Powering electric railcars, the overhead lines running along Fourth and Main in Santa Ana had become a familiar sight to locals by 1910. Whereas a trip to Los Angeles had once been an unpleasant, daylong ordeal, it was now entirely feasible to spend a few hours shopping in the big city and make it home for dinner. Each plushly appointed Red Car seated 57 comfortably on leather-upholstered seats and included a restroom and an ice water tank.

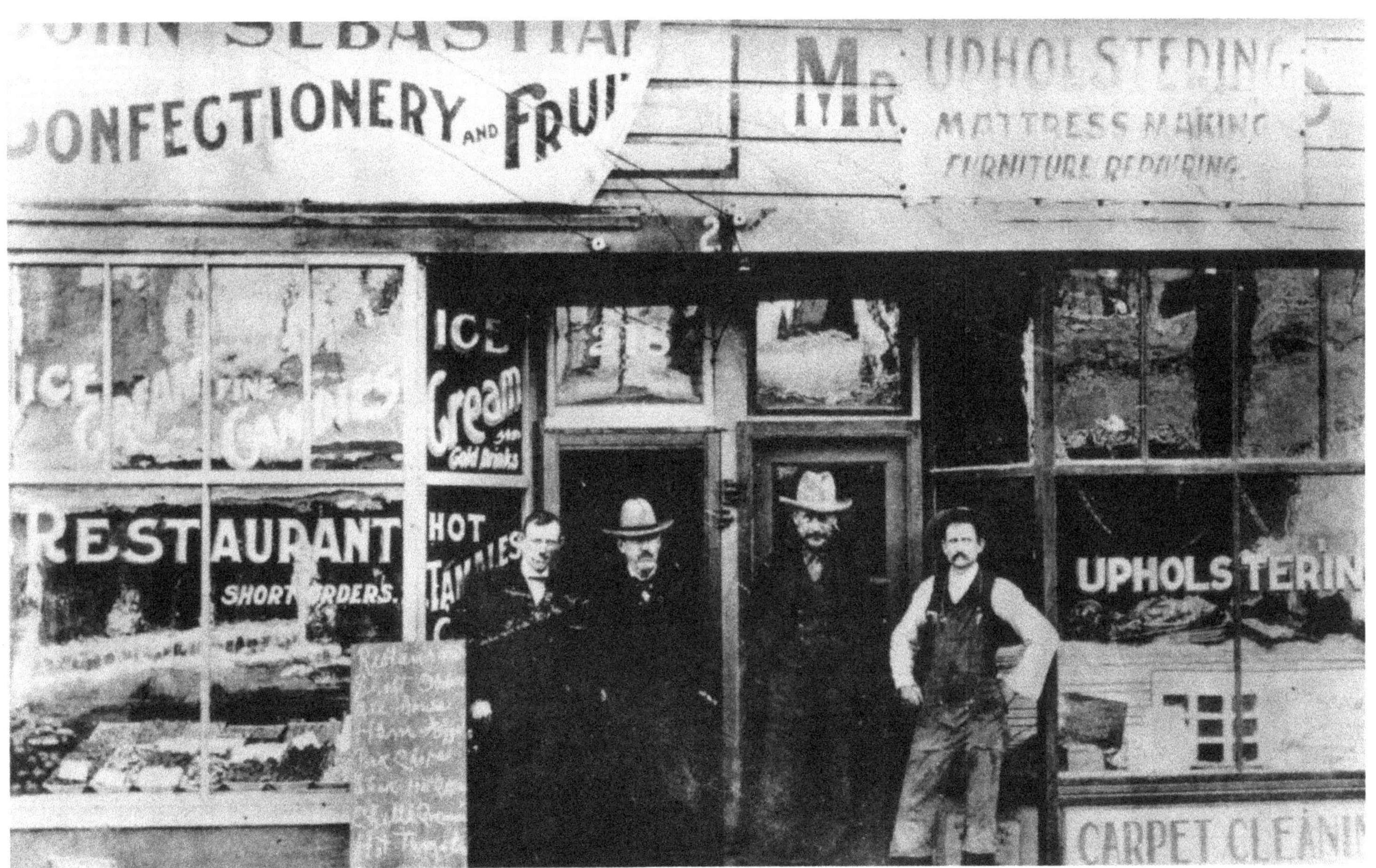

John Sebastian's Confectionery and Fruit Store was located on East Fourth Street in Santa Ana, right next door to John Inman's upholstery business. Both proprietors are pictured here in this photograph, ca. 1910. Sebastian's restaurant and sweet shop reflected the city's Mexican heritage: in addition to ice cream, fine candies, and cold drinks, a sign in the window advertises that the establishment also serves hot tamales.

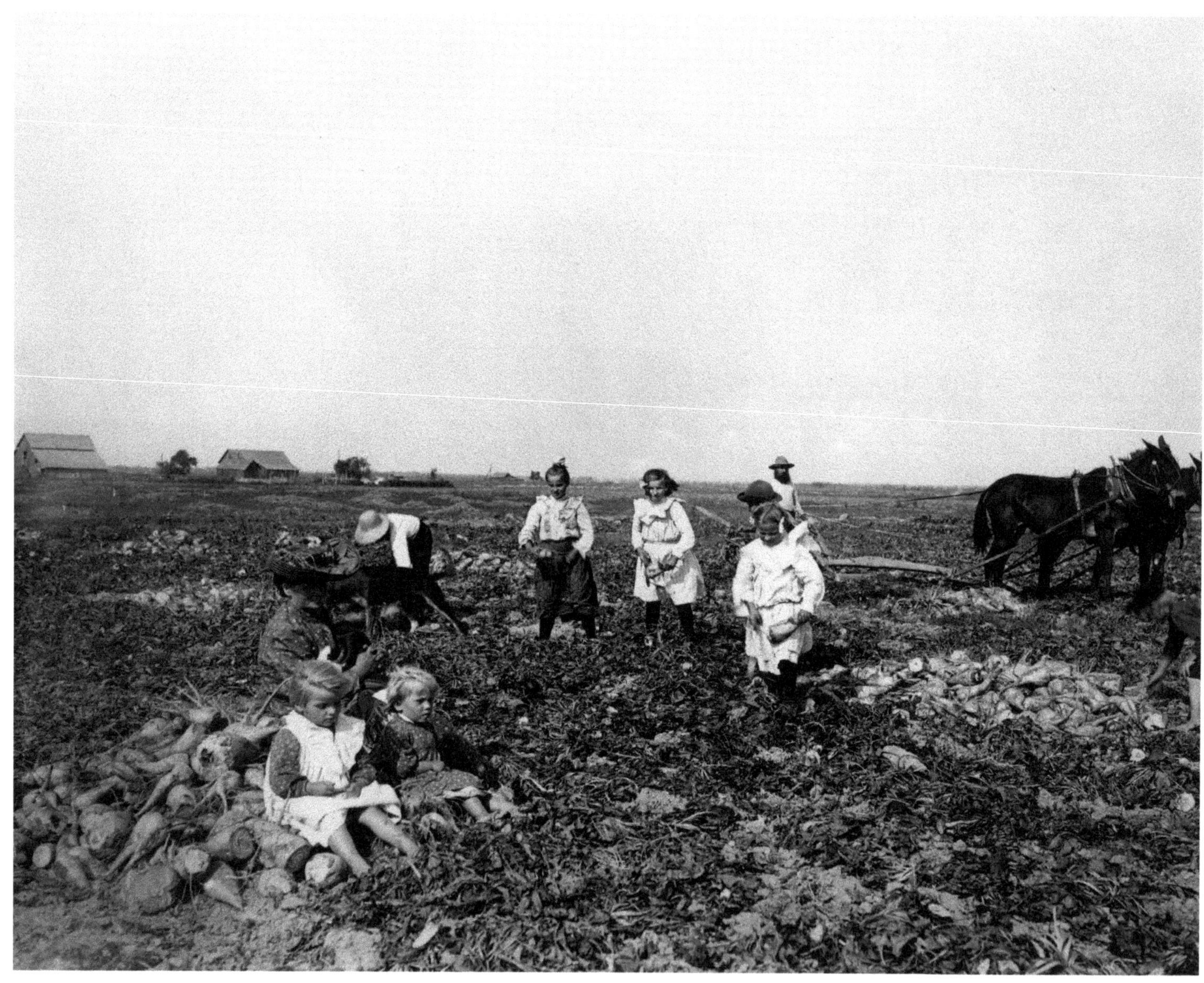

Harvesting sugar beets in the early years of the nineteenth century was a labor-intensive operation that often involved the whole family, as the Jacob Kozina family demonstrates in this 1910 photo. After the father pulls the beets out of the ground with a horse-drawn plow, his daughters cut off the leaves, and his sons stack them for pickup. Even the family dog appears to be helping.

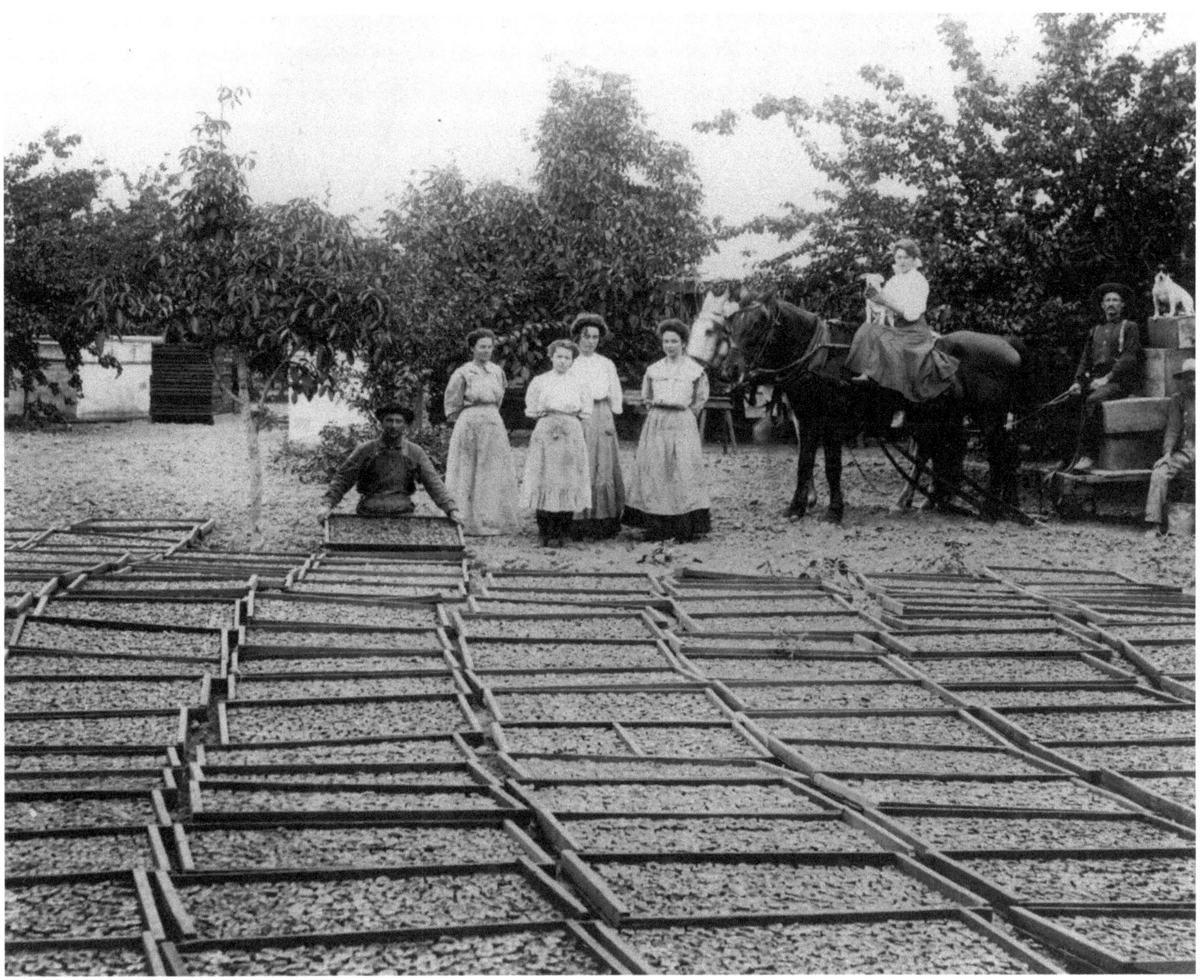

The bulk of Orange County's apricot crop was dried for shipment to Europe, and drying was women's work. The female workers of the George Fox Ranch in Tustin are shown here at center in 1910. Halved, pitted fruit was spread out on redwood trays over a pit of powdered sulfur for preservation, then left to dry under cardboard tenting for three to seven days. Typical pay was about 60¢ a day.

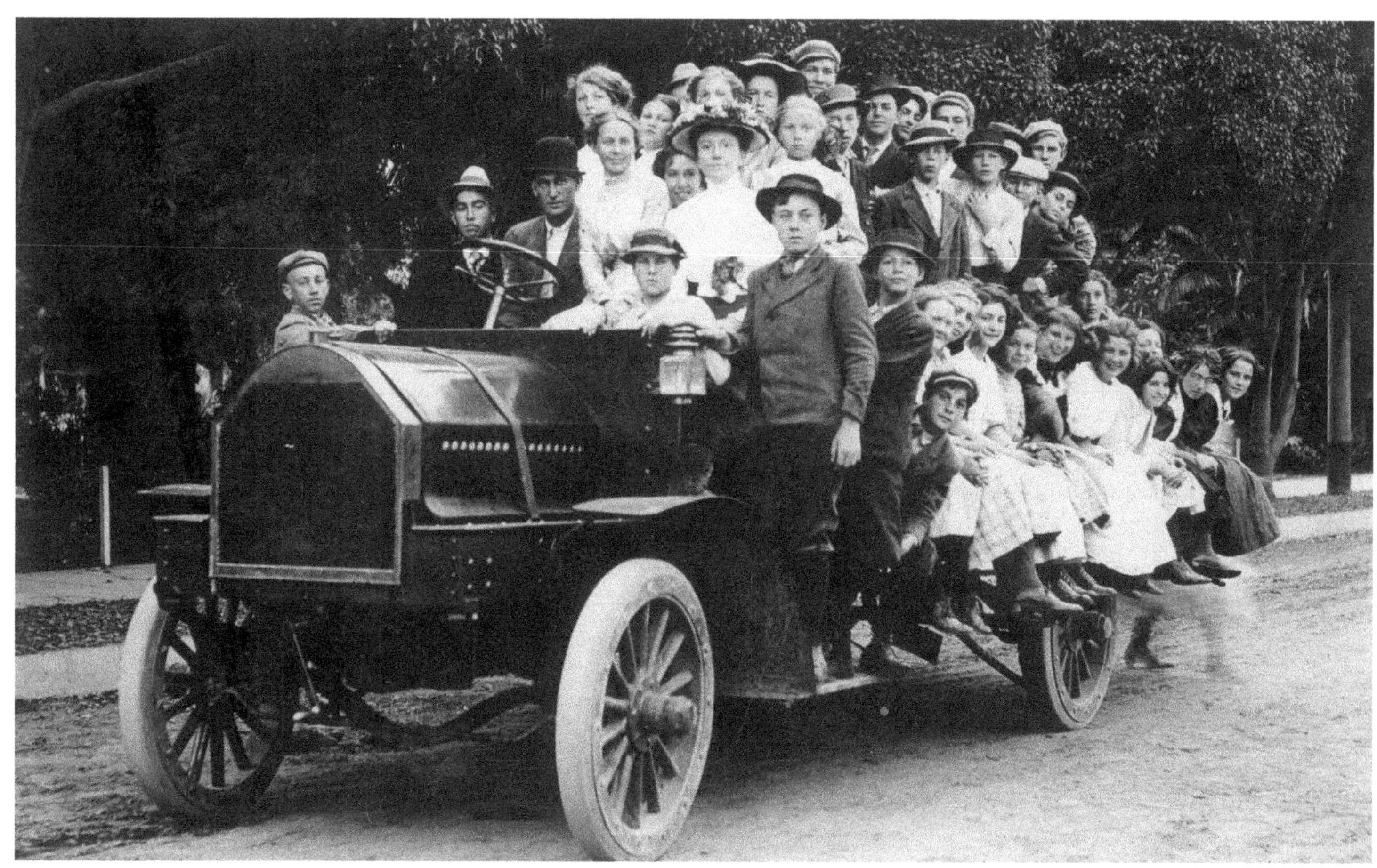

Santa Ana's Birch Park, shown here in May of 1910, was named for A. W. Birch of Illinois, who, like many before him, came to Southern California for the reputed health benefits of the mild climate, and ultimately developed a large and successful farm. Today tiny Birch Park, largely hidden behind a senior center, is all that remains of the 80-acre farm that once covered much of what would become the city of Santa Ana.

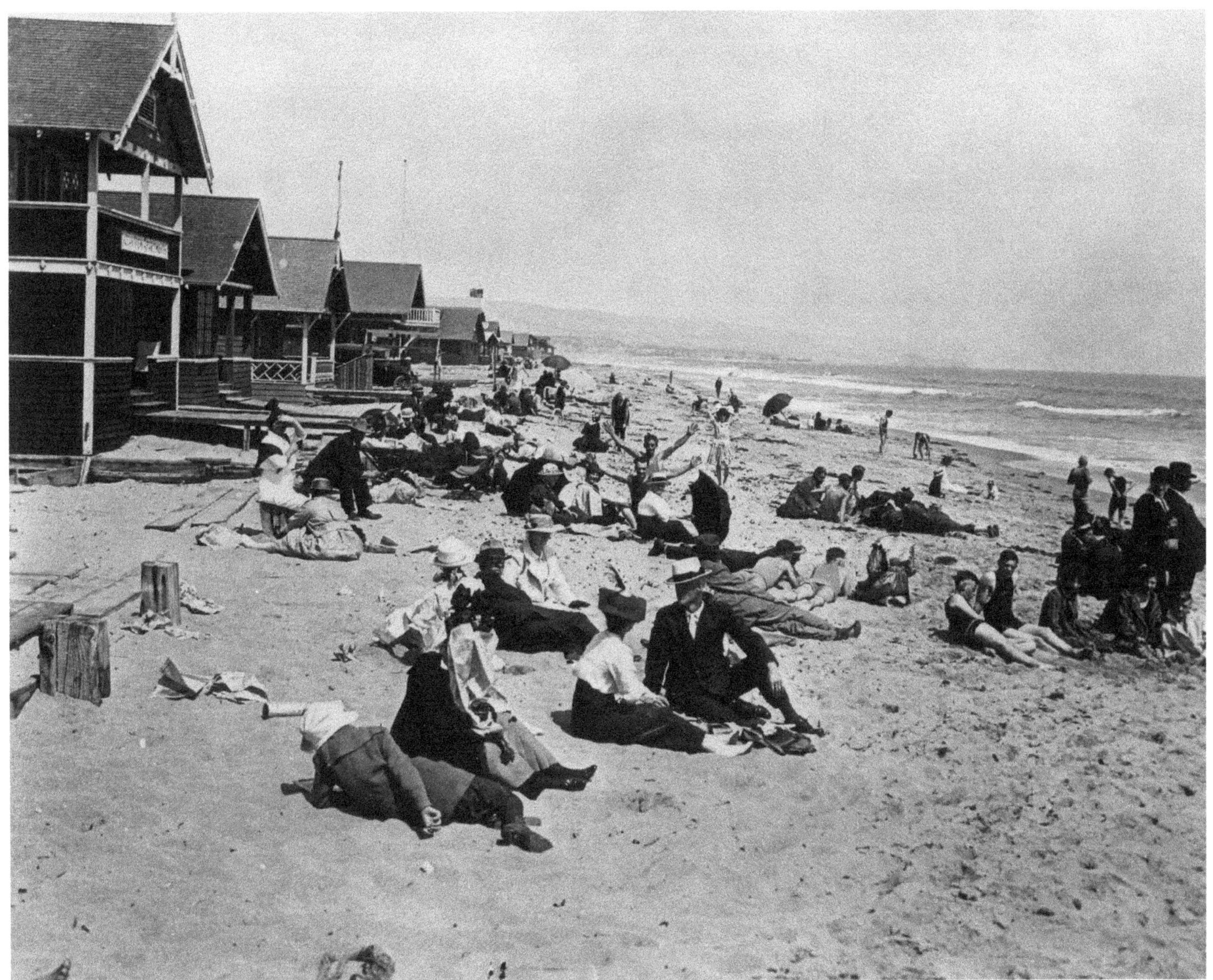

Looking much like a reenactment of Georges Seurat's famous 1884 painting *A Sunday on La Grande Jatte,* Victorian vacationers and day-trippers lounge fully clothed on Newport Beach in the early part of the twentieth century. Since then the attire has changed drastically, but Newport Beach still attracts hordes of weekend visitors—and the attendant traffic jams.

Following Spread: In 1910 the city of Orange held a three-day street fair featuring agriculture exhibits, poultry, sideshow attractions, and speeches from local dignitaries. In 1973 the city resurrected the idea, and today the International Street Fair, held annually over Labor Day weekend, attracts more than half a million people eager to sample exotic beers and cuisine from all over the world. Proceeds from the event go to charity.

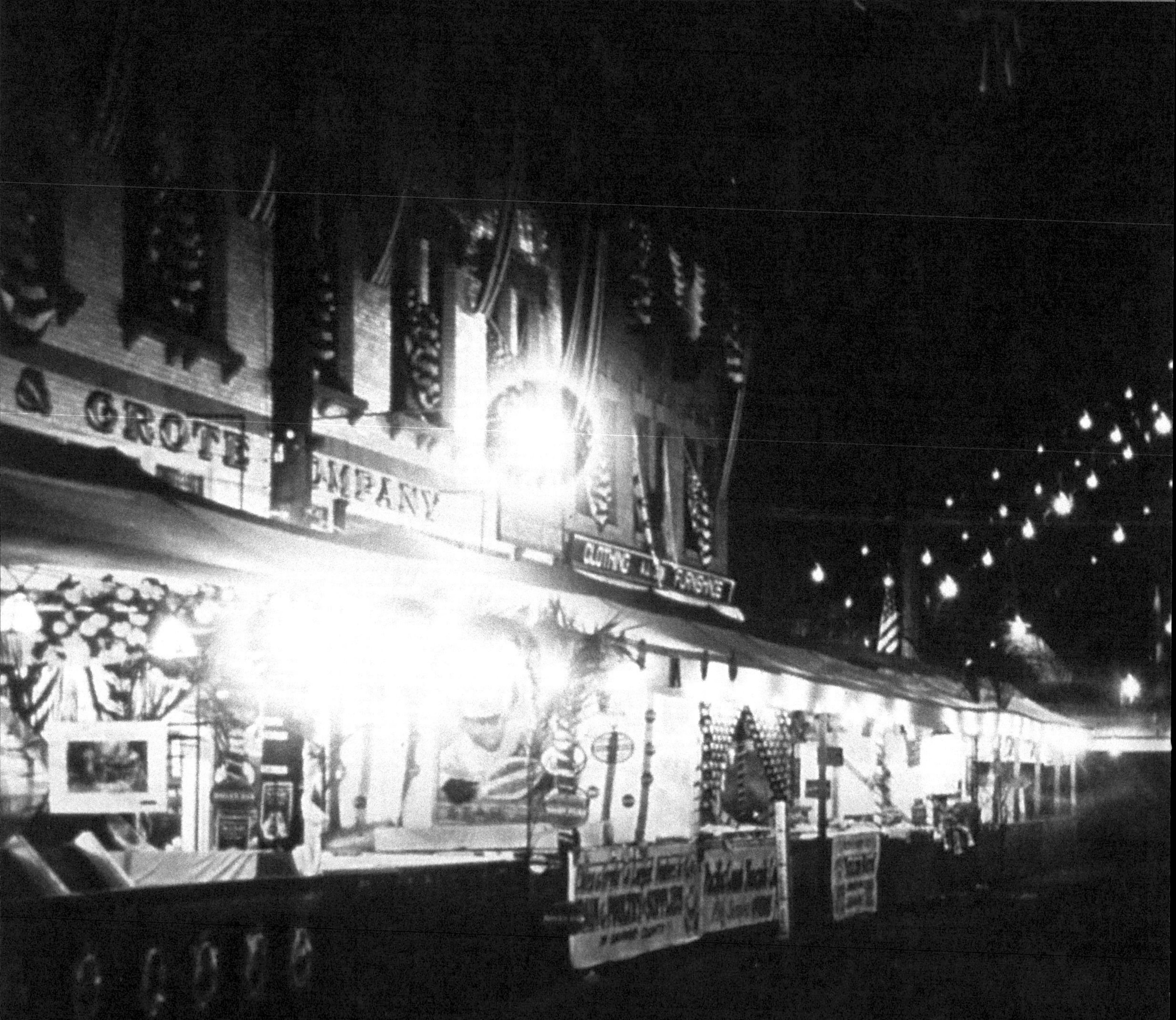
GROTE
CLOTHING

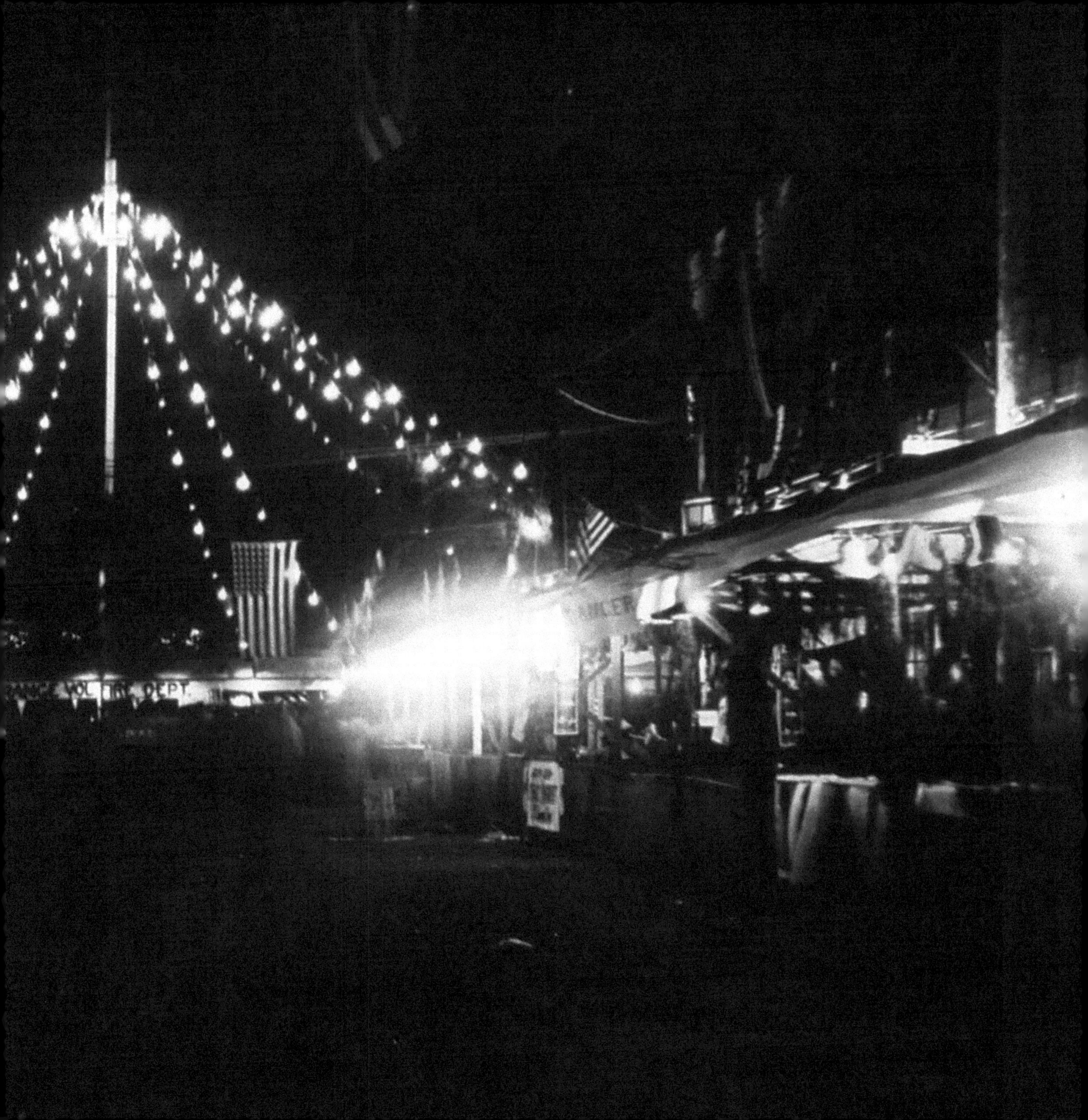

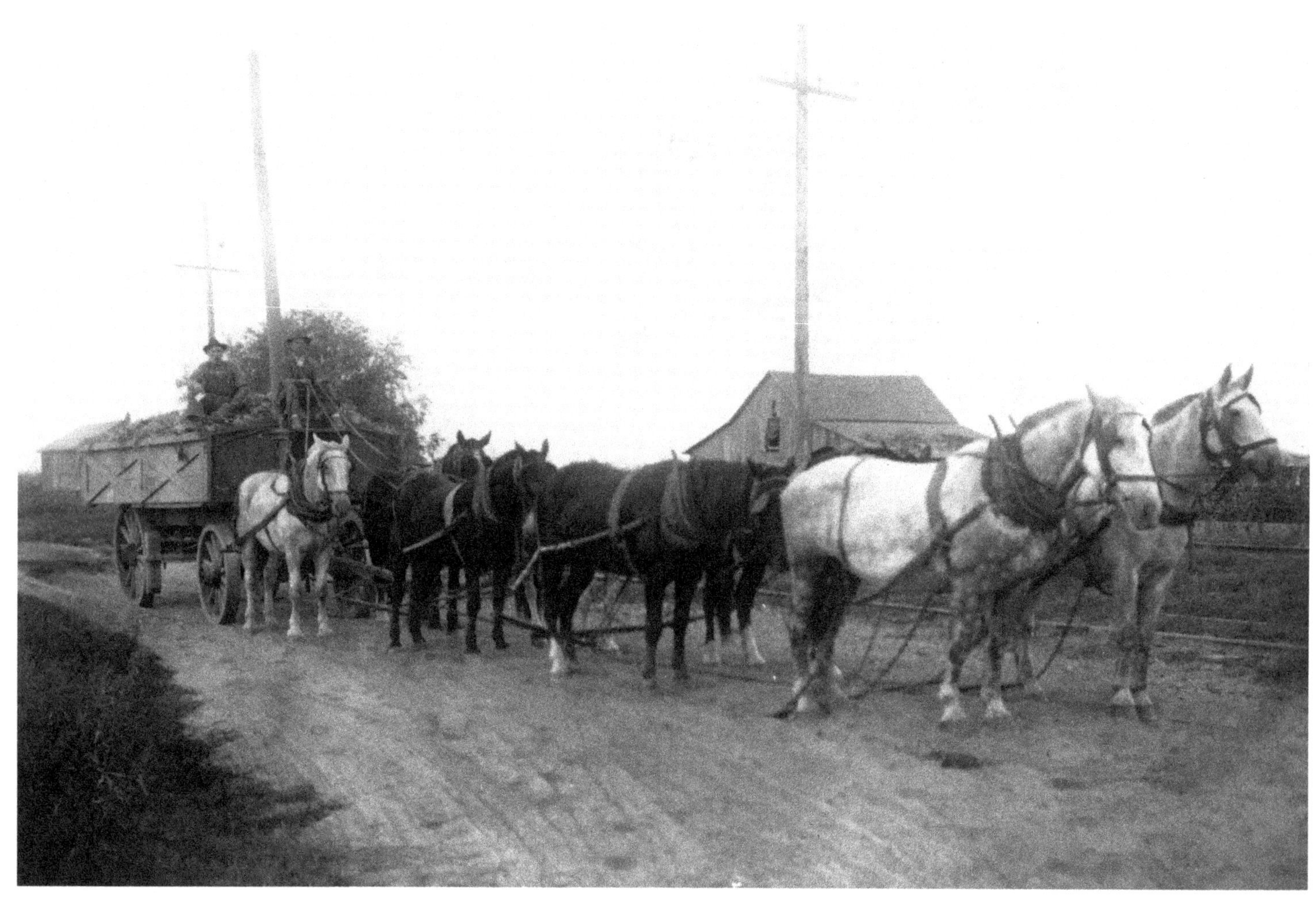

J. N. Davis is en route to the Talbert beet dump in this 1912 photo. The Talbert family played a big role in the development of Fountain Valley and neighboring Huntington Beach. Tom Talbert was a successful farmer, realtor, and oil speculator; he served as mayor of Huntington Beach and later wrote a memoir called *My Sixty Years in California.* His first real-estate office has been restored and is now part of Fountain Valley's Heritage Park.

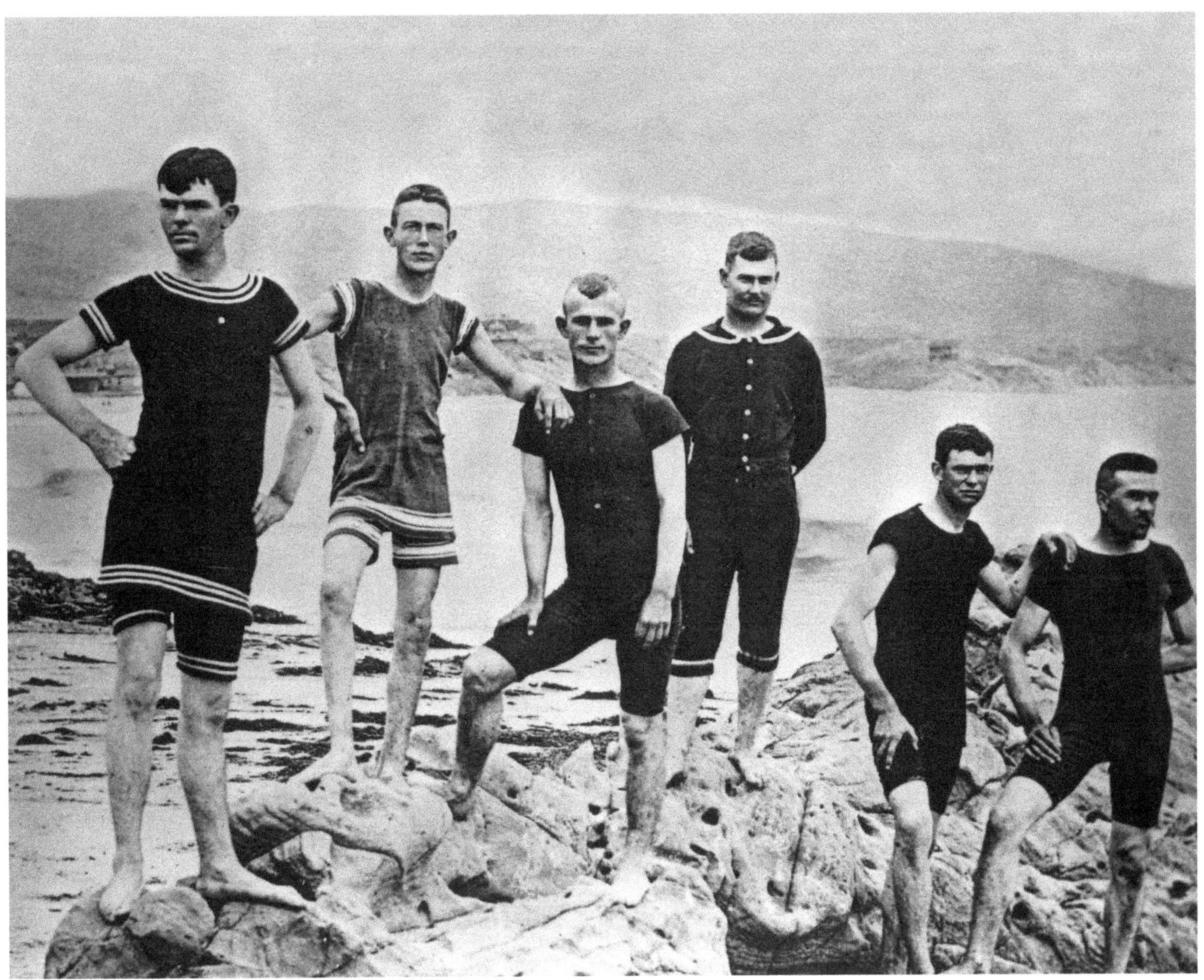

Six strapping young men model the latest in manly swim togs on Laguna Beach in 1912. Despite the bohemian artist colony developing in the city, Victorian mores still prevailed on the beach. The American Association of Park Superintendents' rules of the era forbade suits from exposing the chest below a line level with the armpits. In 1929 a Laguna Beach swimmer was arrested and charged with indecent exposure after scandalously doffing his shirt.

In 1913 much of Orange County suffered through a devastating cold snap that destroyed, by some accounts, as much as 60 percent of the year's orange crop, and turned the fountain on Orange's Plaza into an ice sculpture. Since many local residents had never seen icicles, the frozen fountain provided a bright spot in an otherwise tragic time.

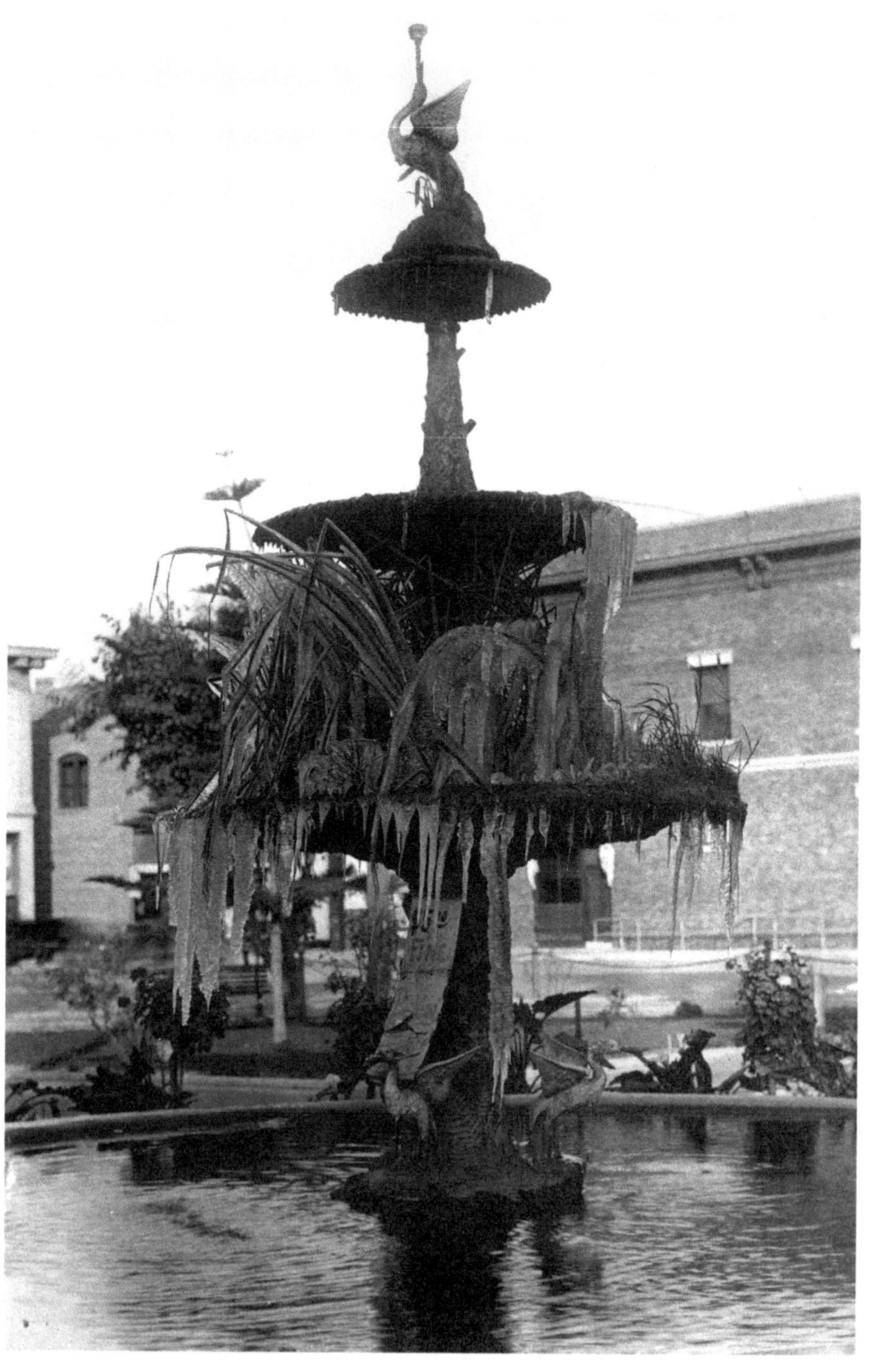

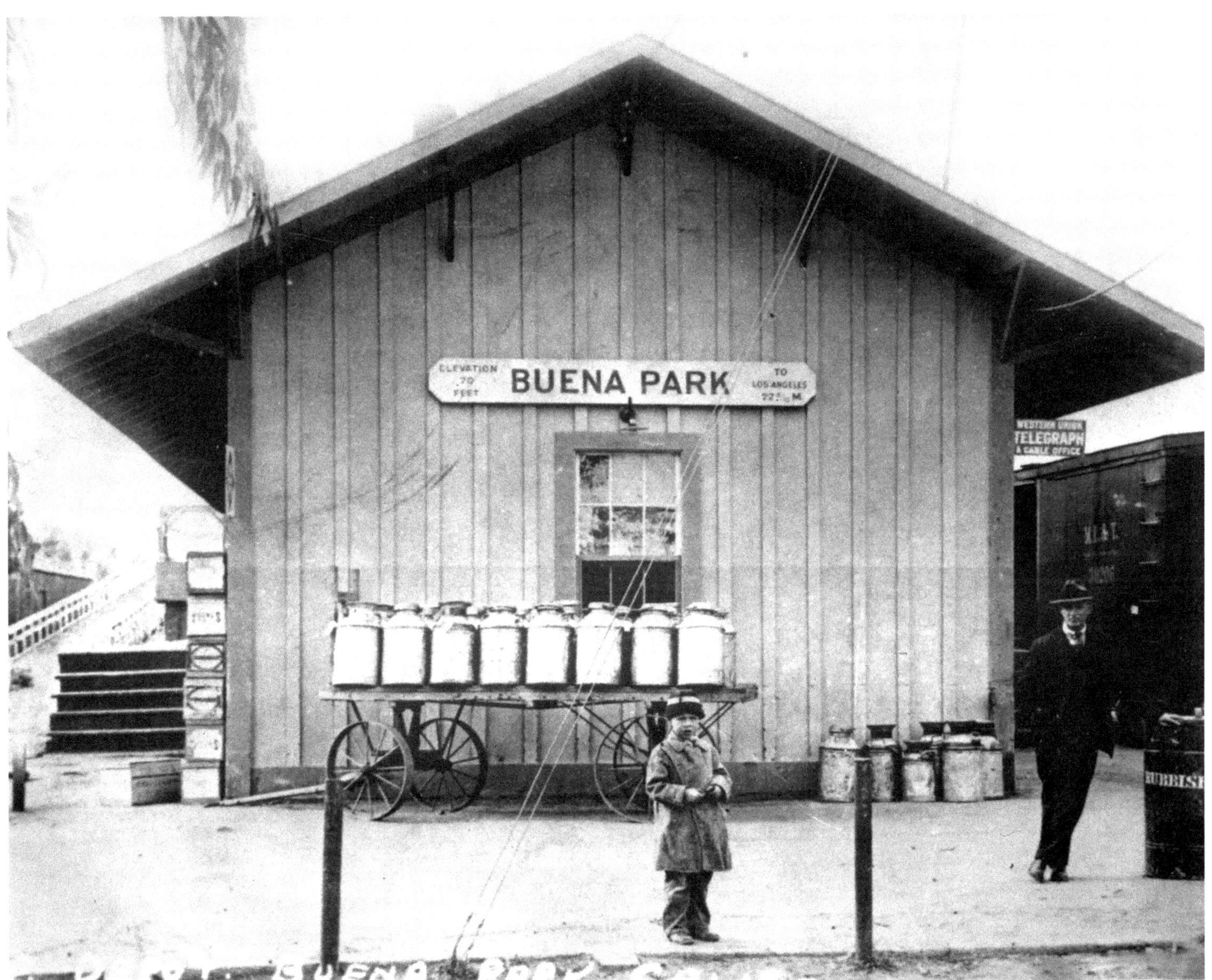

Buena Park founder James A. Whitaker centered the town around this Southern Pacific Railroad Depot only after the Santa Fe Railroad reneged on a promise to build him a depot a mile north. Shown in 1914, the station was the hub of commerce for early settlers, sandwiched between a beet dump on one side and warehouses on the other. The little chap in front of the depot has been identified as six-year-old Percy Owens.

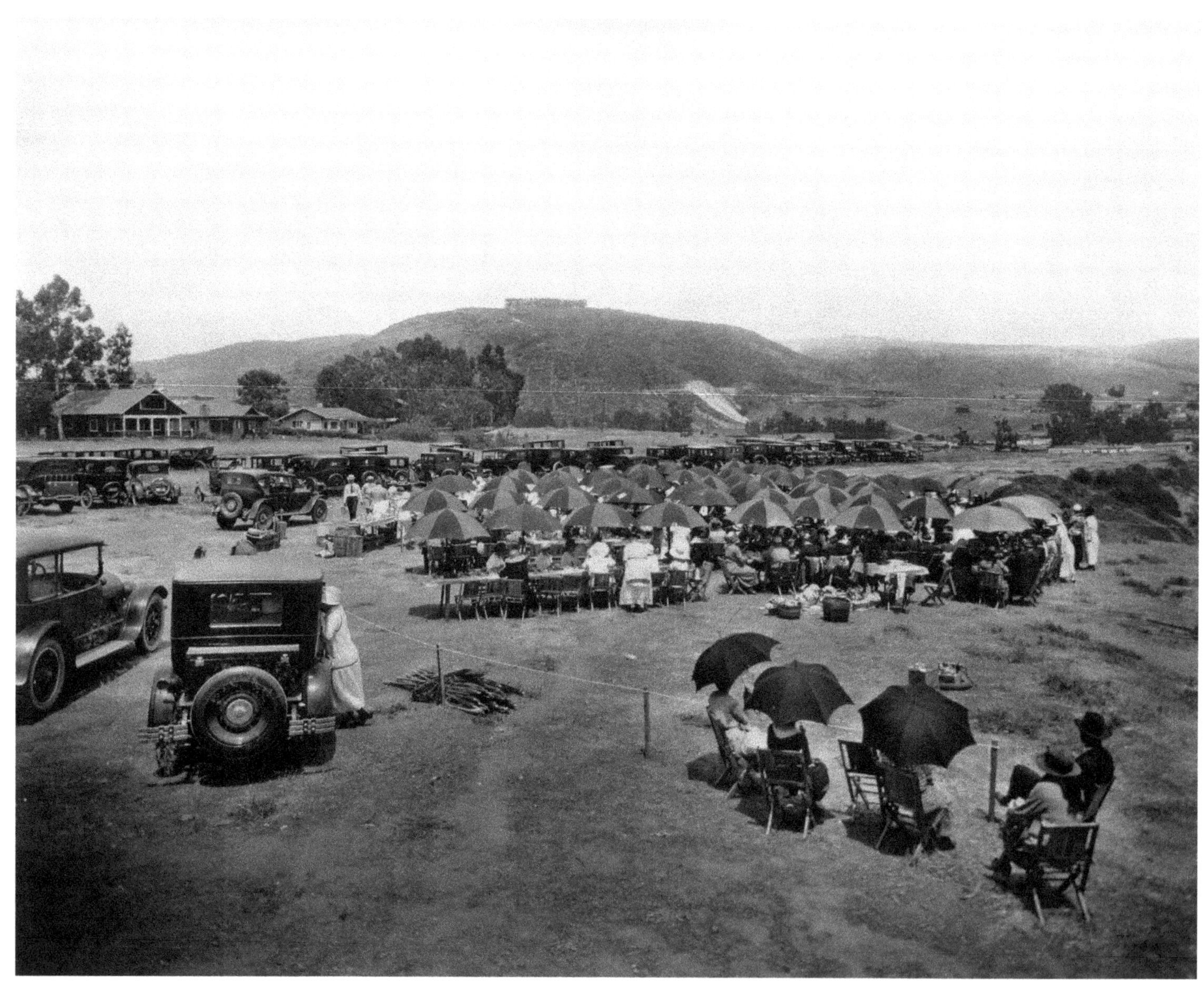

The valuable land of Laguna Beach never stayed fallow for long, as the turn-of-the-century Women's Club could attest. Their original hall was seized by the city and torn down for a new City Hall, and their picnic grounds atop Victor Hugo Point, shown here in 1915, were lost to Victor Hugo Restaurant. The site is currently the home of Las Brisas Restaurant, whose patio diners enjoy one of the finest views in all of Southern California.

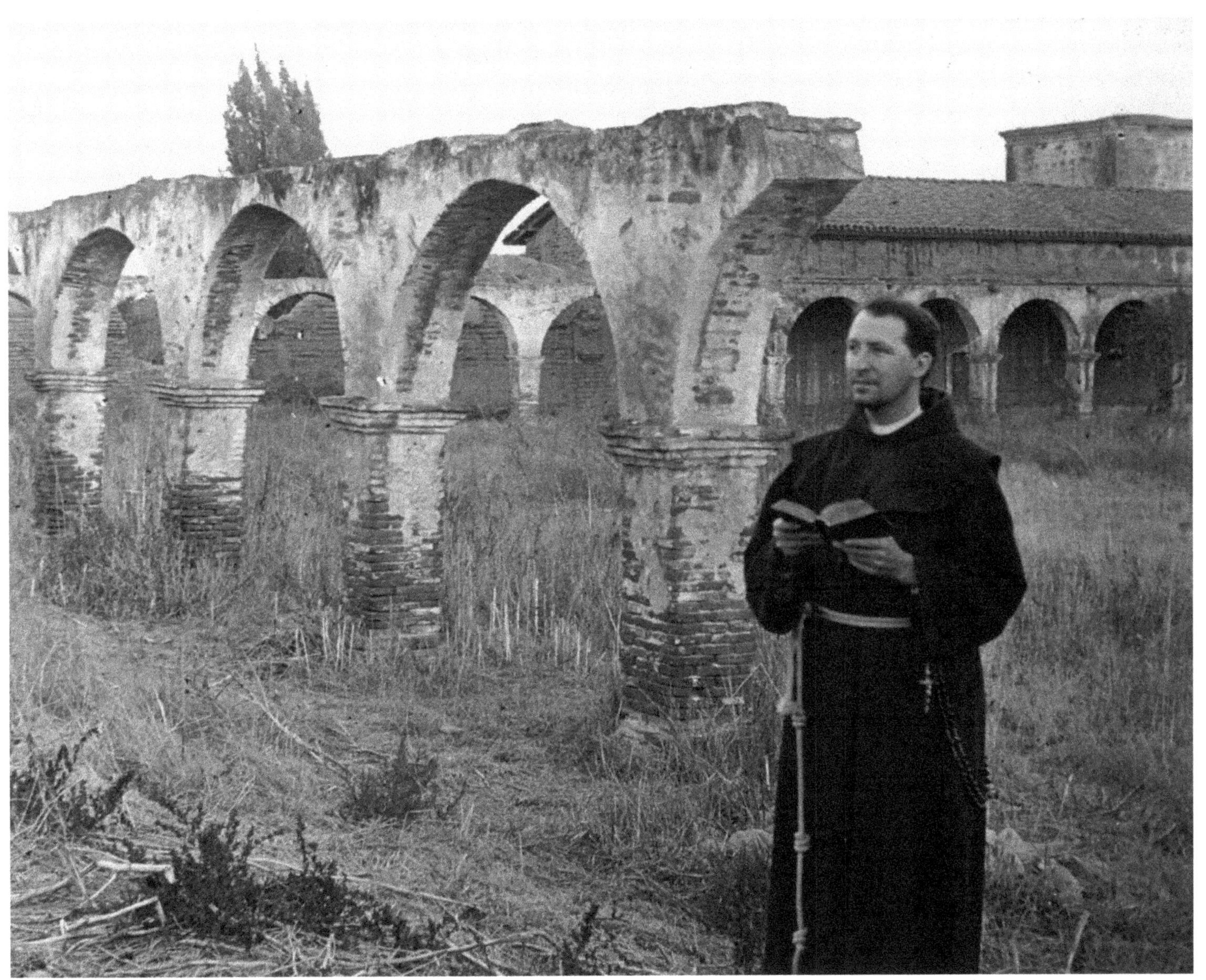

The majestic ruins of Mission San Juan Capistrano, dubbed by architects the "American Acropolis," have served as a favorite subject of painters, photographers, and filmmakers for a century. This photo was taken in 1915 by Philip Brigandi, the great-grandfather of local historian Phil Brigandi, as part of a series on California missions. The picturesque subject at right is a local Franciscan priest, possibly Father Huemulous.

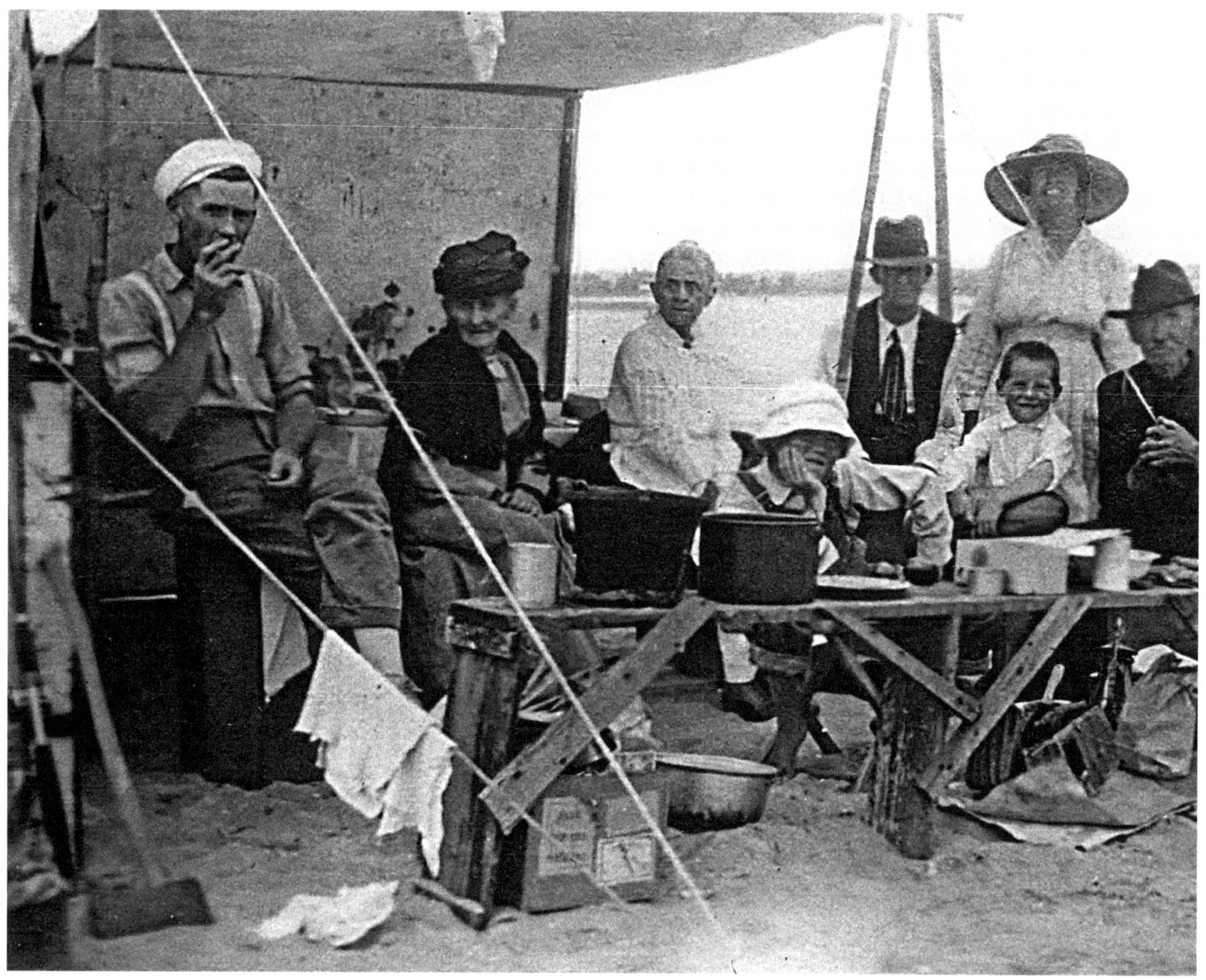

A canvas lean-to and a makeshift table hammered together from scrap wood were all these campers required for an extended stay in Newport Beach in 1916. Prosperous settlers were encouraged by city developers to build homes, but poorer farming families were equally welcome to camp for weeks at a time on the verbena-covered dunes, living off the bounty of the sea and temporarily forgetting the rigors of their hardscrabble lives.

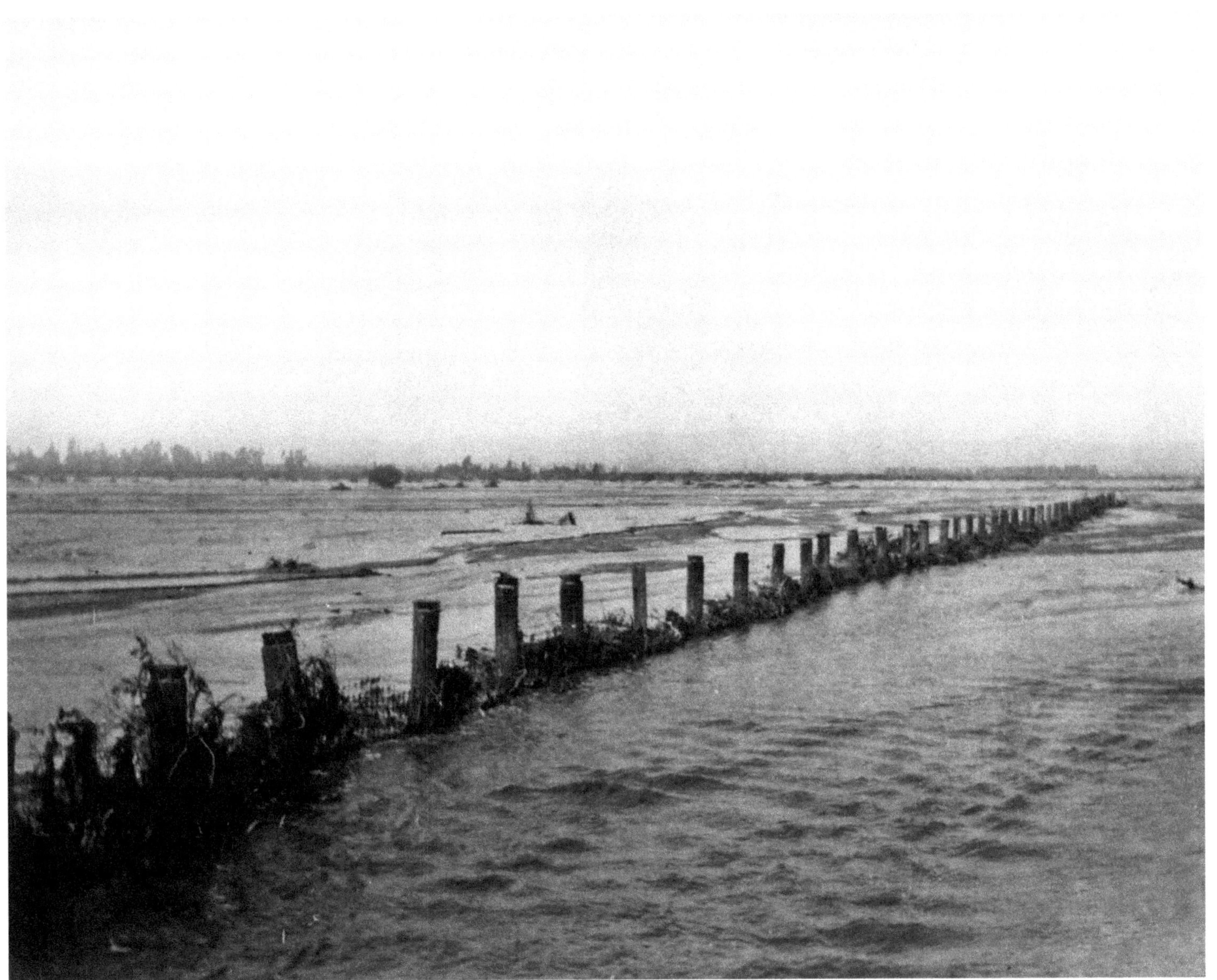

On February 3, 1916, the House Committee on Flood Control was formed to govern the construction of levees and dams in flood-prone areas, but it wasn't soon enough to prevent the mass destruction that occurred just five months later when a series of storms struck the Gulf Coast and swept westward all the way to Orange County, causing millions of dollars in damage to crops and roads and sweeping away topsoil and livestock.

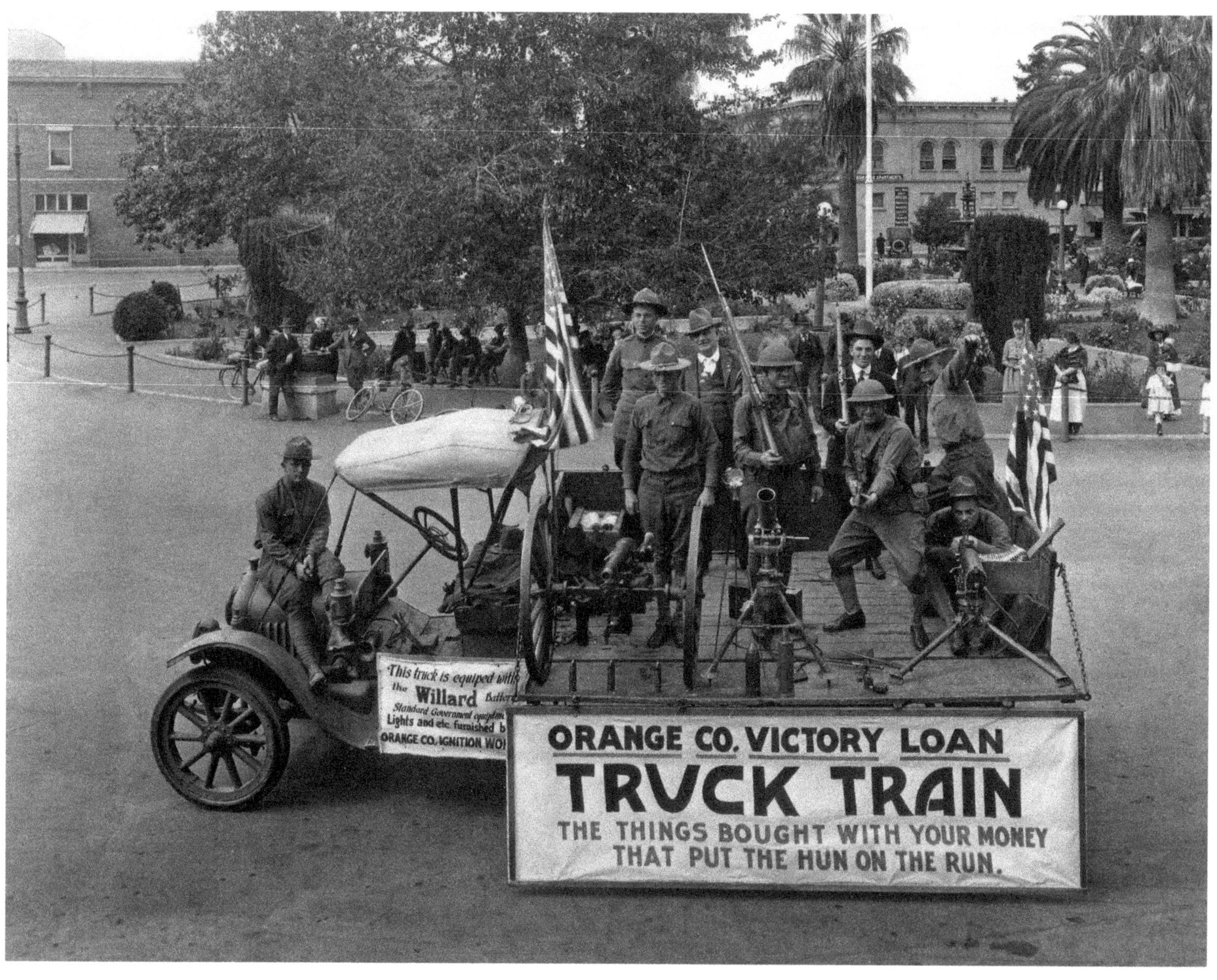

The Plaza in the city of Orange has always played a central role in the life of its residents. During World War I it served as backdrop to four Liberty Loan campaigns (one of which featured teenaged silent-film star Mary Miles Minter) and the Victory Loan campaign of April 21 through May 10, 1919. In this photo a smattering of observers has gathered to watch preparations for a "truck train" in support of the latter fund-raising program.

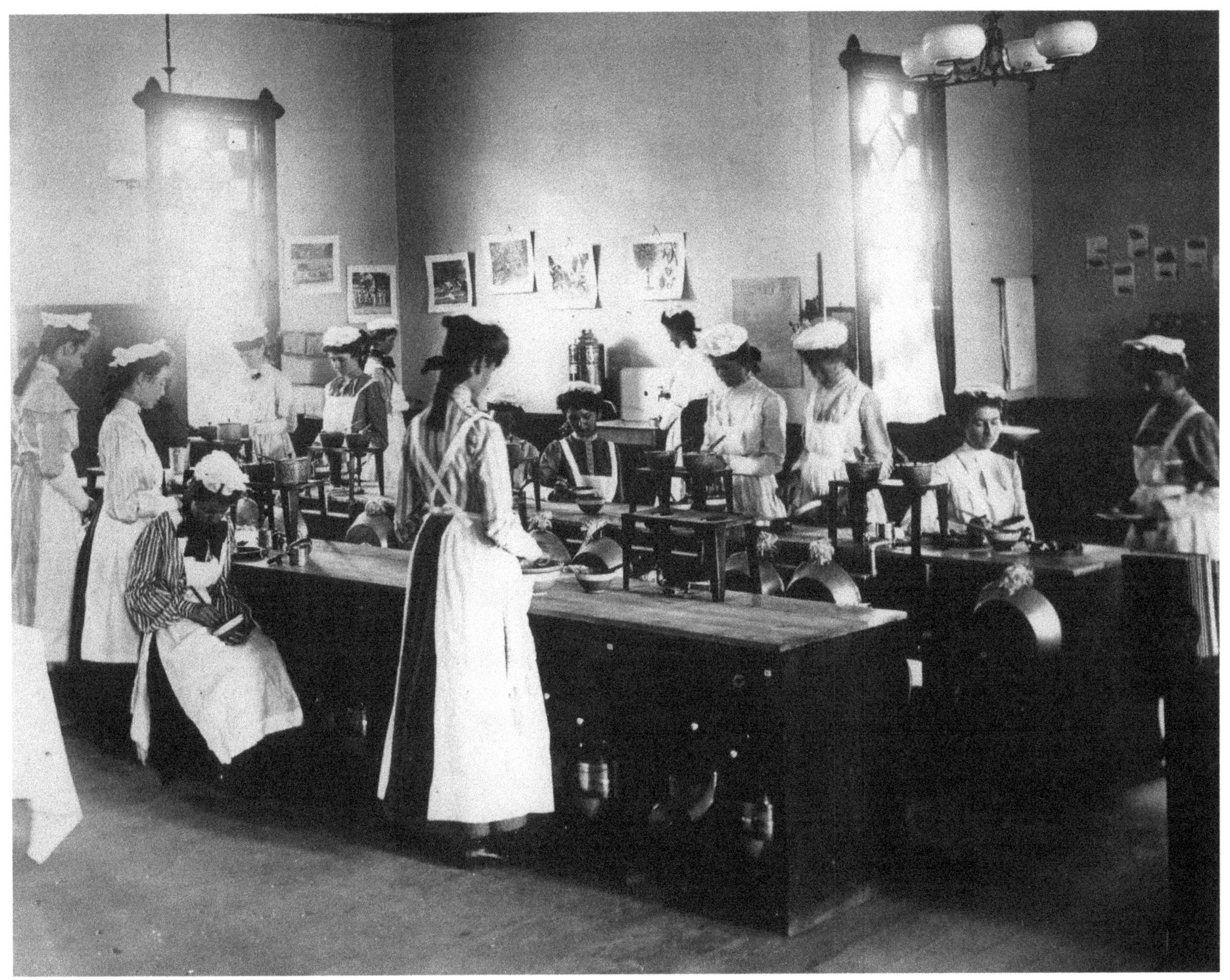

Santa Ana's first high school started life on the second floor of the Central Grammar School in 1889, but moved into its own new redbrick building on the corner of Ninth and Main in 1900. Constructed at a cost of $18,000, the building was demolished in the late 1940s to make way for a Buffum's Department Store. This 1919 photo shows one of the first cooking classes offered to female students at Santa Ana High School.

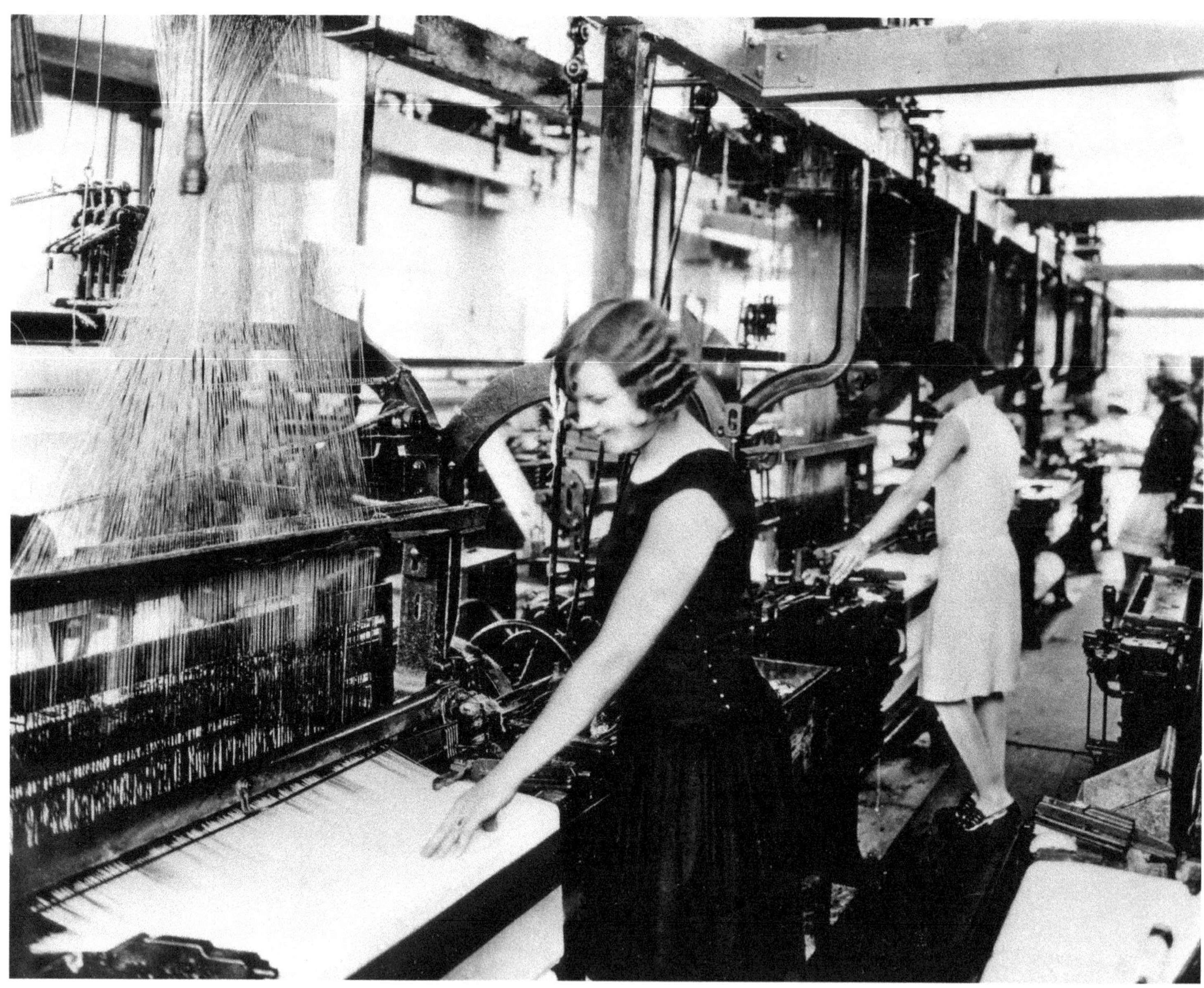

The Mission Woolen Manufacturing Company, located on the corner of Washington Avenue and Santiago Street in Santa Ana, opened in 1917. Manufacturing centered on army blankets and heavy woolen cloth for military overcoats. These fashionable young ladies were among the company's 75 employees doing their part for the war effort. Post–World War I production focused on lap robes and lighter-weight wools used in the manufacture of menswear.

Trials and Tribulations

(1920–1945)

In the Roaring Twenties, Orange County's rugged coastline attracted the interest of Hollywood filmmakers, and many silent movies were filmed at Diver's Cove, Arches Bay, and other scenic locales. Movie stars came to work and play but liked the area so much they never left. Errol Flynn, Humphrey Bogart, James Cagney, and John Wayne all kept yachts in Newport Harbor. Bette Davis, Judy Garland, Rudolph Valentino, and Charlie Chaplin were among the many celebrities who had second homes in Laguna Beach.

Dreams of turning Huntington Beach into "Pacific City," the West Coast equivalent of Atlantic City, were temporarily put on hold in 1920 when oil was struck there. The sleepy little resort town was turned overnight into a forest of wooden derricks, casting their ominous shadows—and noxious by-products—on the beach. Town lots that had been given away 20 years earlier as an incentive to buy a set of encyclopedias were suddenly making their owners very wealthy indeed.

While Orange County was not as hard hit by the Depression as other parts of the country, a pair of natural disasters five years apart tested the mettle of its residents. In 1933, a massive earthquake was felt throughout the county. Though casualties were minimal locally (unlike in Los Angeles County) structural damage was massive. Then in 1938, ten days of continuous rain caused the Santa Ana River to overflow its banks, sweeping away entire communities in the deluge. Both disasters resulted in the passage of laws governing building standards and flood control, making the county much more prepared to handle future catastrophes.

On December 7, 1941, Pearl Harbor was bombed and Orange County prepared for war. Within a year and a half, seven military installations had been built or commandeered for use by Army, Navy, and Marine Corps personnel. While most of these facilities trained troops for overseas deployment, the United States Naval Air Station, Santa Ana, was commissioned as a blimp base. The blimp fleet did sea-rescue work and patrolled the California coastline for submarines, each airship equipped with a crew of nine, a machine gun, and four depth bombs. Hundreds of thousands of young men passed through these bases during the war years, and many would return to live in Orange County after the war.

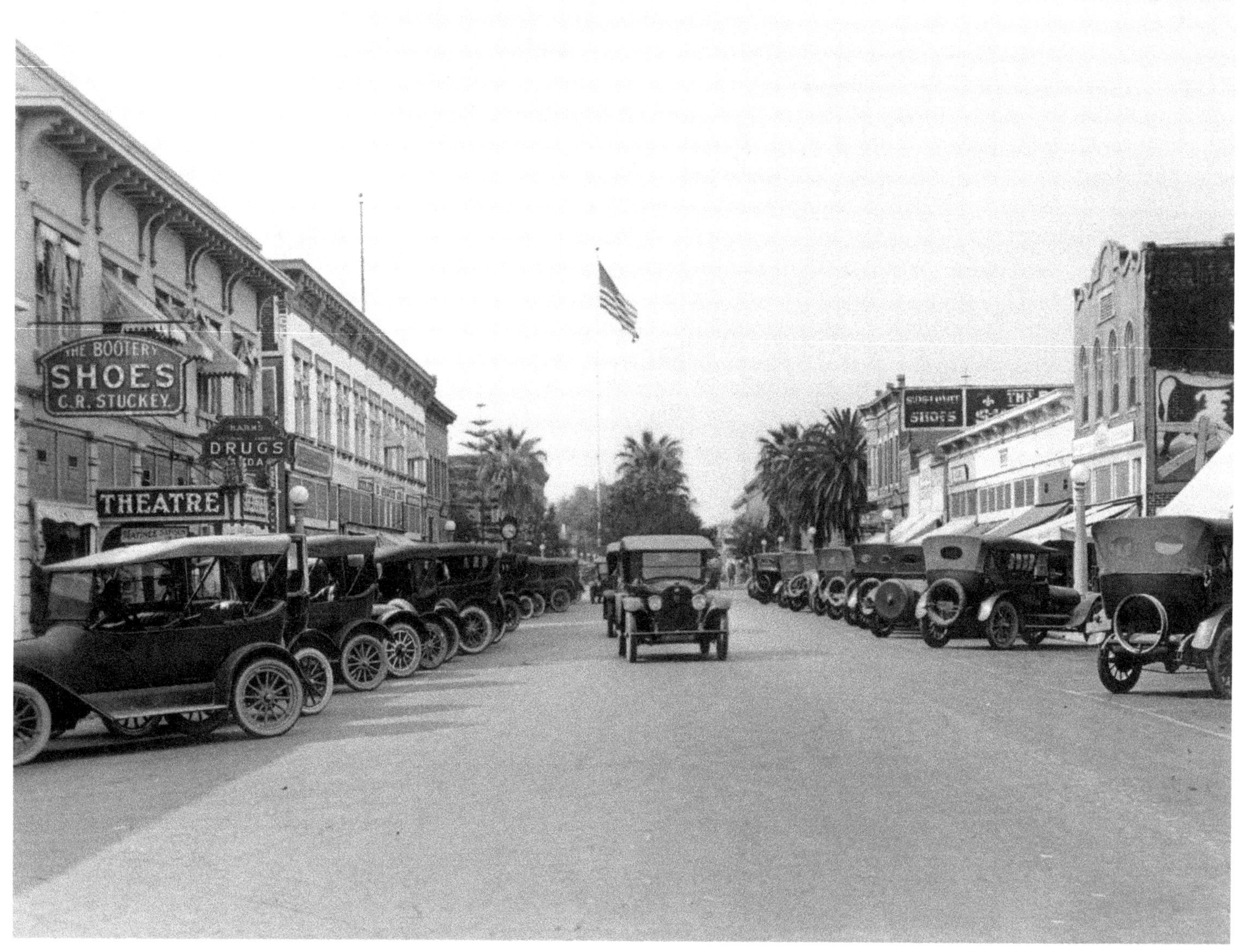

The Old Towne area of the city of Orange was listed on the National Register of Historic Places in 1997. Because it has such a high concentration of historic buildings and has retained a small-town look, downtown Orange is frequently used as a location for television shows and movies, such as the Tom Hanks–directed 1996 film *That Thing You Do!* This is a shot of South Glassell in the 1920s.

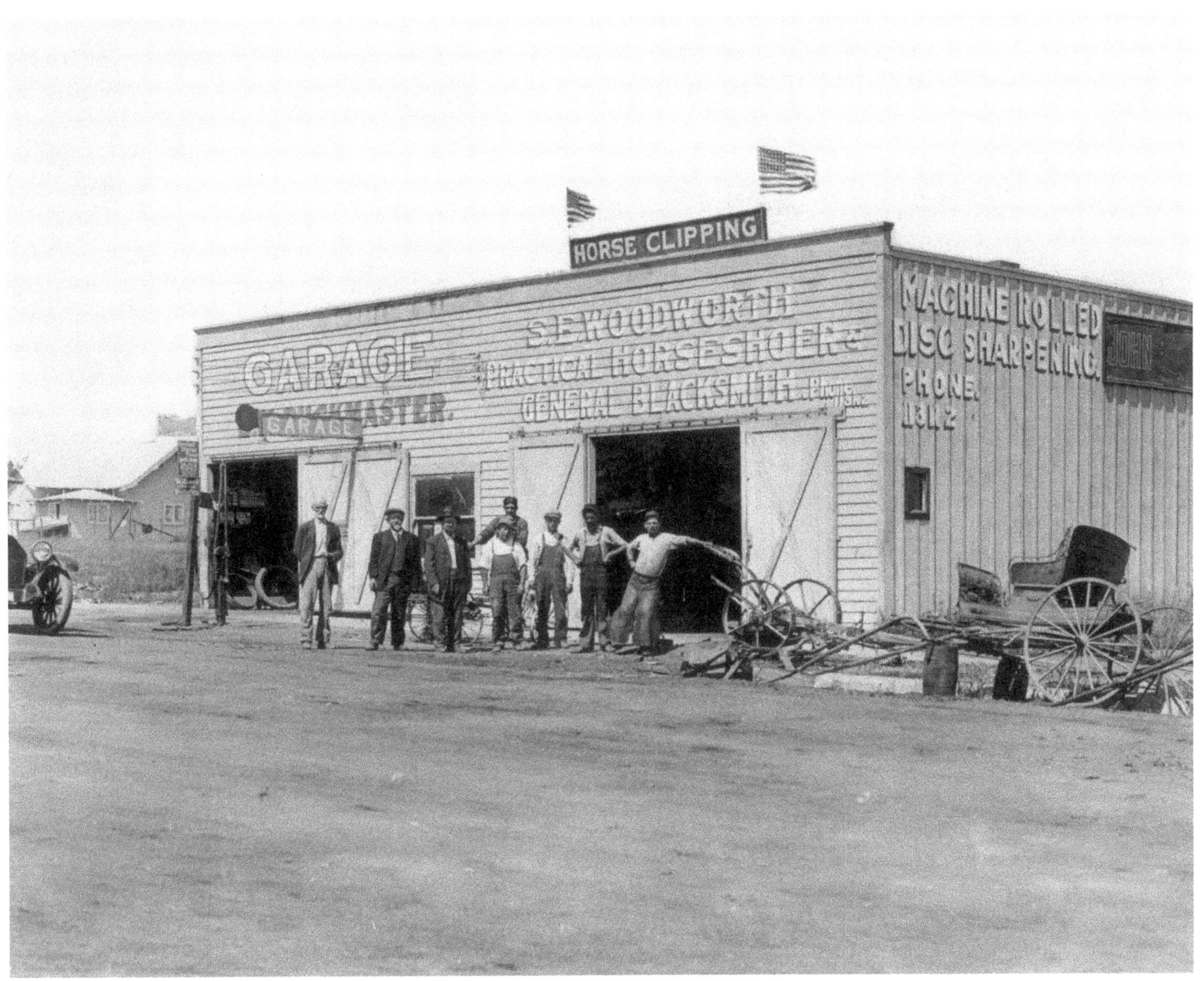

This multi-purpose building was located in Yorba Linda in the 1920s. Yorba Linda, in the northeast corner of the county, is best known as the birthplace of Richard Nixon, whose reconstructed childhood home is now part of the Richard Nixon Library and Museum. In 2005 CNN listed Yorba Linda as #21 among the best places in the United States to live, and the richest U.S. city by median household income.

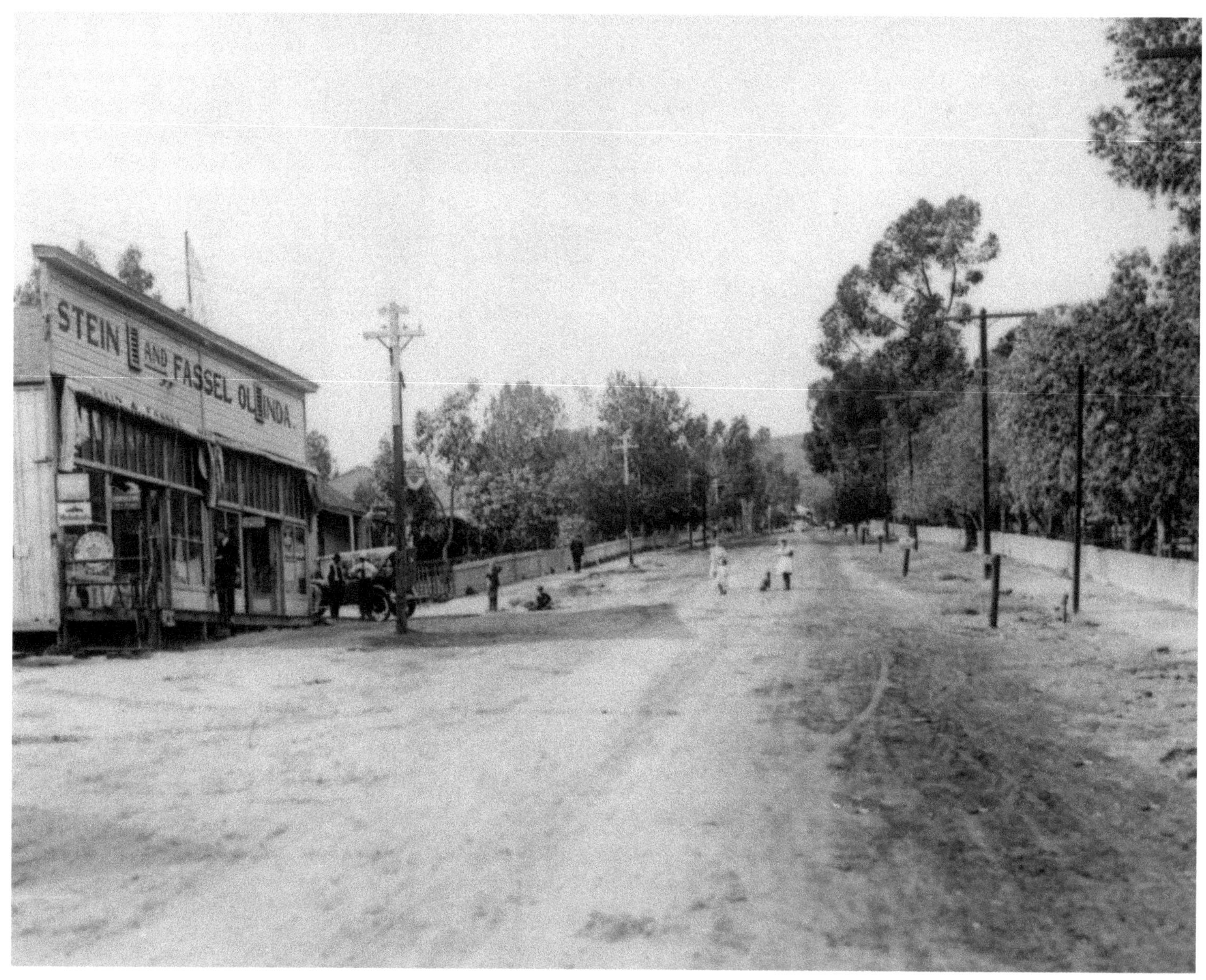

The community of Olinda, located in Carbon Canyon, was once considered prime agricultural land. That is, until oil was discovered in the late 1800s. Pastures quickly gave way to oil derricks, and Olinda, shown here in 1920, was a wealthy little boomtown until the 1940s, when the fields began to shut down. In 1917 Olinda merged with the village of Randolph and incorporated as Brea, Spanish for "tar."

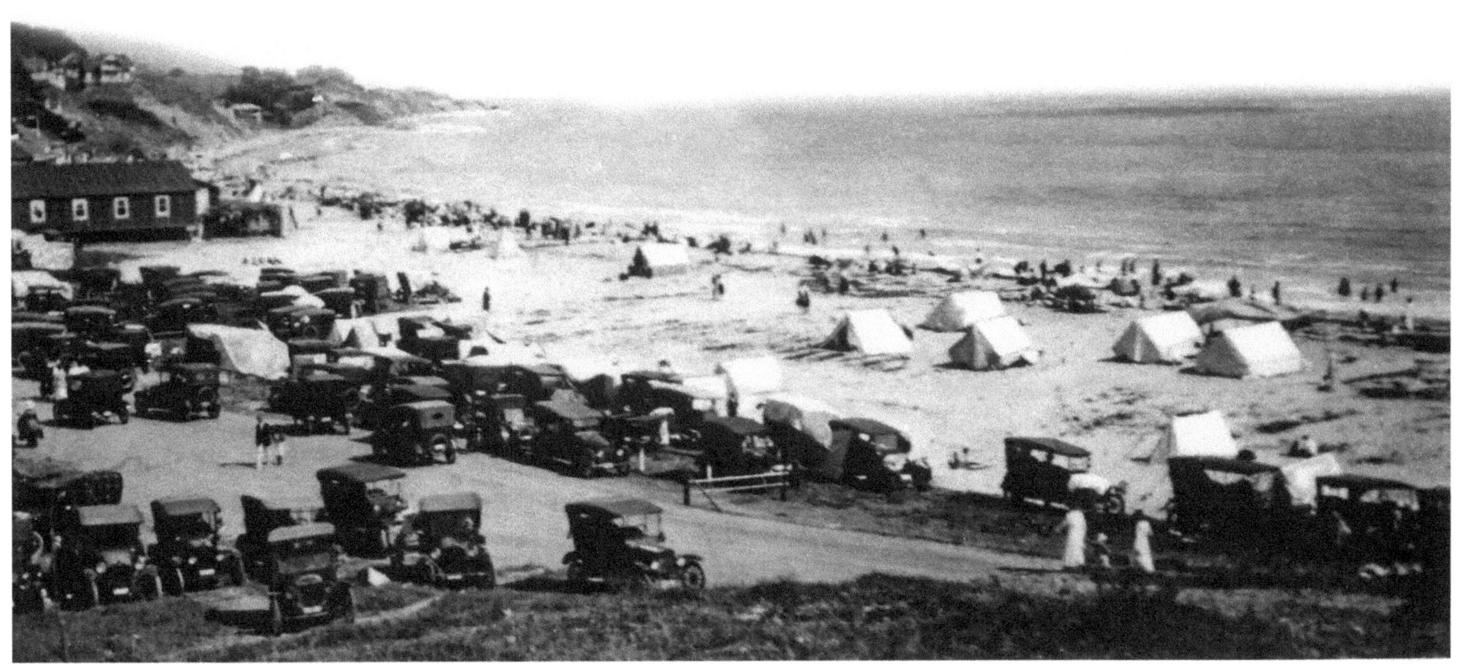

Though parts of what would become Laguna Beach were within the boundaries of the Irvine Ranch, squatters were generally tolerated on the unproductive beach lands. Campers in the early 1920s were mostly from Santa Ana or San Bernardino and would stay anywhere from a few weeks to the whole summer, setting up tents right on the sand. Laguna's first library was formed to provide literary sustenance for these temporary residents.

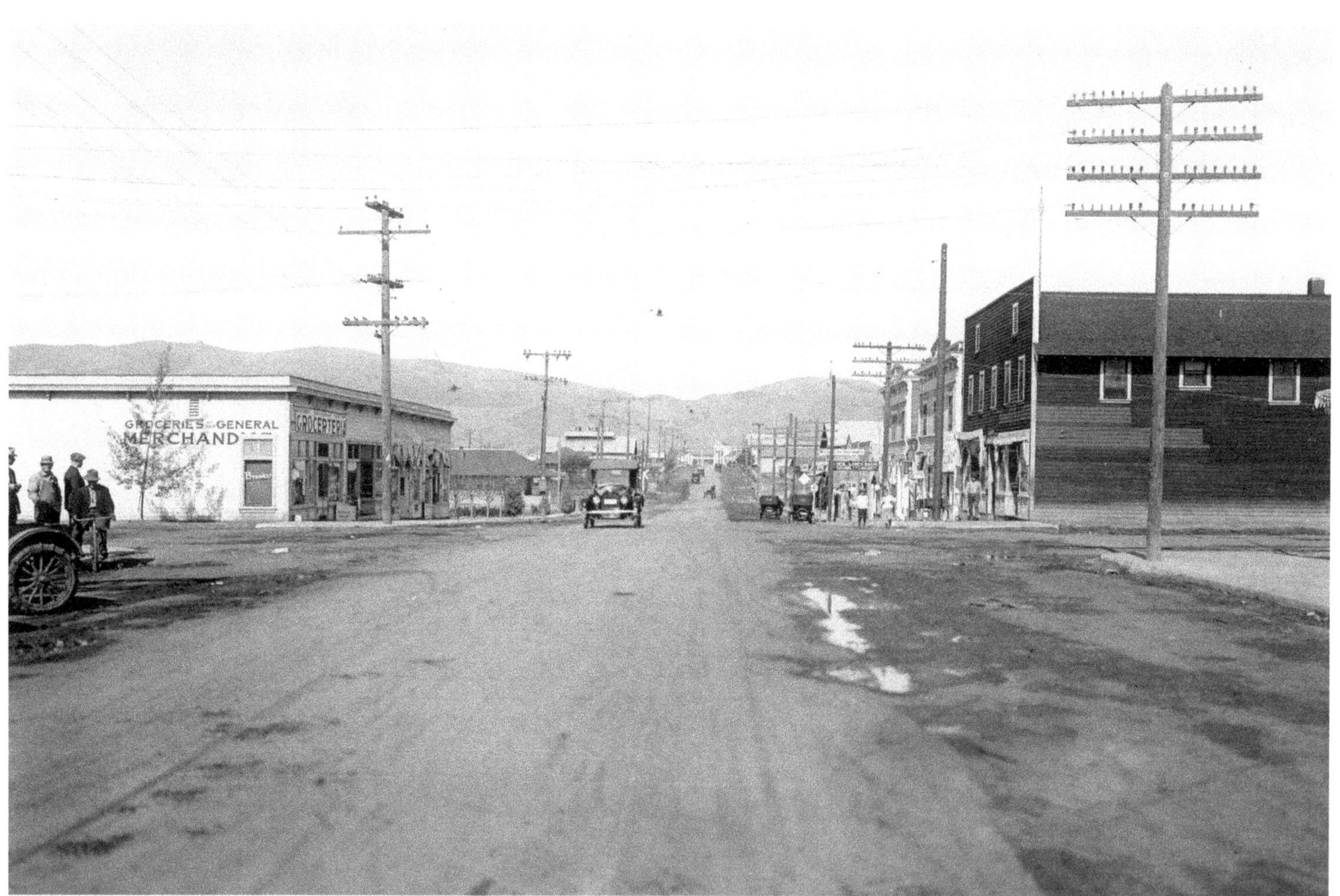

The biggest thing to happen to Brea since the discovery of oil took place on October 31, 1924, at the Brea Bowl, a natural amphitheater owned by Union Oil that has long since been covered over by housing tracts. That day, future Baseball Hall of Famers Walter Johnson and Babe Ruth faced each other in an exhibition game before 5,000 ecstatic fans. A half-day holiday was declared in three towns, and 100 extra officers were needed to police the grounds.

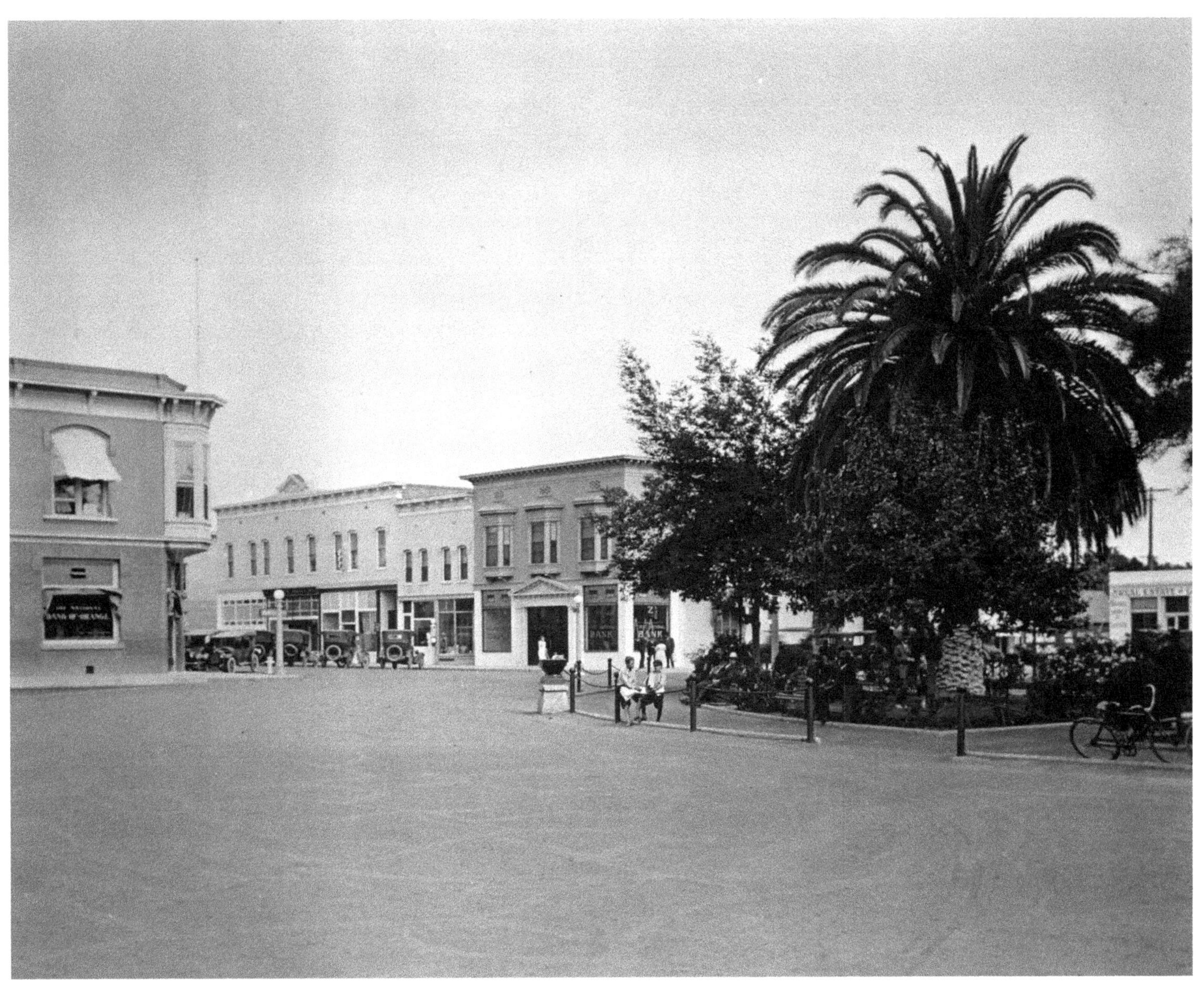

Unlike most cities in the congested northern half of the county, the city of Orange still has an identifiable, central downtown area. Shown here in the 1920s, the Plaza's shaded grassy areas, sidewalks, and famous fountain encourage strolling and social gatherings, while the historically significant architecture ringing the park bolsters civic pride. The Plaza is considered Orange County's oldest dedicated parkland.

This gracious fountain stood in the central Plaza of Orange from 1887 to 1937. The $585 needed to finance its installation was raised by the Orange Women's Temperance Union, largely through the production of an original satiric play called *The Plaza: A Local Drama in Five Acts,* written and acted by townspeople. After several decades in storage the fountain was fully restored in 1981 and currently stands behind the Orange Public Library.

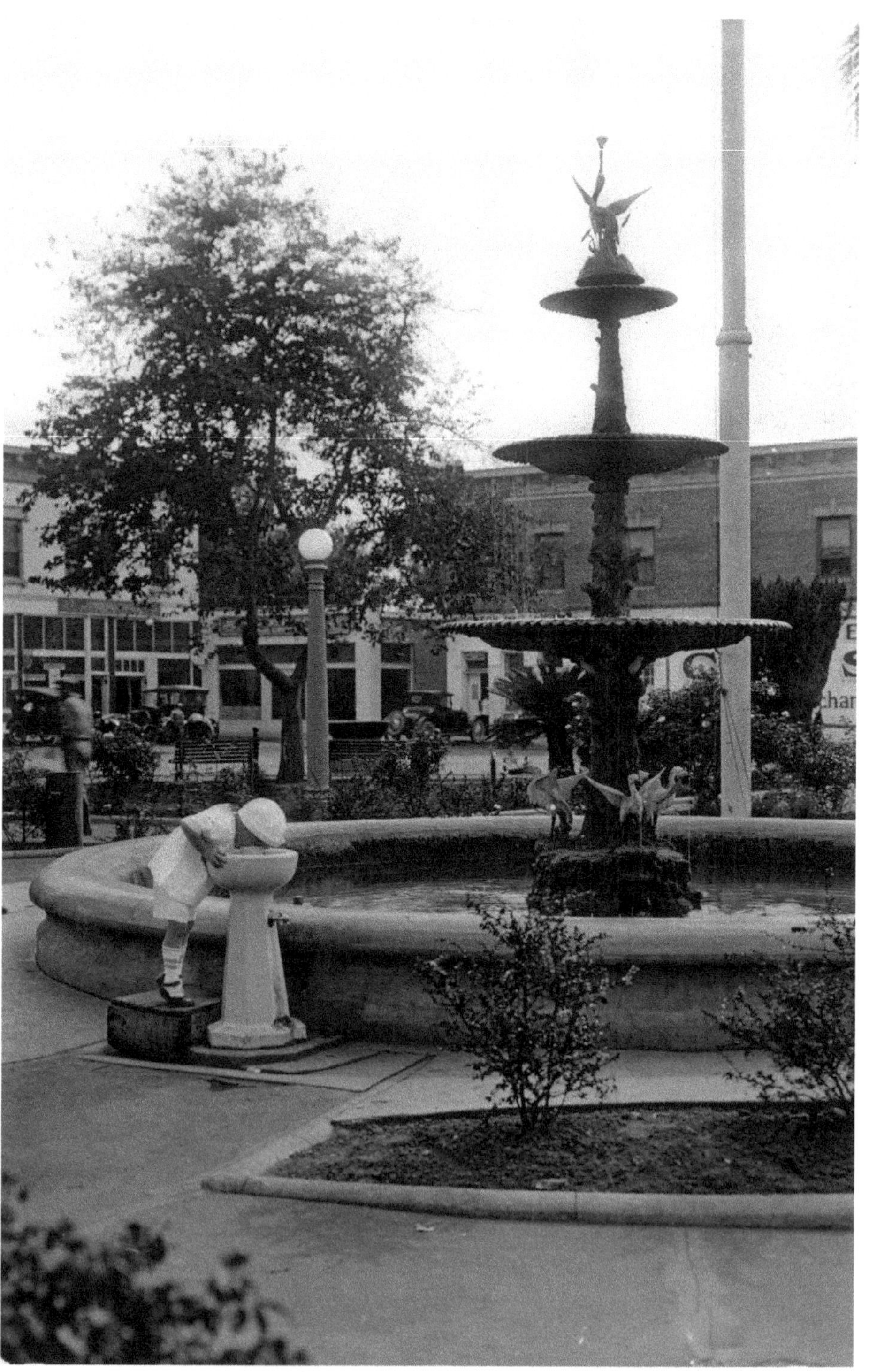

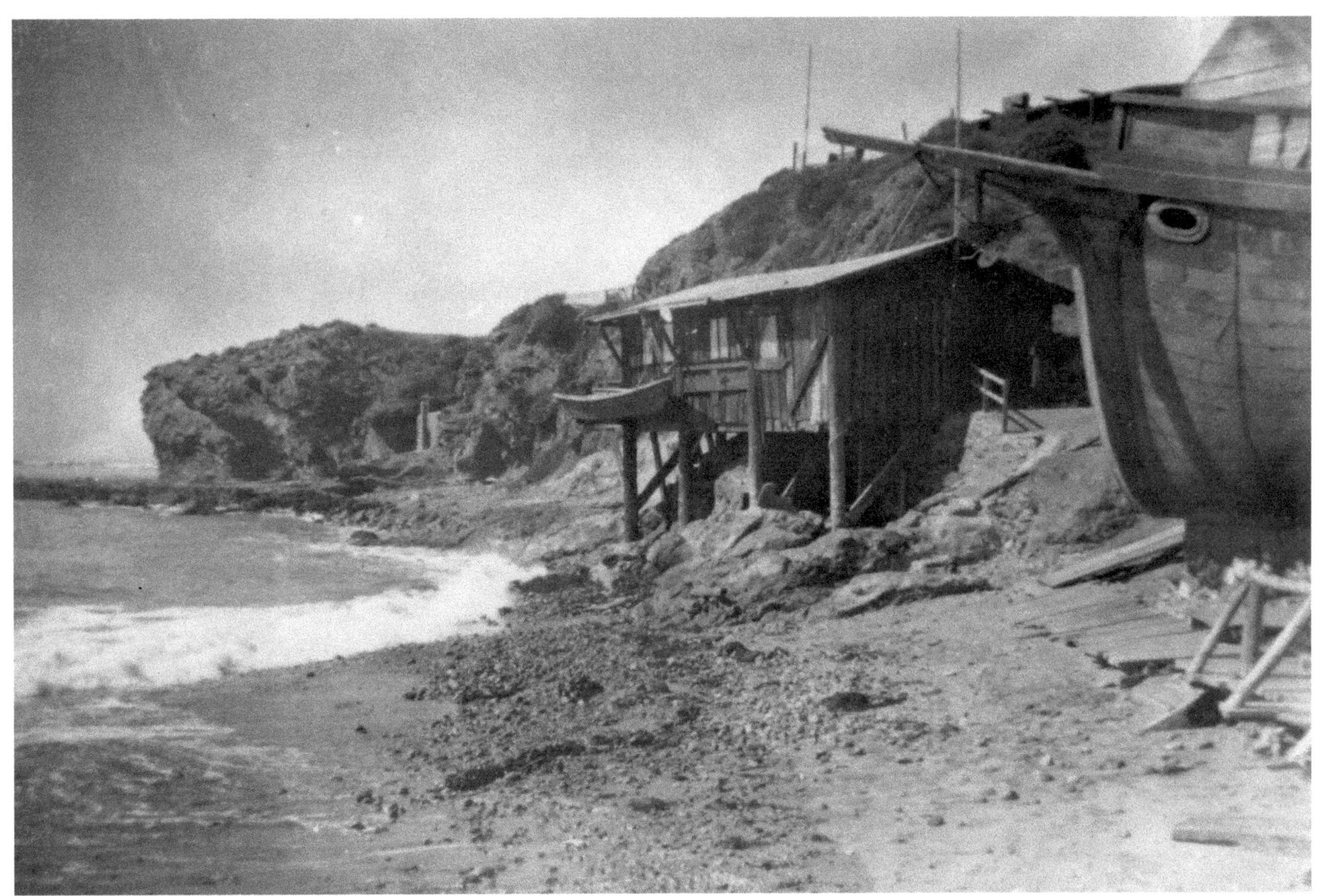

In the 1920s Lagona, as Laguna Beach was known at the time, was still rocky, remote, and difficult to reach by vehicle—and perfect for making movies. This early film set, which included several rustic fishing huts on stilts and the fishing boat whose prow is visible on the right, was possibly for a Buster Keaton silent film, at least one of which is known to have been filmed in the area during this time period.

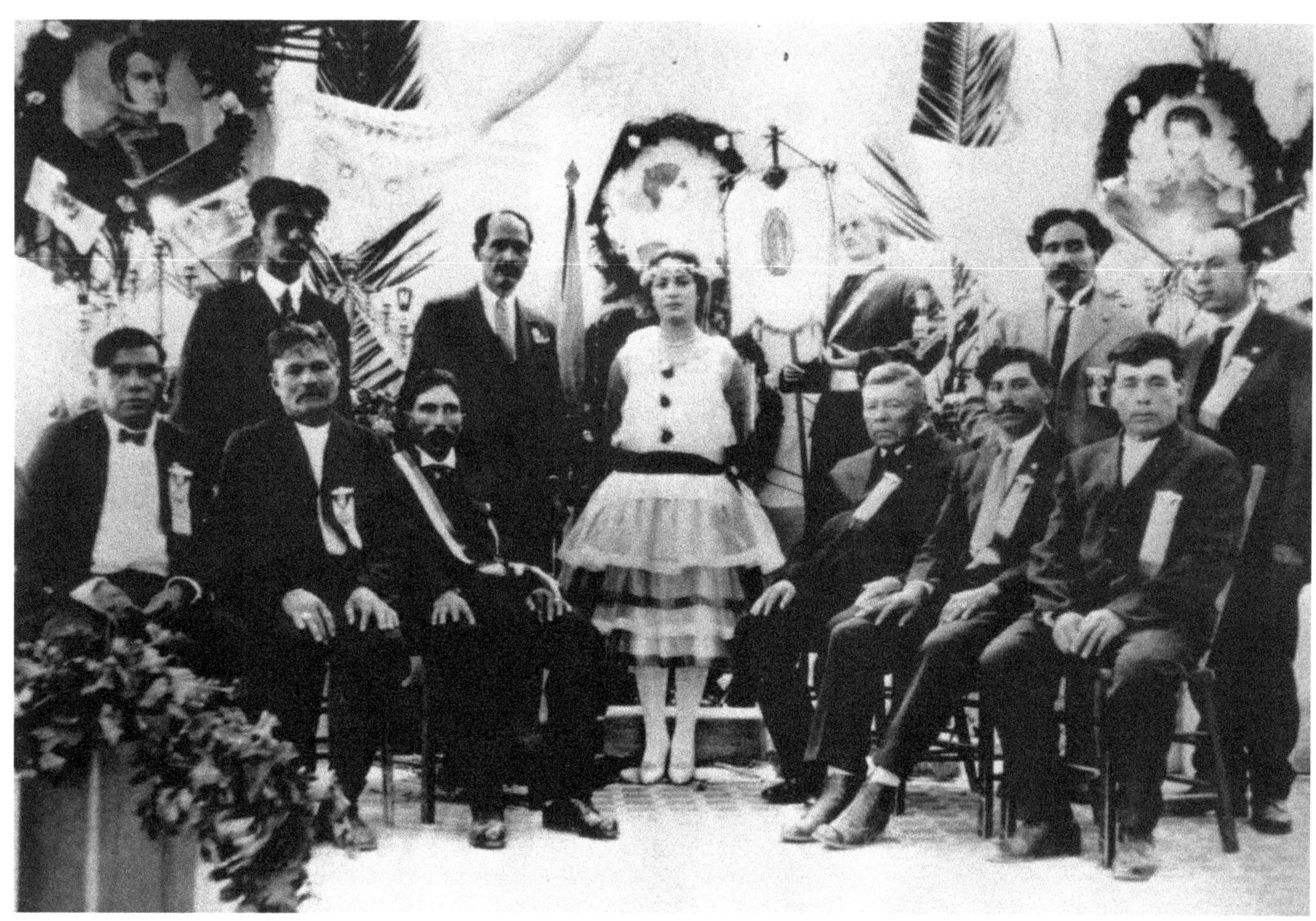

The town of La Habra commemorates Mexican Independence Day in this 1920s photo. Mexican independence from Spanish colonial rule was recognized in 1821, and the annual celebration of this event kicks off with "el Grito" (the Shout) of "Mexicanos, Viva Mexico!" followed by ceremonies, parades, traditional Mexican dances, and mariachi bands. Festivities take place in several Orange County cities, including La Habra, where the population is currently 49 percent Hispanic.

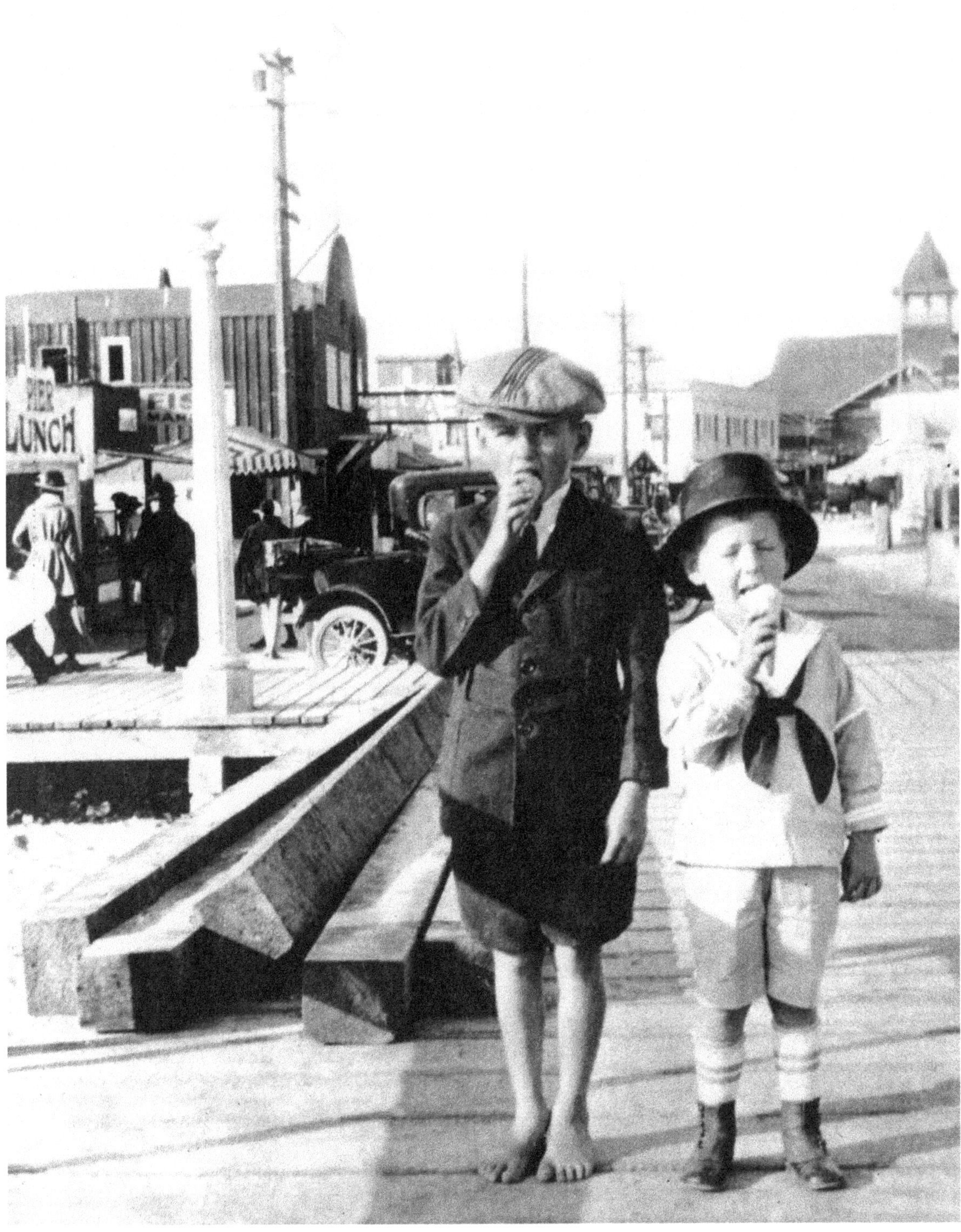

While the grown-ups in the background bundle up in their winter coats on Balboa Pier, it's never too cold for a kid to kick off his shoes on the boardwalk and enjoy an ice cream cone. In the late 1920s, the Rendezvous Ballroom swung with the beat of the big bands, and the harbor was discovered by the Hollywood in-crowd, many of whom docked their yachts there, including Errol Flynn, Humphrey Bogart, and James Cagney.

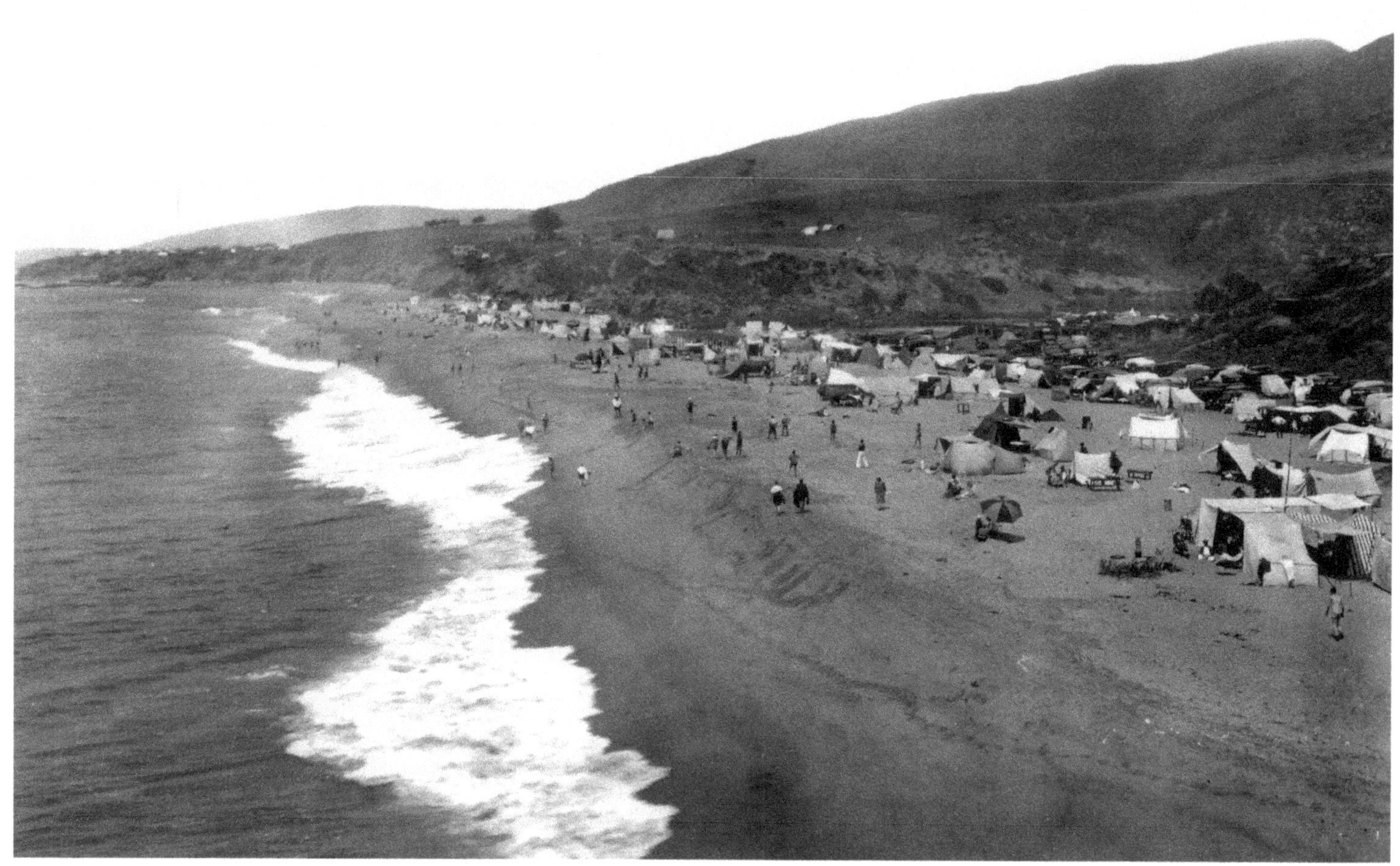

When Mary Pickford cut the ribbon for the newly completed Pacific Coast Highway in 1928, the rest of California discovered the previously hidden gem that was Laguna, and the days of camping free on the beach were over. Tents soon gave way to beach cottages, and these in turn were eventually replaced by the multimillion-dollar homes that now dot the bare cliffs seen behind these campers on Aliso Beach ca. 1922.

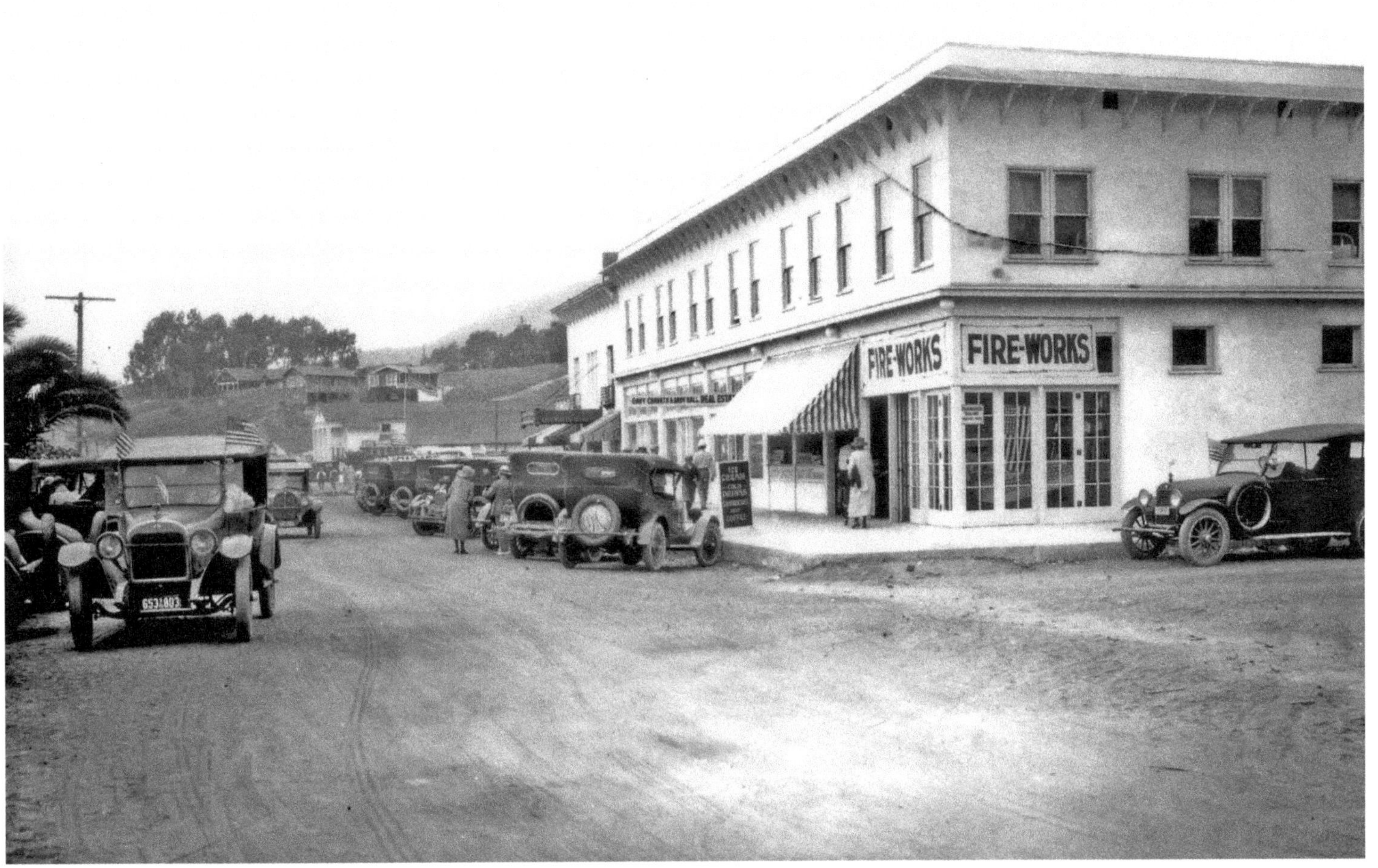

Fireworks, invented in China 2,000 years ago, have been an integral part of American Independence Day celebrations since 1777. This temporary fireworks store at the corner of Pacific Coast Highway and Ocean Avenue in Laguna Beach was doing bang-up business in the 1920s. Though the city was still sparsely populated at the time, the parking lot was full and patrons double-parked to make their purchases.

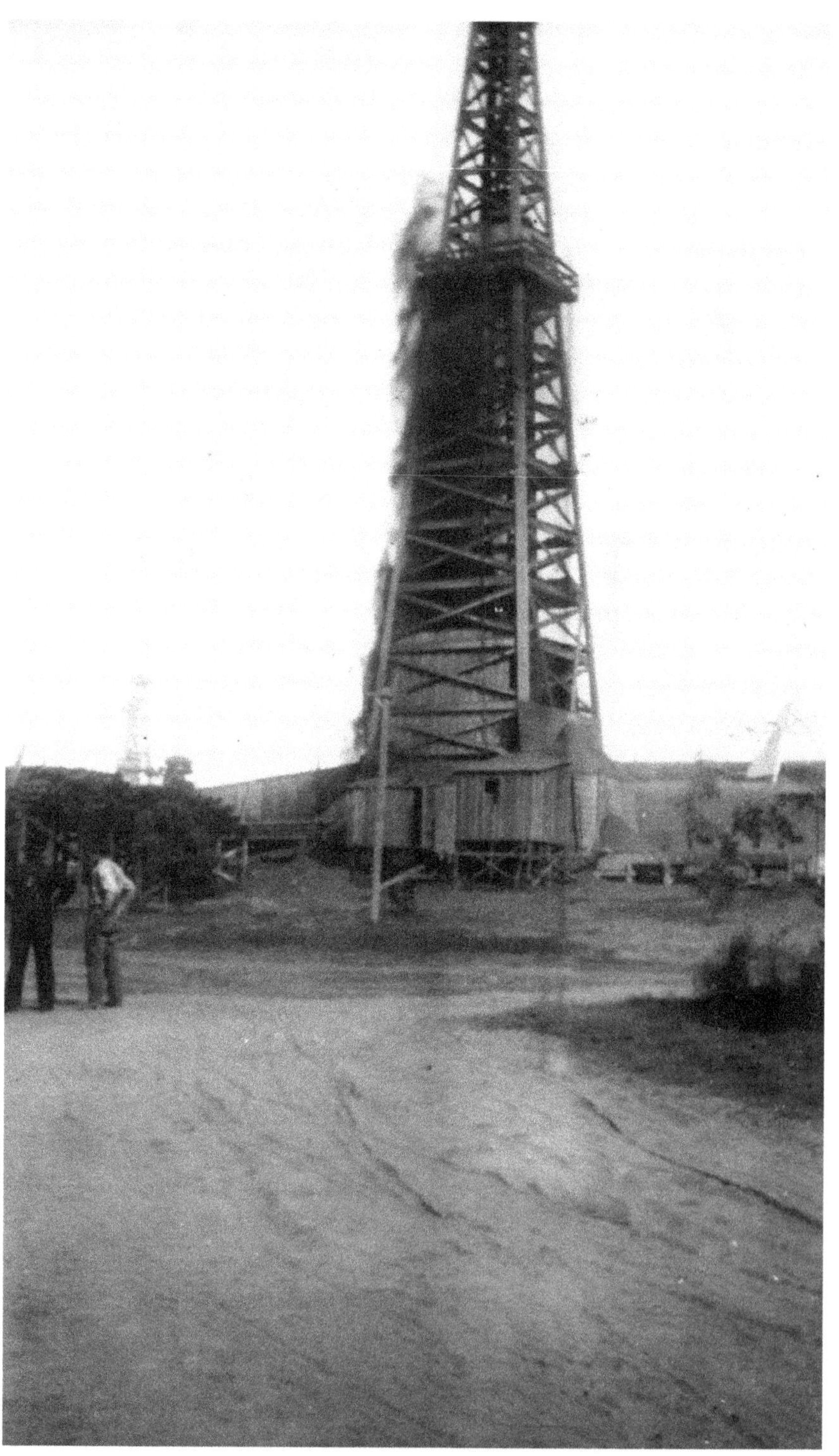

After oil was struck in Orange County, the Talbert #1 oil rig, shown here in 1922, was one of thousands of similar derricks that sprouted in backyards and trailer parks, on street corners and beaches, and even over houses, in Huntington Beach, Brea, and Olinda. Property owners who had been given free town lots in Huntington Beach as part of an encyclopedia promotion two decades earlier suddenly found themselves very wealthy.

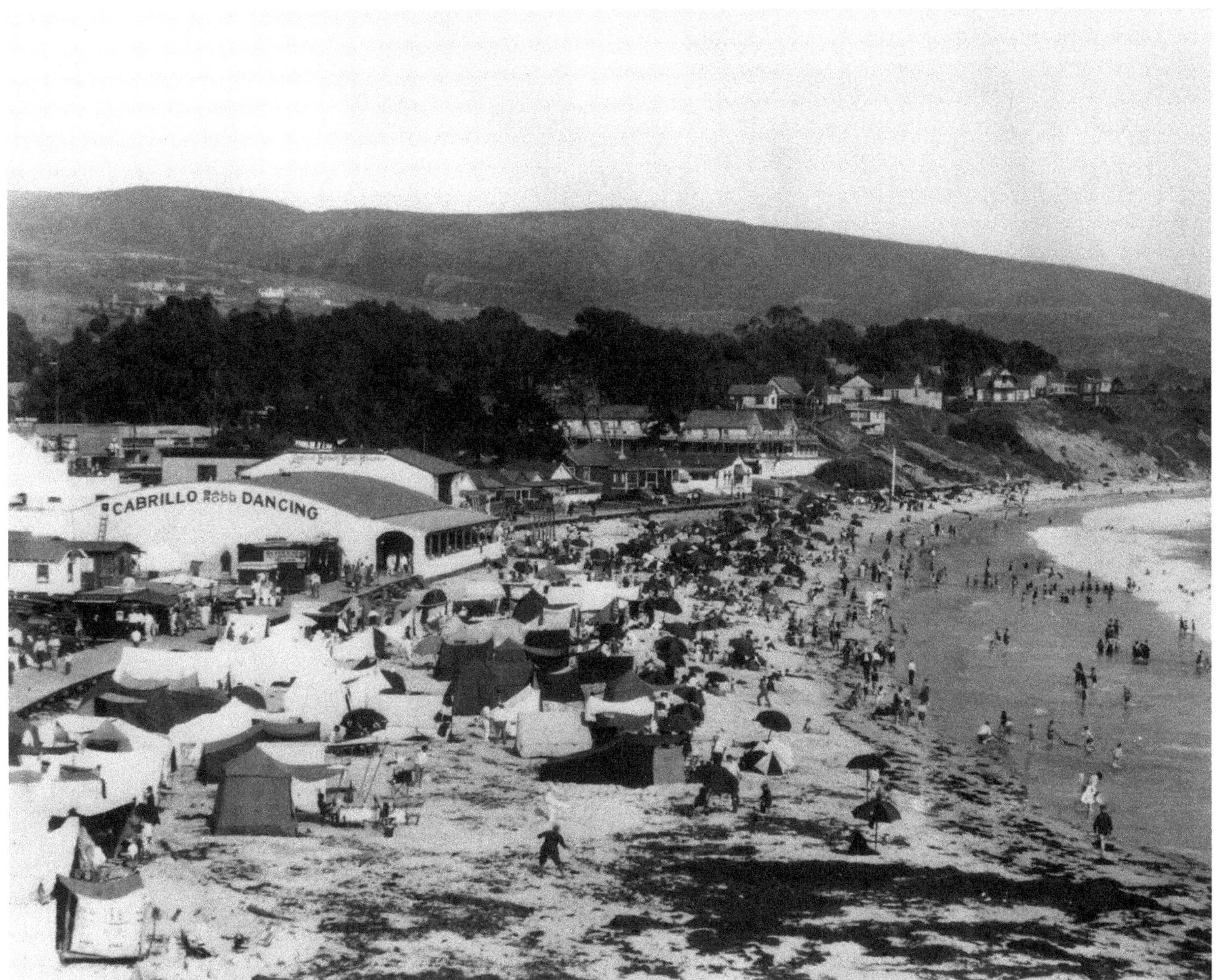

In 1926 the Cabrillo Ballroom, at left, opened on Laguna's main beach and was *the* place to be through the Roaring Twenties for dancing and big-name jazz bands. Before finding fame as an actor, Fred MacMurray played saxophone there, and Mickey Rooney was known to sit in on drums. By 1940 the good times were over and the ballroom was converted into a bowling alley and pool hall. The building was torn down in the late 1950s.

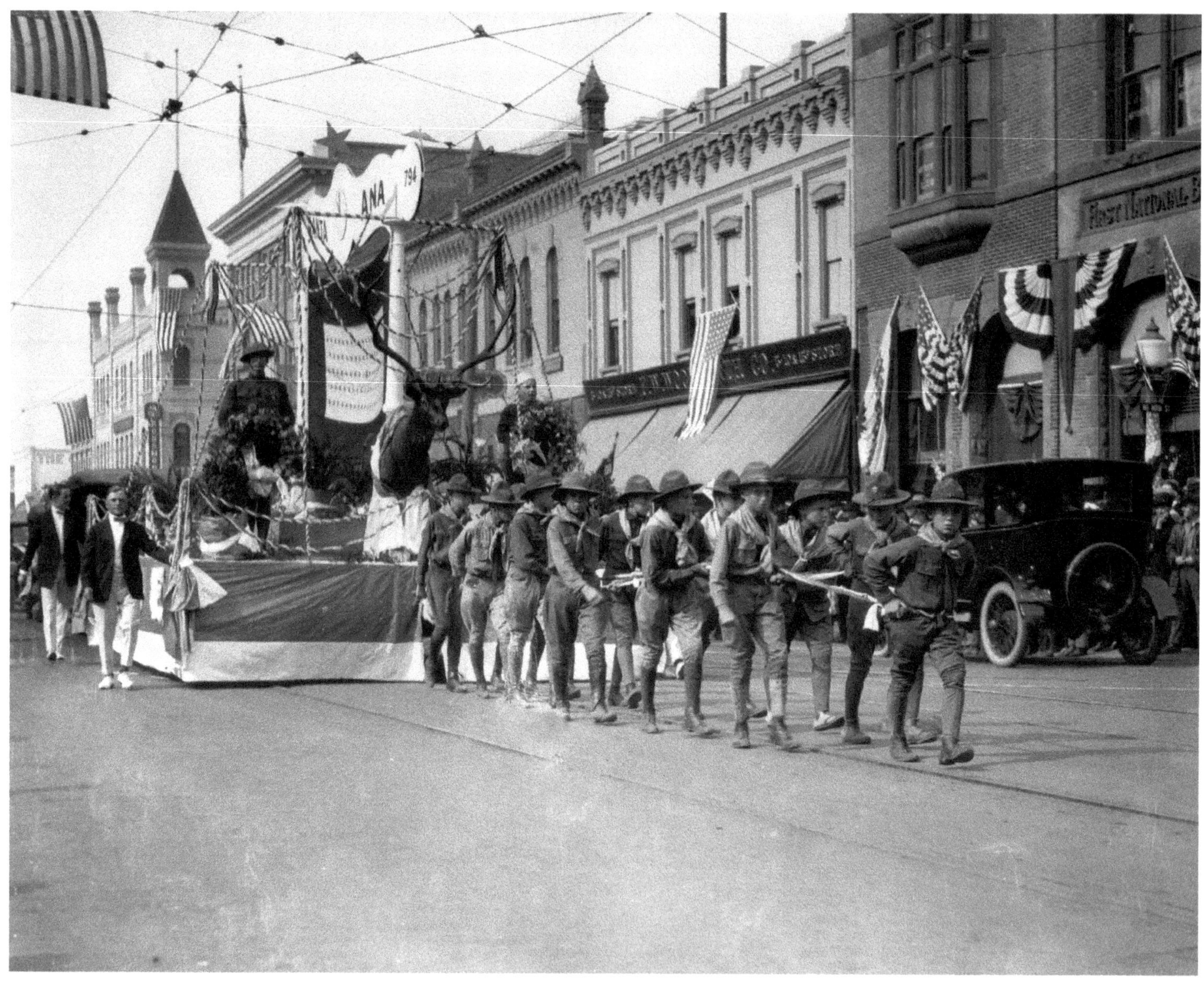

Employing a low-tech form of locomotion, the Elks Float in this 1920s Armistice Day Parade is pulled along by a local Boy Scout troop. Downtown Santa Ana businesses, including F. W. Woolworth and the First National Bank, both visible at right, are draped in bunting to celebrate the anniversary of the end of World War I. Armistice Day was later renamed Veteran's Day.

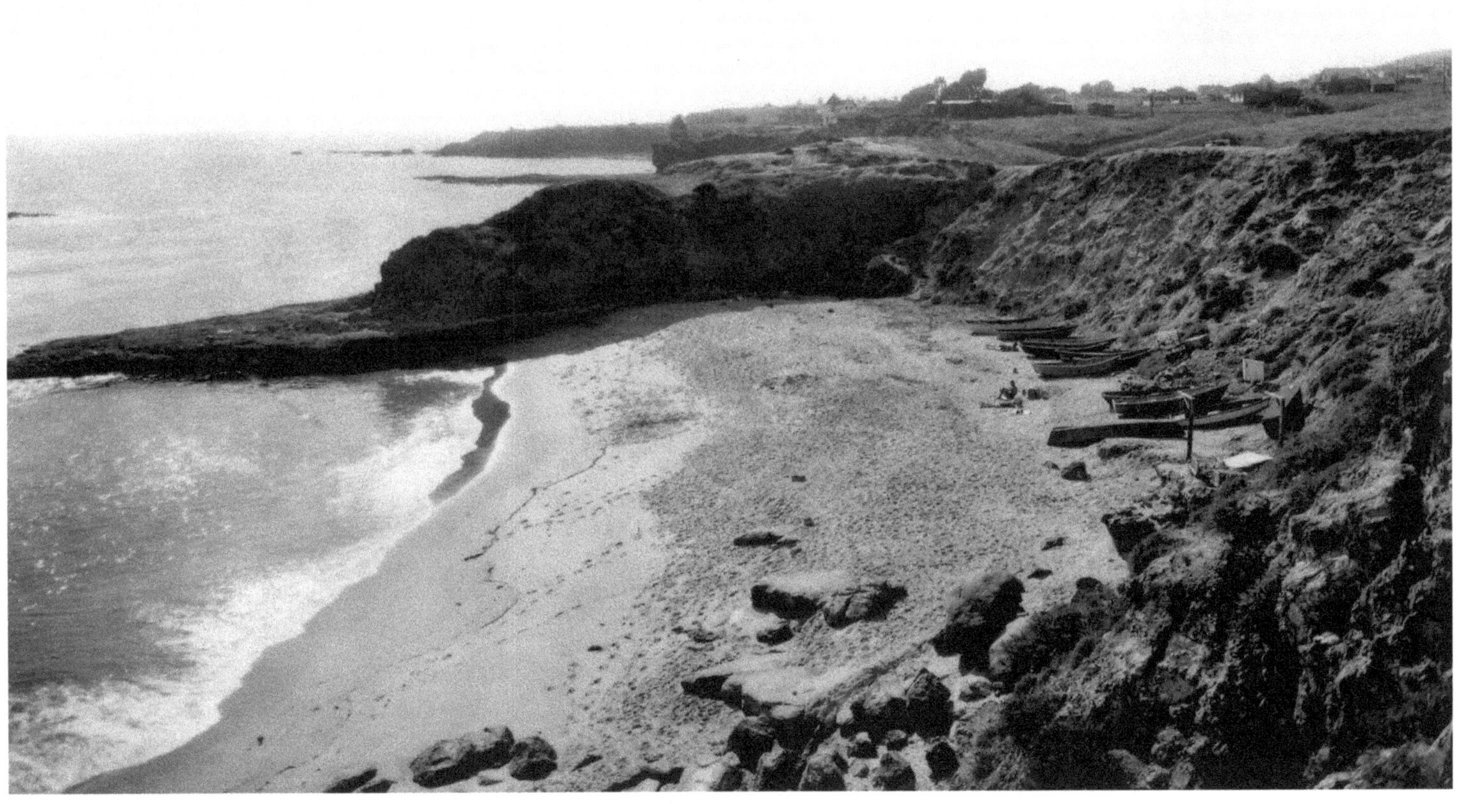

By 1924 Laguna was still sparsely populated and remote, and fishing opportunities at its many beaches were the main draw. It was said that lobster and abalone could practically be plucked from the beach. Today, Diver's Cove is a popular scuba-diving spot with generally calm surf conditions and an offshore reef that teems with colorful sea life such as octopus, spiny cowries, anemones, bat rays, and vivid-orange garibaldis.

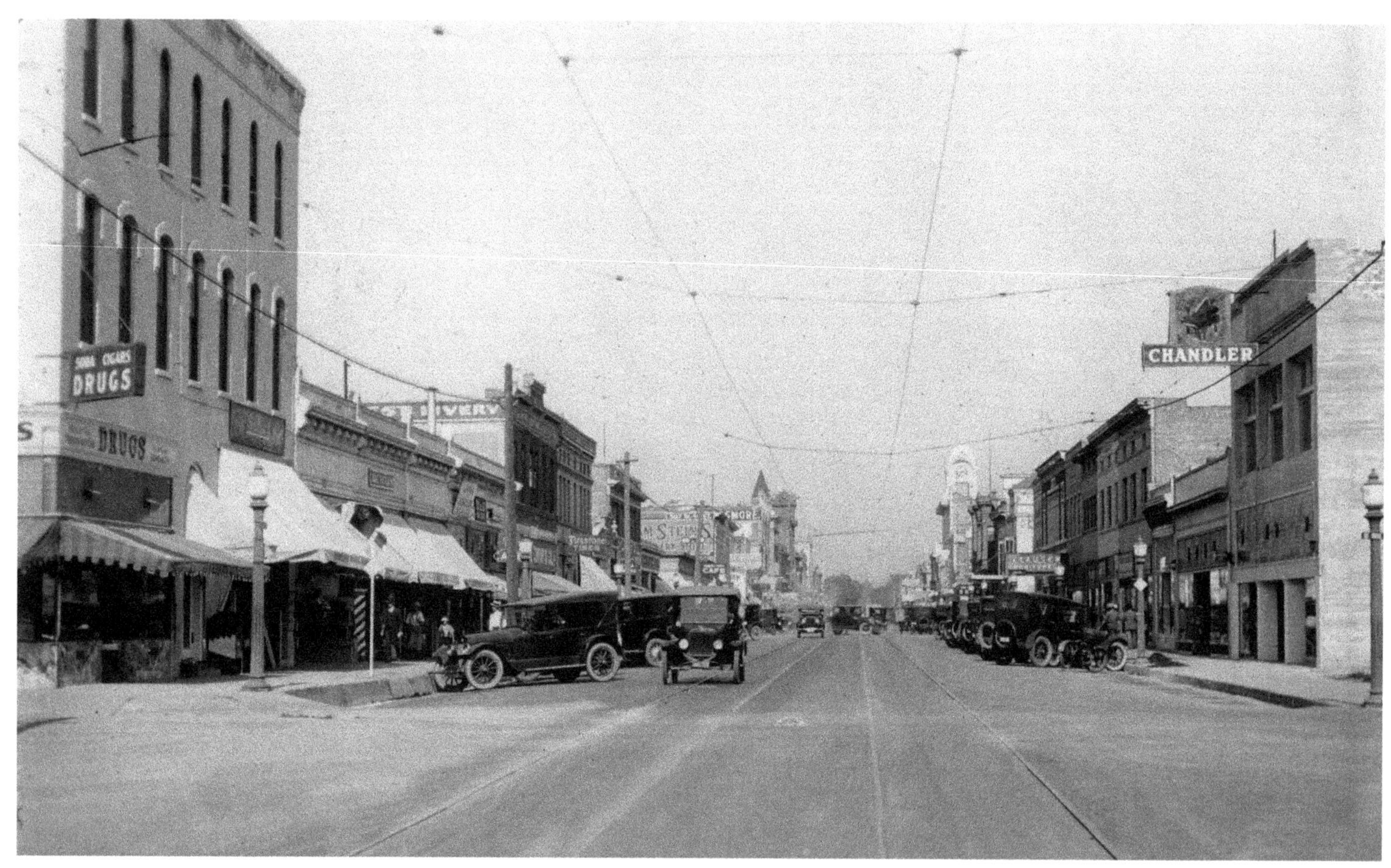

In Santa Ana the view down Fourth Street from Ross is still recognizable from 1925. The Clausen block, right foreground, is intact, and the Spurgeon can still be seen off in the distance. While the block across the street has been replaced by the modern Federal Building, a vibrant historical mural inside links it to the past. A railway spike motif on the surrounding walls pays homage to the tracks that once divided the street.

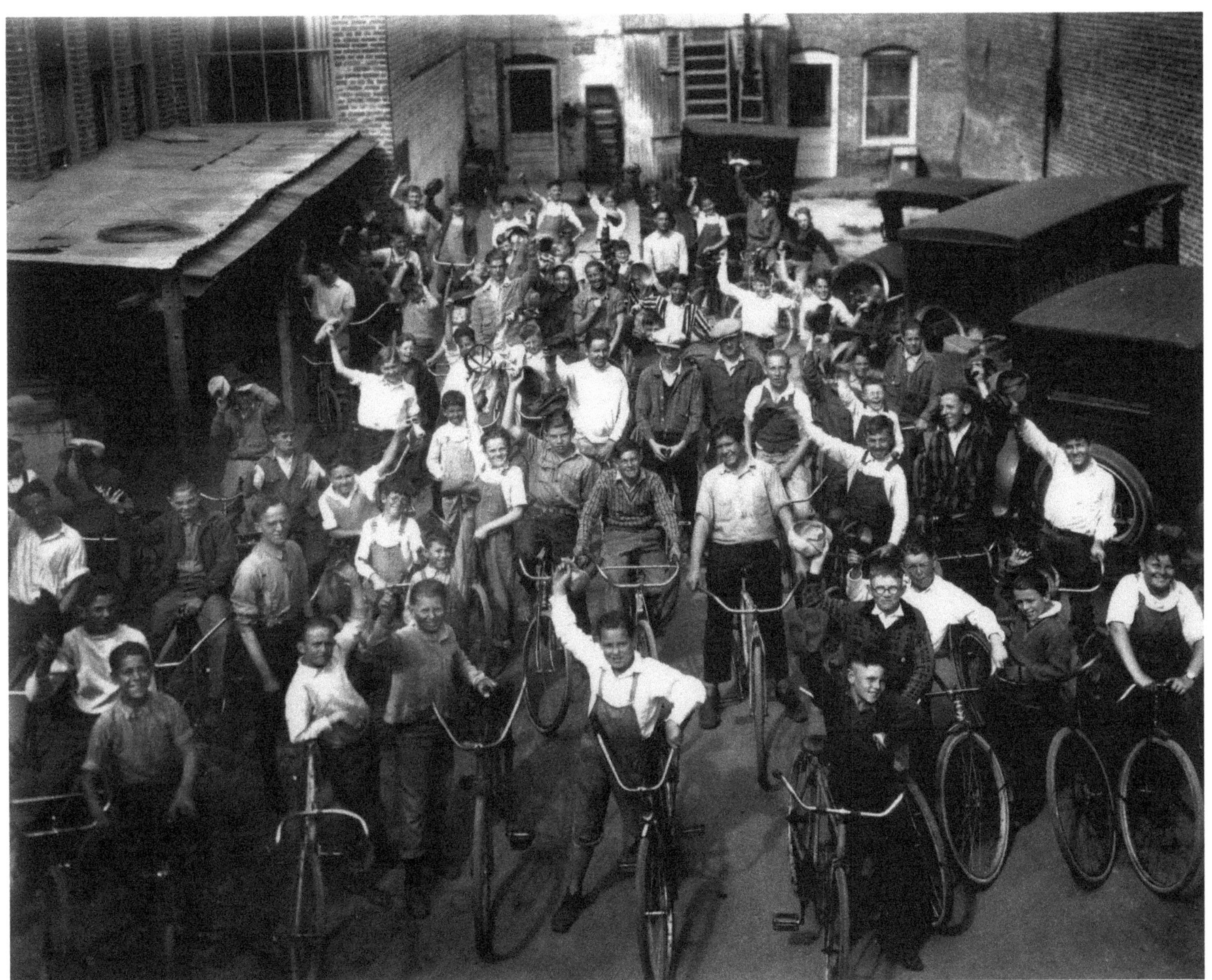

Early nineteenth century bicycle prototypes, known as velocipedes, were uncomfortable and difficult to ride, but the invention of the modern bicycle in the latter part of the century sparked a biking fad, as demonstrated by this crowd of boys outside a Santa Ana fix-it shop in the 1920s. The sunny SoCal weather makes bicycle riding a viable transportation option year-round for environmentally conscious adults as well as fun-loving kids.

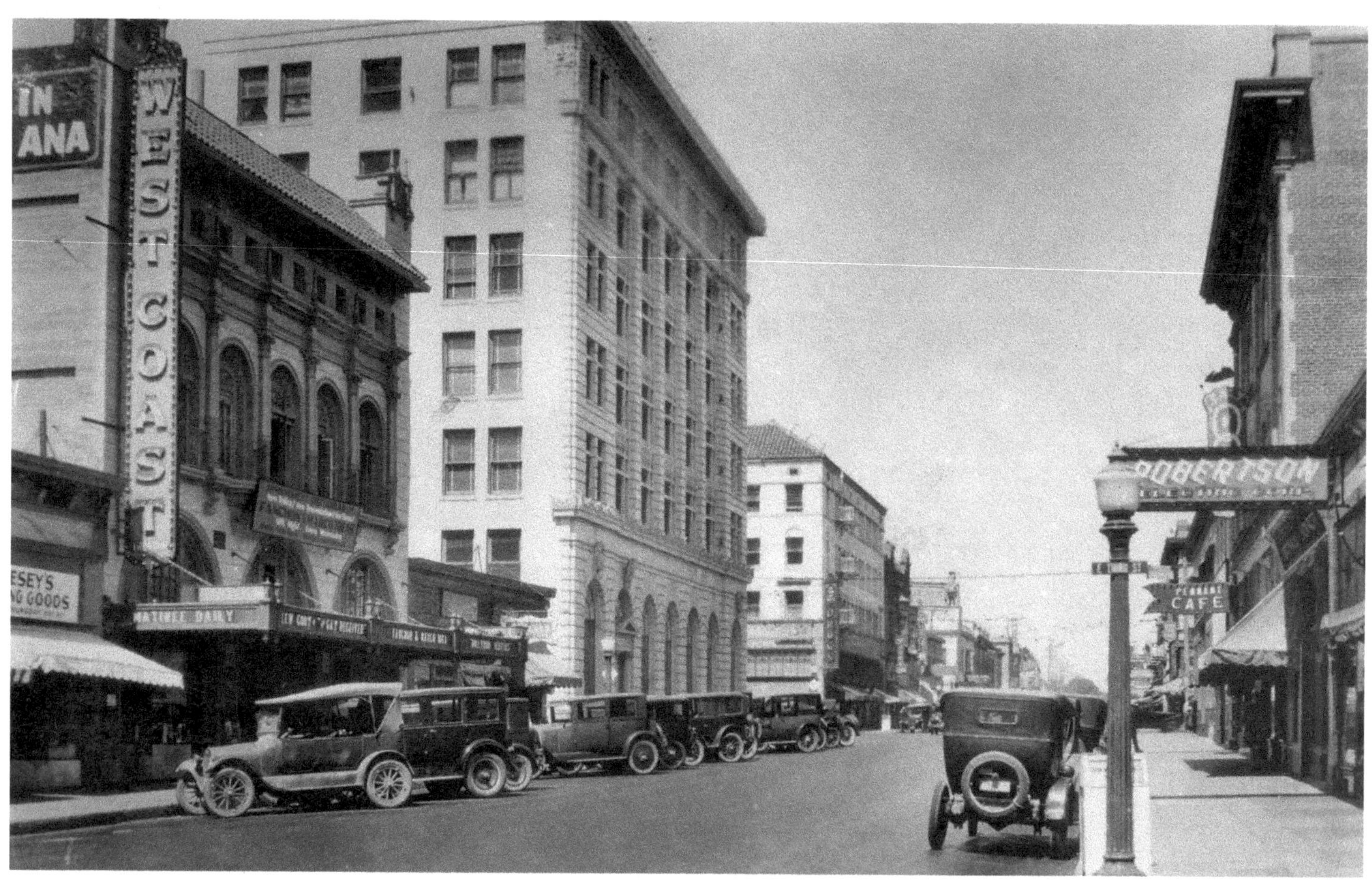

The Boller Brothers–designed Fox West Coast Theater opened on Main Street in Santa Ana in 1924 and showcased vaudeville acts direct from the Orpheum in Los Angeles and silent films such as Will Rogers's *Two Wagons, Both Covered,* which was one of the opening attractions. The theater seated over 1,300 people and featured state-of-the-art cooling and lighting systems, opulent Art Moderne scrollwork, Arts and Crafts stained glass, and a Wurlitzer organ.

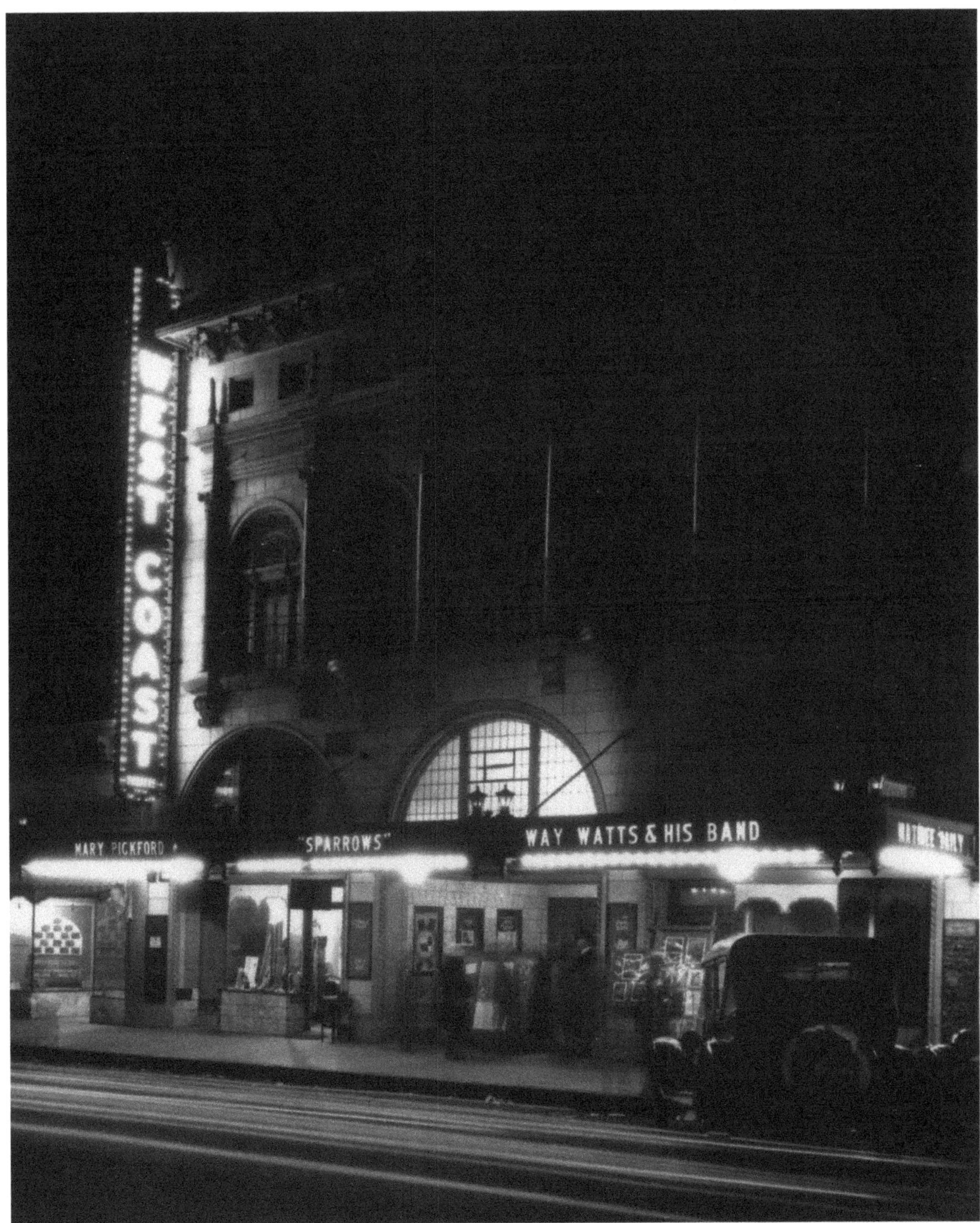

Mary Pickford's silent movie *Sparrows* was the featured attraction in this 1926 night shot of the West Coast Theater. The theater was placed on the National Register of Historic Places in 1982 but quickly fell into disrepair and was closed shortly thereafter. In 1991 the building was restored and converted to a Hispanic church, Tabernaculo Cristiano.

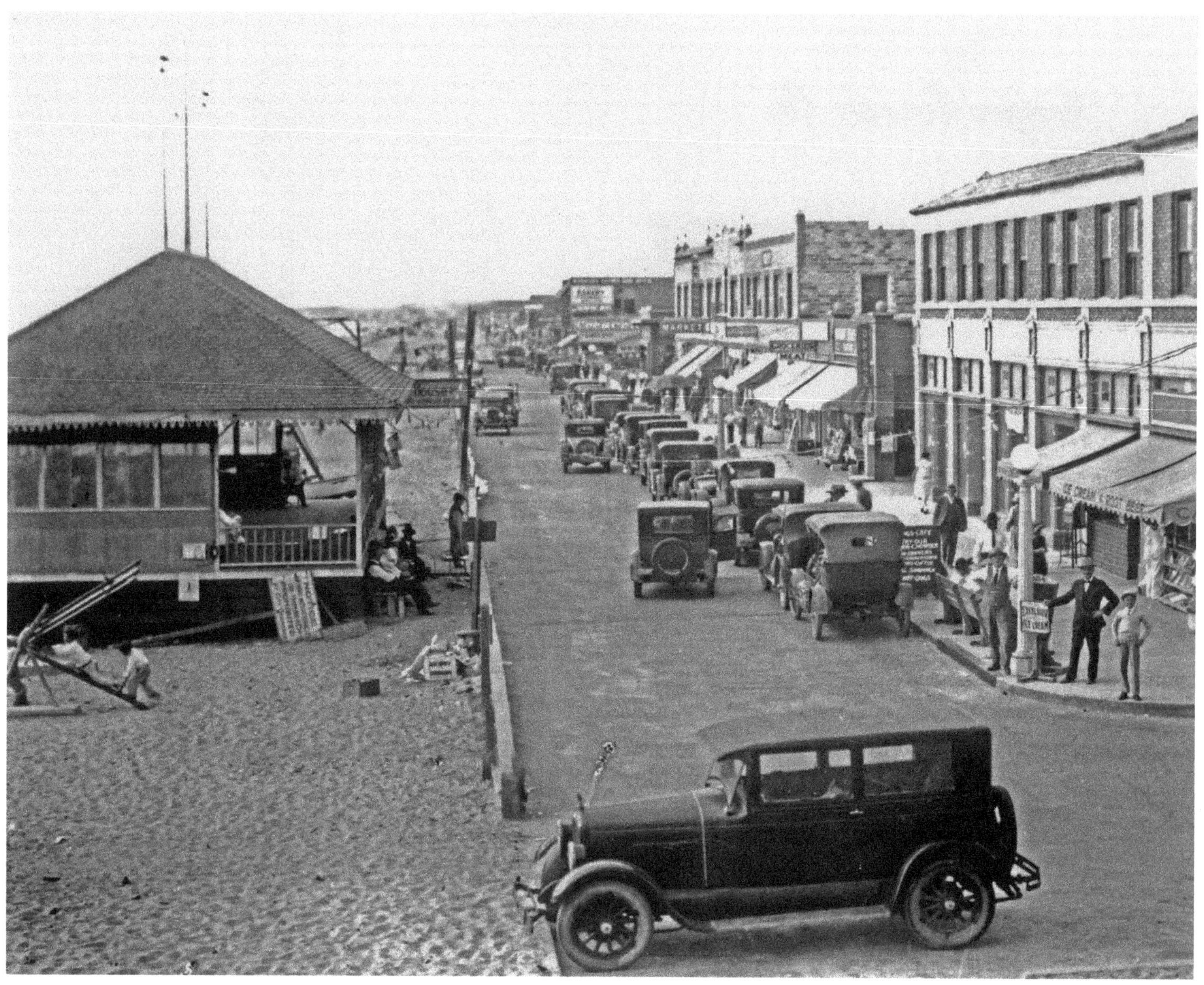

In this photo of Newport Beach, children play on the seesaws, old men sit in the shade of a building, businessmen buy the daily paper from the corner newsstand, and housewives shop for dinner—much like in any American small town. There is little in this scene to suggest the shopping, boating, and entertainment capital that Newport would grow to be in a few short decades.

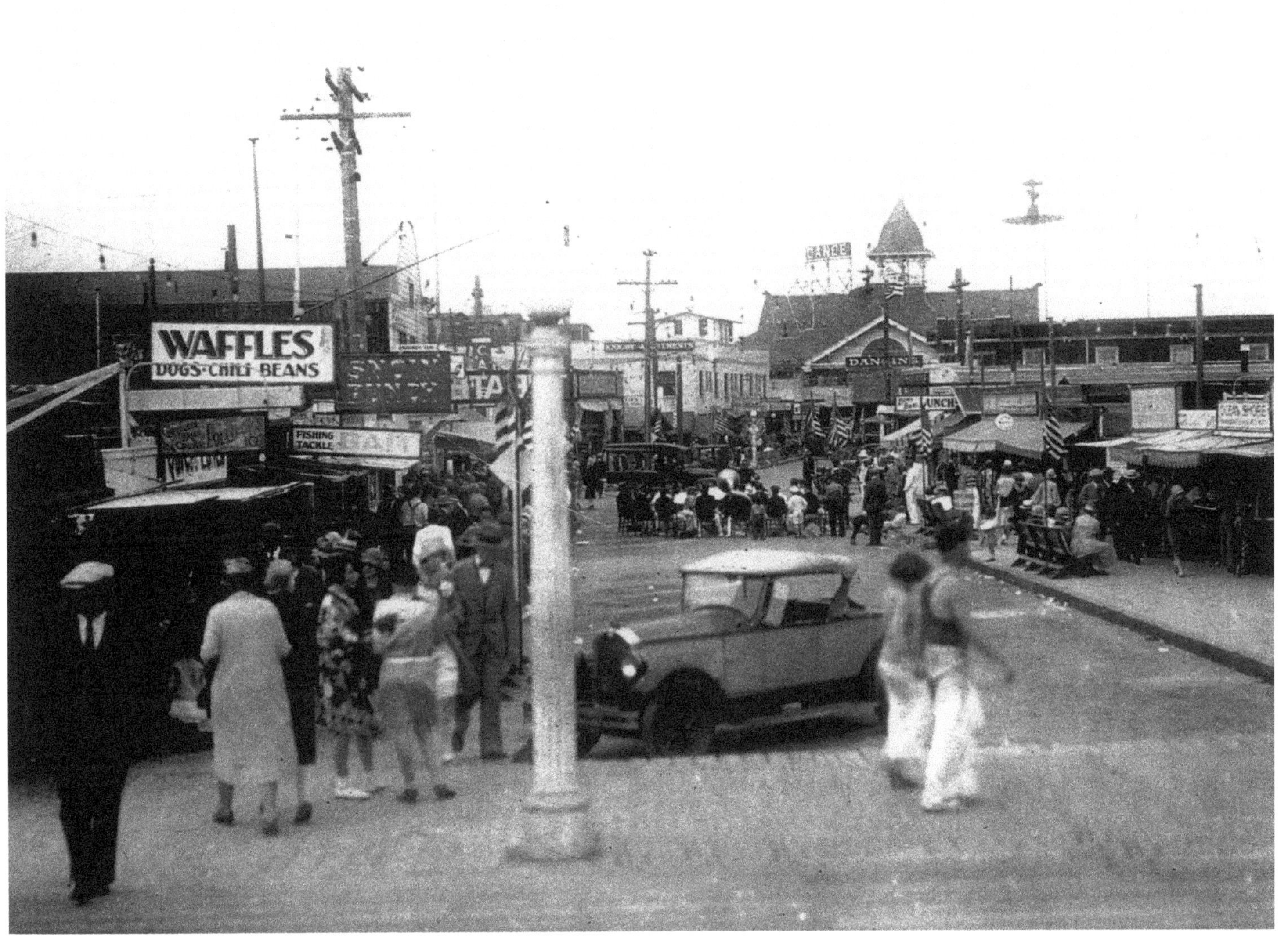

This busy 1920s street scene of Balboa shows the famed Pavilion in the background. The Pavilion's second-floor ballroom was especially popular during the Roaring Twenties and into the thirties. Friday nights featured an eight-piece Dixieland band and appearances by big-name artists like Count Basie and Benny Goodman. The "Balboa Hop," a popular wartime dance, was said to have started there.

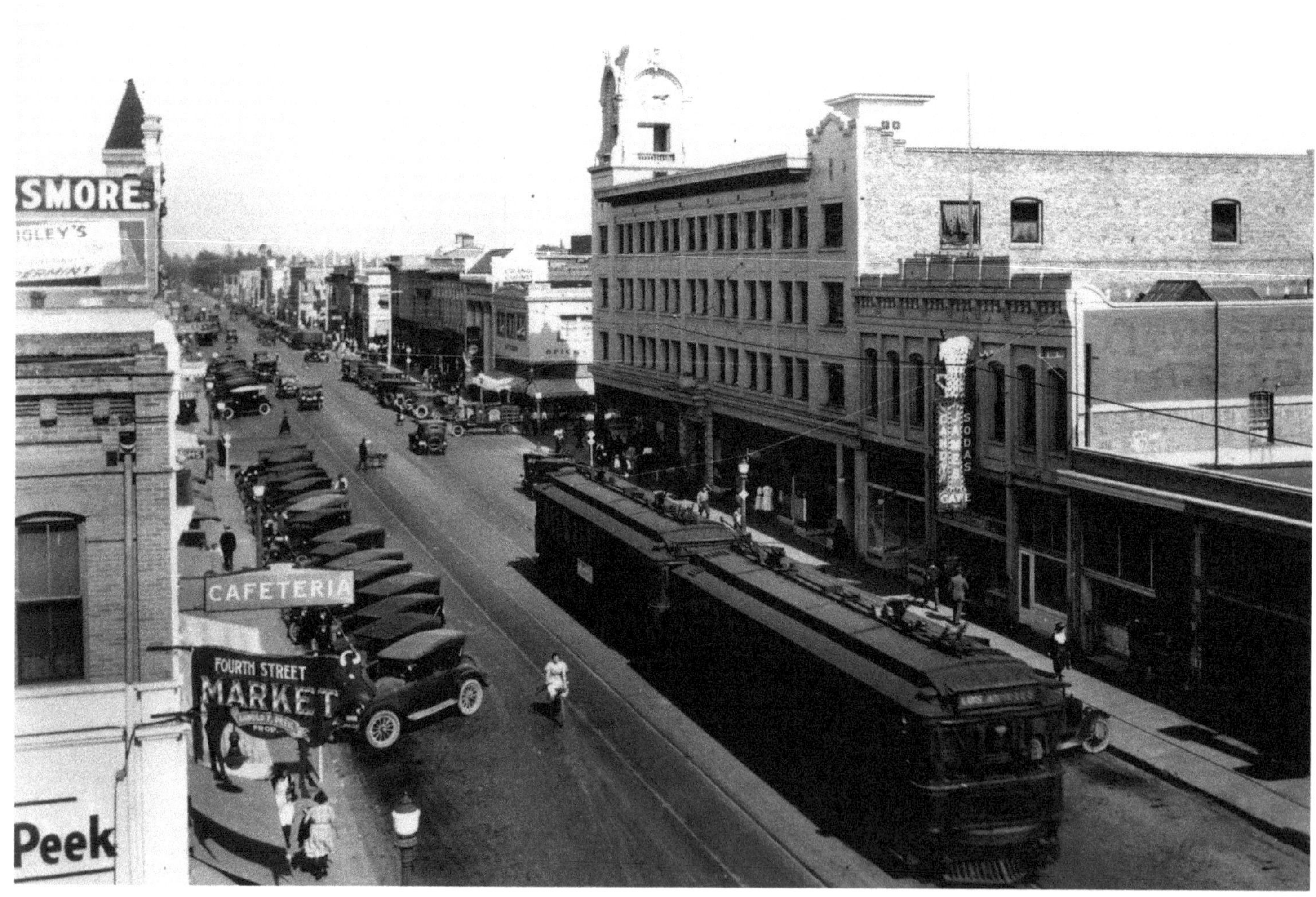

In this late-1920s photograph, the Pacific Electric Red Car passes between the Spurgeon Building, at center, and the Rossmore Hotel, at left, on Fourth Street in Santa Ana, while traveling along its route between Santa Ana and Los Angeles. The Pacific Electric line eventually linked over 150 Southern California communities and was the primary means of intercounty transportation for four and a half decades.

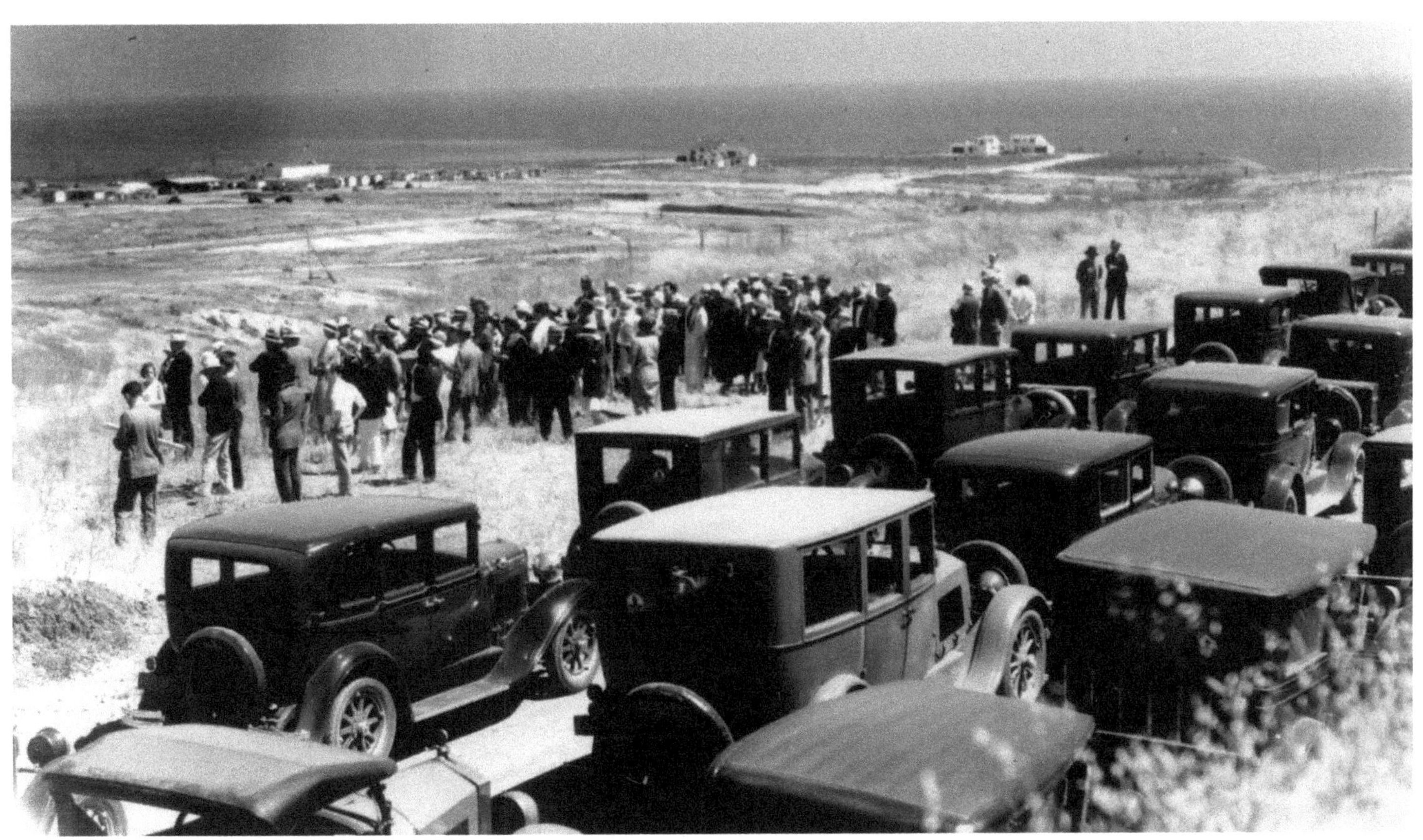

Dana Point was named for Richard Henry Dana, whose 1840 travelogue referred to the rugged coastline as "the only romantic spot in California." Several unsuccessful attempts were made in the 1920s to promote Dana Point, including the 1927 grand opening of a subdivision planned by Hollywoodland builder Sidney Woodruff. It wasn't until the late 1950s, when the San Diego Freeway was extended through southern Orange County, that Dana Point was finally opened to new residents.

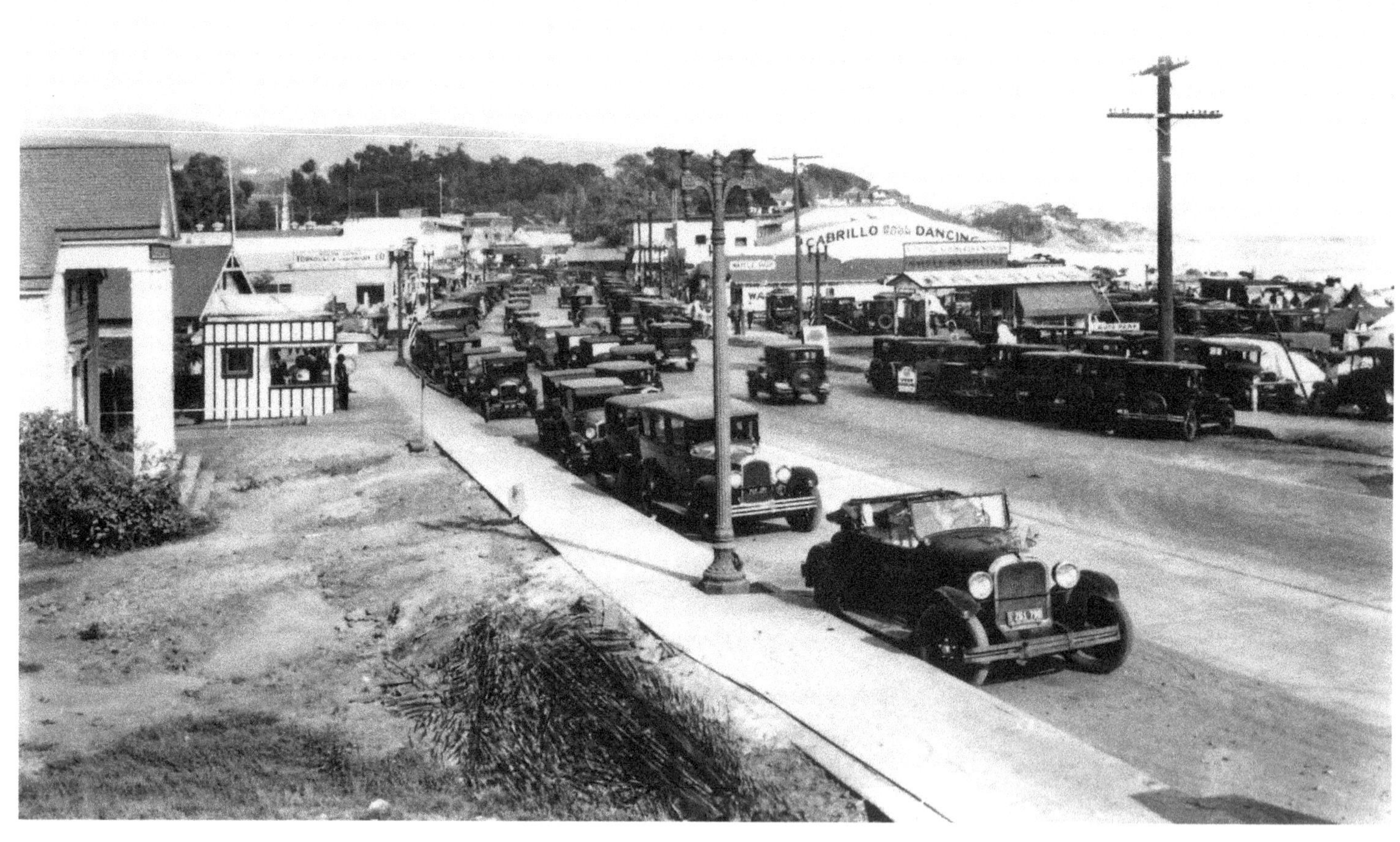

Many Laguna Beach locals opposed the construction of the Cabrillo Ballroom, shown here at center in 1927, fearing it would lead to hot dog vendors and cheap-souvenir stands, essentially turning the rustic artist colony into a second-rate Coney Island. The townsfolk needn't have worried: the pristine sands where the dance hall once stood have been restored, and dining and shopping opportunities today are definitely not of the cheap variety!

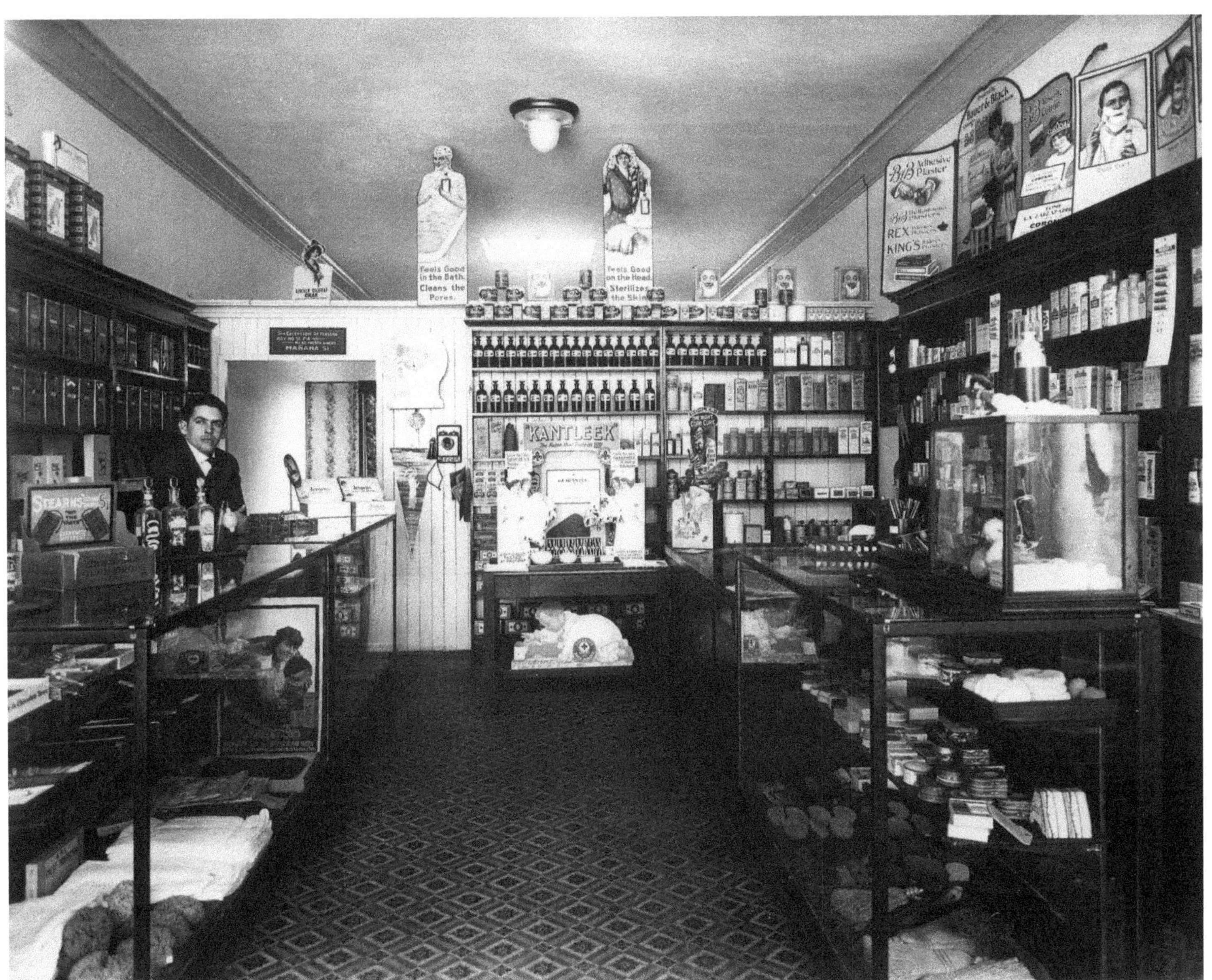

In Orange County as elsewhere, the period between the world wars was the golden age of hucksterism. In this 1929 image, a shop clerk in Santa Ana sits surrounded by dubious potions and lotions promising to cure corns, clean pores, and sterilize skin. Ironically, many of the early twentieth century buildings that housed these purveyors of empty promises still stand, but their occupants are now twenty-first century lawyers, ready and willing to sue over false advertising.

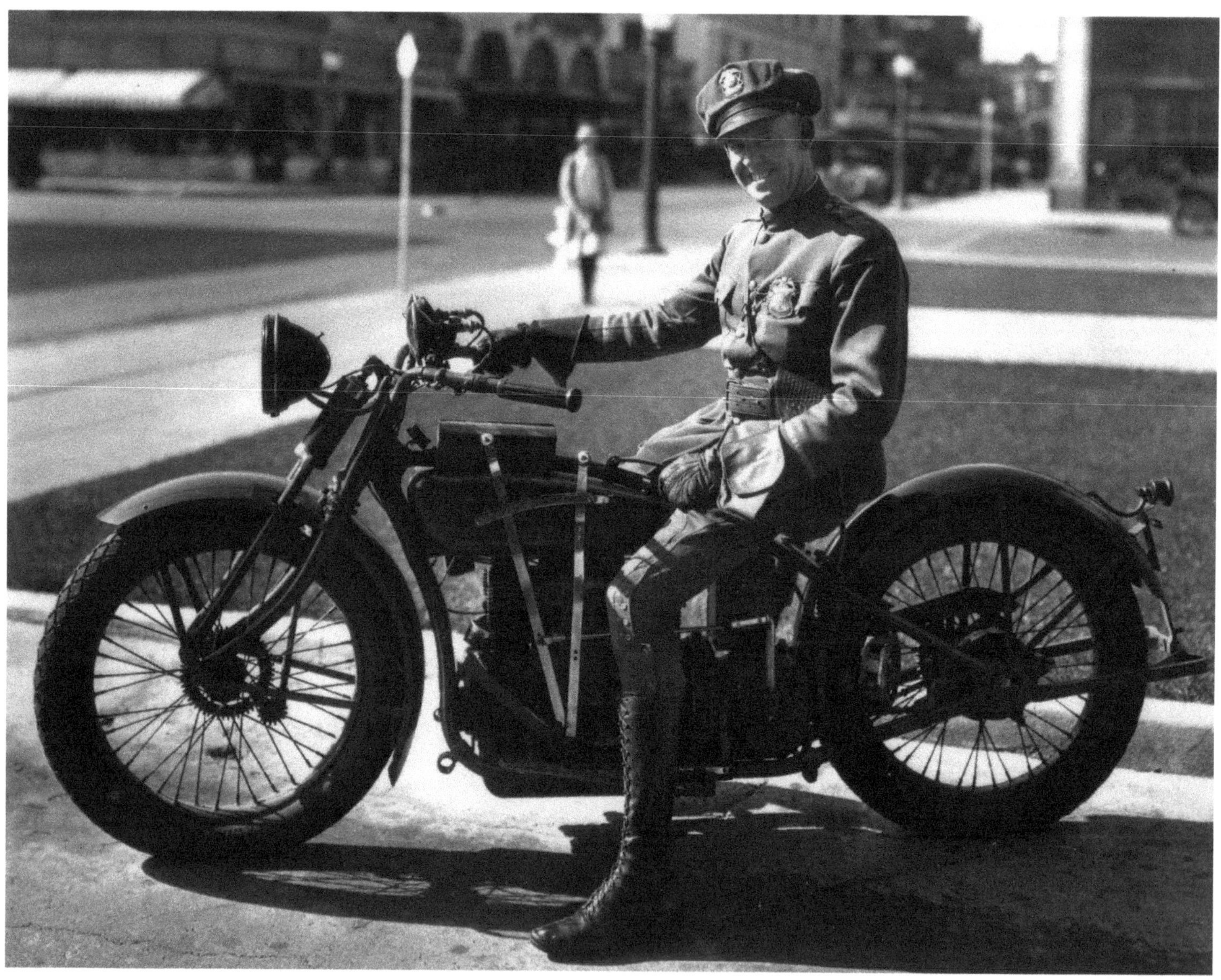

When Santa Ana's police department formed in the 1880s, horseback patrols enforced laws against leaving park gates open and keeping pigeons within city limits. By the 1930s, when this photo was taken, the mode of transportation had changed, and the issues confronting residents had grown in scope. Between the Depression, the 1933 earthquake, the end of Prohibition, and the 1938 flood, Santa Ana's finest had their hands full maintaining law and order.

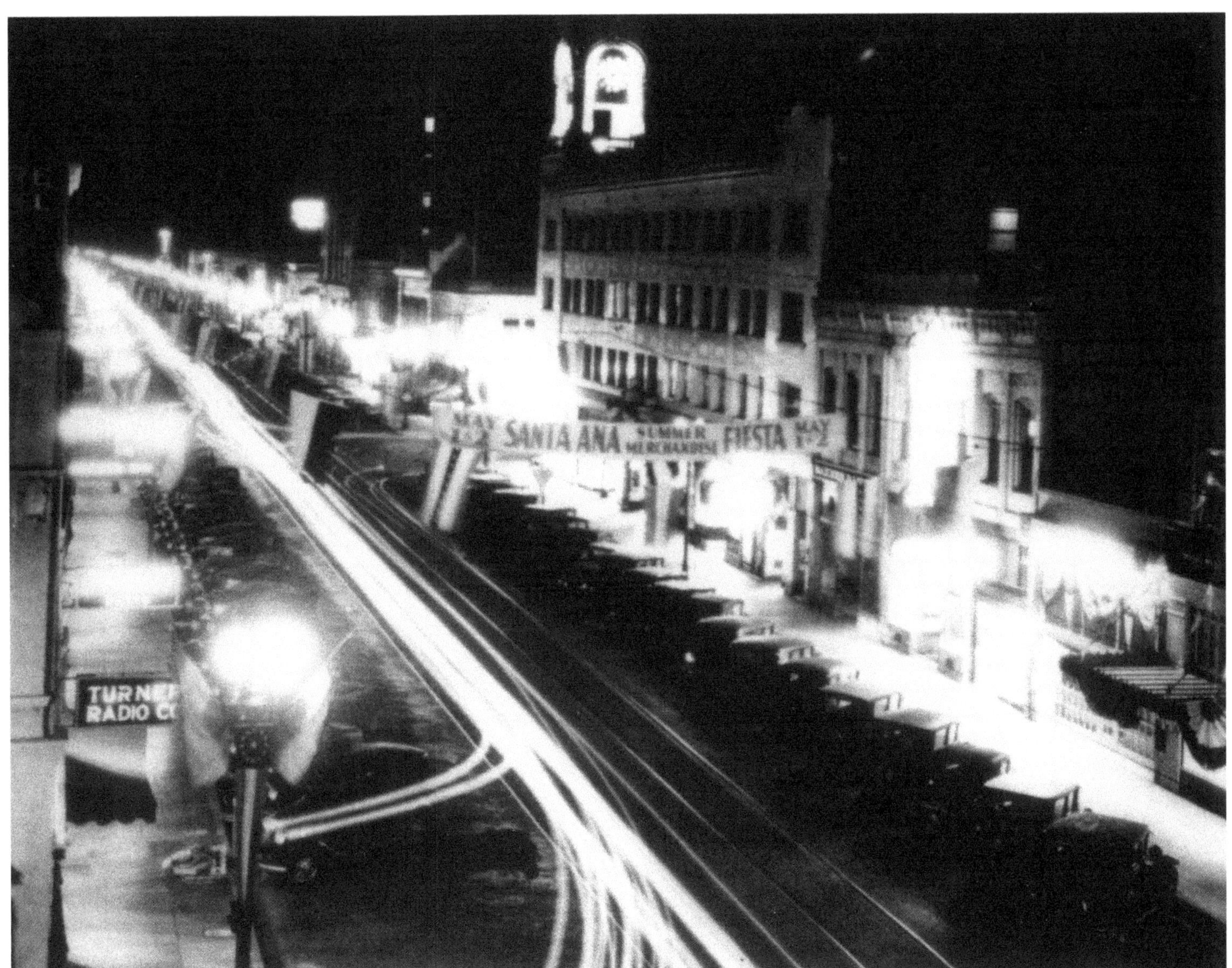

This night shot of Fourth Street in Santa Ana viewed toward the lit-up Spurgeon clock was taken in the 1930s. Light poles are draped with banners, and every parking space is filled, in preparation for the "Santa Ana Summer Merchandise Fiesta." Cognizant of the city's Mexican and Spanish roots, Santa Ana retailers strove to appeal to the rapidly growing Latin demographic. The city's population is currently 80 percent Hispanic.

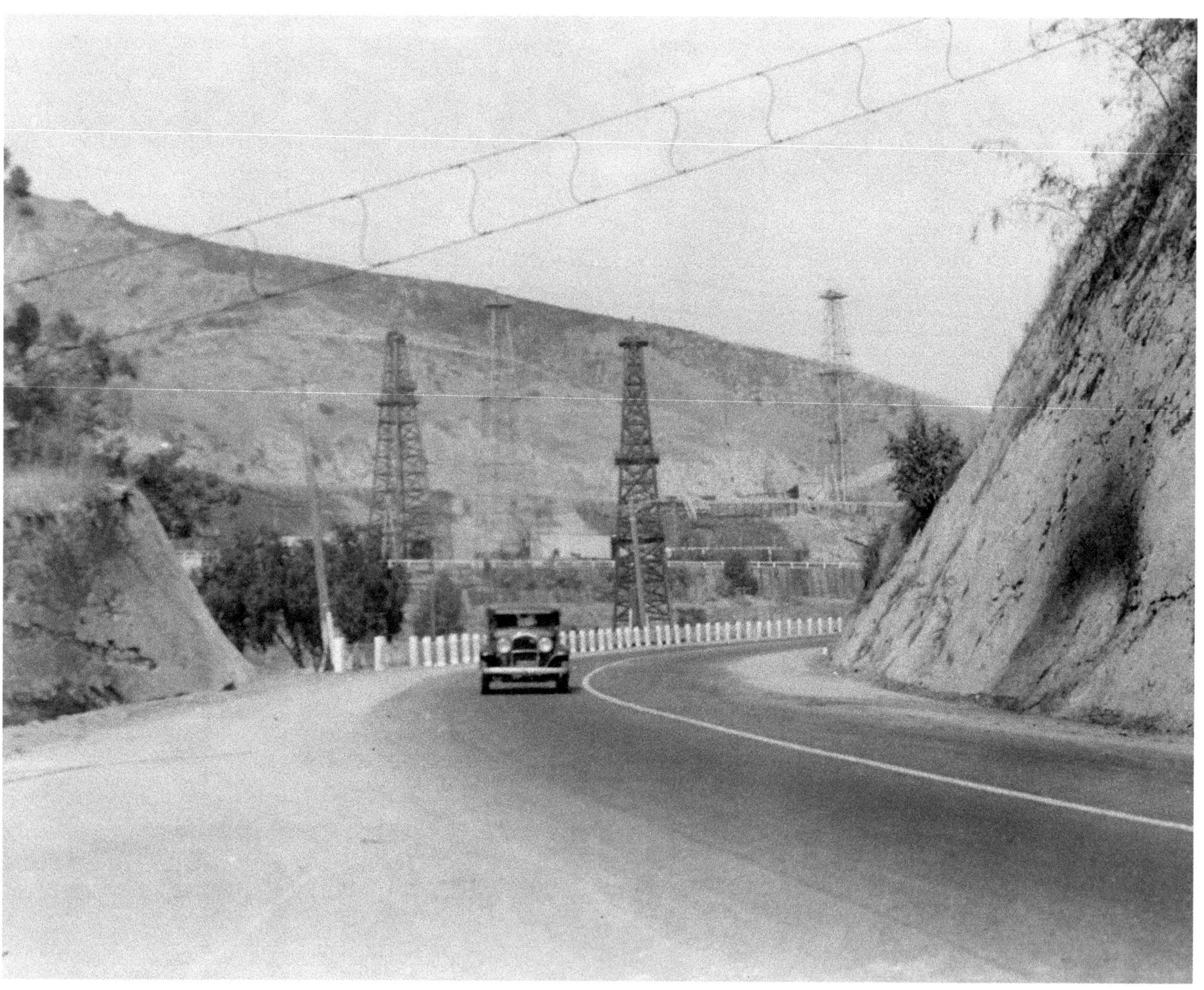

The barren hills and scattered oil rigs in this 1930 photograph of Brea Canyon give little indication that *Sunset* magazine would one day name Brea one of the top five places to live in the western United States. Today, the city unprepossessingly named after tar has become known for the upscale Brea Mall, a modern shopping and dining destination featuring fountains, vaulted skylights, and Italian-tiled floors that is California's second-most-visited mall.

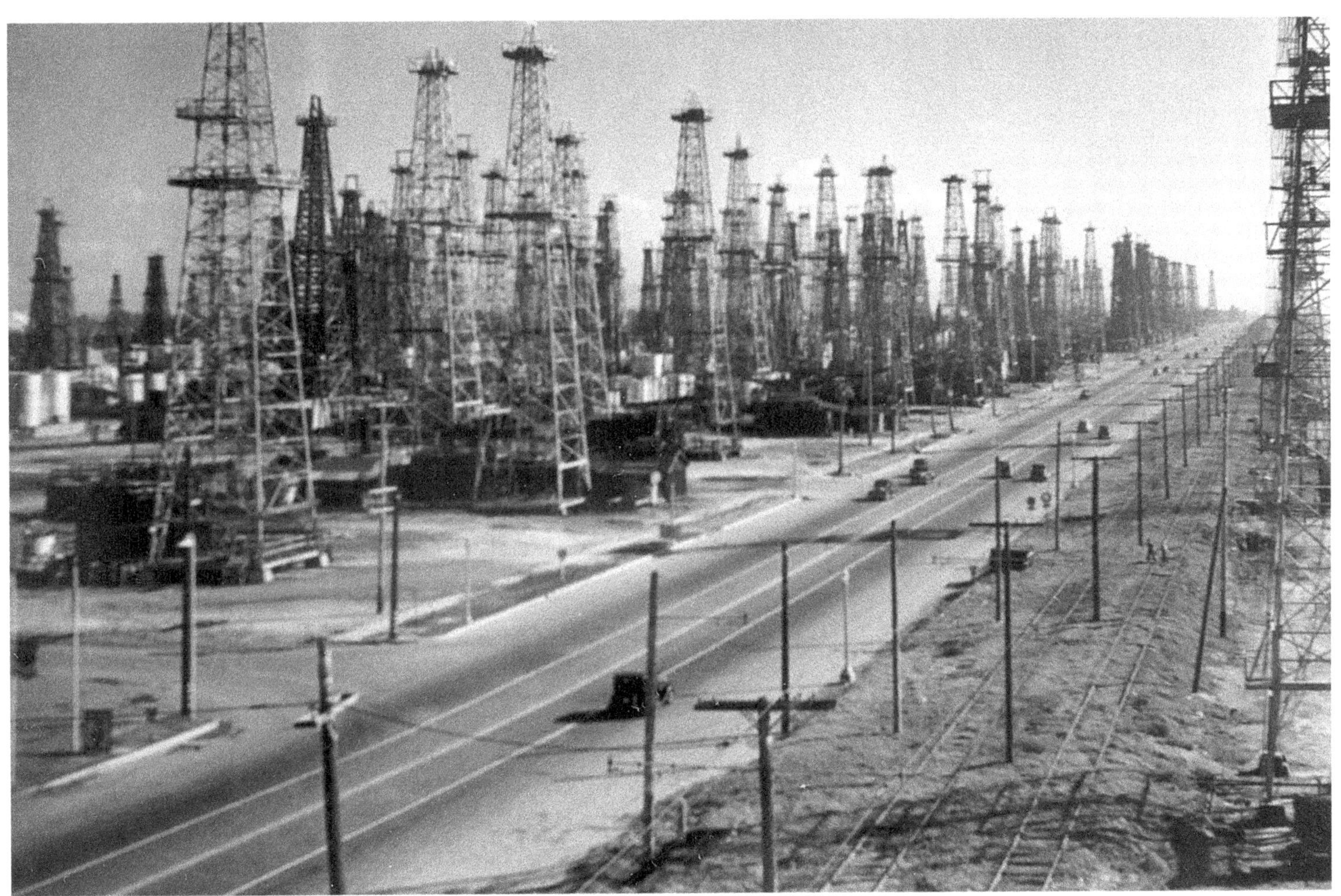

The skyline of Huntington Beach changed forever in 1920 when oil was struck. Seemingly overnight, palm trees were replaced with a forest of 120-foot-tall wood-frame derricks, marching in lockstep down the Pacific Coast Highway, as shown here in 1930. Within a year of the discovery, the city's population had quadrupled from 2,000 to 8,000, and a severe housing shortage developed. Neighboring communities scrambled to fill the void.

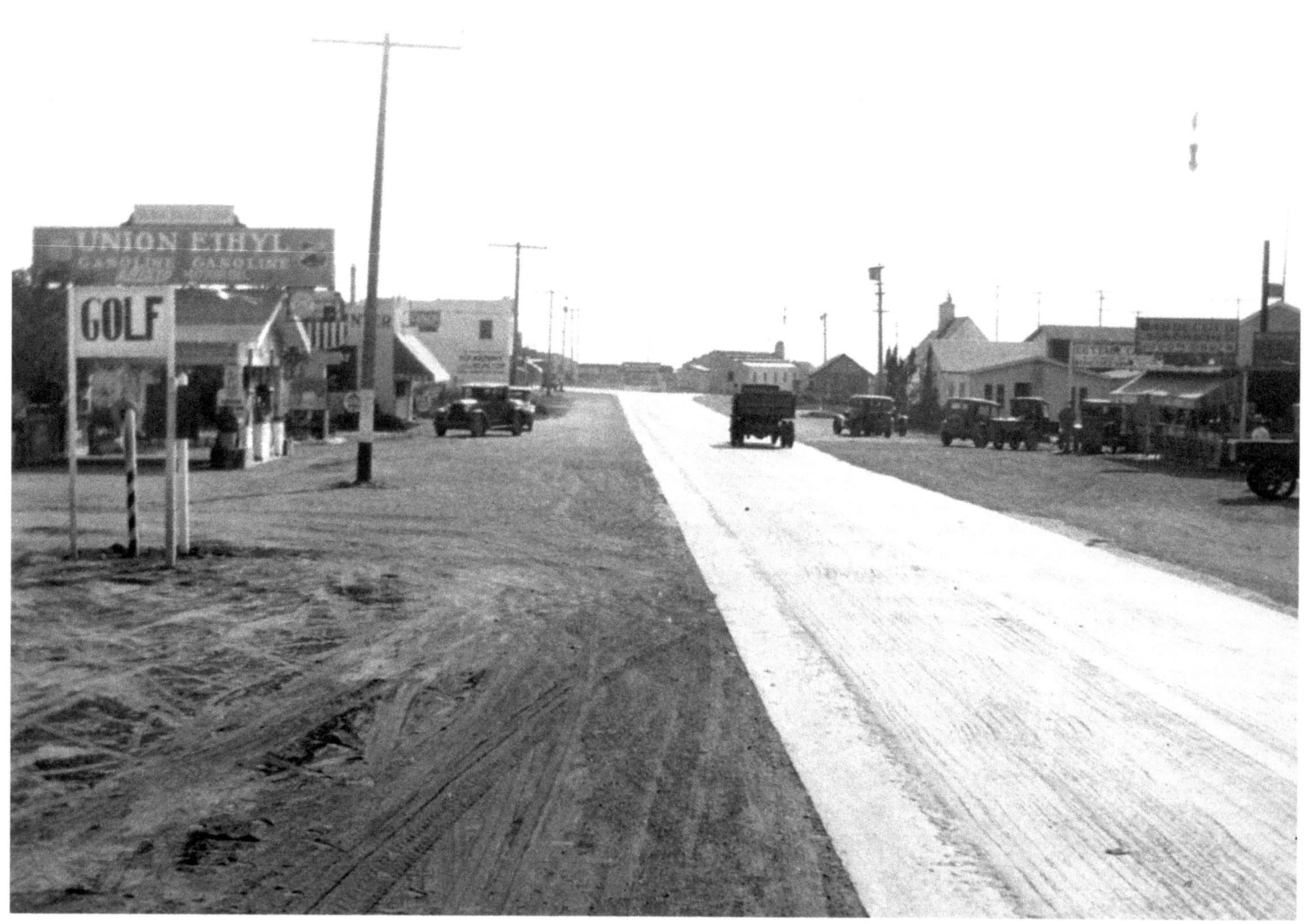

For better or worse, the 1956 Interstate Highway Act would transform Orange County. The sleepy hamlet of Capistrano Beach, shown here in 1930, was but one of many isolated towns along the coast before completion of the 5 Freeway, which would run the length of the state. In 1989 Capistrano Beach and neighboring Laguna Niguel voted to join newly incorporated Dana Point and today have a healthy combined population of 35,000.

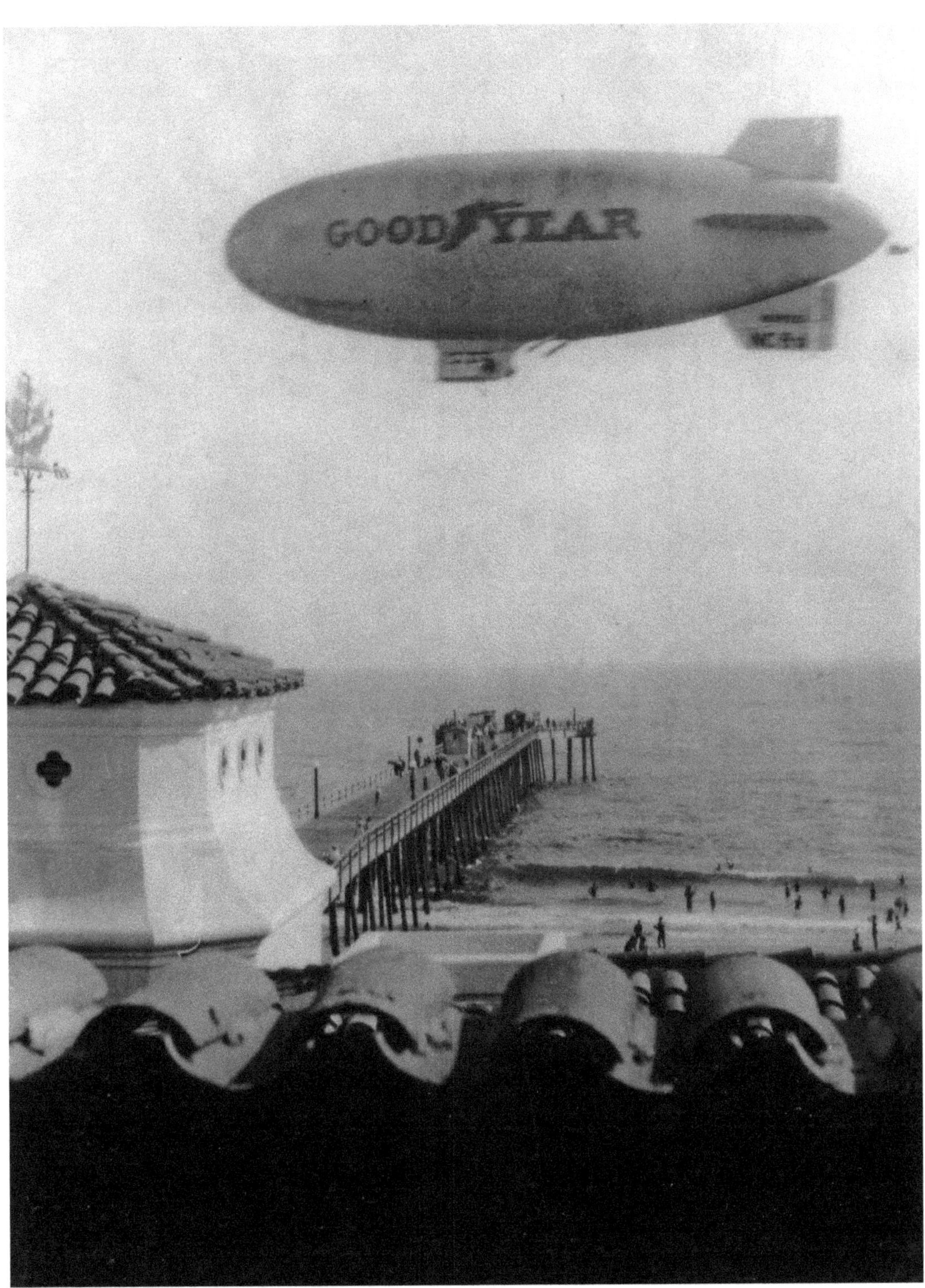

This photograph of the Goodyear blimp passing over Balboa Pier was taken on August 21, 1930, from the roof of El Portal Hotel. In the 1930s blimps were outfitted with lighted signs for advertising. During World War II they patrolled the coast. More recently, the now-empty blimp hangars outside Tustin have served as the site of an *X Files* convention and as a location for the 2001 movie *Pearl Harbor.*

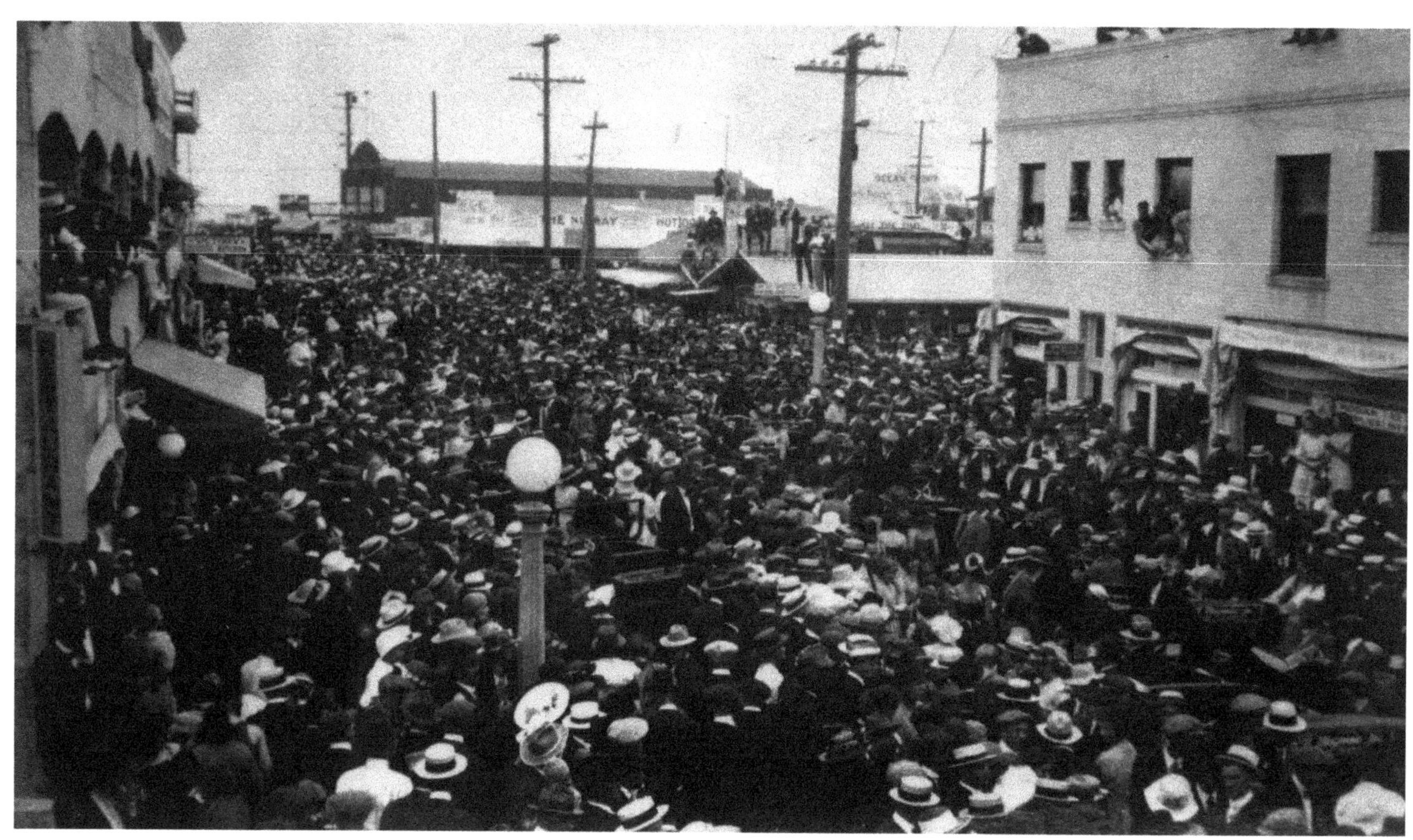

Modern rush-hour traffic on the 5 Freeway pales in comparison to this scene of an unidentified 1930s-era event in Newport Beach. People hang from windows and stand on rooftops to get a better view of the proceedings below, and others are trapped in their cars by the impenetrable mass of humanity clogging the streets. The photo was likely taken from the Balboa Pavilion.

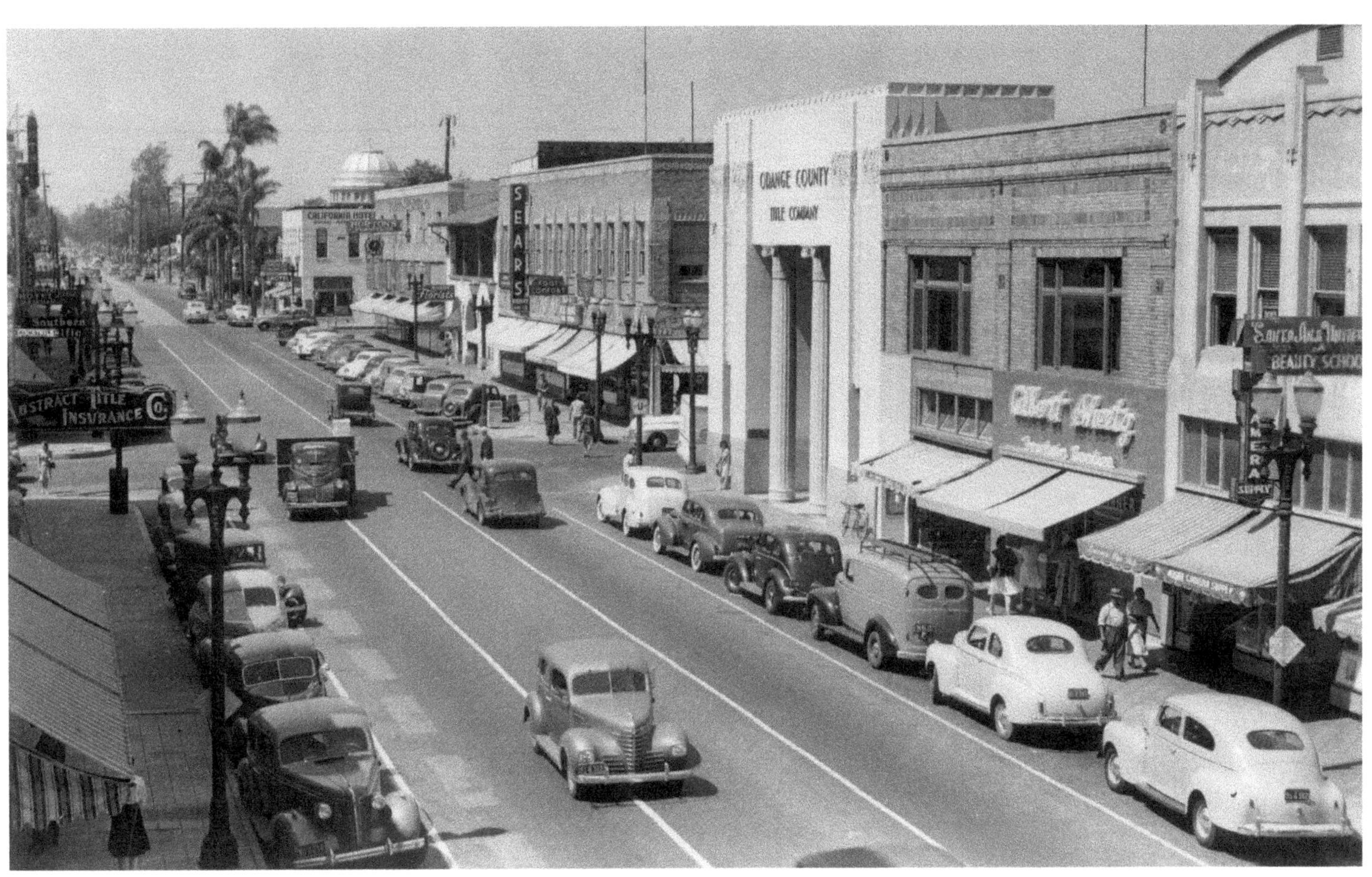

In 1931, Santa Ana's Orange County Title Company moved into its new, gleaming white, Zigzag Moderne headquarters, shown at right in this photo, directly across from the company's chief competitor, the Orange County Abstract Title and Insurance Company. The two later merged to form First American Title Insurance Company, possessors of an extensive photographic archive from which many of the images in this book were taken.

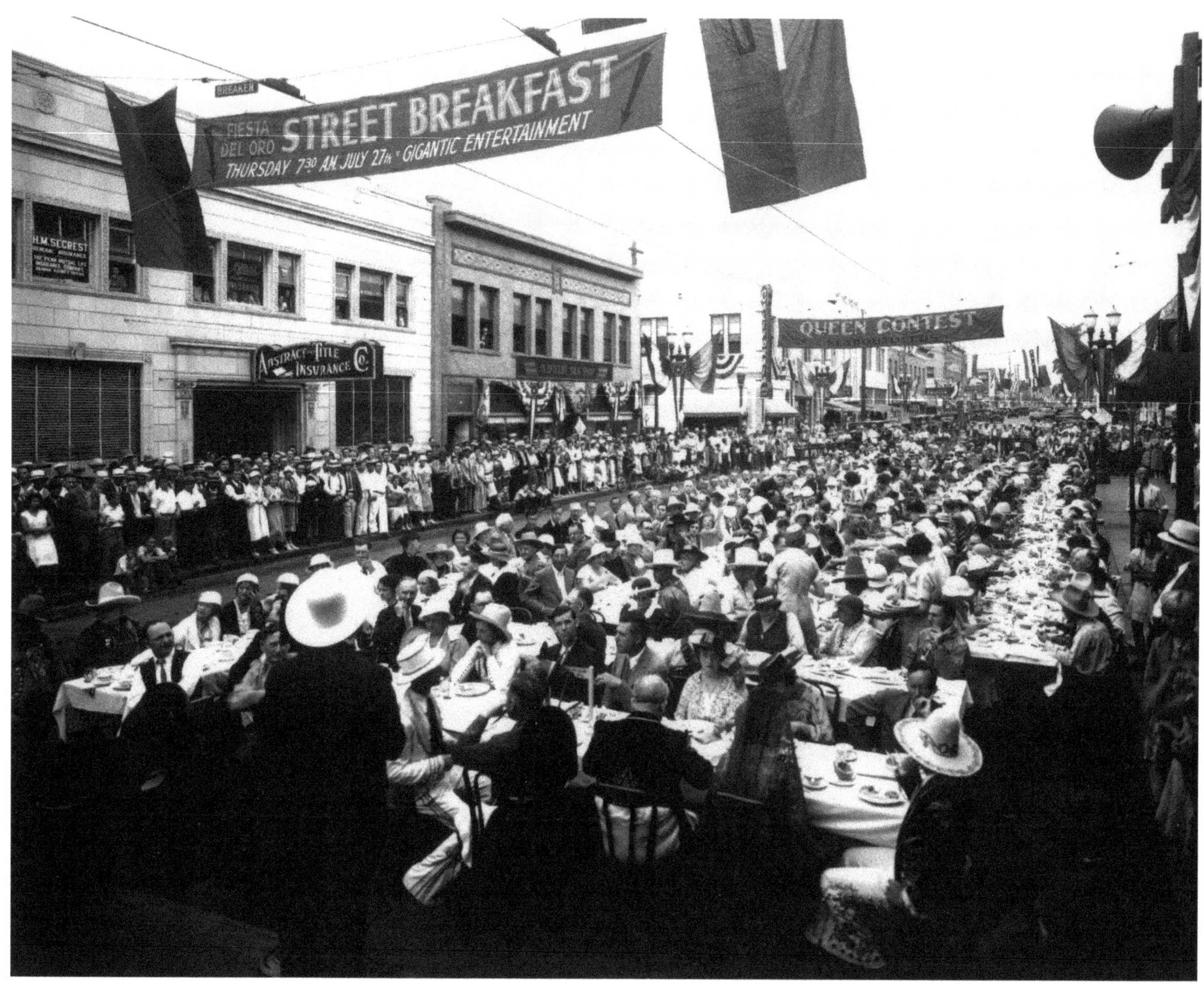

The Santa Ana Breakfast Club, founded in 1925, was an informal civic group that became known for its al fresco breakfasts. From these humble beginnings arose the three-day Fiesta del Oro of 1933, which kicked off with this standing-room-only street breakfast at 7:30 A.M. on a closed-off block of North Main Street, between Fourth and Fifth streets. Honorees at the event included Fiesta Queen Margaret Sawyer and James B. Utt, future congressman.

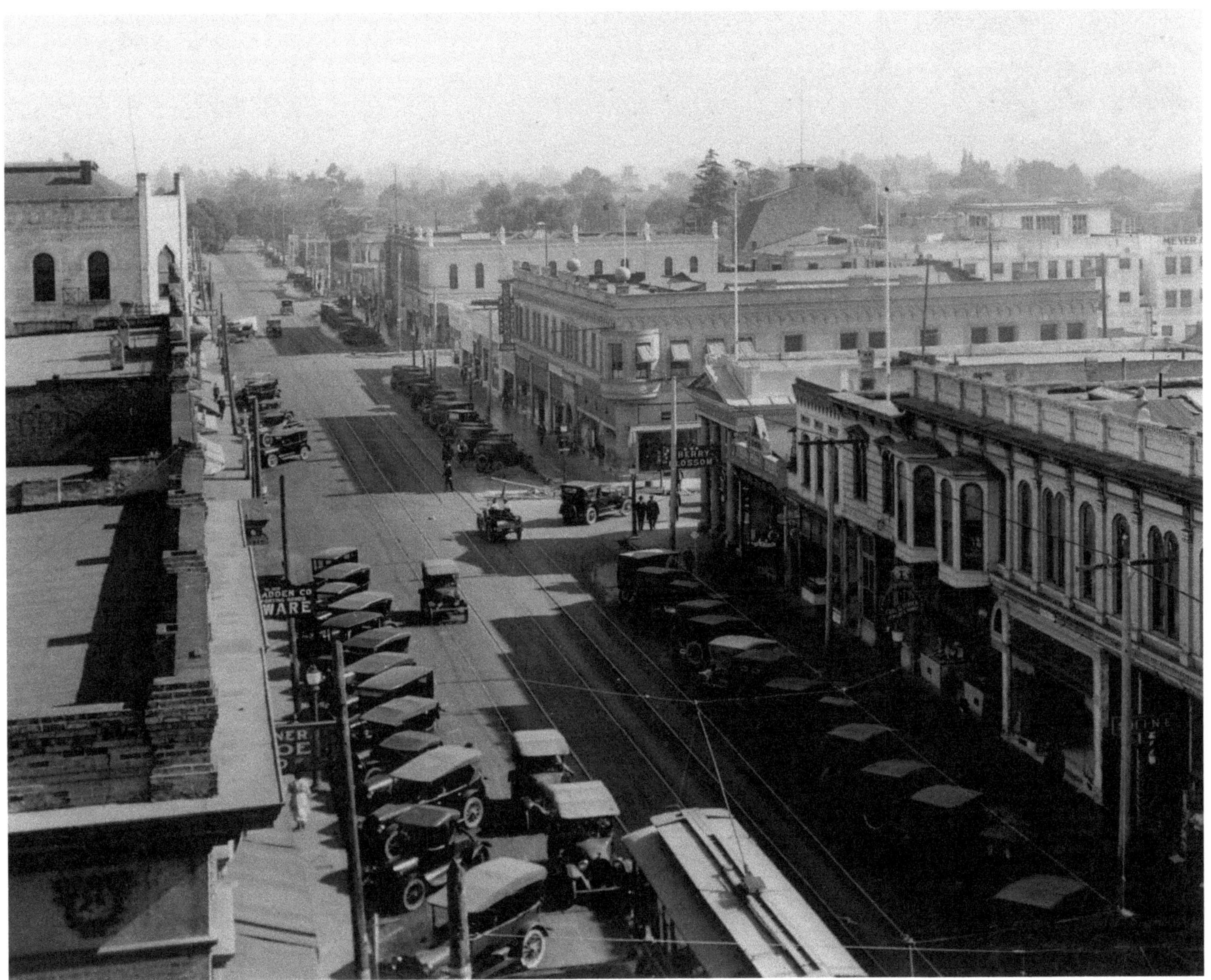

This photo of Fourth Street in Santa Ana was taken in 1932, three years into the Great Depression. Though building activity greatly declined and the population leveled off during this period, Santa Ana appears to be holding its own, with automobiles filling the shopping district. In another year, the beautiful brick facades of many of the buildings at right would topple down in the Long Beach earthquake, crushing dozens of similarly parked cars.

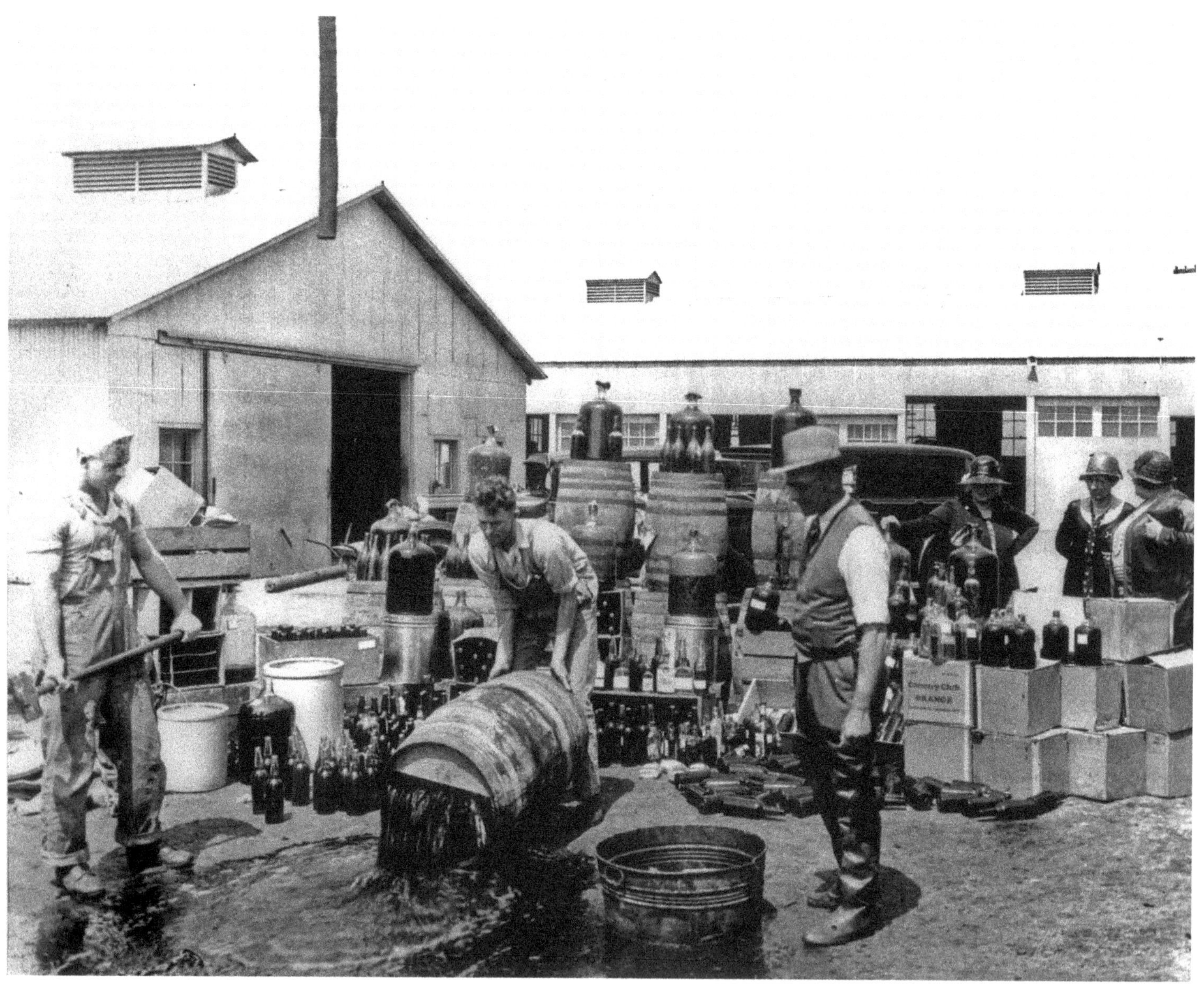

The Women's Christian Temperance Union, founded in Fredonia, New York, in 1873, was instrumental in the passage of the Eighteenth Amendment, ushering in the era of Prohibition. The local Santa Ana chapter of the WCTU was very active and succeeded in making Santa Ana a dry town 17 years prior to the national legislation. The three ladies at right in this 1933 photo of liquor being dumped were likely members of the organization.

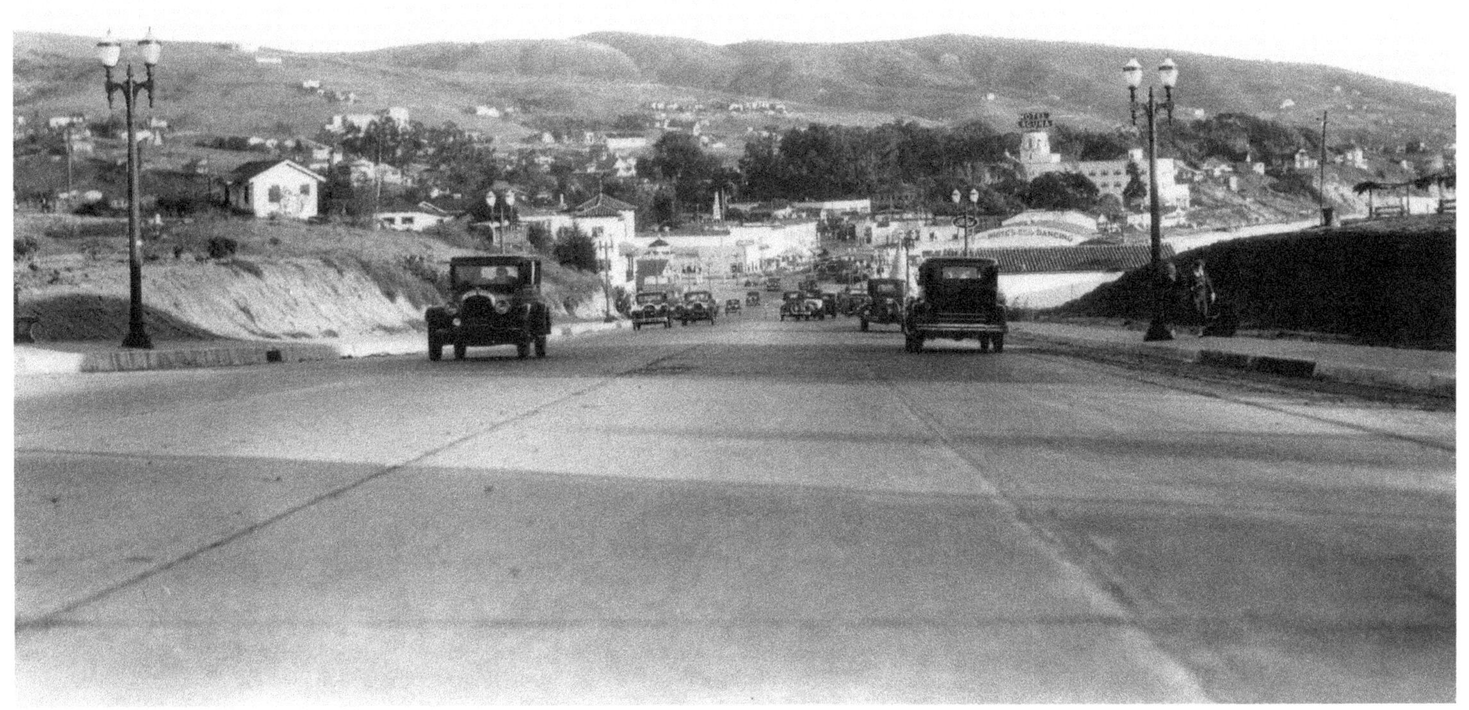

This shot looking south on the Pacific Coast Highway shows Laguna Beach at the height of the Depression. It was during this time that local artists inaugurated the Festival of Arts as a means of generating income. The Festival has since grown to encompass three major art shows and the Pageant of the Masters, the tableaux-vivant production that shows nightly every summer in the Irvine Bowl, a natural amphitheater in the Laguna hills.

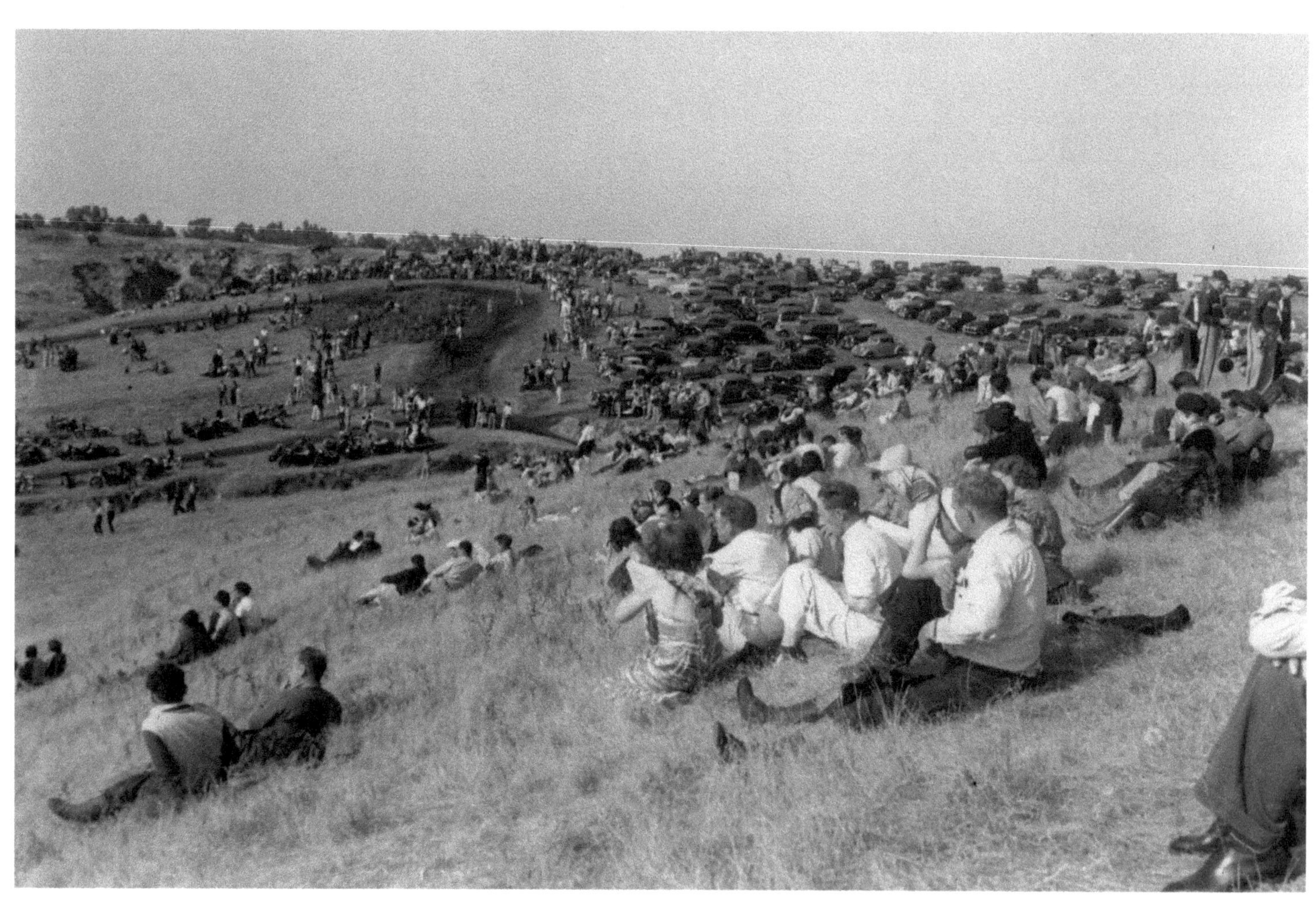

Motorcycle racing was an inexpensive entertainment during the Depression years, and races held in the hills surrounding what would become Costa Mesa drew large crowds, as this 1930s photograph shows. These unofficial gatherings were a precursor to the current Costa Mesa Speedway races, held every Saturday night from April through September since 1969 at the Orange County Fairgrounds.

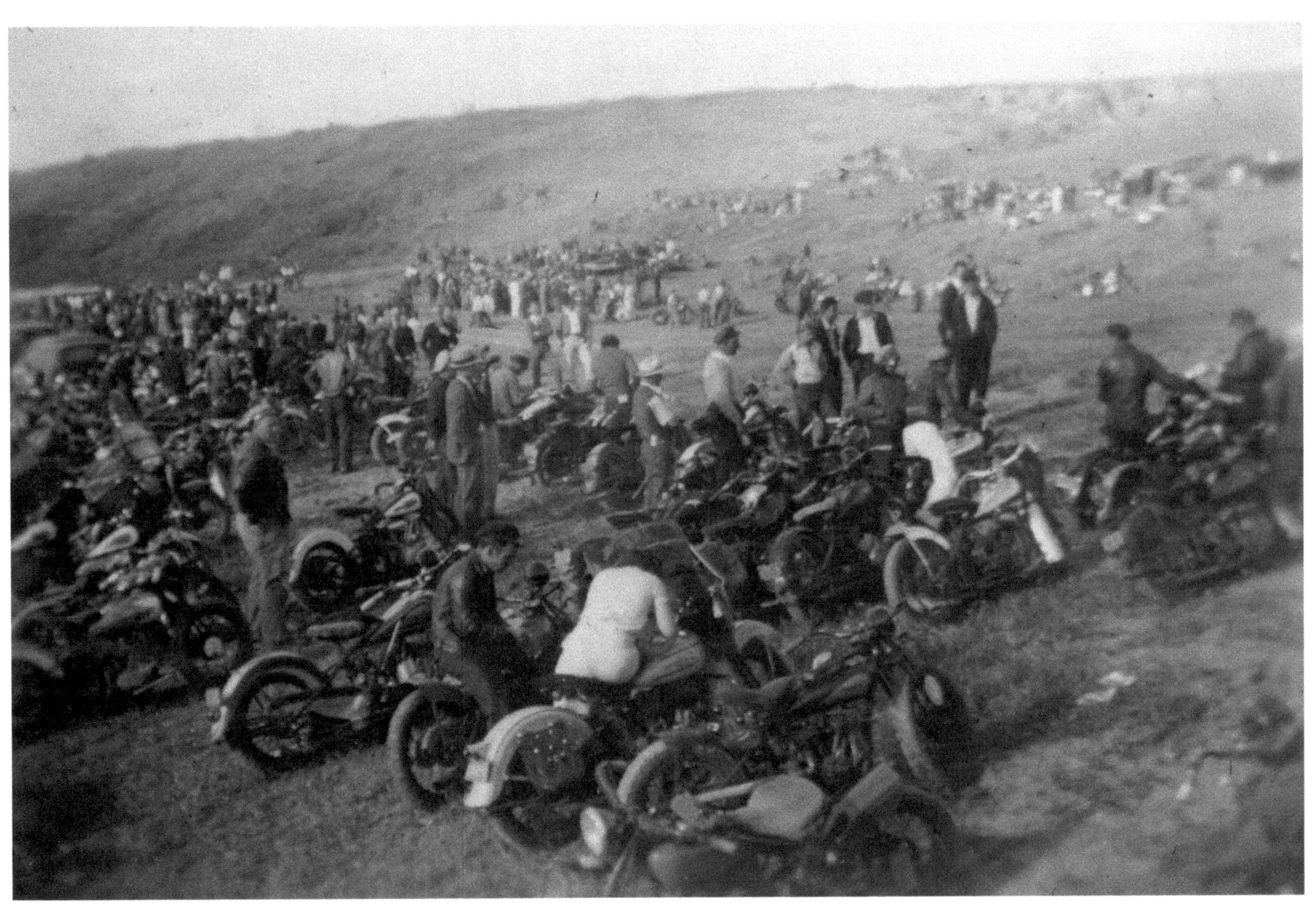

Following their use in World War I, motorcycle sales boomed in the United States, especially in Southern California where temperate weather made year-round riding possible. Motorcycles were marketed as a cheap alternative to the automobile. By the end of the 1930s, when this photo was taken, the American Motorcycle Association was sanctioning almost a thousand dirt-track races a year, almost all of them for amateurs.

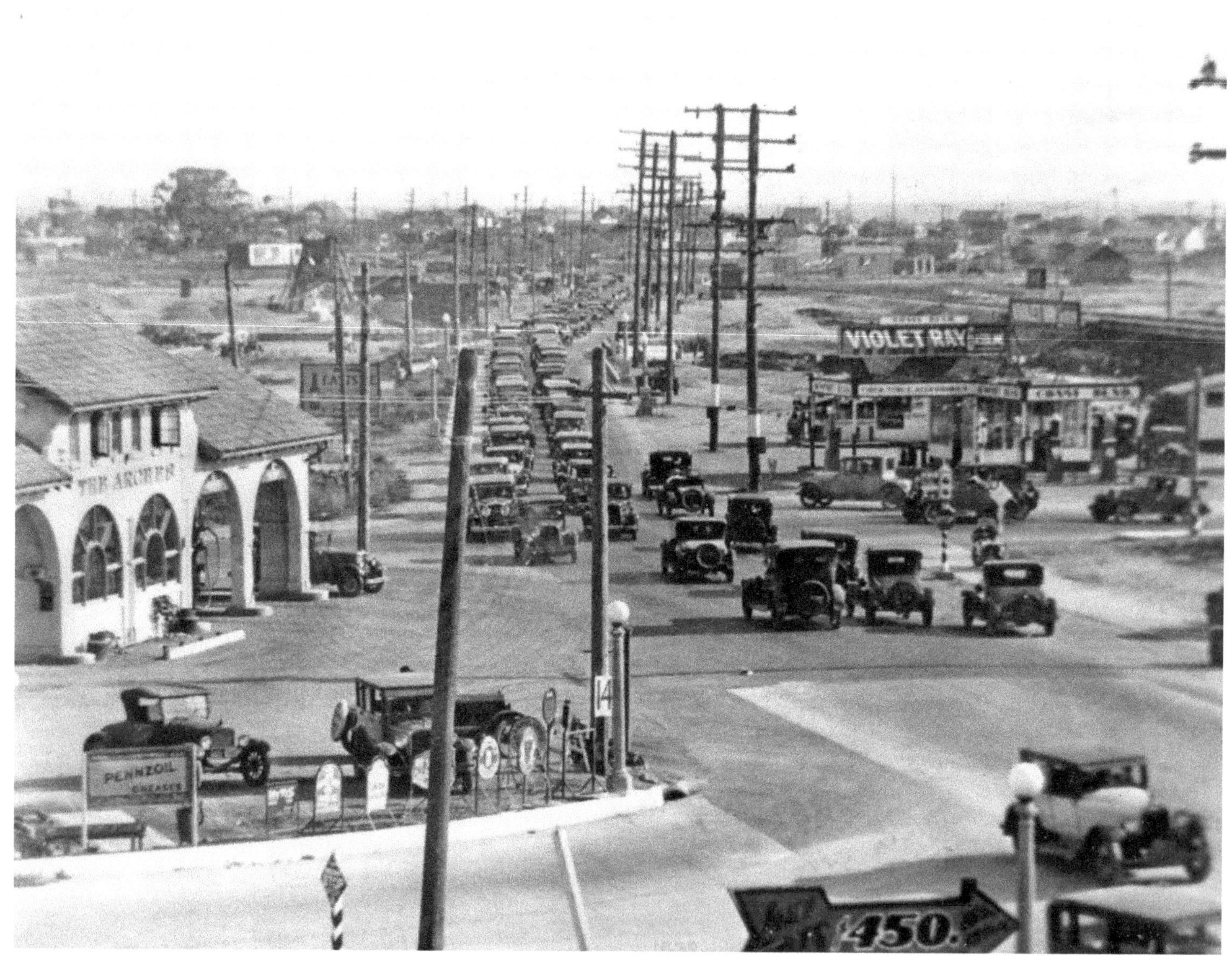

The Arches, at left in this 1930s photo, was a service station–restaurant combo that featured Spanish-Mediterranean styling complete with arches—hence the name—and that catered to traffic on the newly completed portion of the Pacific Coast Highway that ran between Newport Beach and Laguna. The restaurant eventually developed a celebrity clientele that included Humphrey Bogart, John Wayne, and the Rat Pack.

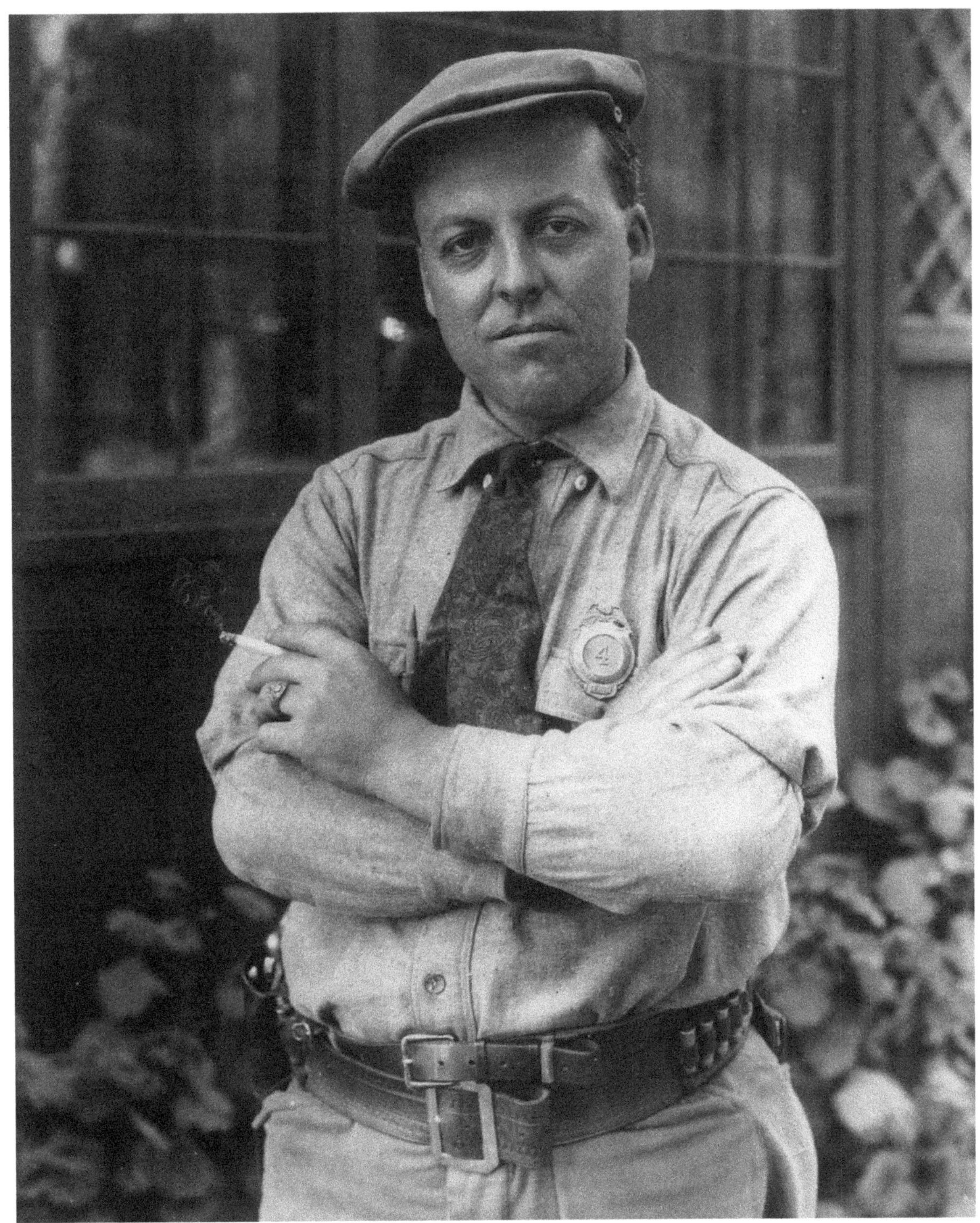

During Prohibition, Laguna Beach police officers, such as this one, had their hands full when the long, rugged coastline became a hotbed of bootlegging activity. Suppliers would anchor three miles off the coast at night to wait for fishing boats, which would ferry the moonshine ashore in gunnysacks. Lookouts on the cliffs kept watch for "revenuers." Locals were sometimes pleasantly surprised to find a stray bottle or two washed up on the beach in the morning.

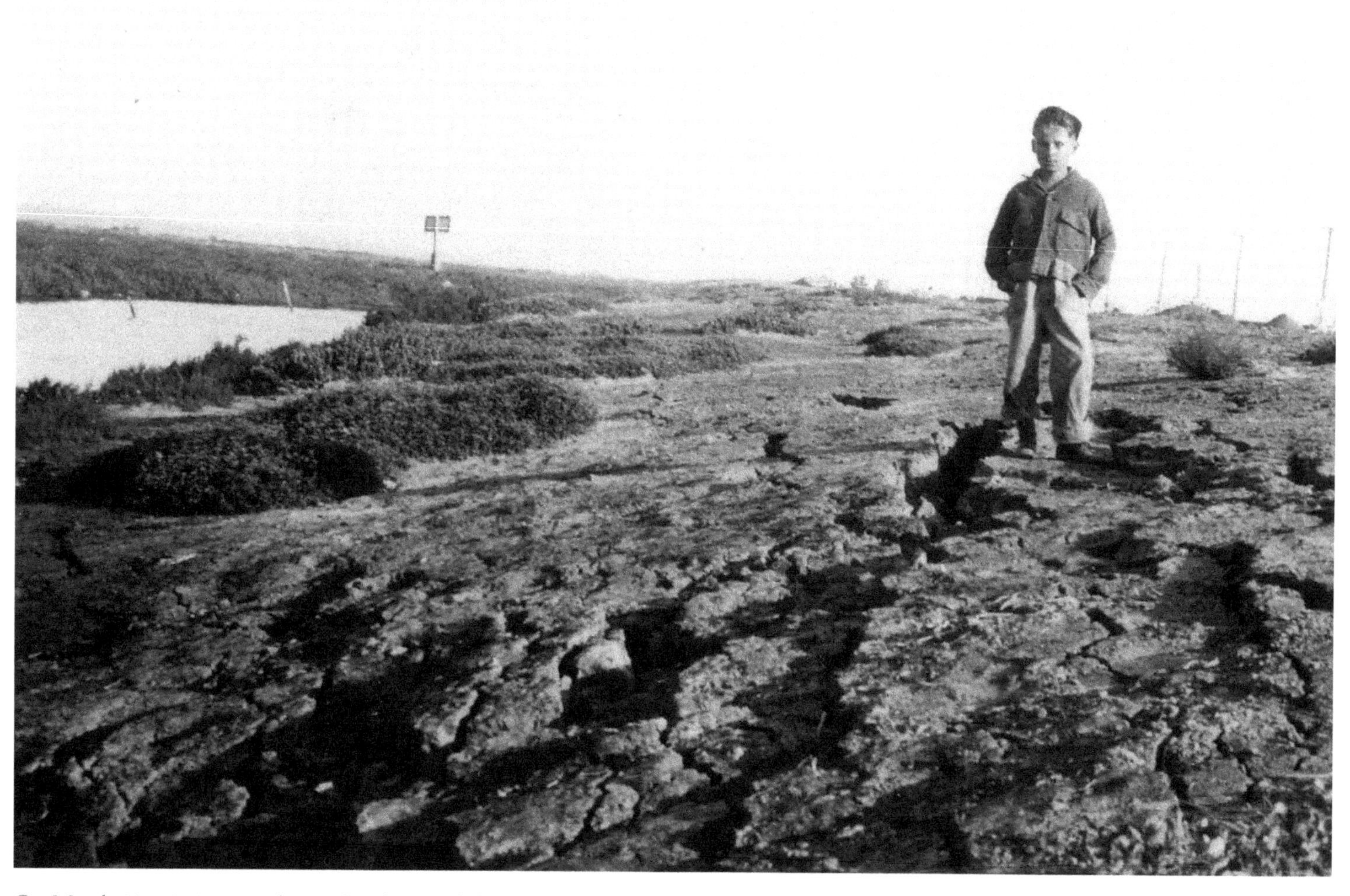

On March 10, 1933, at 5:54 P.M., Southern California experienced its deadliest earthquake in recorded history. At least 120 people were killed. Damage from the offshore fault line was concentrated in the beachfront cities of Long Beach and Huntington Beach. Aftershocks continued for months, traumatizing recent arrivals and earning the greater L.A. region its reputation as "earthquake country." Pictured is the fault line running through Huntington Beach.

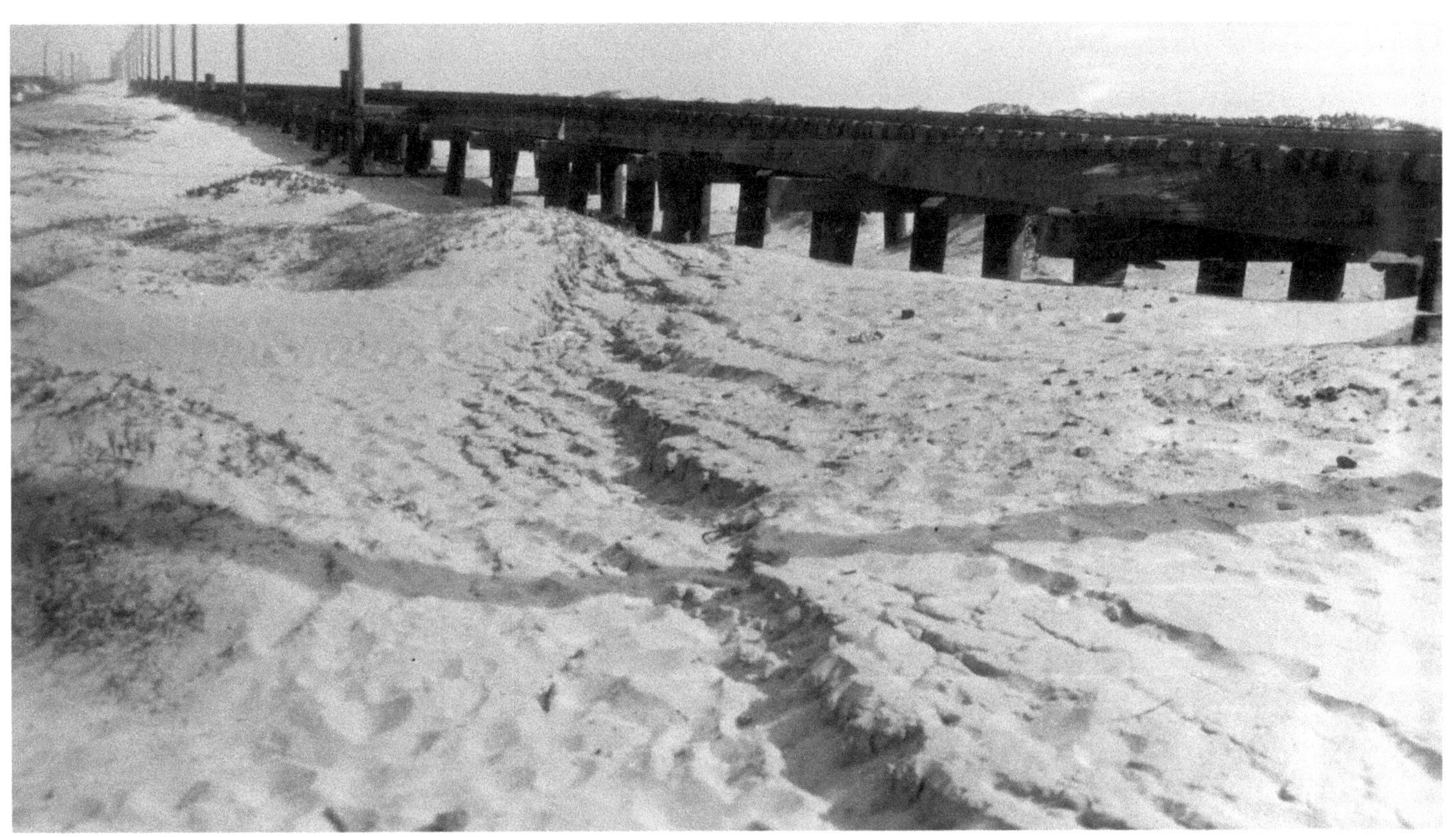

In addition to loss of life, the Long Beach Quake, as it came to be known, caused millions of dollars in property damage, primarily to coastal communities such as Huntington Beach, shown here, where liquefaction shook oil rigs and telephone poles out of the ground and ruptured water mains, leaving residents without utilities for days. This photo was taken east of Huntington Beach, near the Coast Highway.

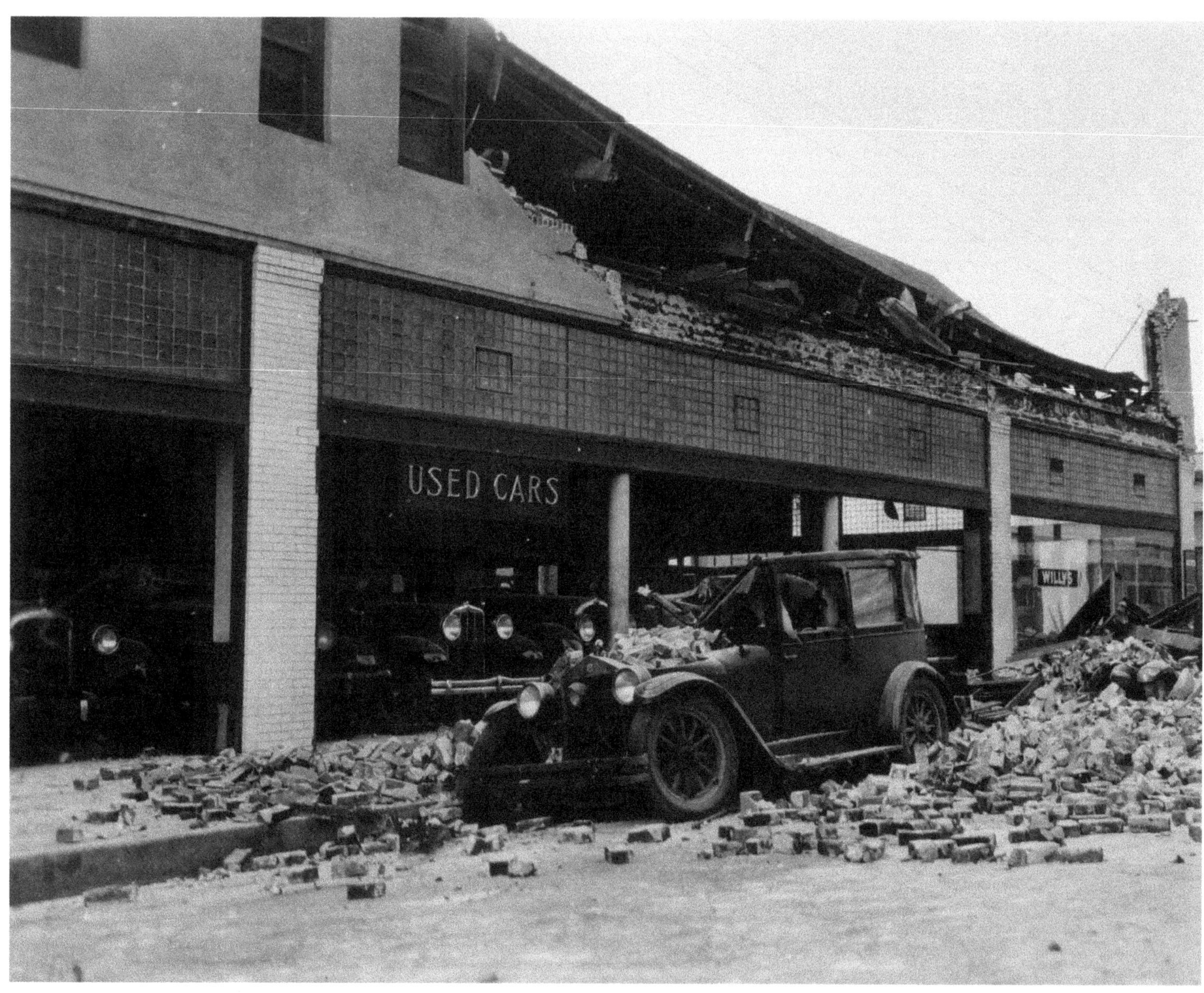

Of the inland cities, Santa Ana was particularly hard-hit by the 1933 earthquake, due to the large number of unreinforced brick buildings lining its downtown streets. This photo shows the damage to the Haley Building at the corner of 5th and Bush. Scenes such as this led to the passage of the Field Act one month later, establishing rigorous building codes for public buildings and greatly reducing property damage and loss of life in subsequent quakes.

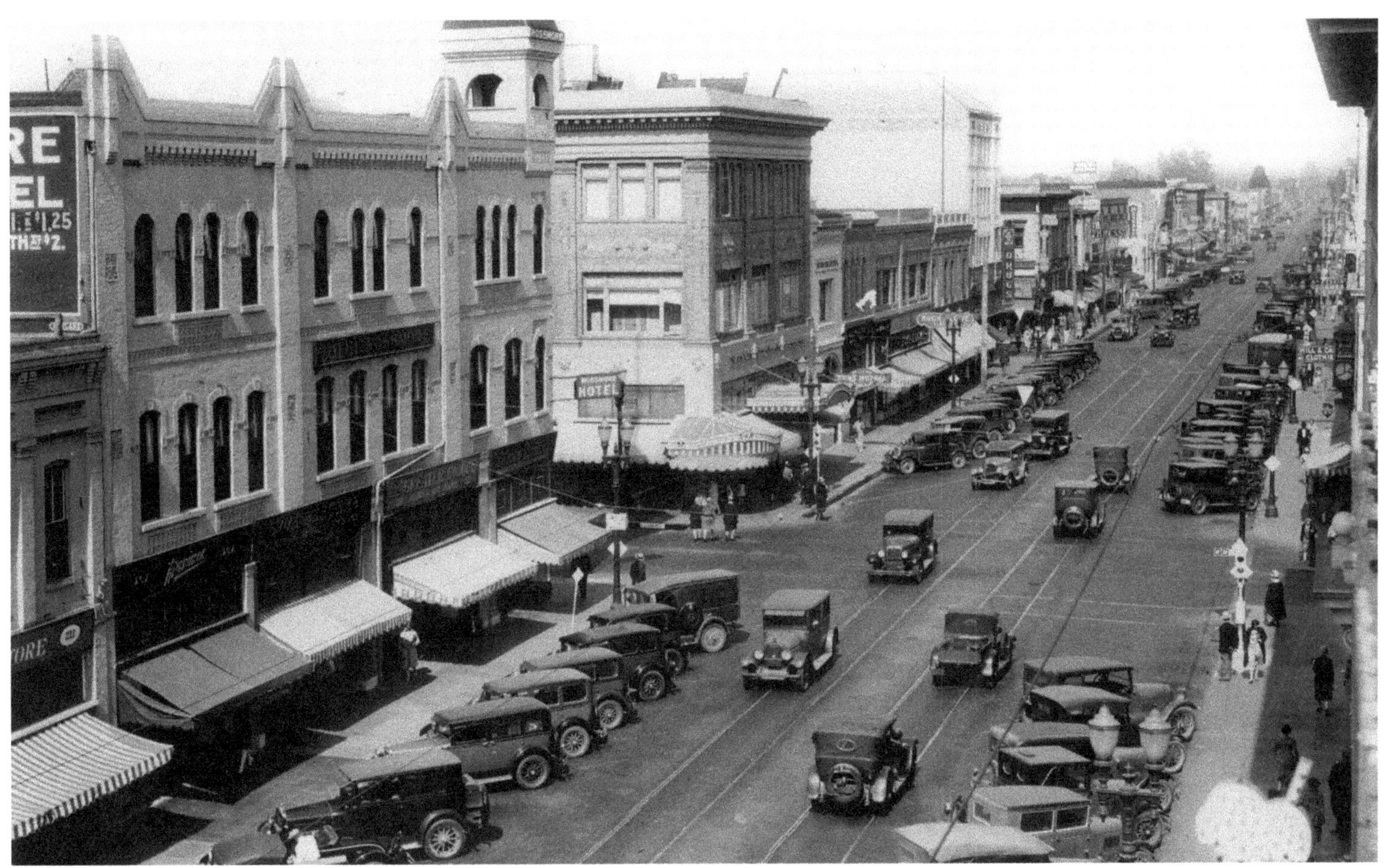

Seen here in 1930, the Rossmore Hotel, at left, would be the site of two of Santa Ana's three fatalities in the 1933 earthquake. On March 10, Jess and Yetta Ellison, a honeymooning couple from Oakland, were on their way to the hotel restaurant when they felt the tremors and ran outside, into the path of falling bricks. The restaurant itself sustained little damage.

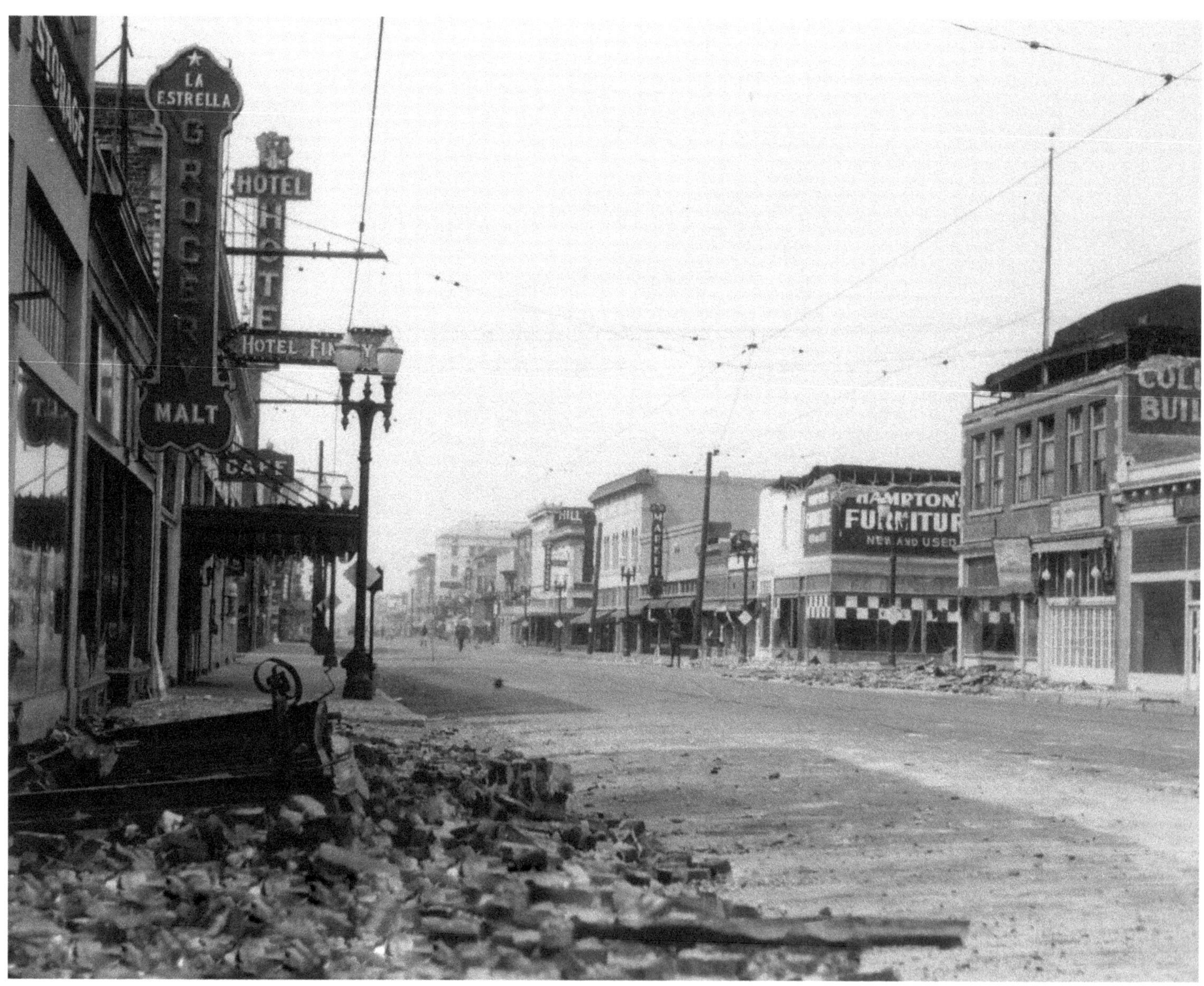

All over downtown Santa Ana, windows shattered and unreinforced buildings lost their facades in a shower of plaster dust and crumbling bricks. Earl Wilson Adamson was buried under the debris while walking along Fourth Street and became the city's third casualty. So many buildings were deemed unsafe and were subsequently demolished that the city's skyline was forever changed, the razed structures replaced by Art Moderne buildings that complied with stringent new codes.

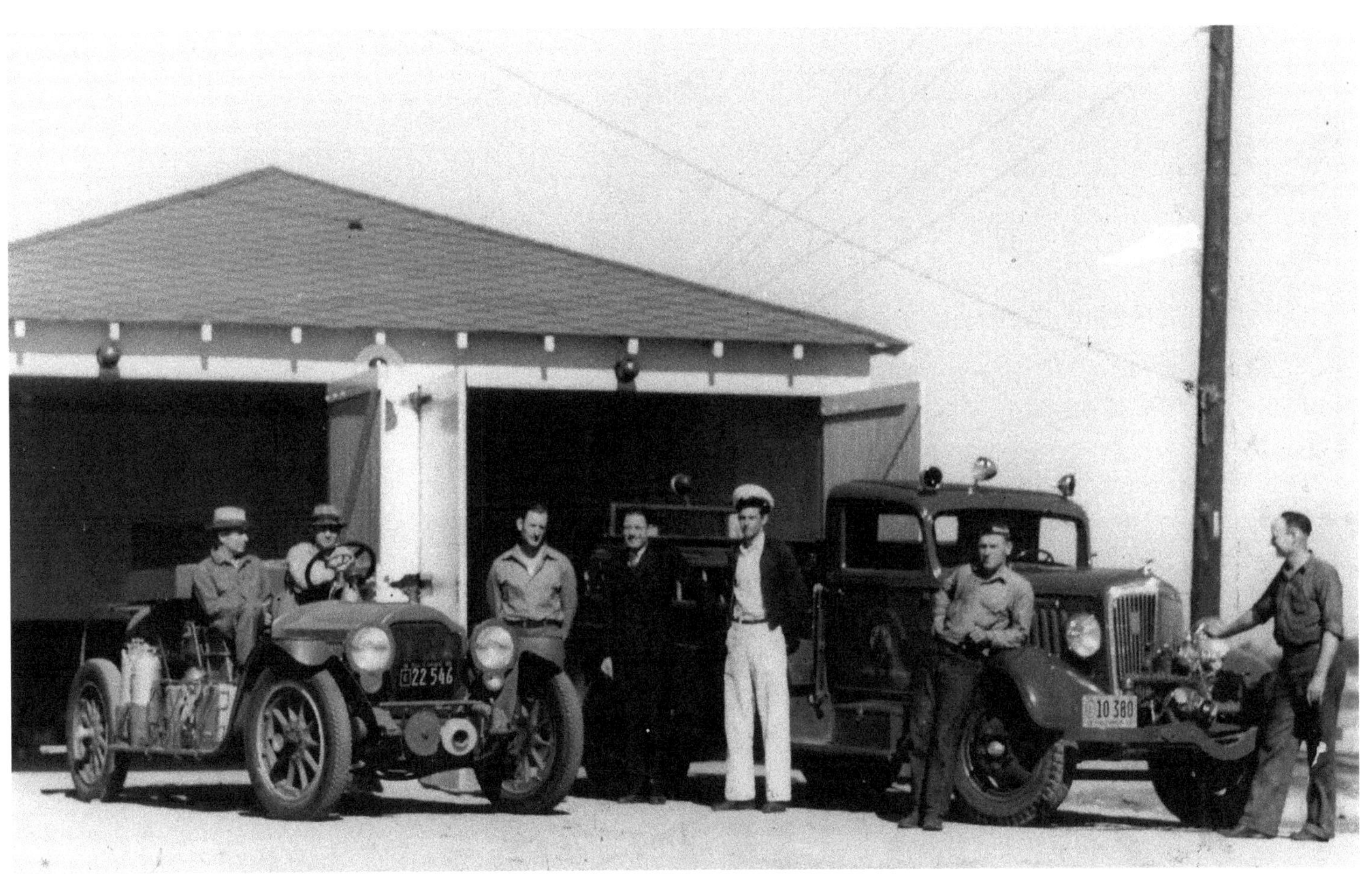

Midway City is an unincorporated community so named because it is midway between Santa Ana and Long Beach. The area has been fighting off annexation attempts almost since its inception, most recently by neighboring Huntington Beach and Westminster. Though fire protection today is provided by the county, in 1936 it was undertaken by this volunteer fire department, proudly posed with their equipment in front of their firehouse.

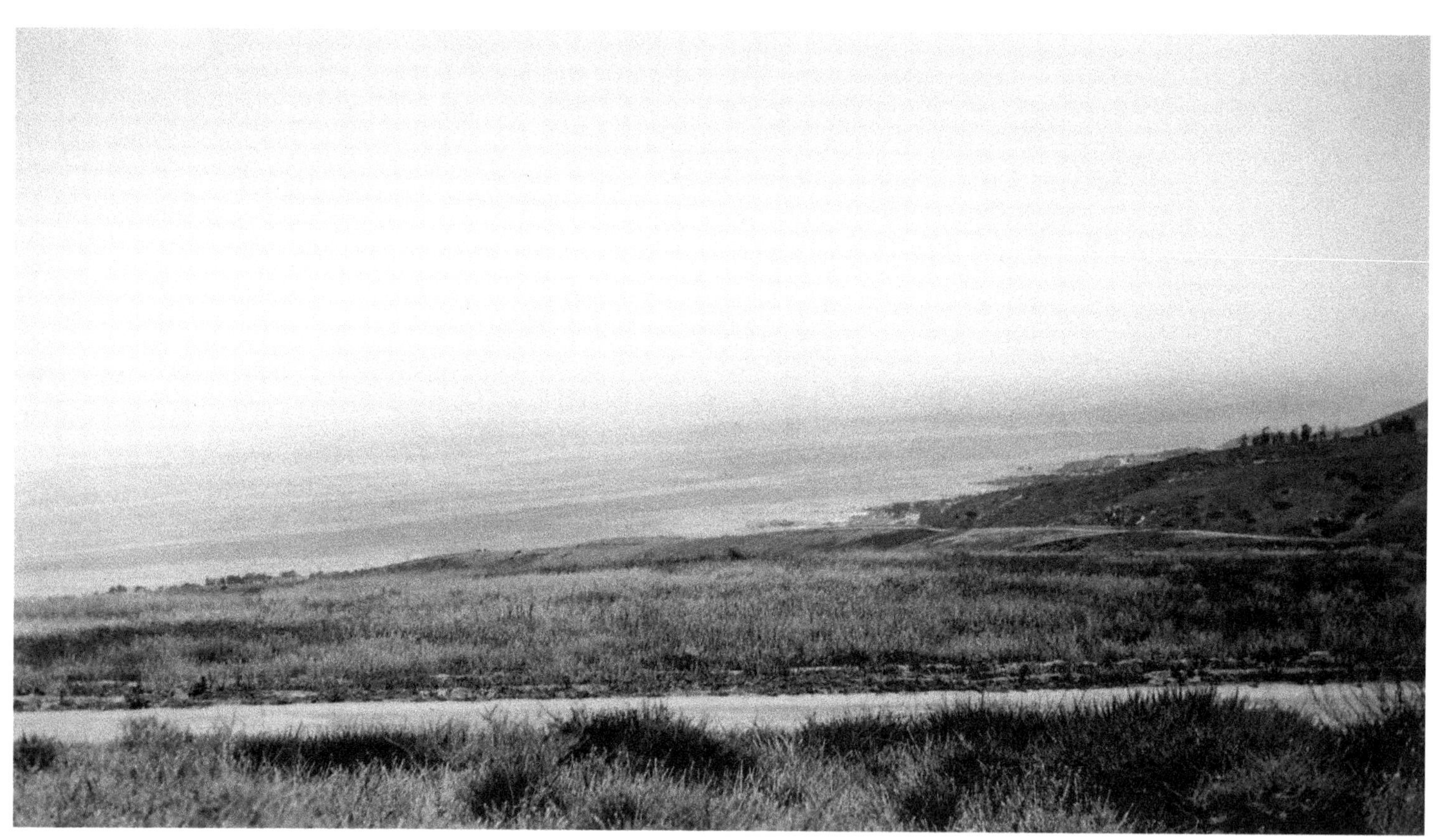

By the 1920s the rugged and varied coastline of Laguna Beach had been discovered by Hollywood to be the perfect stand-in for just about anywhere, and many movies were filmed there. An early Buster Keaton silent movie substituted Laguna for Italy; *The Life of Emile Zola,* winner of the 1937 Oscar for Best Picture, was set in France but filmed among Laguna's bluffs; and the 1942 Bette Davis flick *Now, Voyager* replaced multiple worldwide locales with Laguna sites.

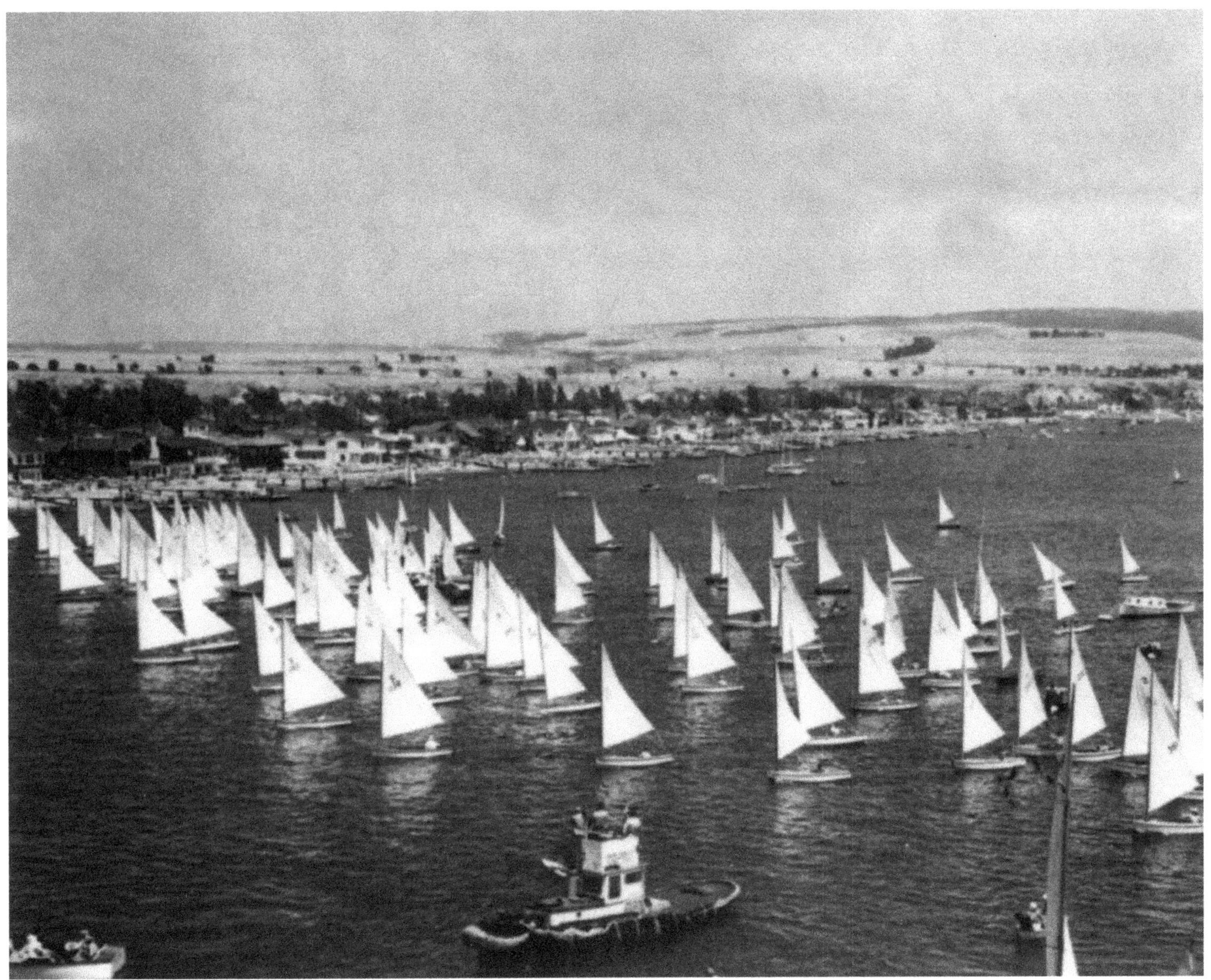

To many residents of Newport Beach, boating is a way of life. Newport's sheltered harbor allows children as young as five to participate in boat racing. The Flight of the Snowbirds, a sailboat race for young people, was initiated in 1935 as a stimulus to tourism by Harold Beek, Newport's first harbormaster. He was paid a whopping $25 a month for his services when first appointed in 1911.

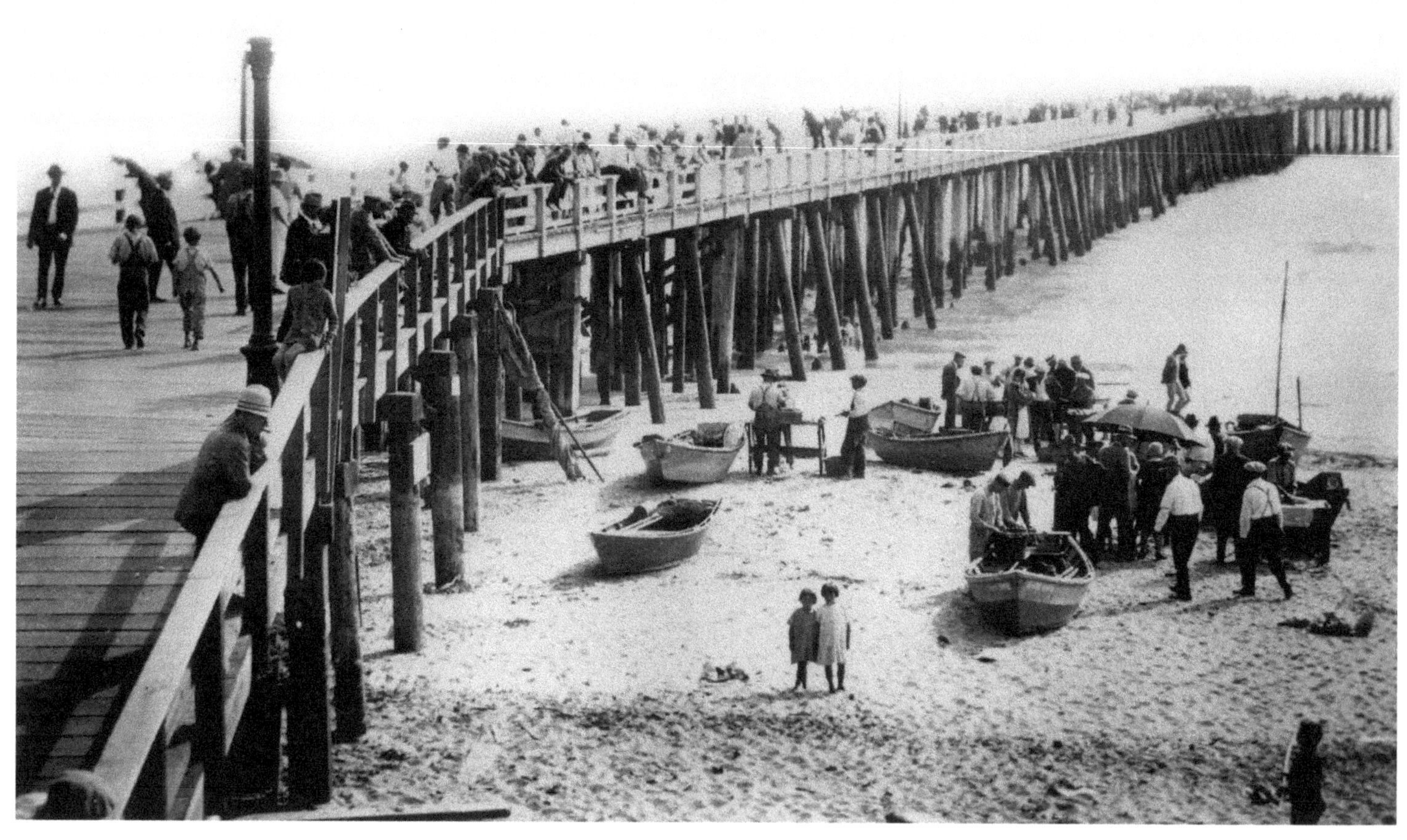

Newport's Dory Fleet is an institution that dates back to the construction of Newport Pier, then known as McFadden Wharf, in 1888. Named for the small, flat-bottomed boats they use, the dory fishermen still go out to sea every morning, returning to sell their catch to locals right on the beach, using their weather-beaten boats as sales counters. The practice originated as a way to eliminate the middleman and has evolved into a time-honored tradition.

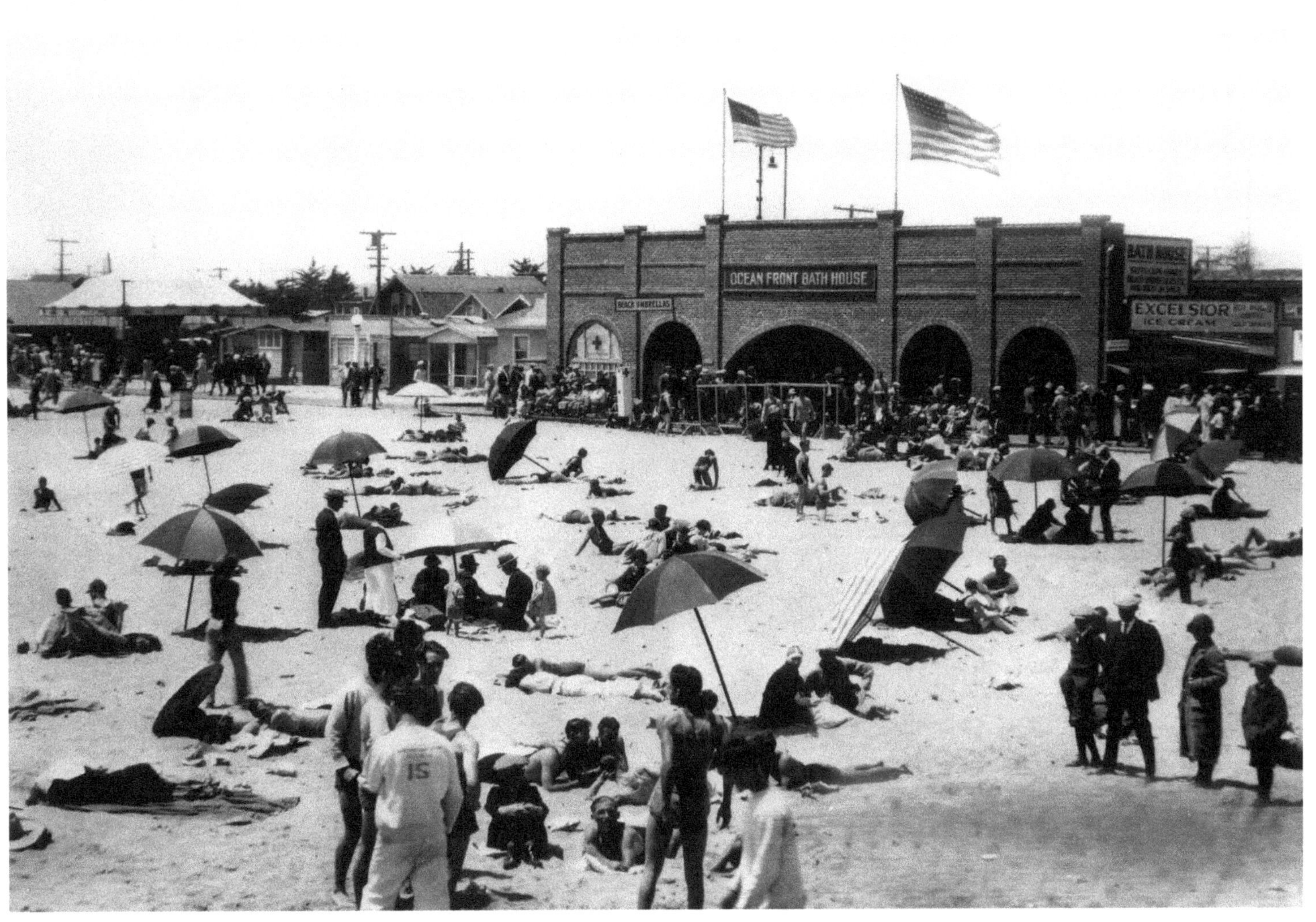

Bathhouses of the 1930s like this one on Balboa provided a safe alternative to swimming in the cold, rough waters of the Pacific Ocean, a task made even more difficult by the heavy, wool swimsuits of the era that tended to weigh an extra 20 pounds when wet. Orange County's coastal bathhouses typically offered a heated saltwater pool, swimsuit and beach-umbrella rentals, lockers and changing facilities, and a basic lunch menu.

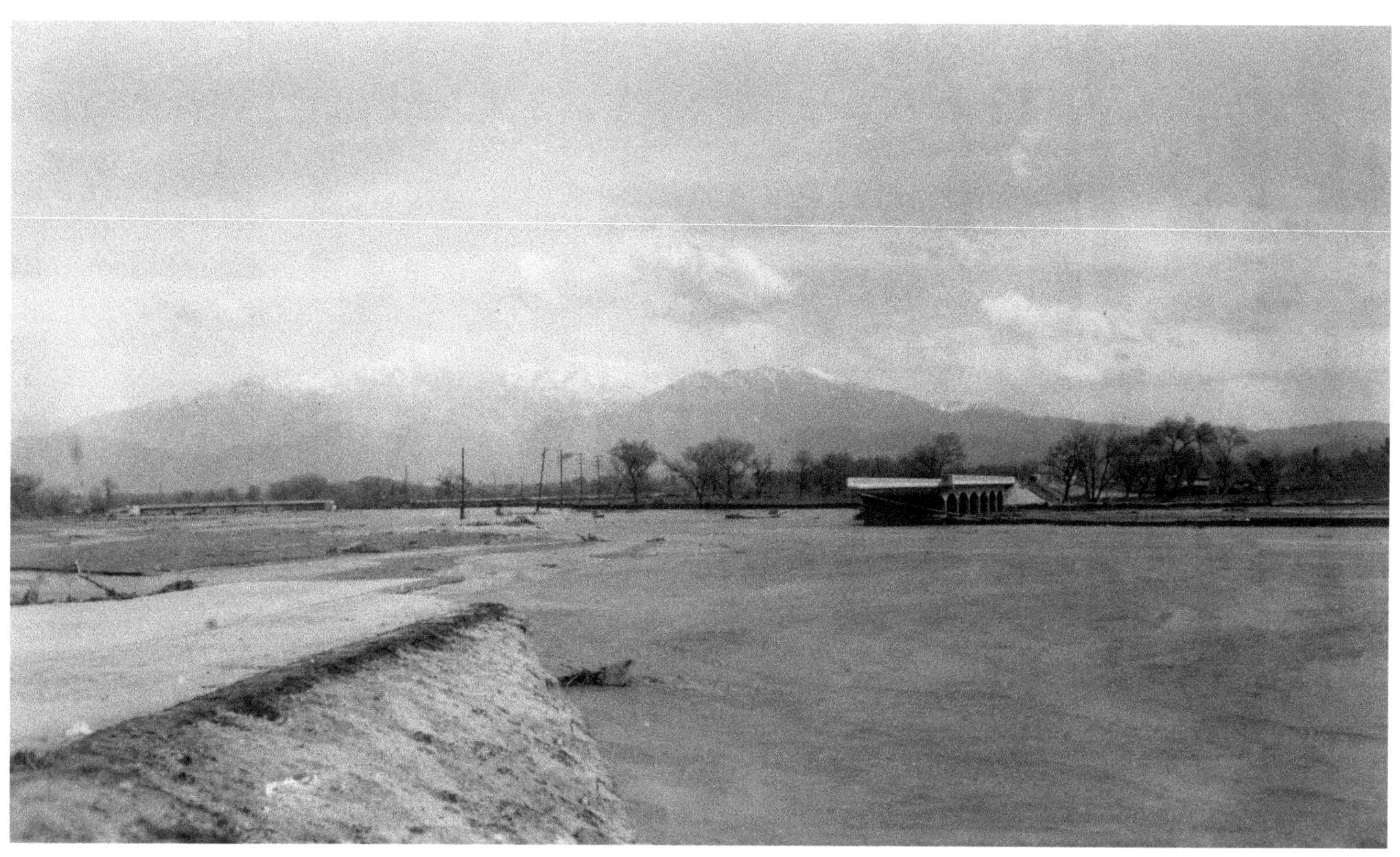

The city of Anaheim lies in the flood plain of the Santa Ana River, which originates in the San Bernardino Mountains and flows nearly a hundred miles before emptying into the Pacific Ocean between Newport and Huntington Beach. Though dry most of the year, ten days of heavy rain in February 1938 caused the river to overflow its banks, sweeping away the little town of Atwood and destroying nearly every bridge in Anaheim.

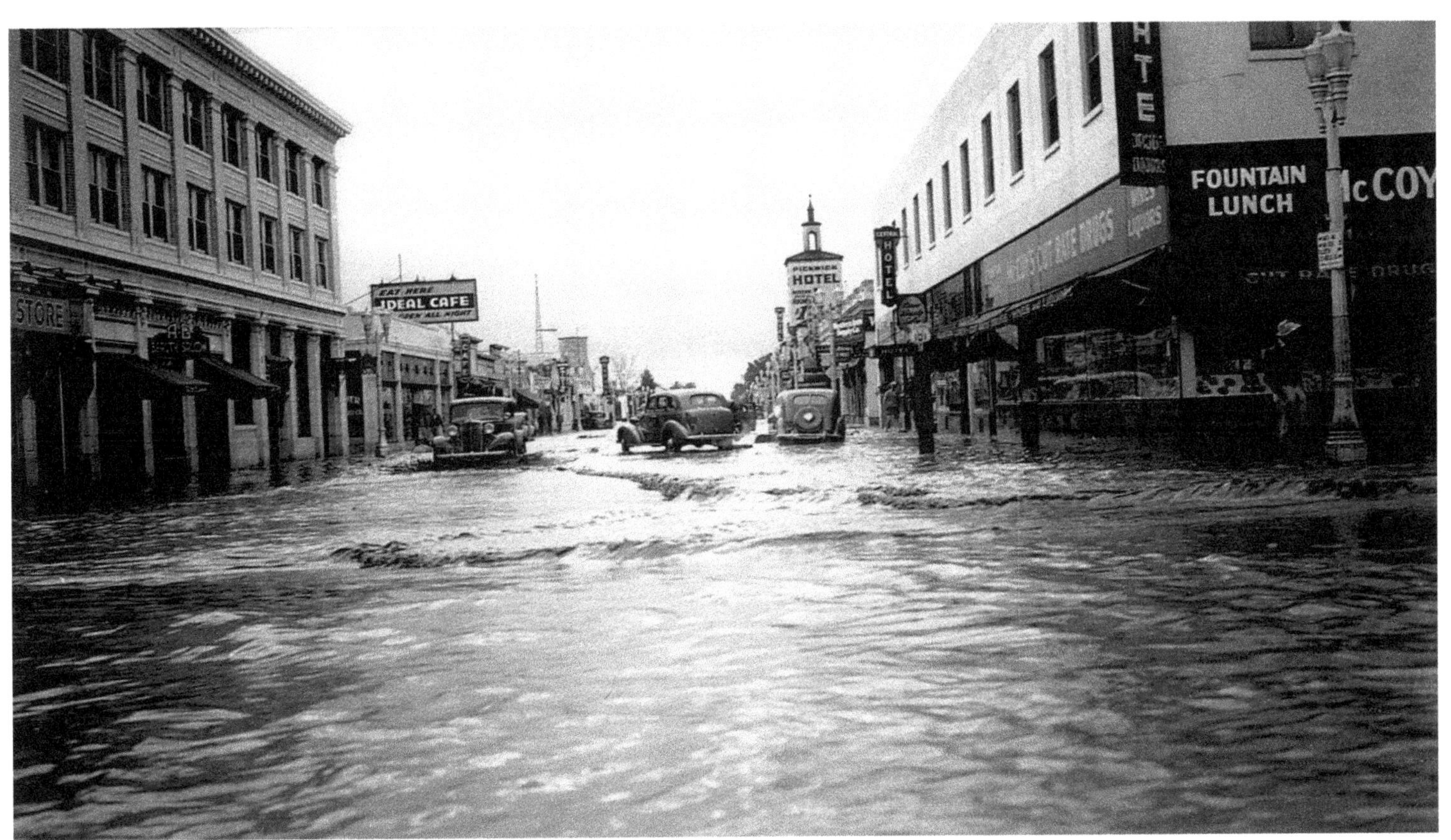

Five minutes after the Anaheim fire department whistled a warning, a wall of water four feet deep crashed through homes, sweeping away vehicles, livestock, and barns. Moments later the floodwaters hit downtown, filling basements and rising several feet into the first level of nearly every business establishment. State militia held looting to a minimum, placing the city on virtual lockdown till order could be restored.

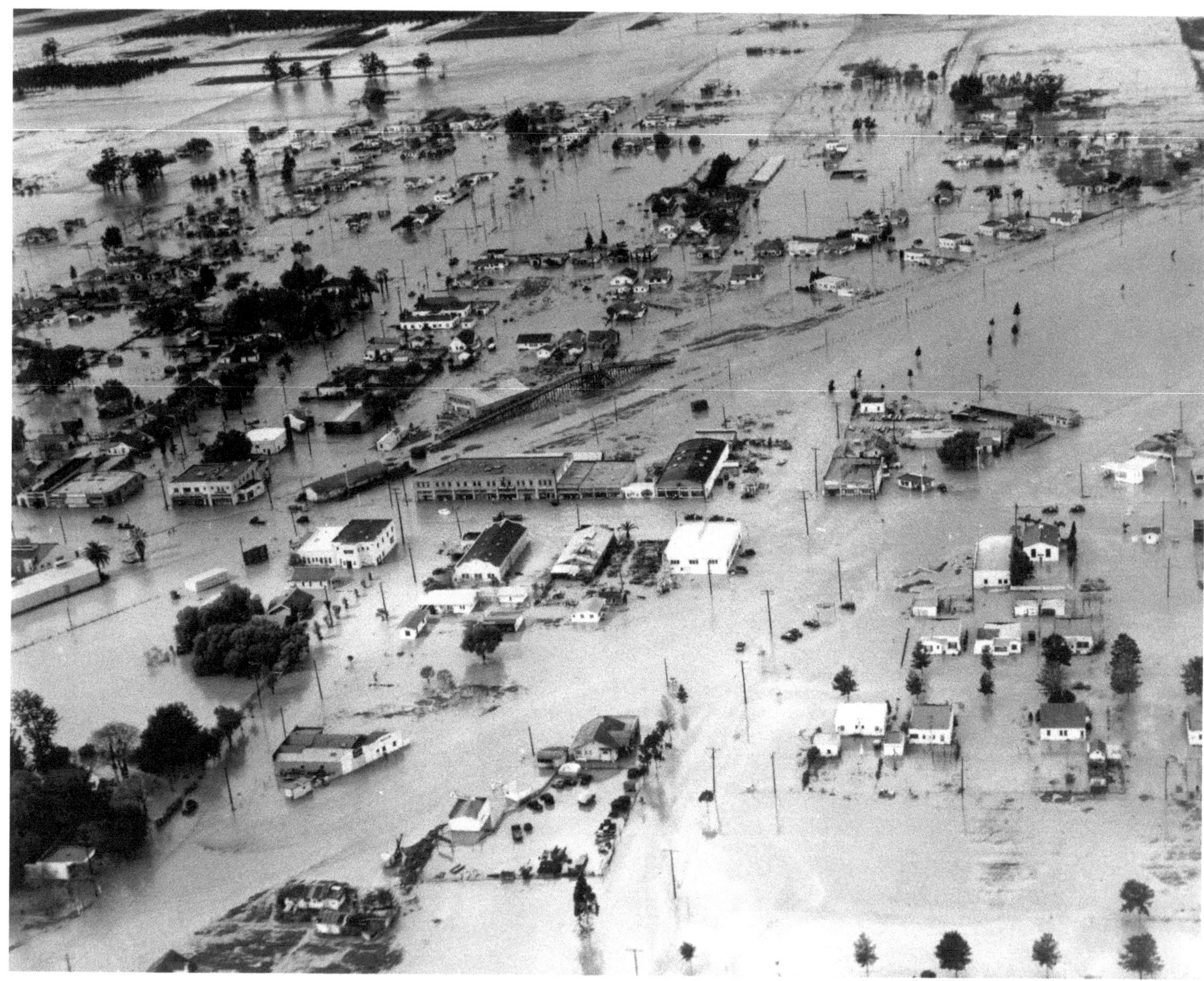

The February 1938 storms resulted in the Santa Ana River overflowing its banks and unleashing a torrent of water that swept away bridges and piers and devastated much of Orange County. This photograph shows Buena Park's downtown area underwater. The flood, the second to affect Buena Park in just over a decade, was the catalyst for the construction of citywide flood-control channels.

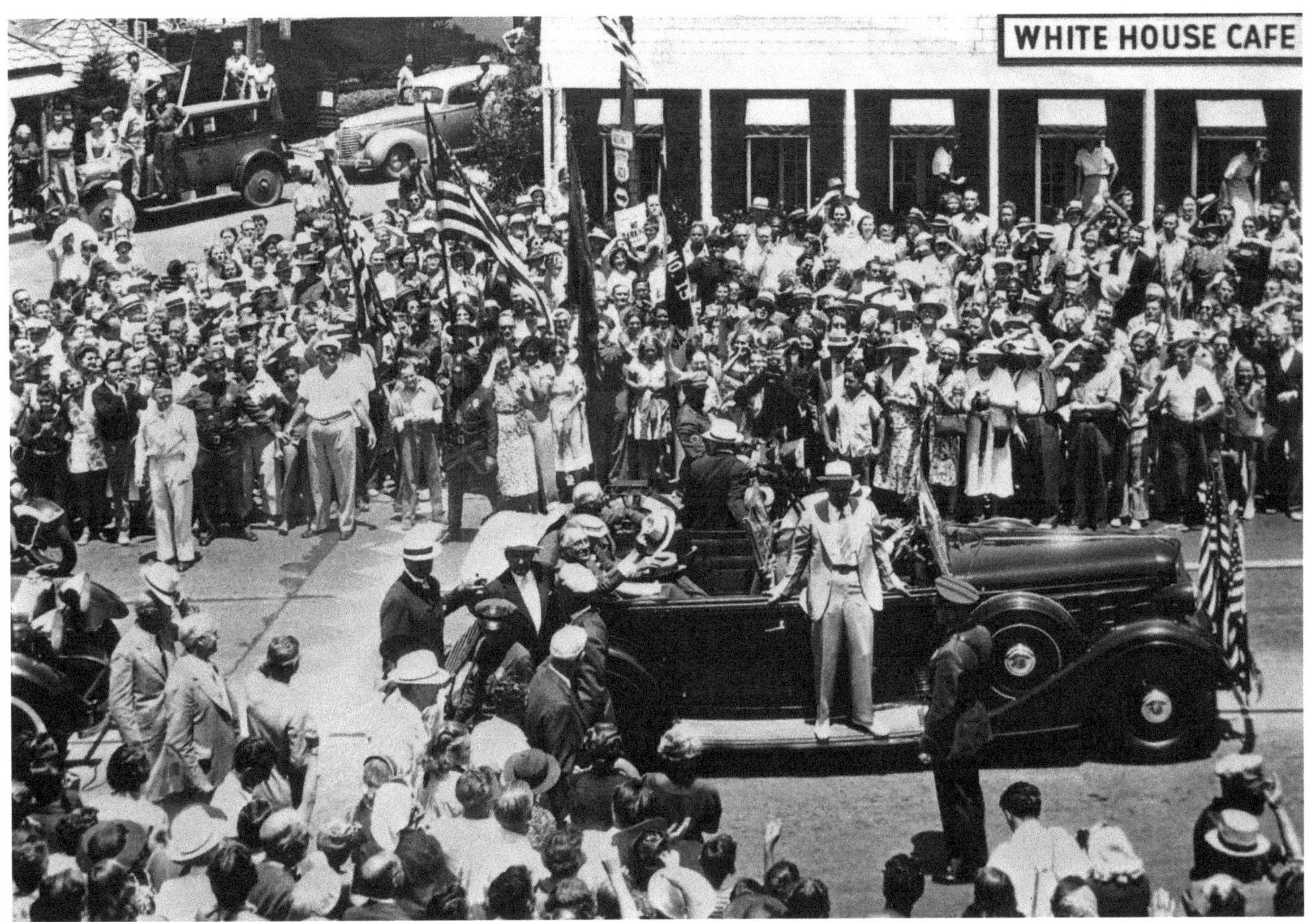

Following the flood of 1938, President Franklin D. Roosevelt toured the disaster areas and later signed into law the Flood Control Act of 1938, which authorized the construction of dams, levees, and dikes through the management of the U.S. Army Corps of Engineers. He is shown here in Laguna Beach, in front of the White House restaurant, which opened in 1918 and is still a popular nightspot, known for offering live music seven nights a week and for showcasing local art.

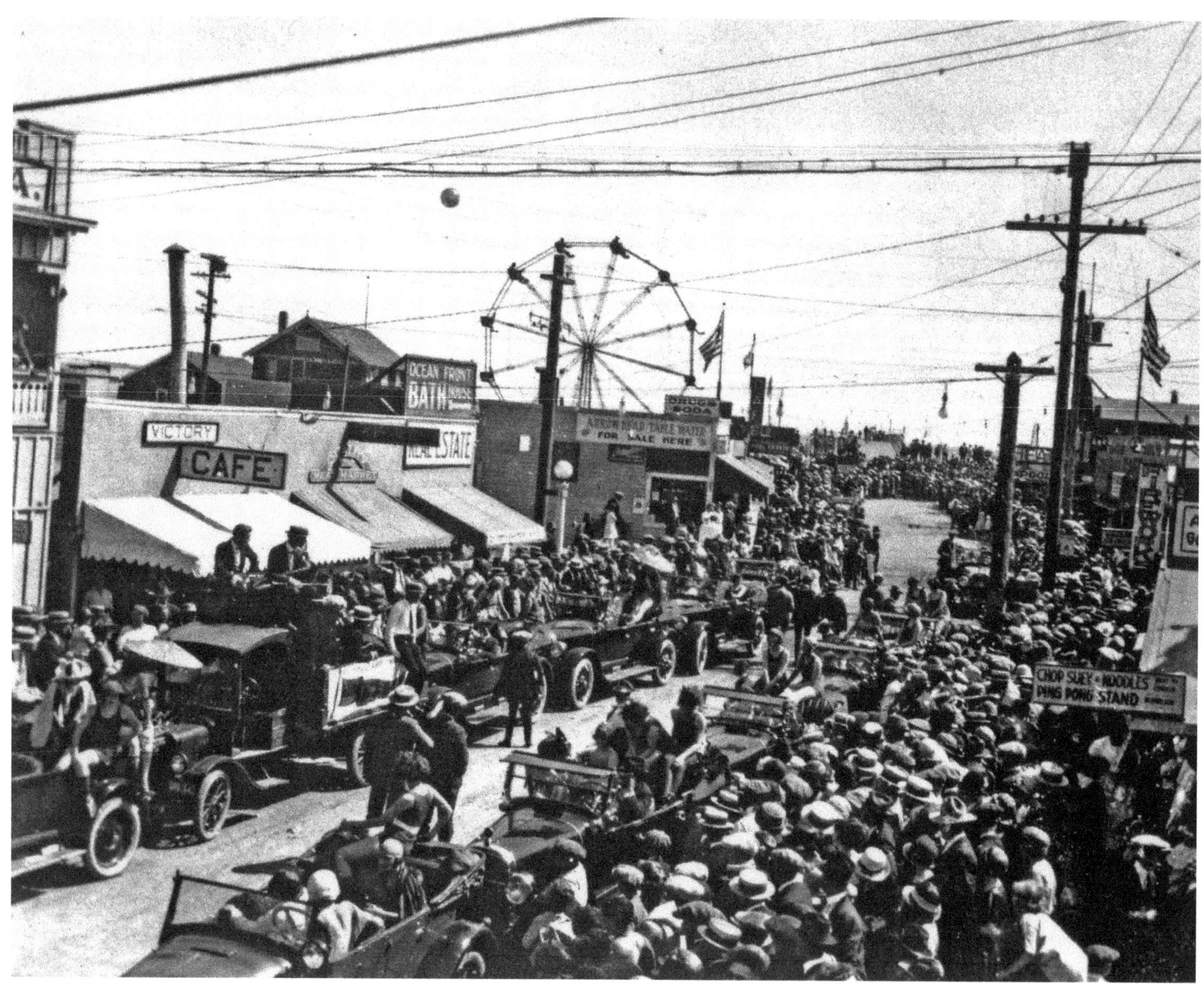

One of the earliest of Orange County's many tourist attractions was the family-owned-and-operated Fun Zone on Balboa, shown here in the late 1930s. Opened in 1936, the park featured such colorfully named rides as Punk Rack, Spill the Milk, and the Bird Cage Ferris Wheel. After a major refurbishing in 1986, the Fun Zone is still going strong and is currently owned by the Newport Harbor Nautical Museum.

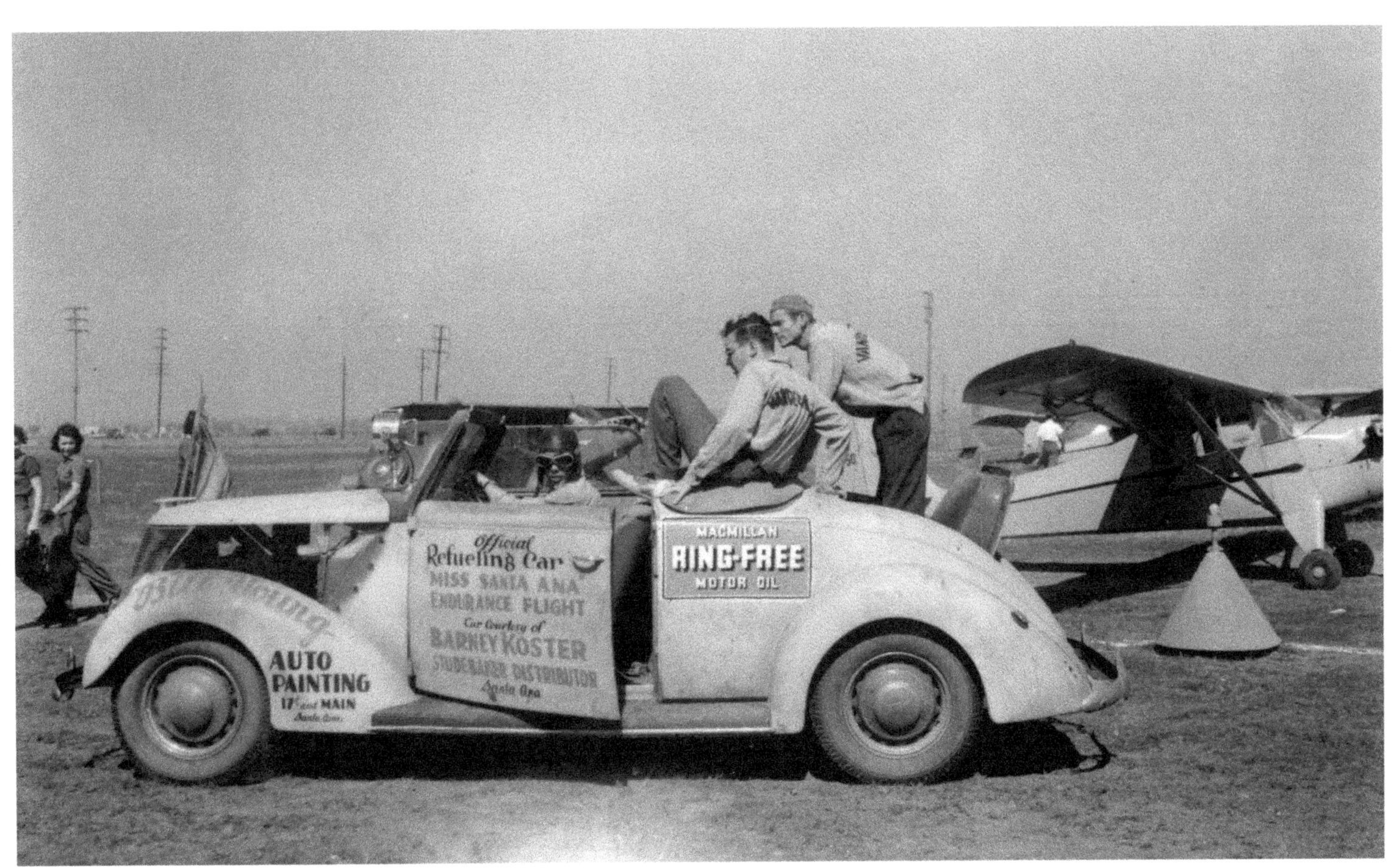

Shown here in 1939 is the support car for the Miss Santa Ana Endurance Flight. Santa Ana played a big role in early aviation history. In 1924 resident Eddie Martin built OC's first airport, the Eddie Martin Airport. Howard Hughes crashed into a Santa Ana beet field in 1935 after setting a speed record. And Douglas "Wrong Way" Corrigan, inspiration for the 1939 movie *The Flying Irishman,* settled in Santa Ana after his 1938 transatlantic flight.

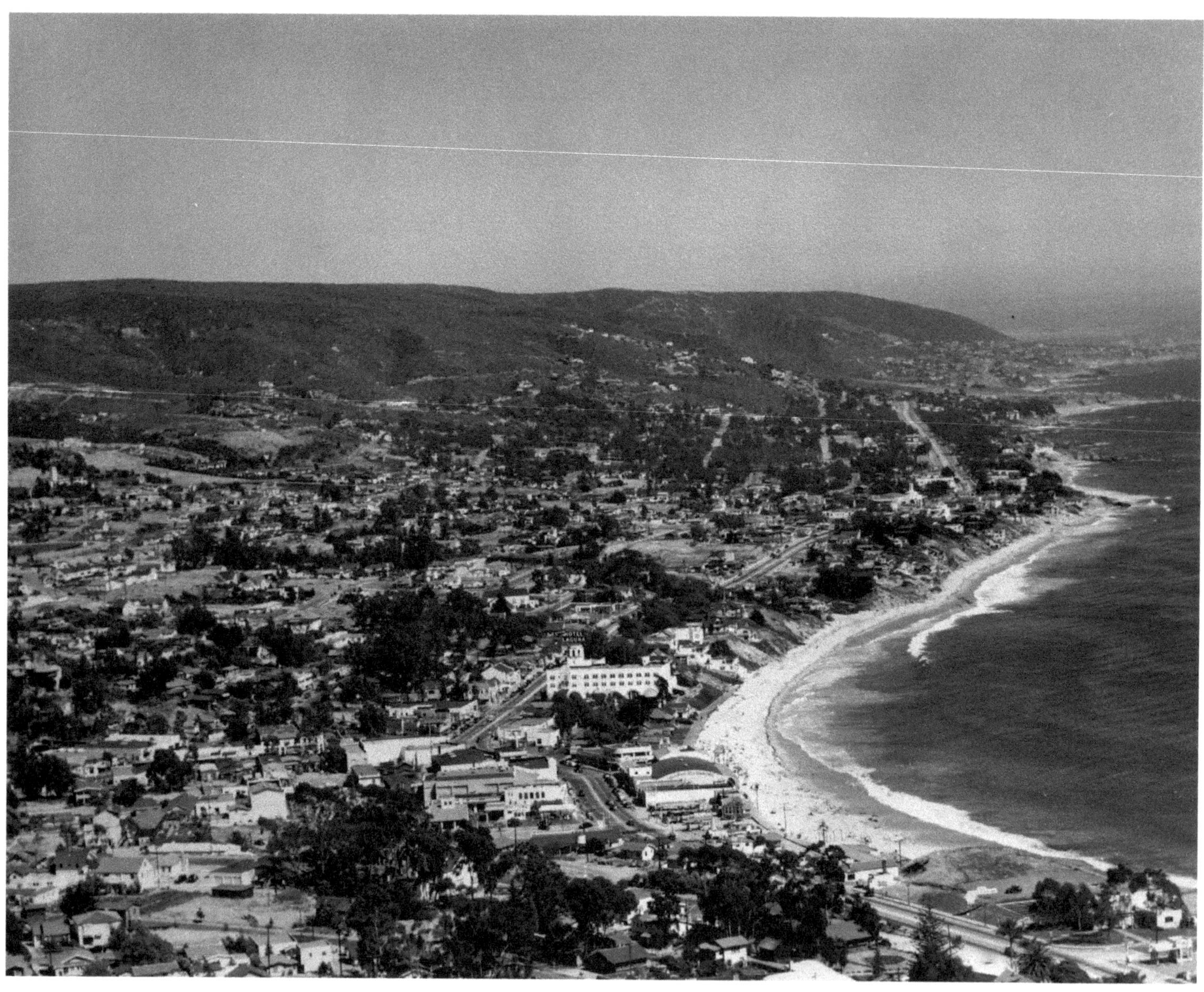

Over the years Laguna Beach, seen here in 1939, has been home to many celebrities, including Bette Davis, Judy Garland, and Rudolph Valentino. But the town's most famous resident is the Laguna Greeter, a Danish immigrant who arrived in 1940. For the next 33 years this eccentric character stood by the Coast Highway and welcomed all visitors to town with a booming "Hellooooo, How Are You?" A statue in his honor stands in front of the old Pottery Shack.

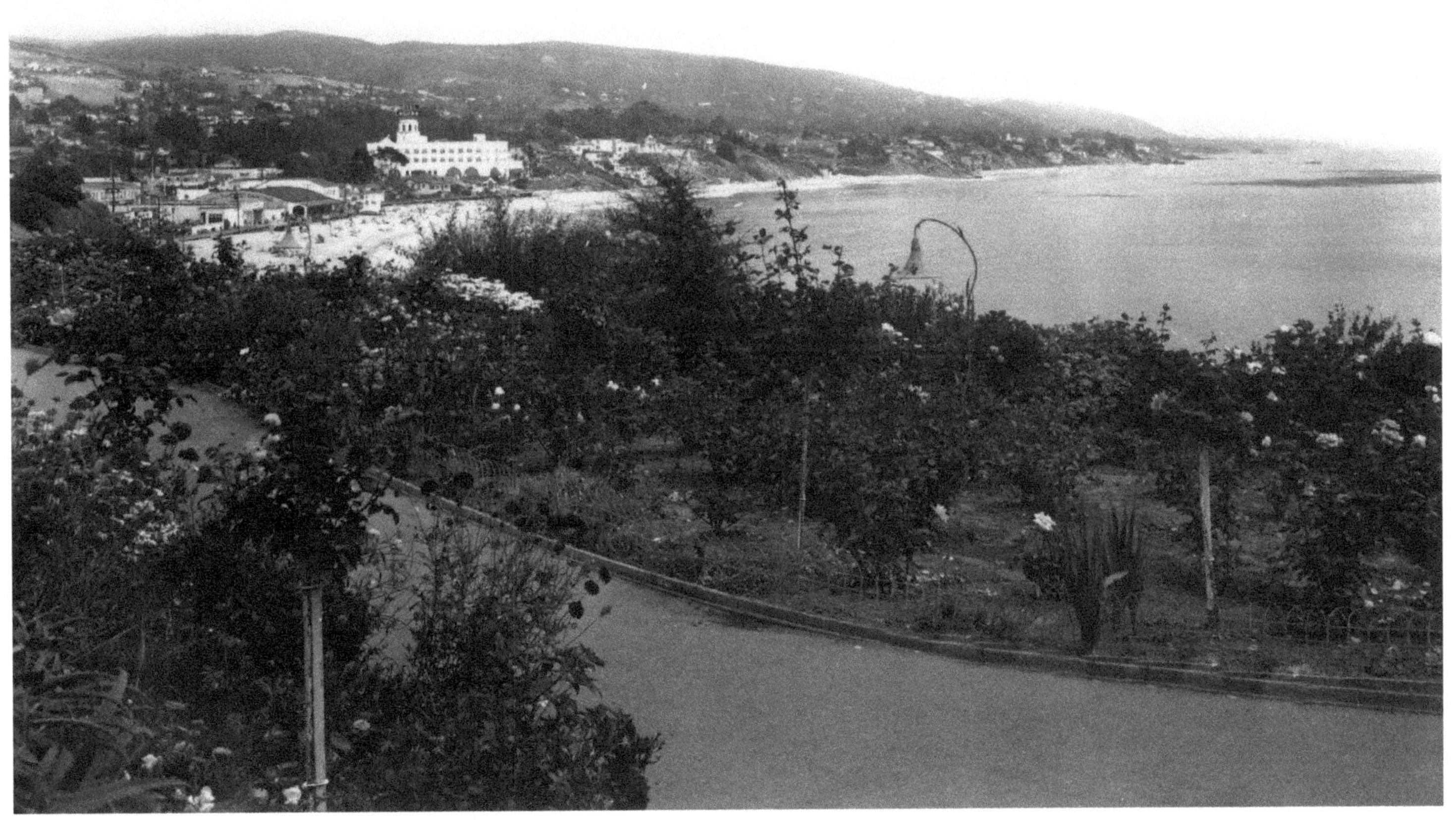

The view from Las Brisas restaurant looks much the same today as it did in 1939, one year after it opened as Victor Hugo Restaurant. The walking path shown here connects the sheltered Main Beach at left to a cliff-top gazebo at Heisler Park at right (not shown) that overlooks stunning vistas of the rock formations below and has been providing tourists with photo opportunities for decades. It's also a popular wedding site.

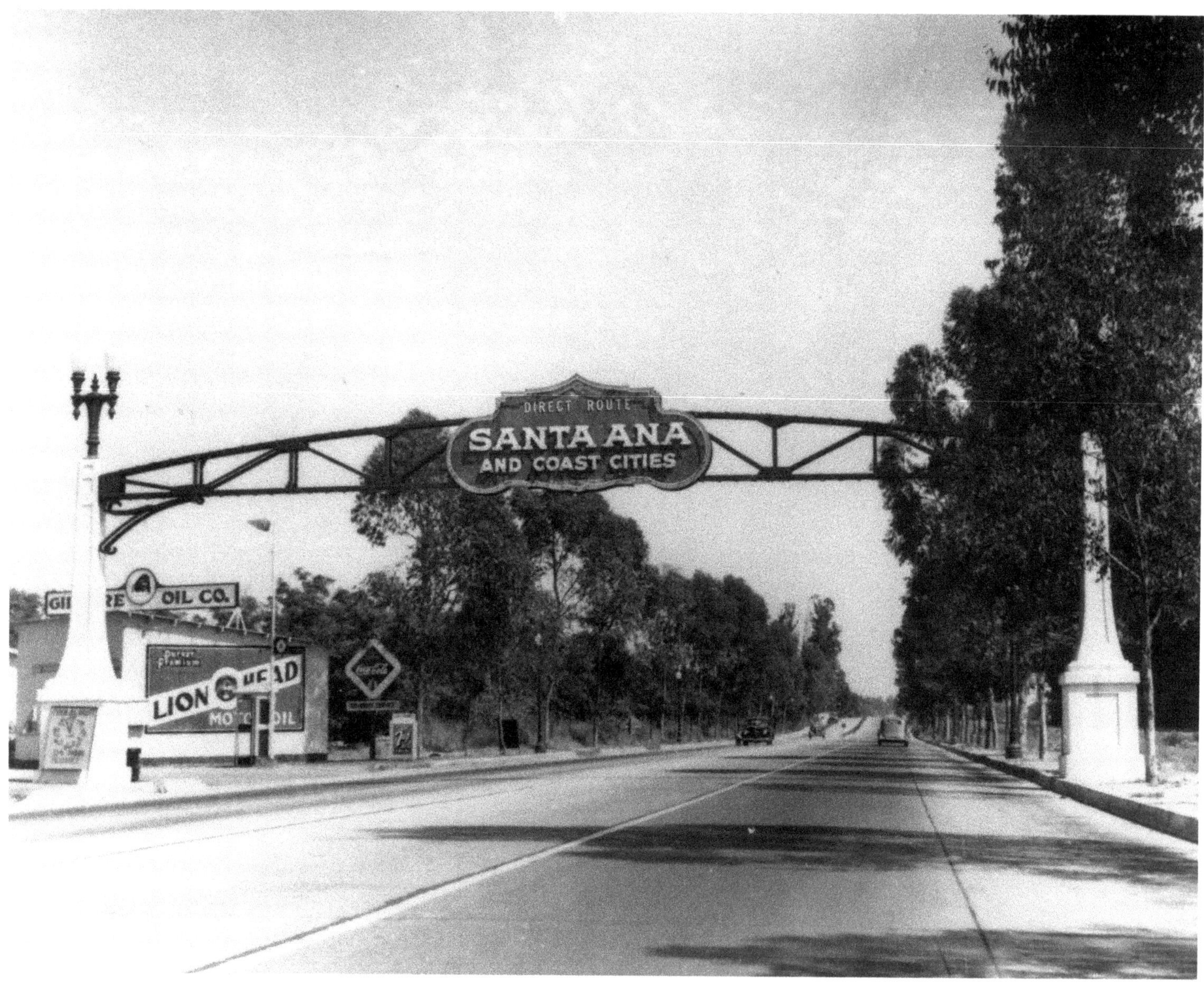

This sign, shown in 1940, once welcomed visitors to Santa Ana as they turned onto Santa Ana Boulevard from Highway 101 (now the 5 Freeway) on the northwest edge of town. Though the original sign is long gone, a near-exact replica was installed in 2007 on Main Street, identifying the Historic South Main Business District.

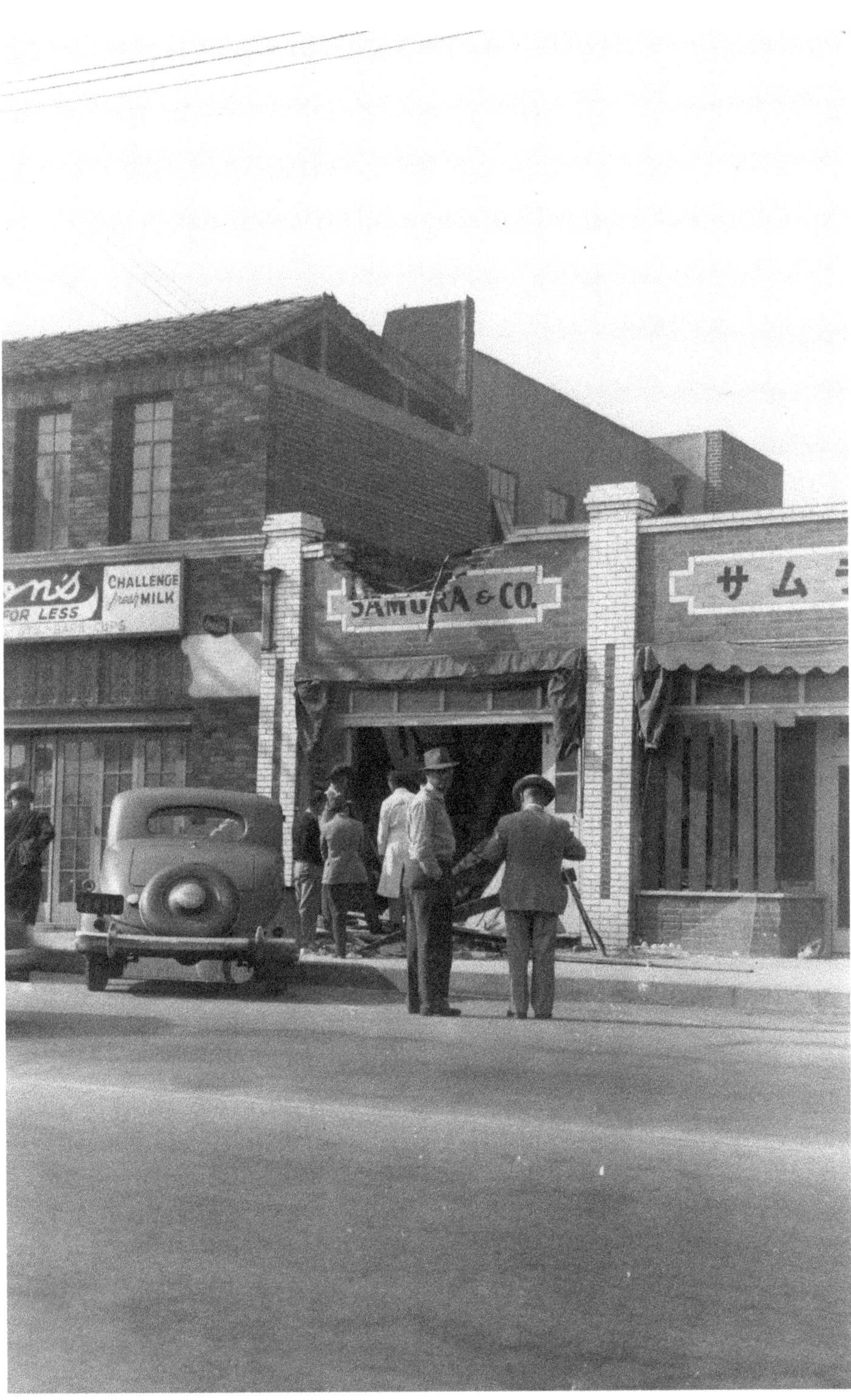

On November 14, 1941, a minor earthquake, centered in Los Angeles County, caused structural damage to Samura and Company in Garden Grove. Just a few months later, the owner of this business, along with all the other 1,854 Japanese Americans living in Orange County at the time, would be sent to Poston Relocation Camp in Arizona as part of California's wartime evacuation program.

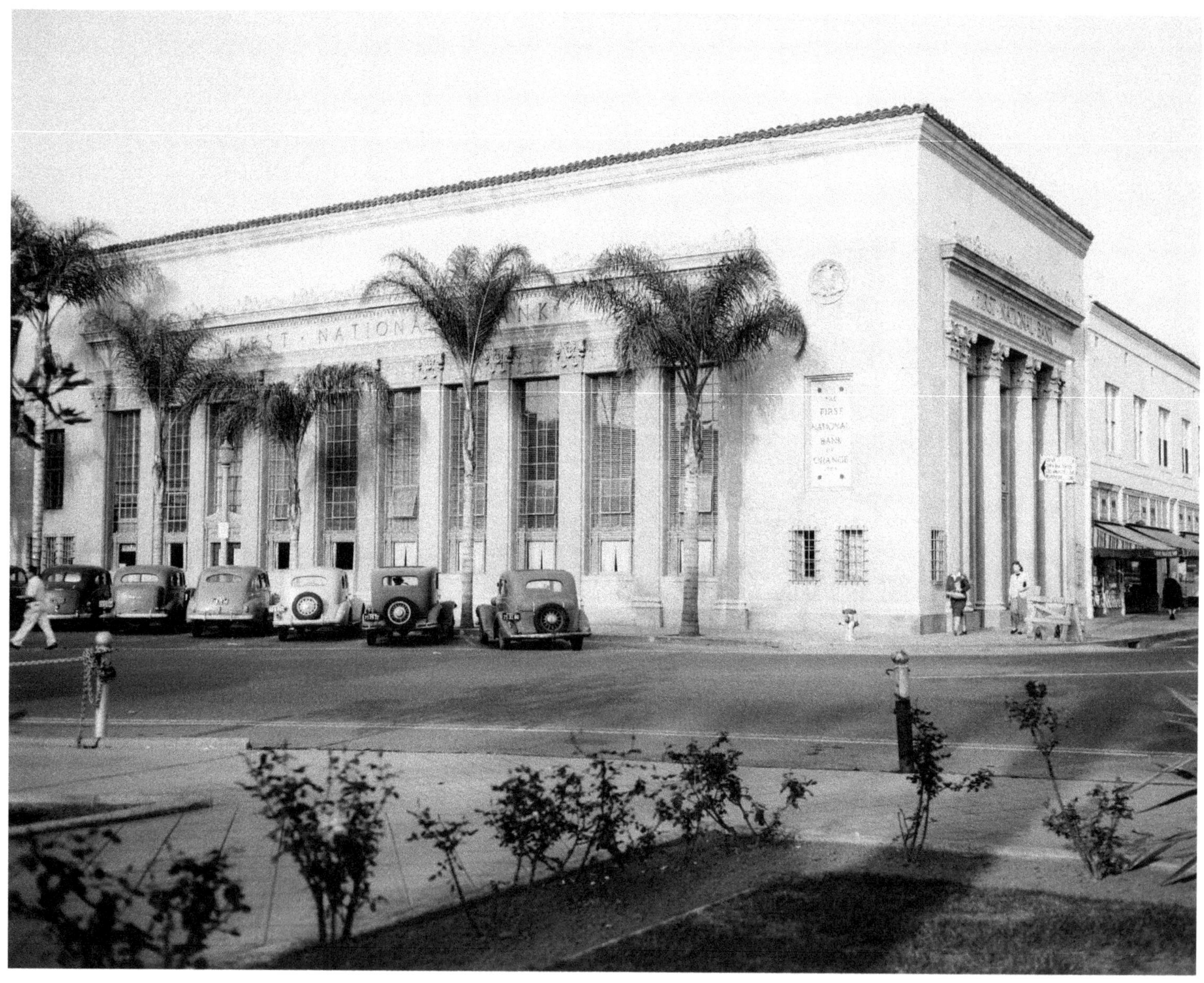

This Beaux Arts structure was built in 1923 by the architectural firm of Morgan, Walls, and Clements, designers of such Los Angeles icons as the Mayan, Belasco, and Wiltern theaters (all L.A. historic cultural monuments), and the Atlantic Richfield Oil Building. Shown here in the 1940s, it was home to the First National Bank of Orange at the time, and was a rare example of a foray into Orange County on the part of the renowned architectural trio.

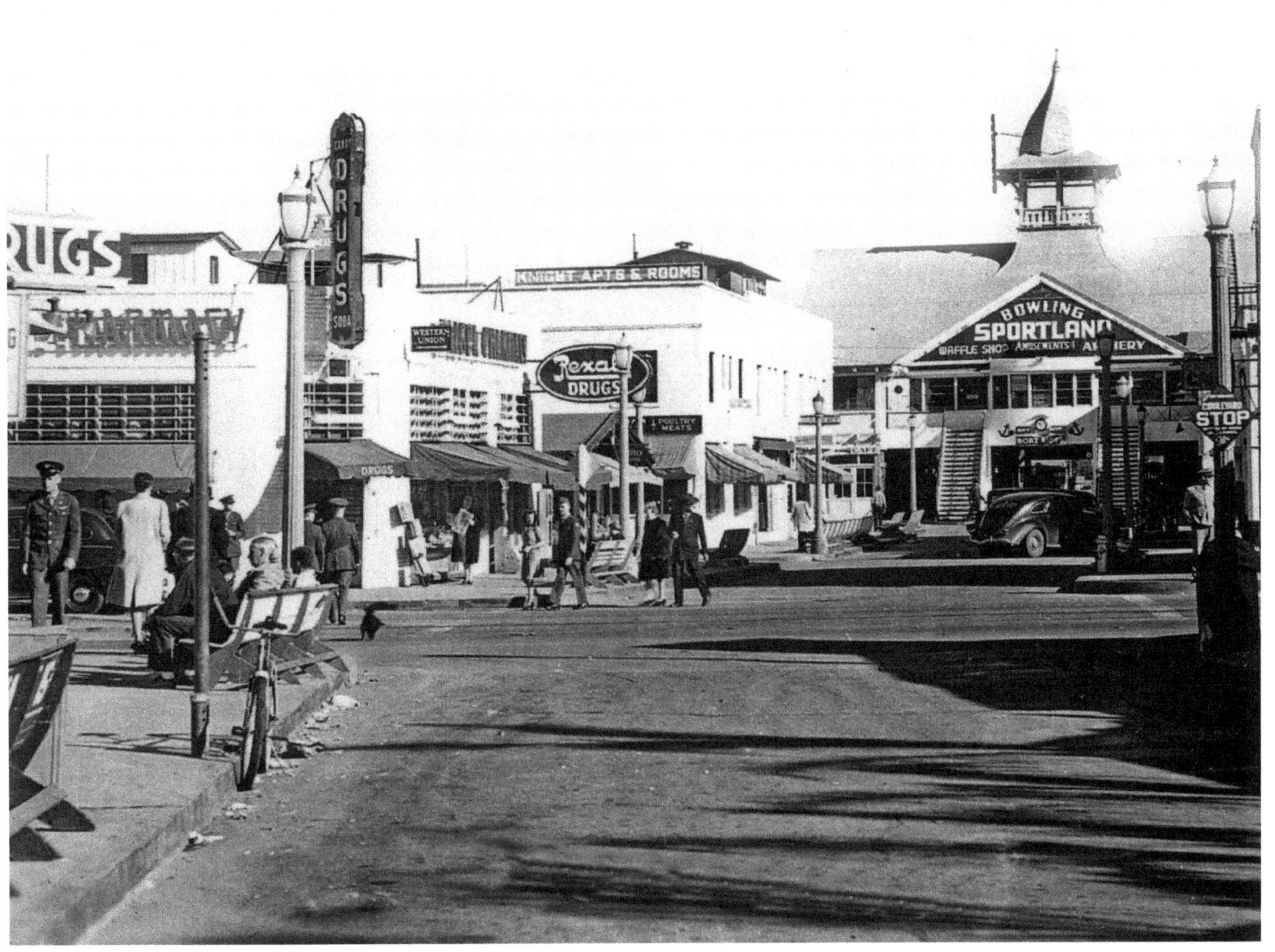

In 1928 competition from the newly opened Rendezvous Ballroom ended Balboa Pavilion's heyday as a dance hall. By the 1940s, when this photo was taken, the peninsula landmark had become "Sportland," offering bowling, archery, and other "amusements" that tied it thematically to the newly opened Fun Zone immediately adjacent. An upstairs room briefly offered "Skil-O-Quiz" bingo.

Corona Del Mar, Spanish for "Crown of the Sea," is shown here behind a beachgoer in 1940 or 1941. Located east of Balboa, just across the entrance to Newport Harbor, Corona Del Mar is officially a neighborhood of Newport Beach but has its own post office and Chamber of Commerce. The area is famed for Crystal Cove State Park, which features tide pools, a 1,140-acre underwater scuba park, and 13 newly renovated, 1930s-era beach cottage rentals.

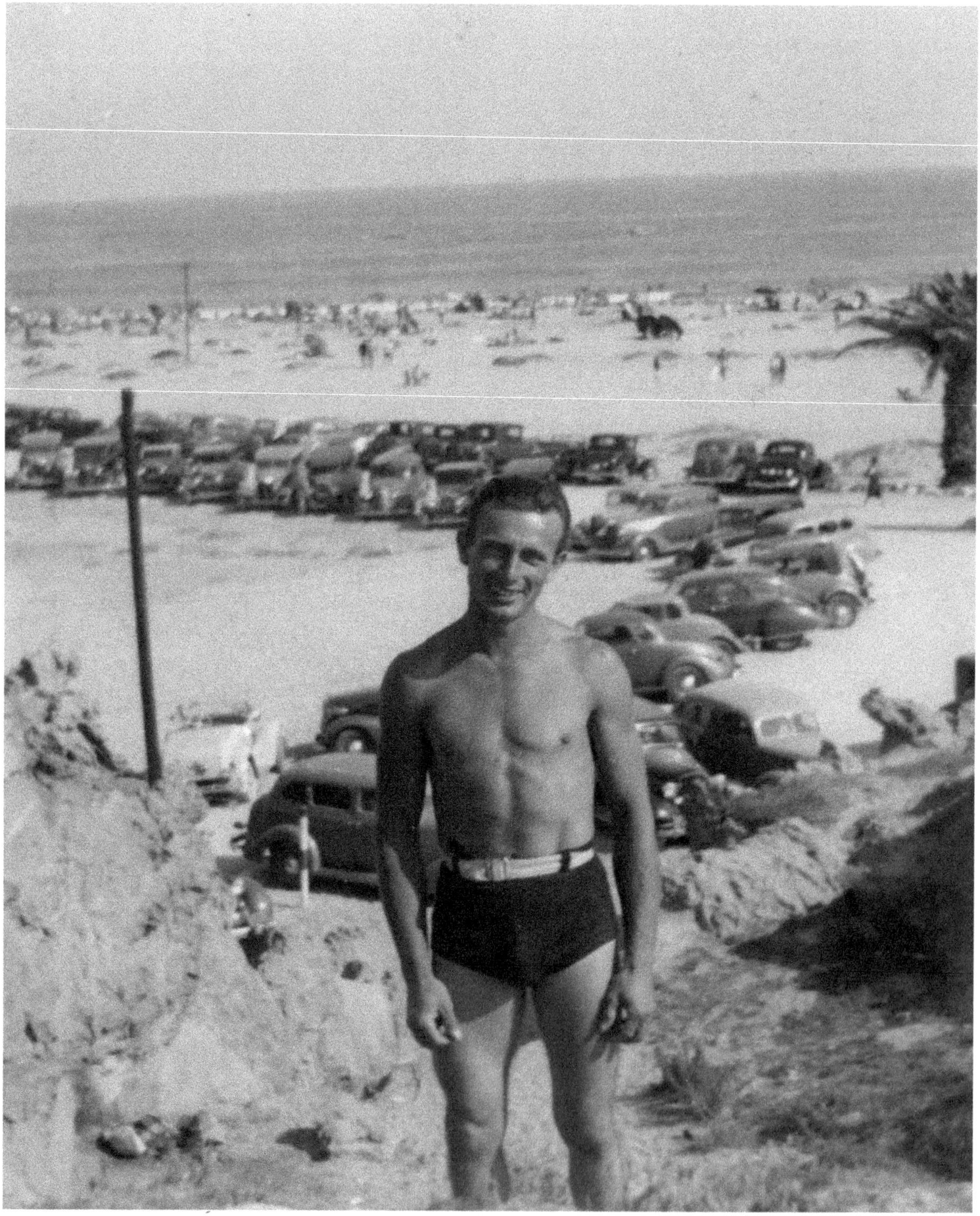

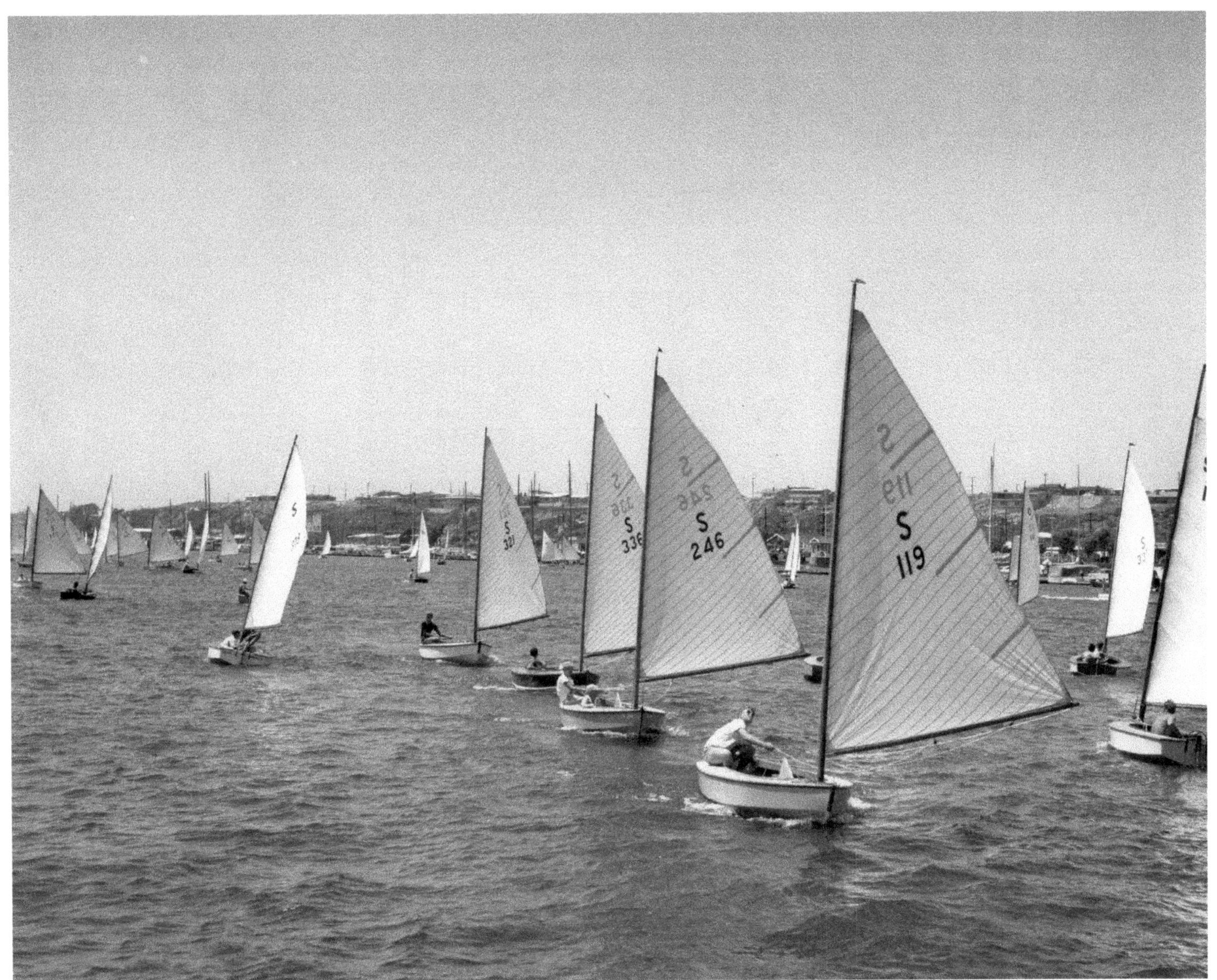

Most yachting activities in Newport Harbor ceased during World War II, but the annual Flight of the Snowbirds sailboat race, shown here in the 1940s, continued throughout the war years. Renamed the Flight of the Lasers in 1970, the event remains a Newport tradition and is now an all-ages event with prizes awarded in such categories as "First Married Couple," "First Parent/Child Team," and "Best Decorated Boat."

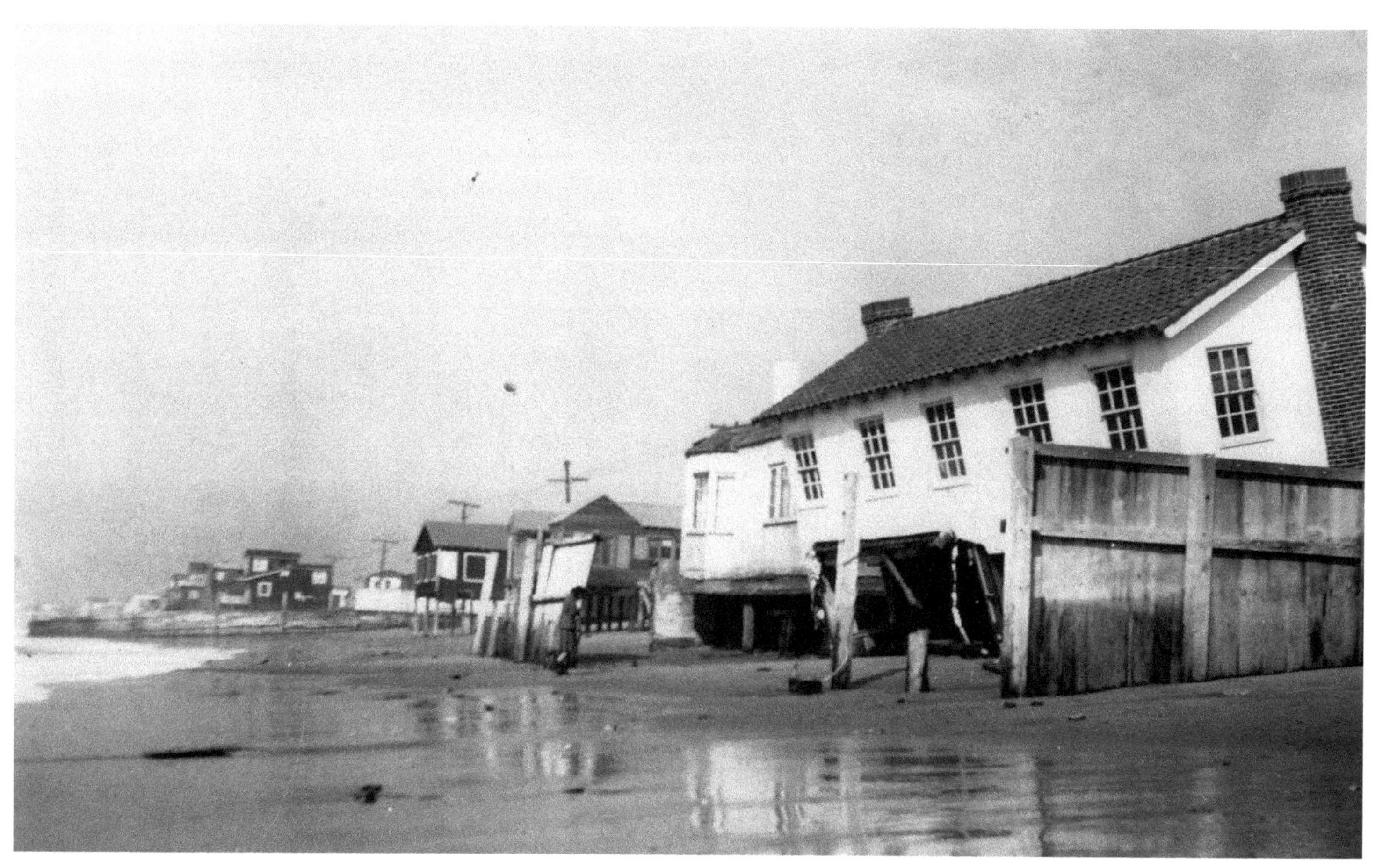

Like many Orange County communities, Sunset Beach owes its existence to the Pacific Electric Railroad. The tracks arrived in the early 1900s, and houses quickly sprang up on either side of them, many built on pilings perilously close to the surf. This dwelling, complete with chimneys on each end, keeled over in a 1942 storm. The quirky housing trend continues to this day; Sunset Beach's most recognized landmark is a high-rise home built inside a water tower.

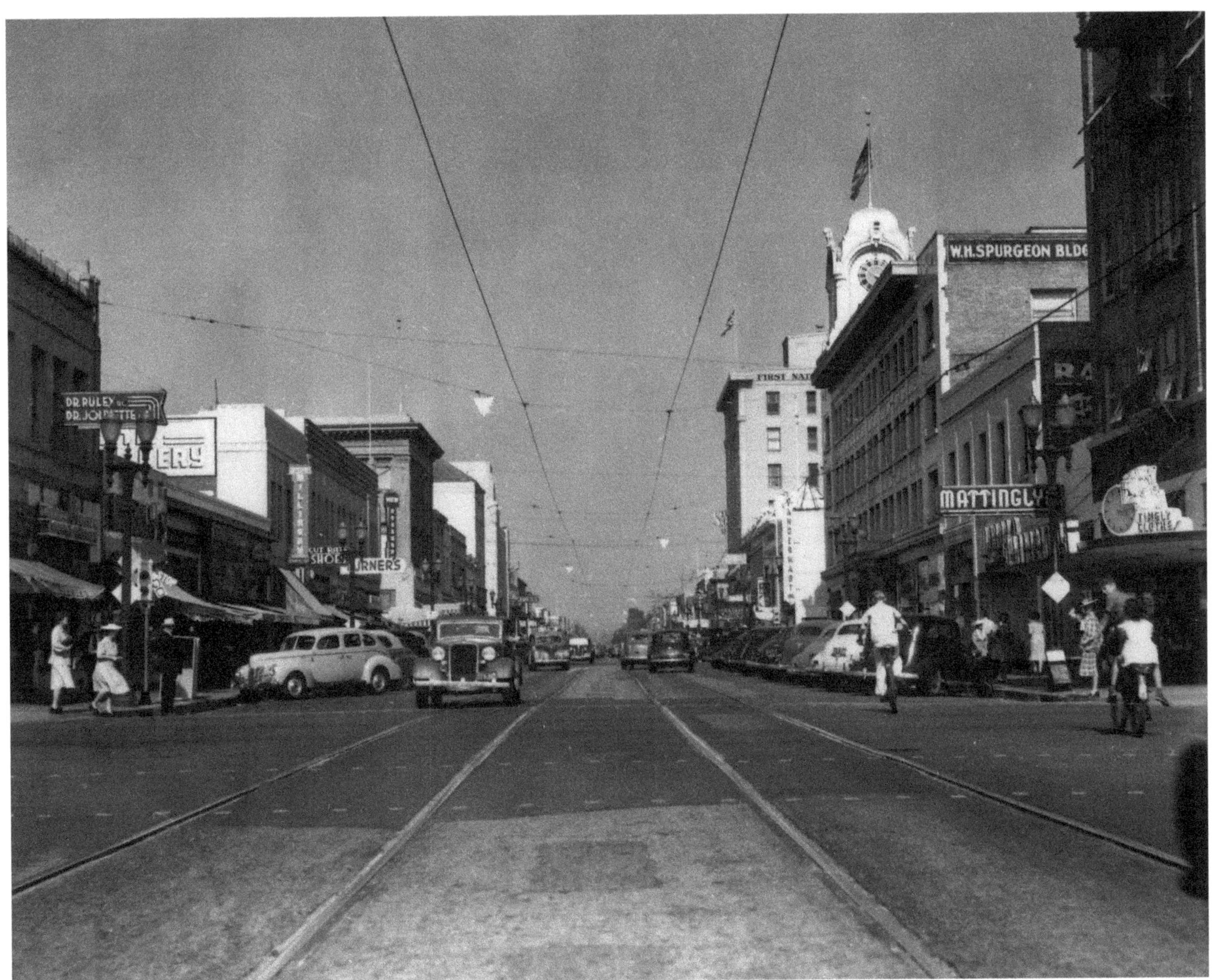

Santa Ana's four-story Spurgeon Building, shown here at right, was erected in 1913 by William Spurgeon, the town's founder. In the 1920s and 1930s the Spurgeon was a fashionable business address. Today it houses artists' studios. For many years the four-sided clock tower crowning the building chimed and played military marches on the hour. A $90,000 restoration was undertaken in 1999 to restore the clock to its former glory.

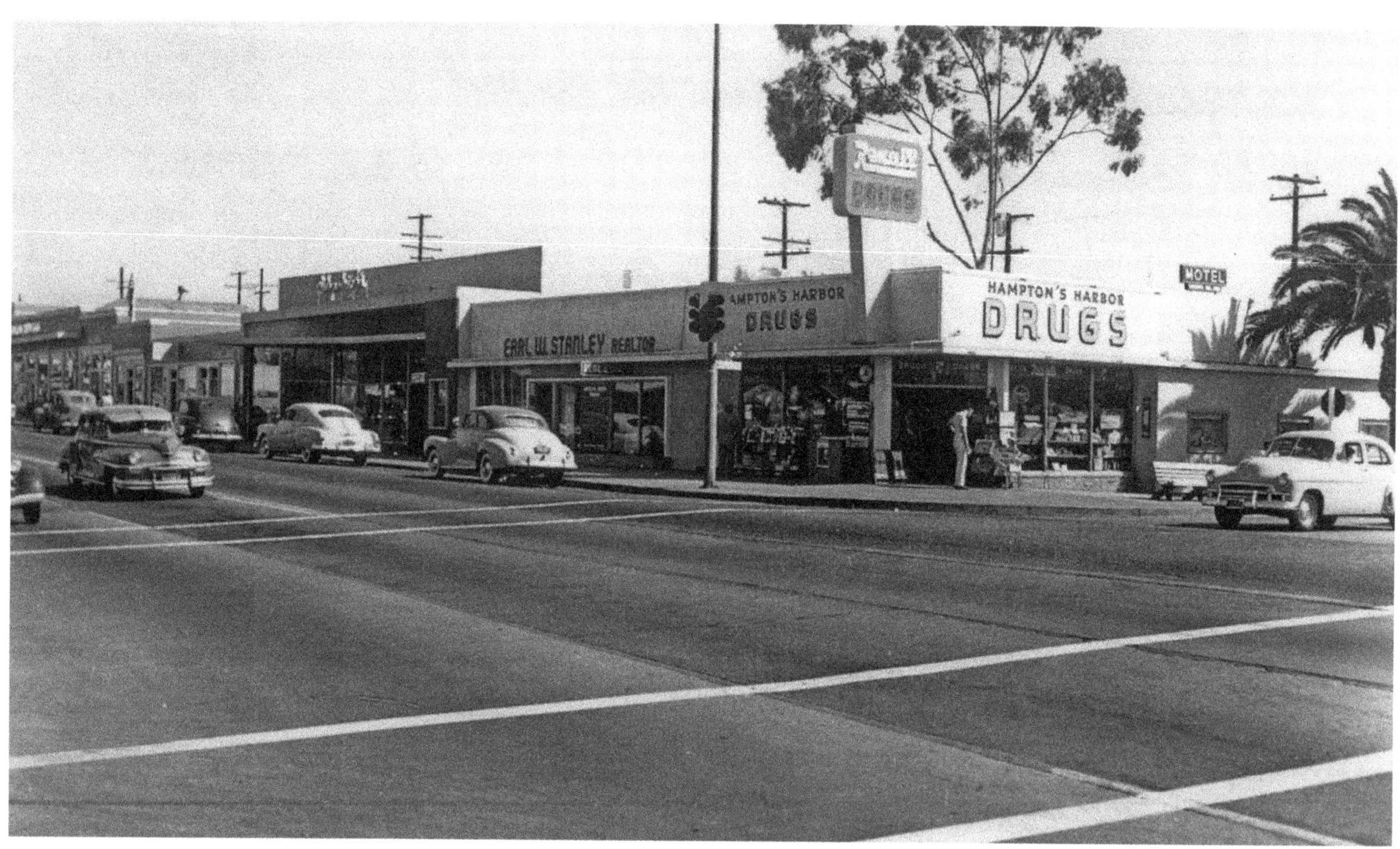

This photo of Corona Del Mar shows the business and shopping district along the Pacific Coast Highway. All streets that cross the highway in the downtown area are named after flowers, in alphabetical order from Acacia to Poppy, and each is uniquely landscaped. Corona Del Mar is home to the Sherman Library and Gardens—a nonprofit garden, library, and historical research center dedicated to the flora of the Pacific Southwest.

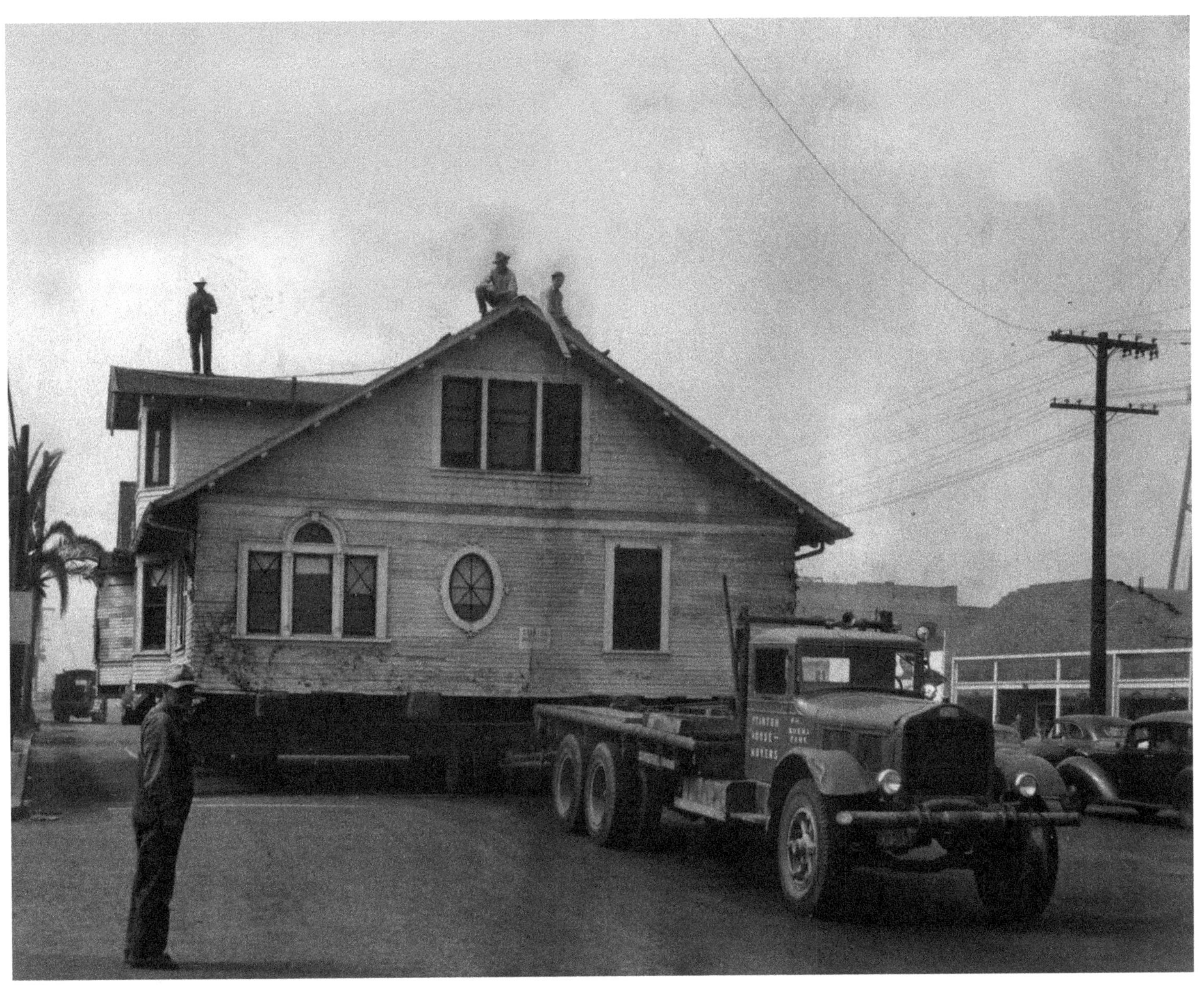

Shown here in 1943, the Weatherly House of La Palma is being sloooowly moved through Buena Park by Stanton House Movers. The historic districts of many Orange County towns, including Buena Park, were created by relocating historically significant buildings from areas threatened by development.

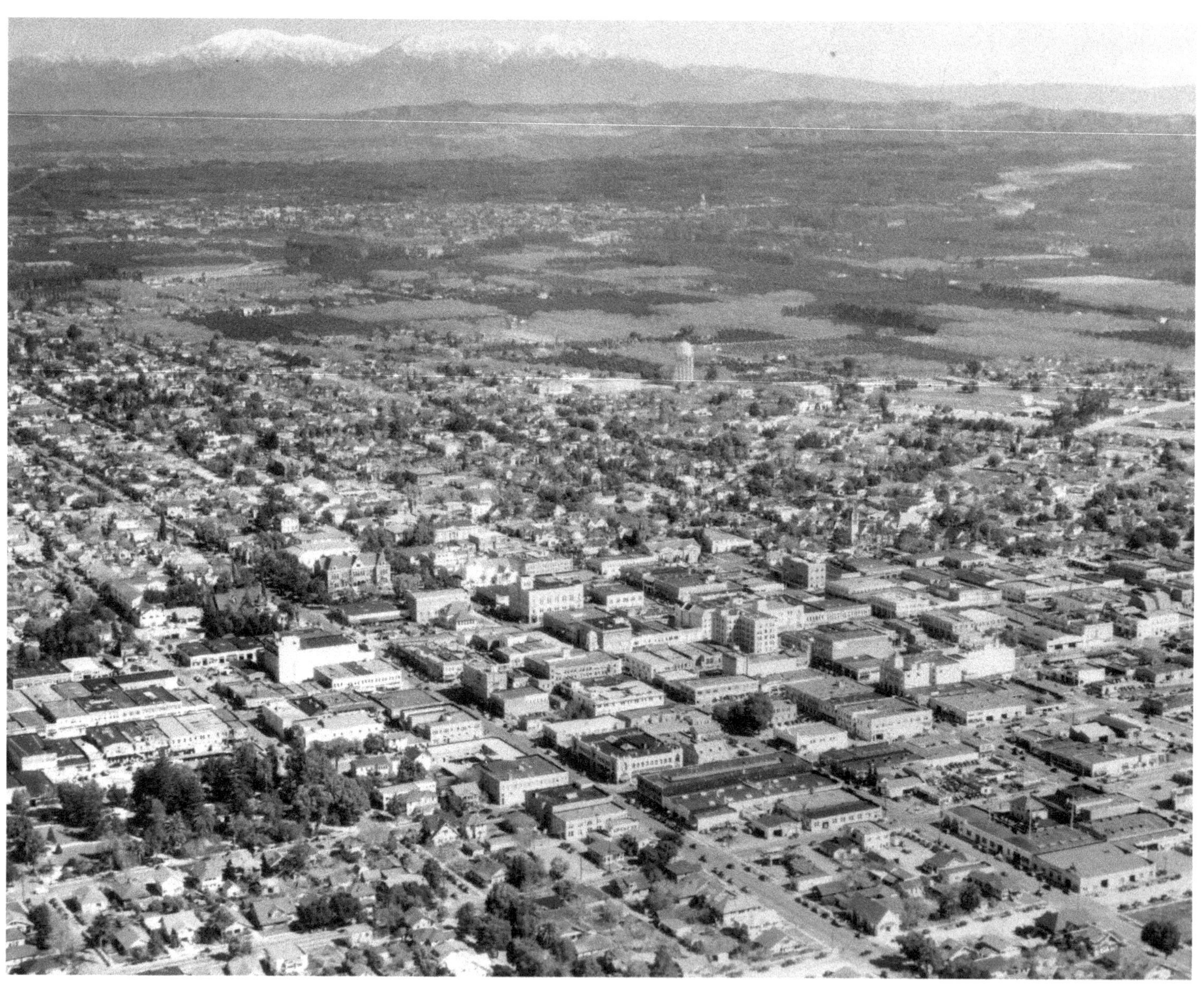

On the day of its incorporation in 1886, Santa Ana counted just under 3,600 people living within the city limits and on the surrounding farmlands. Some 50 years later, around the time this aerial photo was taken, the population had jumped to 32,000. Another 50 years hence that number would be ten times greater. The unprecedented growth of the postwar years would blur the borders of OC's cities and make annexation the only viable means of expansion.

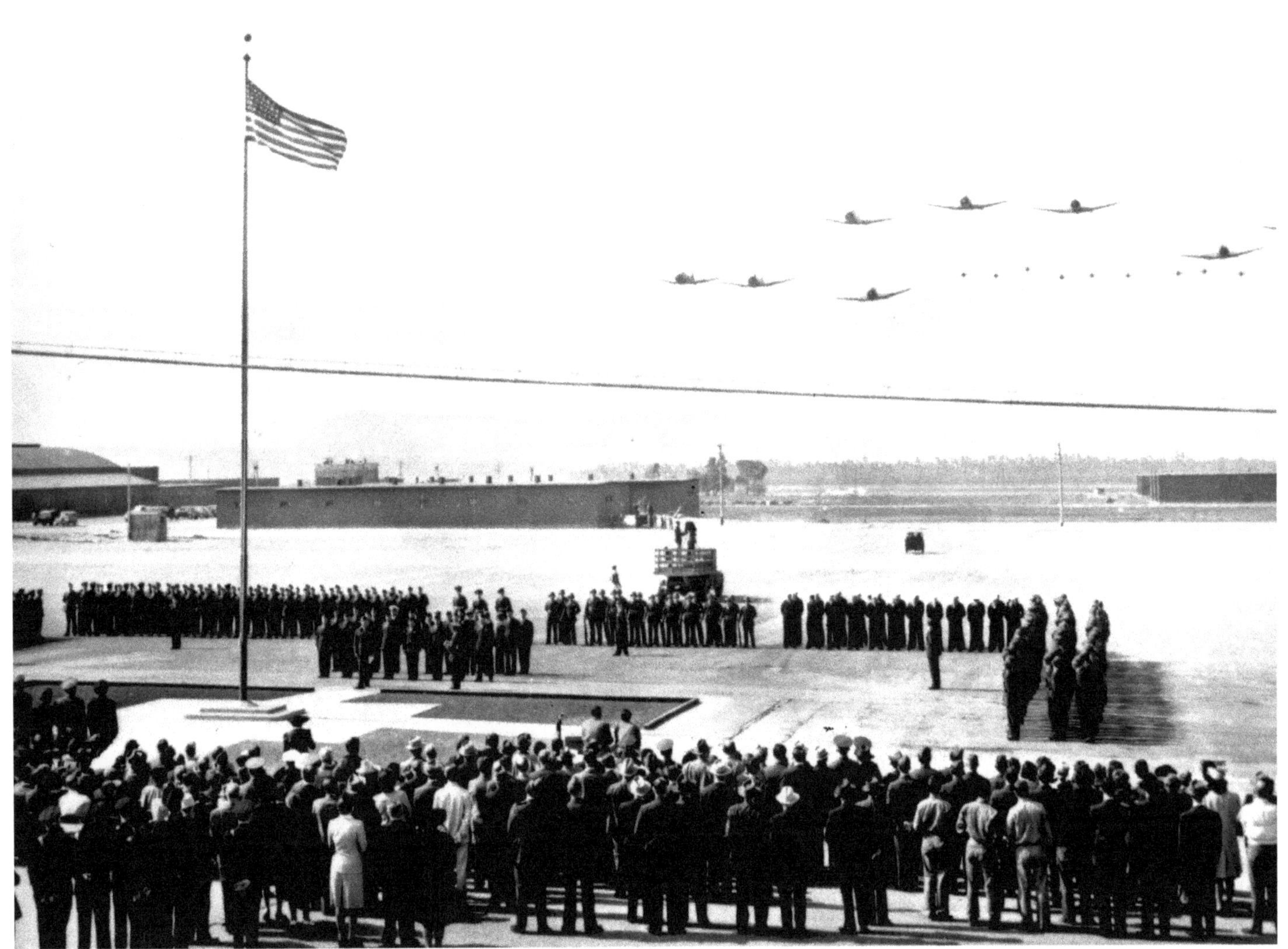

In 1942, when Lieutenant Colonel William Fox flew over Orange County searching for a suitable site on which to locate a Marine Corps air station, the area was still largely orange groves and wide-open spaces. By the time the El Toro station, shown here on opening day, March 17, 1943, officially closed in 1999, suburbia was encroaching on all sides, and a decade of controversy ensued over the facility's future. Further complications arose with the discovery of the base's contaminated groundwater.

Following Spread: Downtown Orange today looks much the same as it did in this 1944 shot of Glassell Street, viewed north from the plaza. Despite the solid line of parked cars on both sides, the street is devoid of people, emblematic of the mass overseas exodus of the city's male population during World War II. Approximately 50 Orange residents lost their lives in combat.

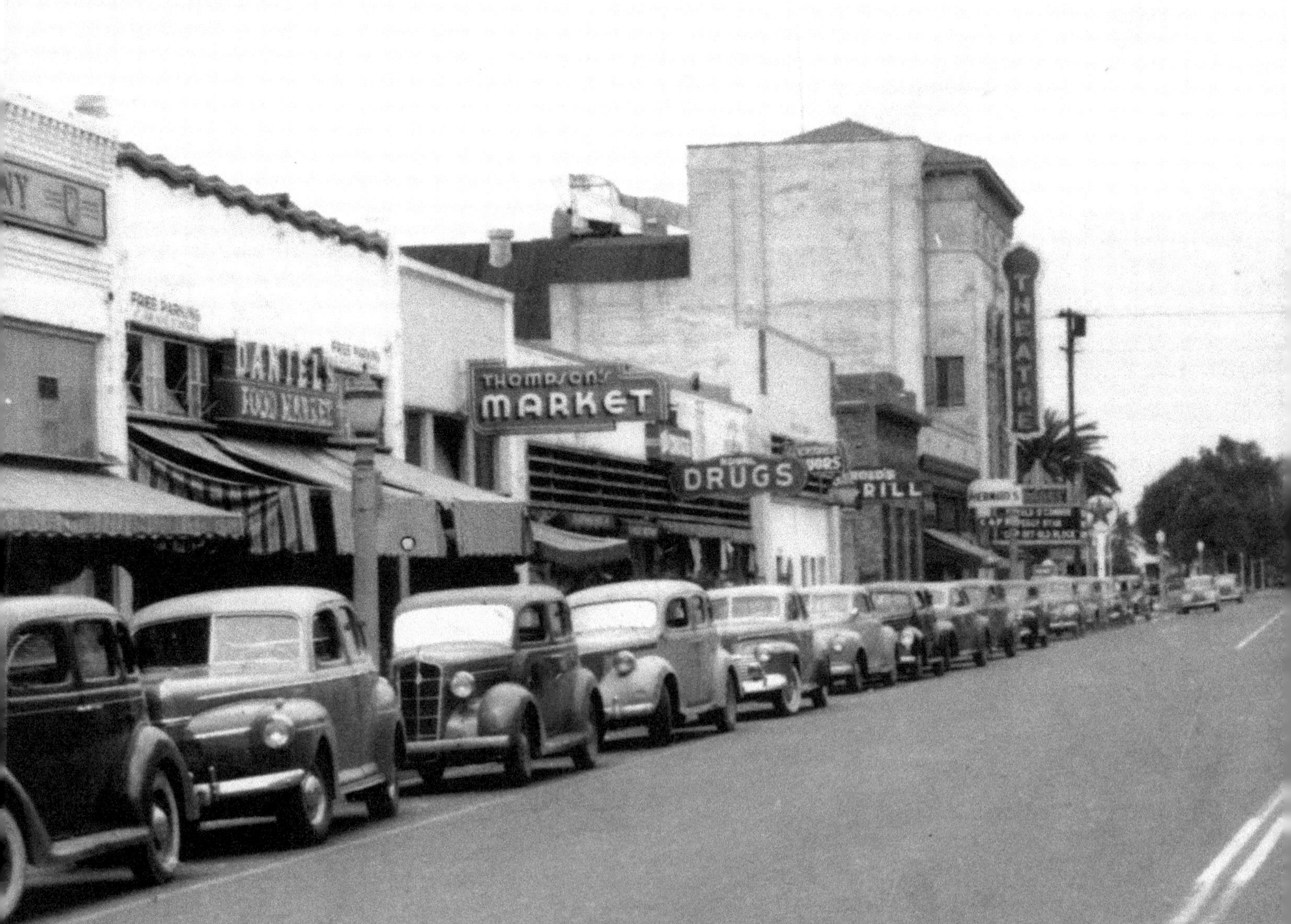
FREE PARKING
DANIEL'S
FOOD MARKET
FREE PARKING
THOMPSON'S
MARKET
DRUGS
RILL
THEATRE

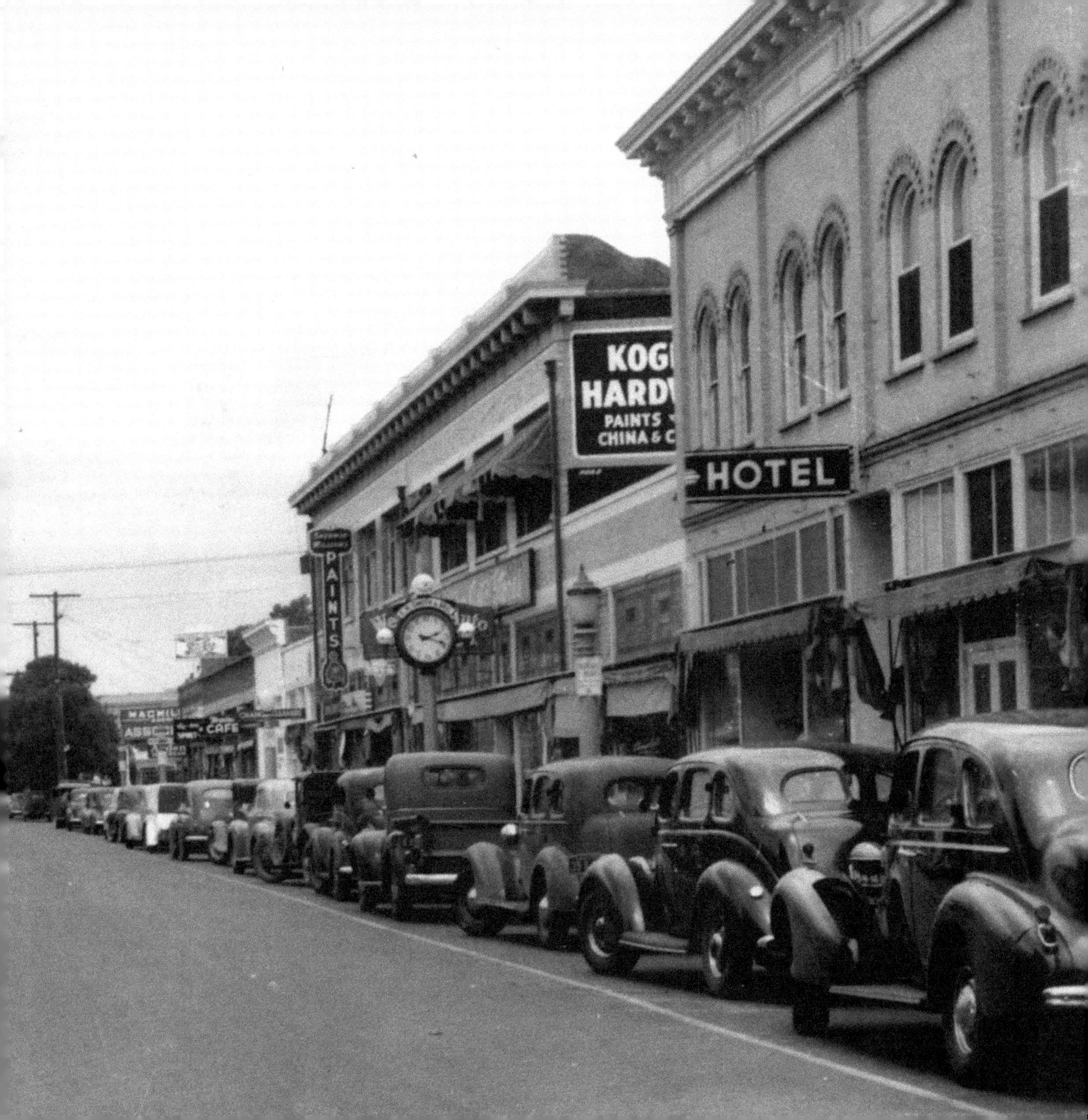
HOTEL
PAINTS
CAFE

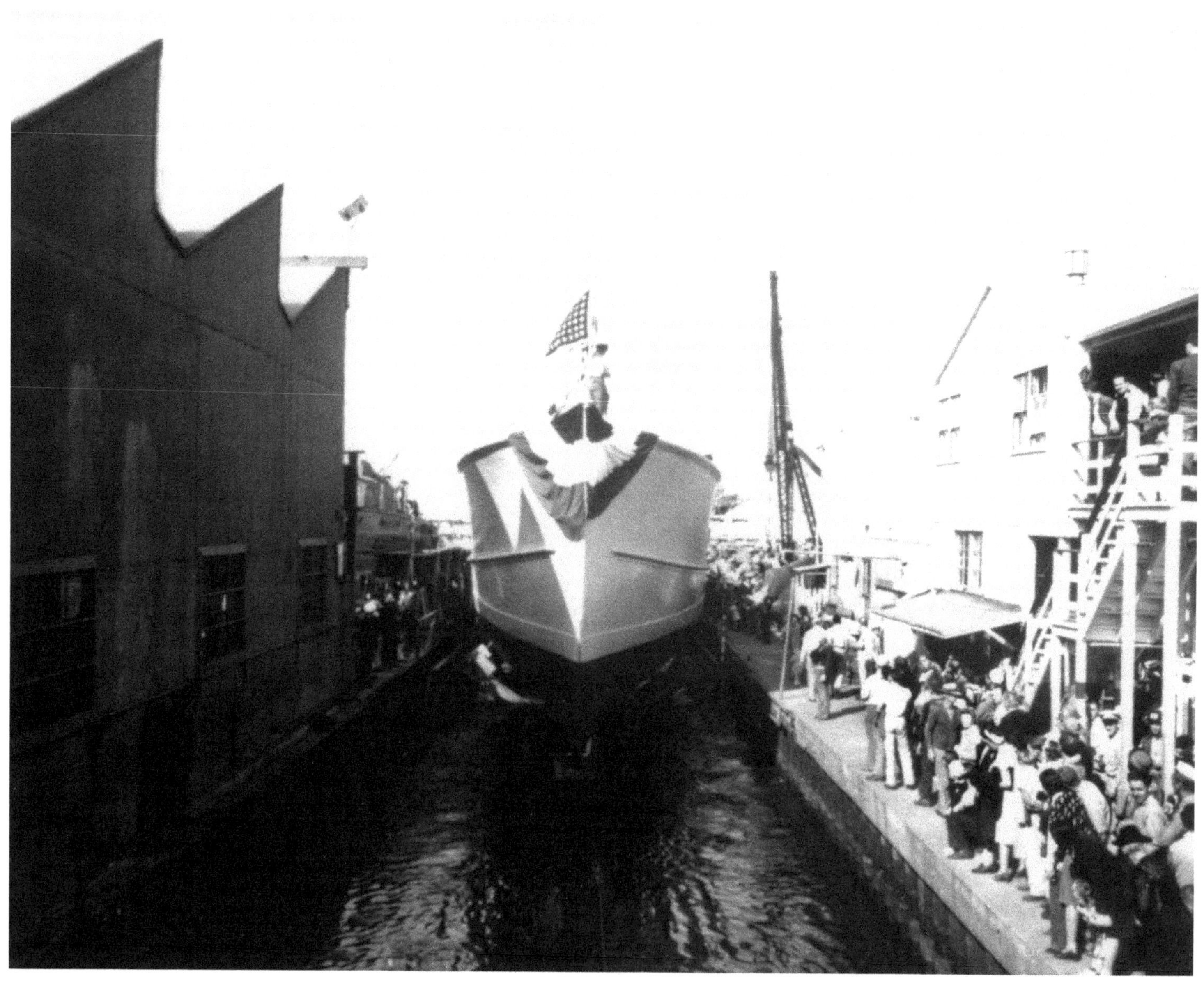

The South Coast Boat Building Company operated out of Newport from 1933 to 1964. During World War II the boatyard produced 28 Yard Minesweepers such as this one that patrolled the California coastline for Japanese submarines. Many were later converted to private use, such as YMS 328, which became John Wayne's yacht *Wild Goose. Wild Goose* is currently available for charter and said to be haunted by the Duke himself.

Endless Summer

(1946–1967)

After World War II, thousands of GIs who had been stationed in Orange County and liked the year-round temperate climate and laid-back lifestyle returned here to live, causing an unprecedented population boom. The intense demand for housing led to the development of the mass-produced California ranch house, characterized by an open floor plan, indoor/outdoor living spaces, and an attached garage to accommodate Southern California's growing obsession with the automobile.

The 1956 Eisenhower Interstate Highway Act ushered in the freeway age. By the end of the 1960s the 5 Freeway would stretch from San Diego almost to the Canadian border. The 22, 55, 57, and 405 freeways appeared shortly afterward, and Orange County gridlock soon rivaled that of Los Angeles. Environmental concerns and shrinking funds finally halted the freeway-construction onslaught in the 1970s.

The 1950s saw the birth of "tiki" culture. The popularity of Trader Vic's and similar restaurants soon filtered into mainstream architecture. Entire tracts of mid-century homes exhibited elements of toned-down tiki bar architecture. By the end of the 1960s there were 17 motels and 42 apartment complexes in the Anaheim phone book with names containing some combination of the words palm, beachcomber, Tahiti, paradise, or island.

In the 1960s Orange County became known worldwide for surfing, thanks to the lyrics of the Beach Boys and the tireless promotion of surfing pioneer Duke Kahanamoku, to whom a surfing museum is dedicated in Huntington Beach. The same time period saw an influx of theme parks. The Fun Zone on Balboa was joined by dozens of unique tourist attractions, many of them in Buena Park where the success of Knott's Berry Farm served as inspiration. The California Alligator Farm, Movieland Wax Museum, Palace of Living Art, Cars of the Stars and Planes of Fame, and the Japanese Village and Deer Park formed Buena Park's Entertainment Zone. Disneyland debuted in 1955 in neighboring Anaheim.

The 1970s and 1980s brought increasing awareness of Orange County's architectural legacy, especially in Santa Ana and Orange, where Art Deco sits cheek by jowl with postmodern. The downtown districts of both cities are designated national historic landmarks. Once considered a backward cousin of Los Angeles, Orange County today is internationally recognized for its beaches, shopping, and cultural and entertainment opportunities.

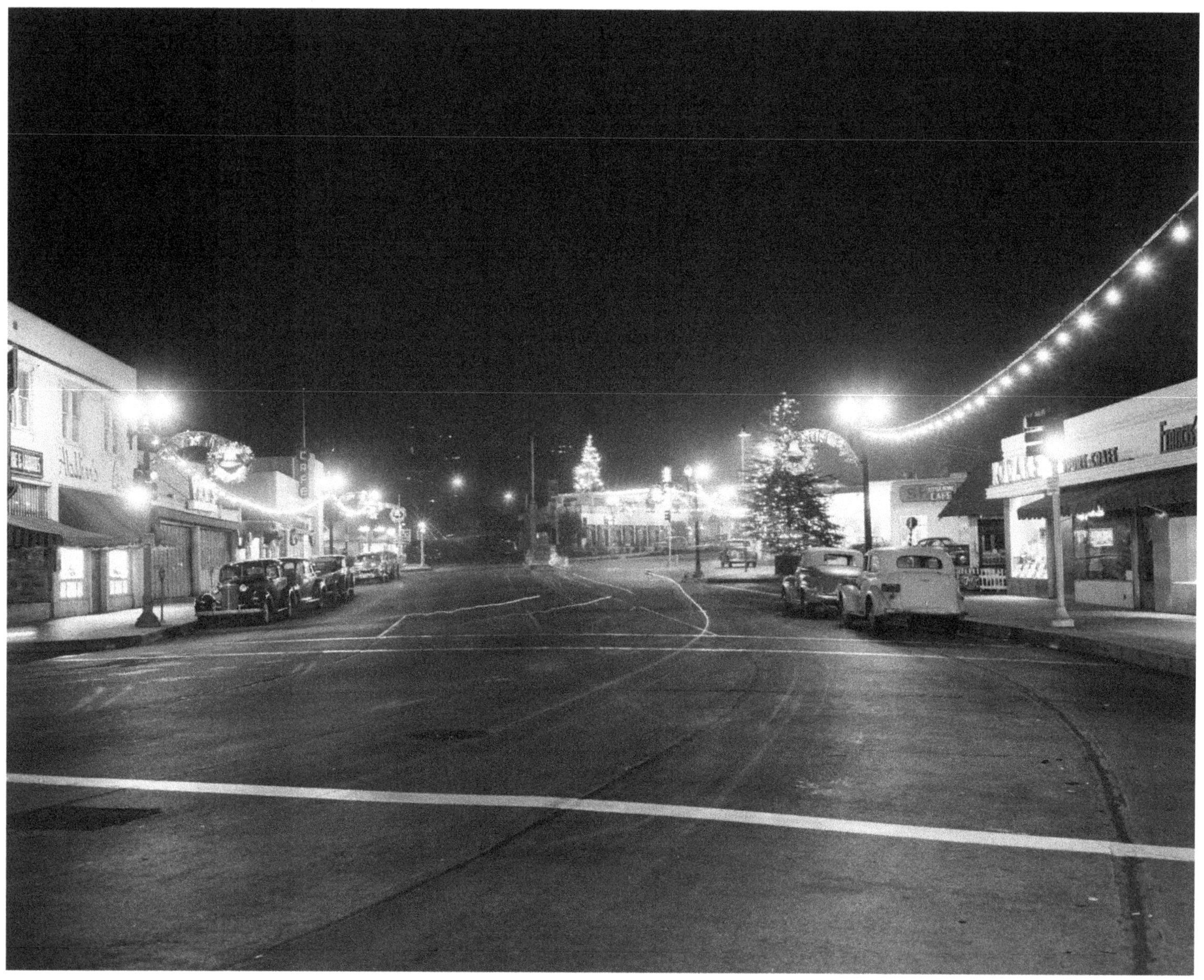

The war had been over for a year and a half when this peaceful shot was taken of downtown Laguna Beach lit up for the holidays. In the postwar boom that would soon overtake most of Orange County, the city of Laguna Beach would become a top tourist destination, renowned for art, stunning ocean-view property, fine dining, and dozens of beautiful beaches, each unique.

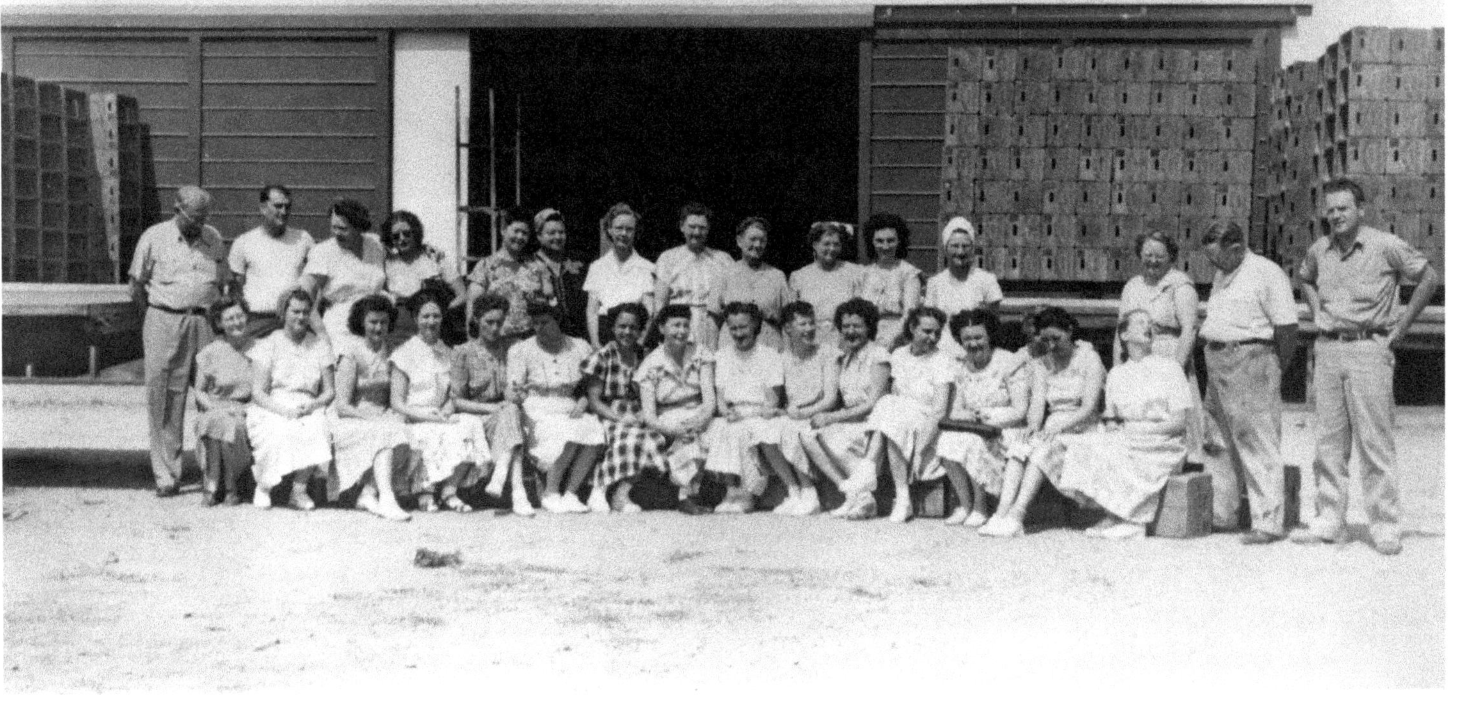

The city of Placentia, from the Latin for "a pleasant place," organized its first orange growers cooperative in 1894. Thirty-six local ranchers banded together to package, advertise, and deliver citrus to a national market. Typically located near rail spurs, packinghouses such as this one, shown in 1949, sorted, stamped, and individually wrapped oranges for shipment in wooden crates. Crate labels evolved over time into works of art, highly prized by collectors today.

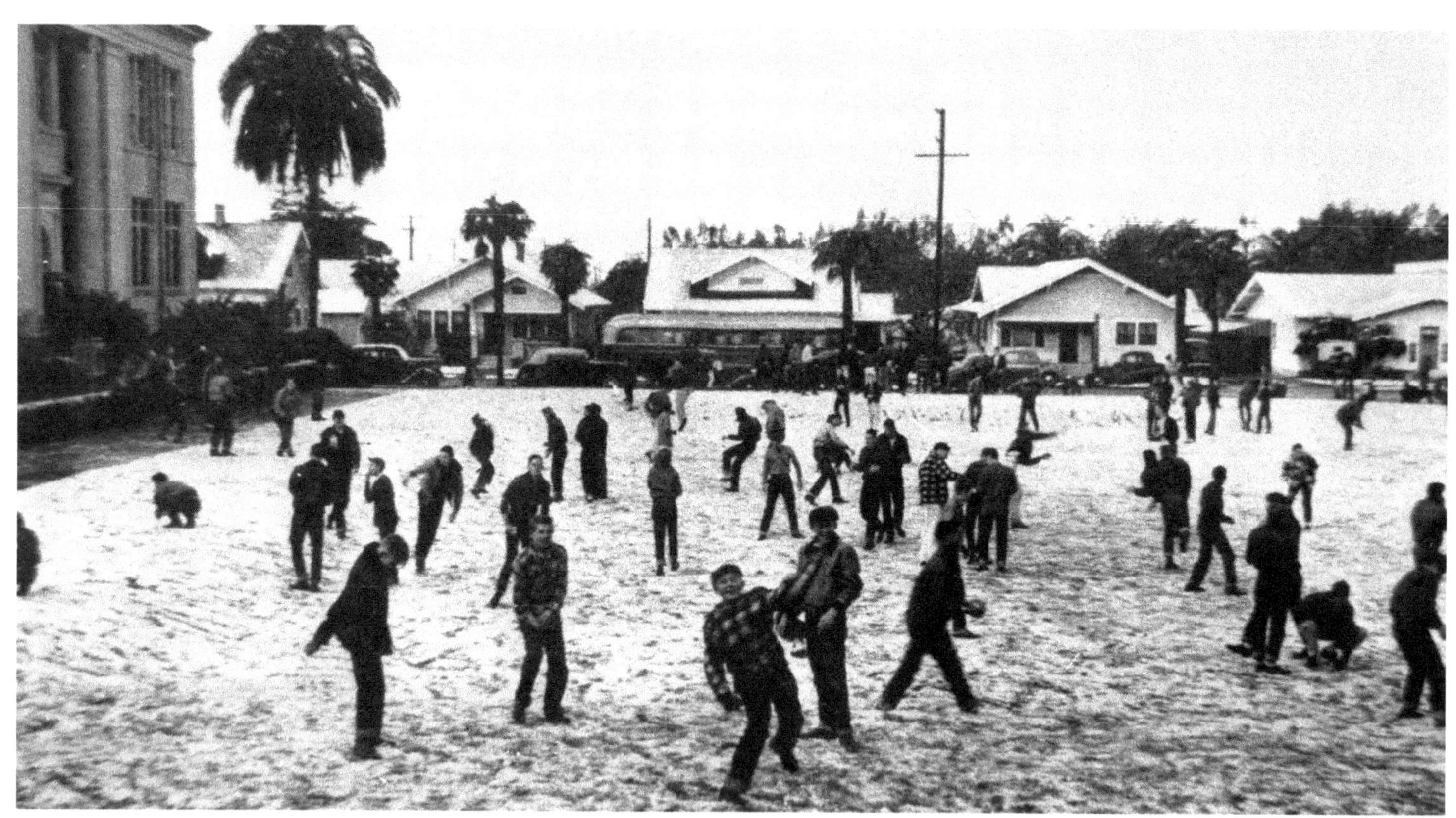

In 1949 students at Orange Union High School witnessed a rare event—the area's only recorded snowfall in decades. OUHS was one of the first high schools built in Orange County and produced an Olympic gold medalist, Fred Kelly, who won the 100-meter hurdles in 1912. Since 1954 the neoclassical building has been part of Chapman University, located at 333 North Glassell, and is on the National Register of Historic Places.

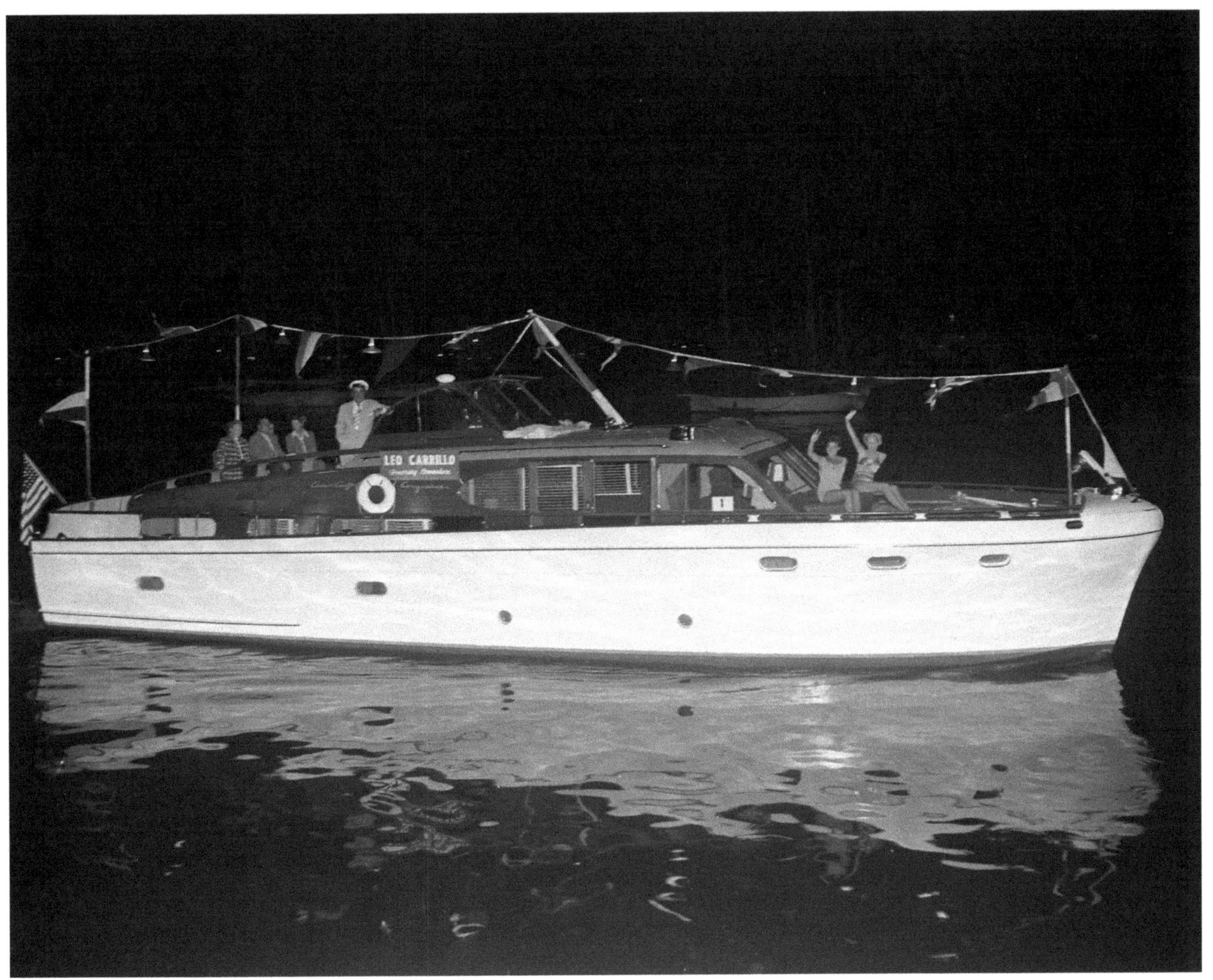

Actor Leo Carrillo, best known as Pancho in the 1950s television series *The Cisco Kid,* was an ardent preservationist (a state park near Malibu is named for him) and boater. He is shown here participating in a late-1940s Newport Harbor boat parade, a predecessor of today's Newport Beach Christmas Boat Parade, a five-day event featuring up to 150 lighted boats. This Yuletide classic attracts 200,000 people annually.

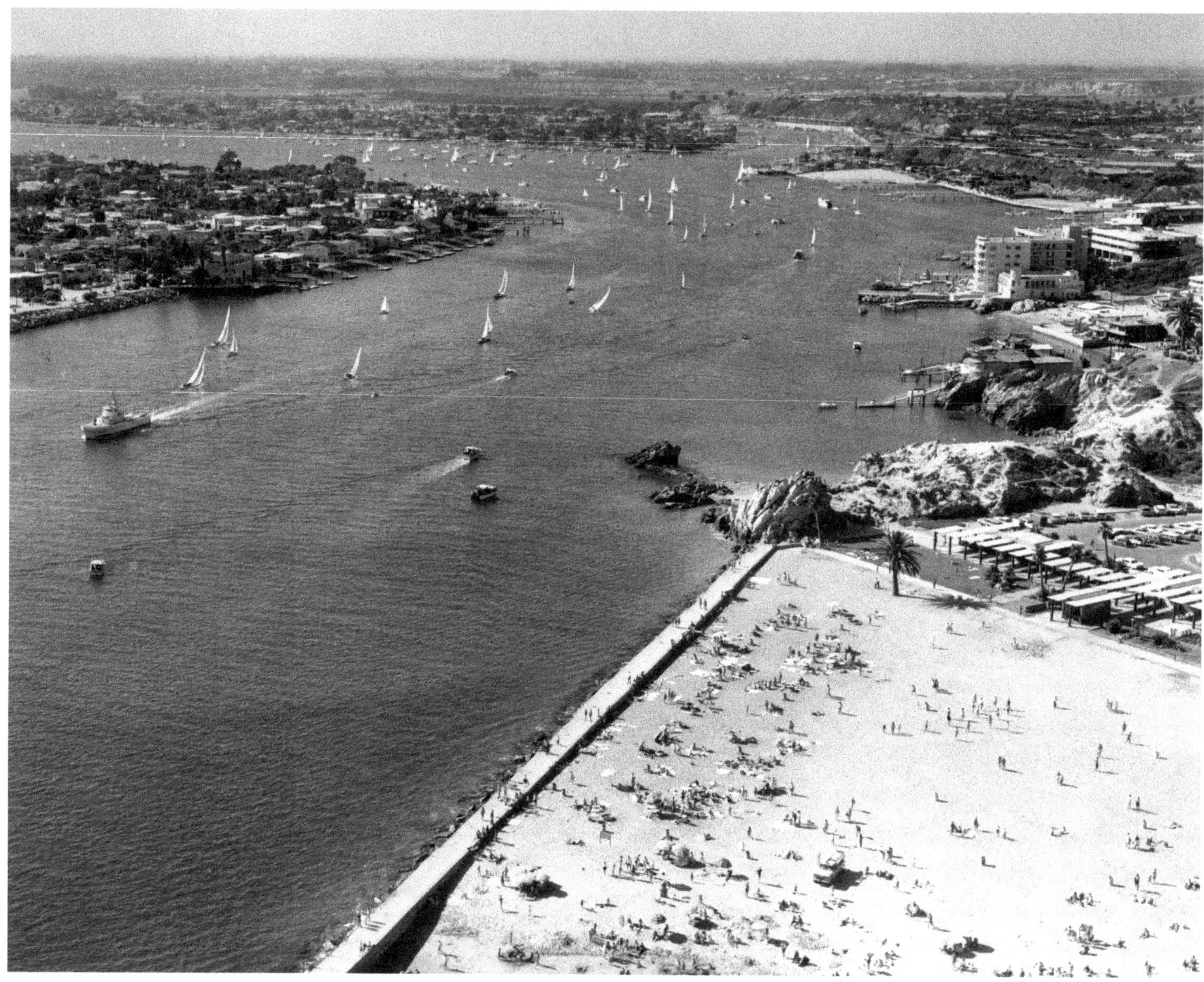

This gorgeous 1950s shot of Corona del Mar, seen at lower-right, was taken looking northwest across the channel to Balboa Peninsula. The most daunting challenge faced by early developers of Newport Harbor was the treacherous channel, which was shallow and riddled with hidden sandbars. Many lives were lost attempting to navigate it before the jetties were improved and the harbor dredged in the 1930s. Balboa Island was created with the sand that was removed.

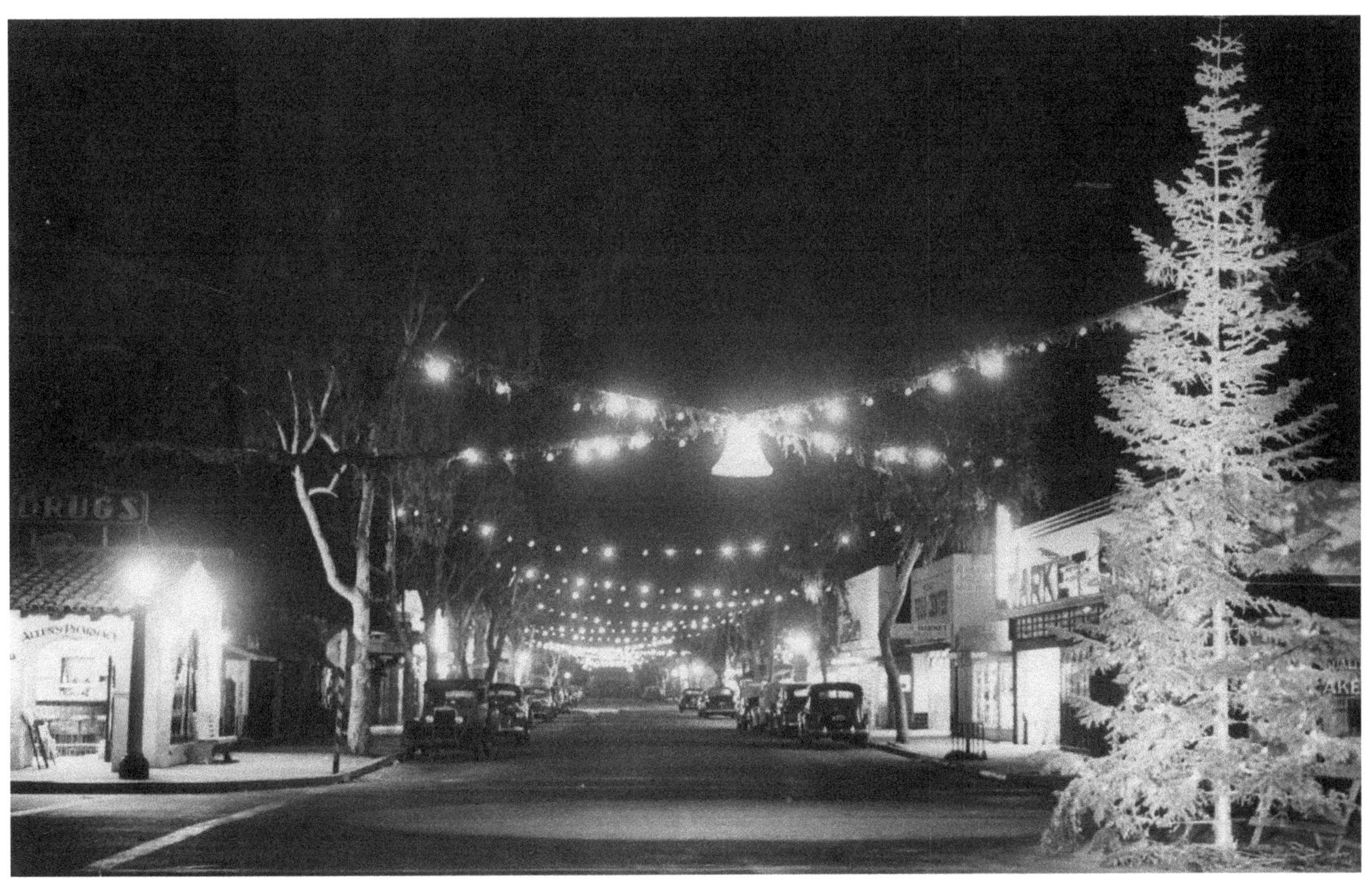

Though temperatures in Orange County in December are typically in the 60s, and the chance of snow is remote (to say the least), the residents of the tiny island of Balboa in Newport Beach have Christmas cheer in abundance. This 1950s view of Marine Street from Park Avenue reveals a town eager to put wartime rationing and blackouts behind it.

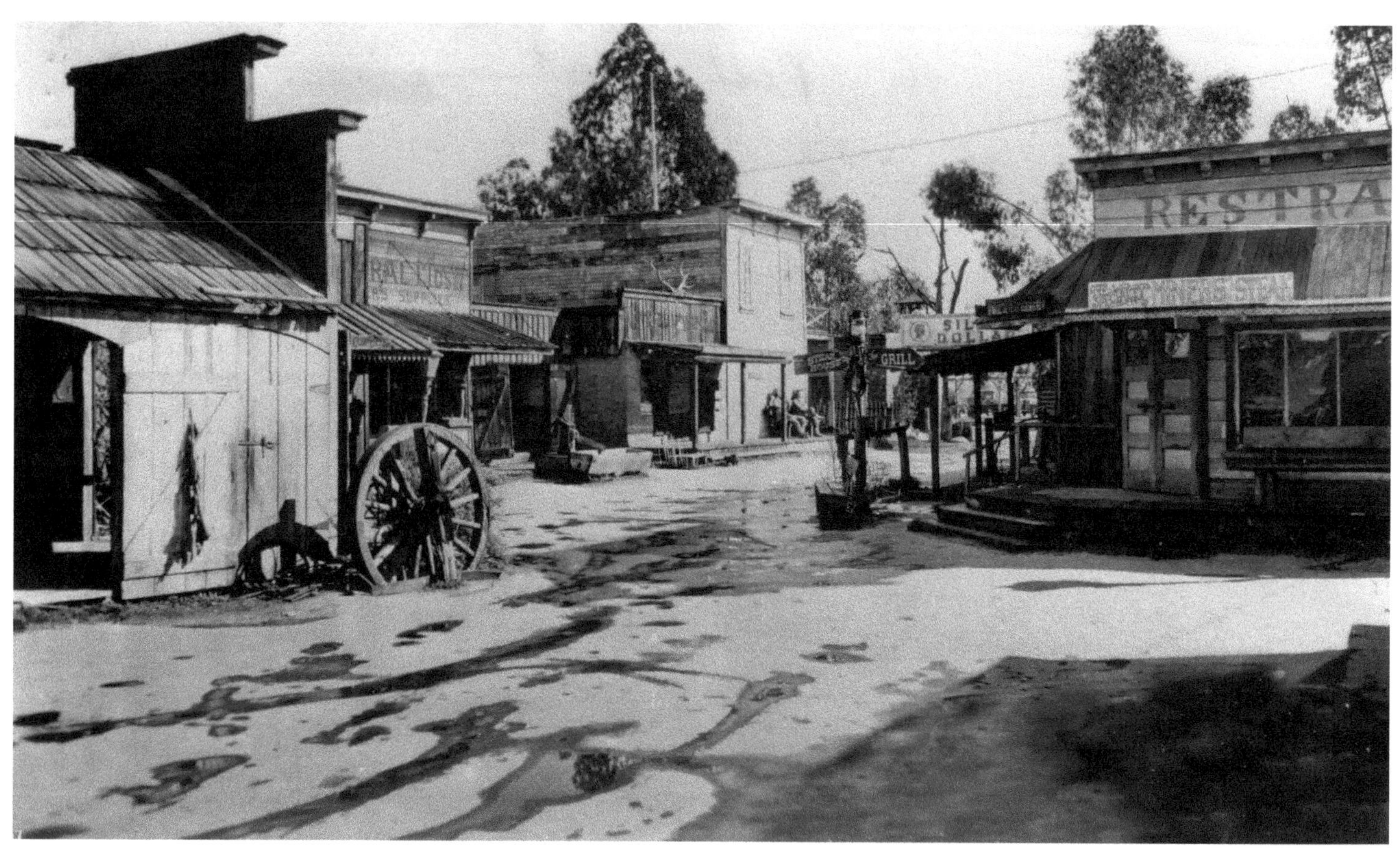

The Ghost Town section of Knott's Berry Farm, built in 1940, is composed of buildings and artifacts relocated from actual Arizona and California ghost towns by founder Walter Knott. The success of Knott's, considered "America's first theme park," paved the way for a slew of other tourist attractions that would follow in the 1960s. Although other areas of the park have succumbed to modernization, Ghost Town today looks much as it did in this 1950s photo.

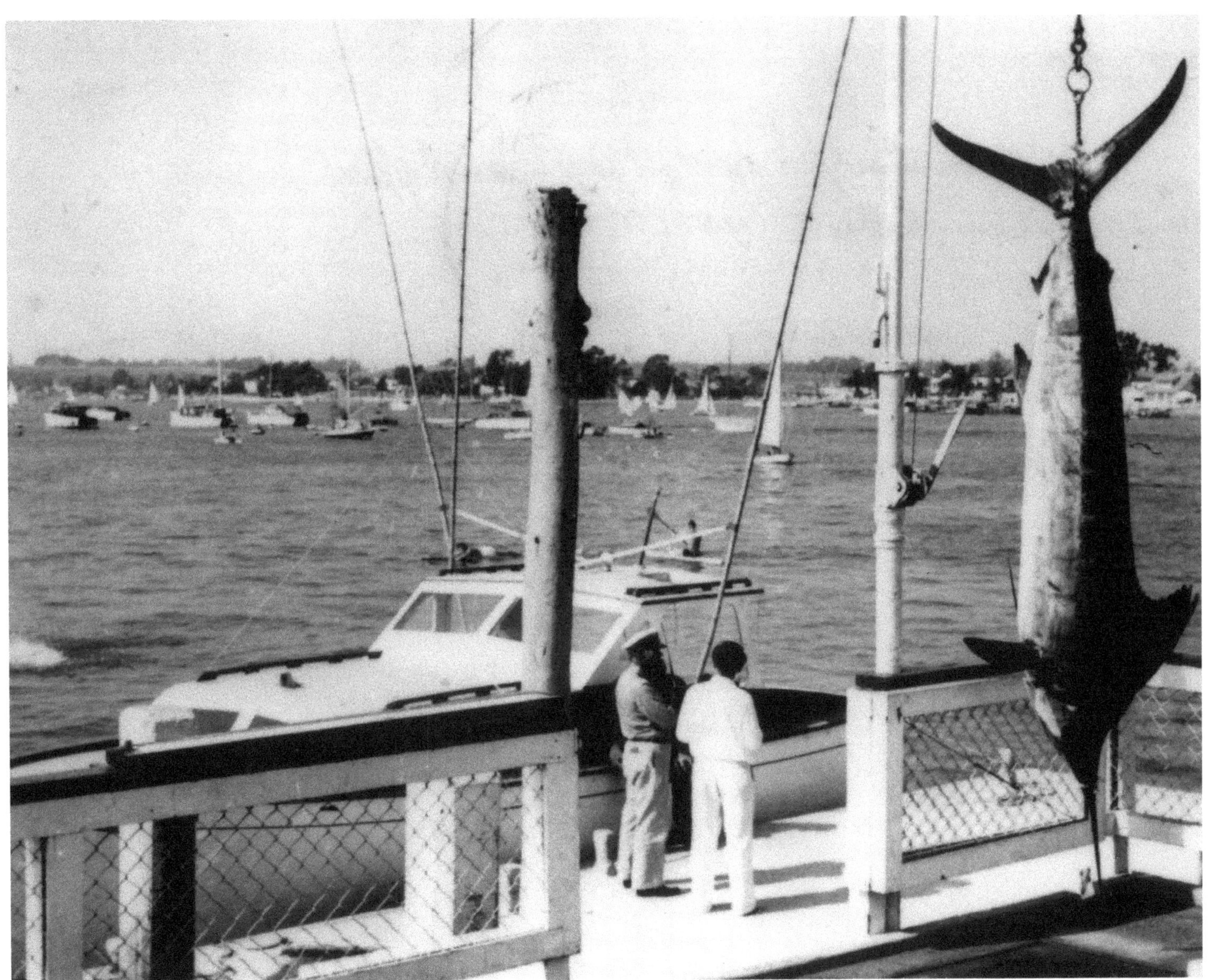

The Balboa Angling Club was formed in 1926, and the first official weigh station was located on Washington Street next to the harbormaster's office. Newport Harbor at that time was close to sport-fishing heaven, and marlin catches like this one, ca. 1950, not uncommon. Overfishing and increased regulations have since impacted the sport. The Balboa Angling Club today promotes conservation and the catch and release program.

A single-engine Piper aircraft sits in front of the control tower at Orange County Airport in this 1950s photograph. The airport originated in the 1920s as a private landing strip built by aviation pioneer Eddie Martin. During World War II it was seized for military use. Renamed John Wayne Airport in 1979 in honor of one of the county's most famous residents, the facility features a larger-than-life bronze statue of the actor, created by sculptor Robert Summers.

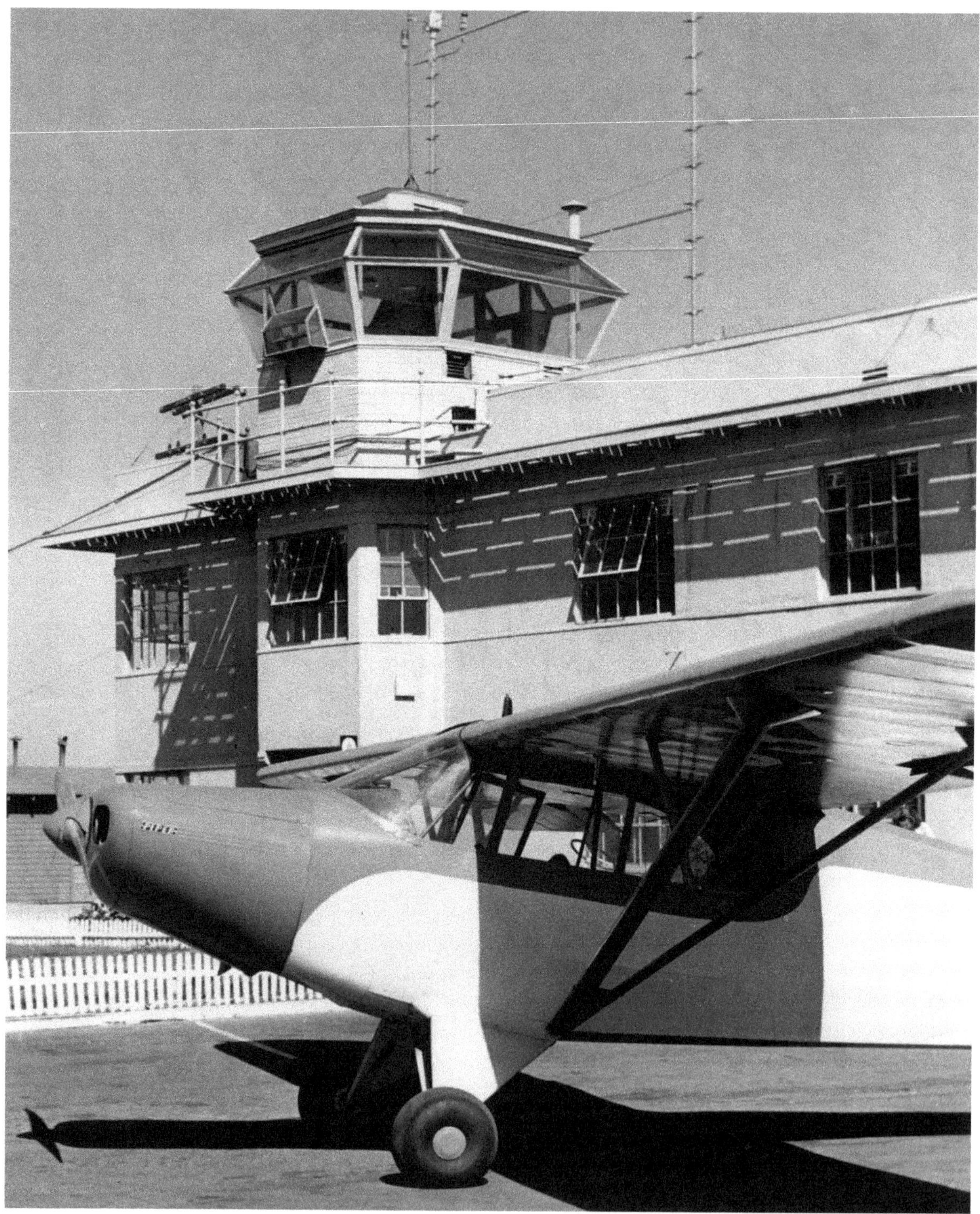

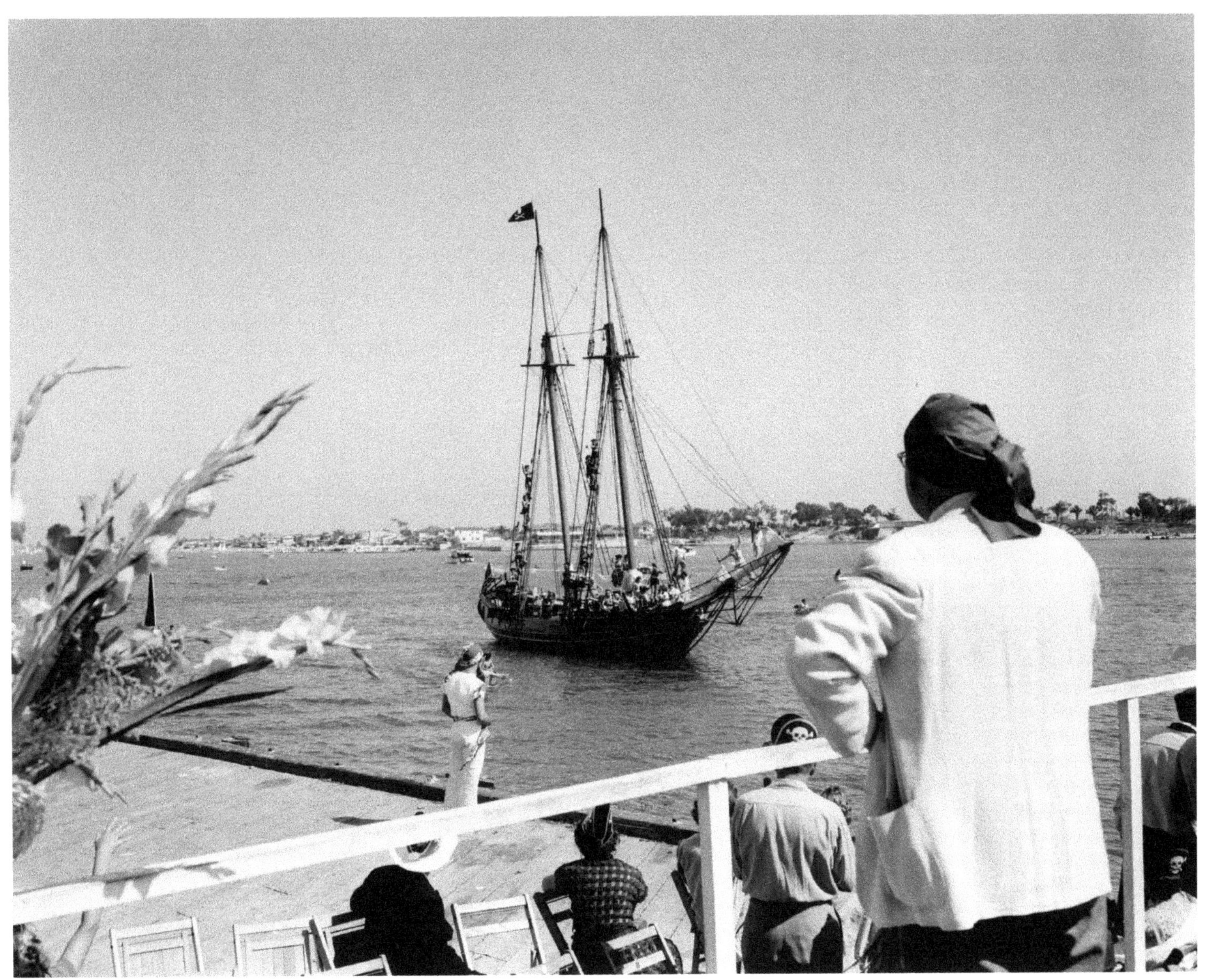

Shown here in 1953 is James Cagney's boat the *Swift,* a replica of an American-made brig captured by the British in 1783. Recreated as a topsail schooner in 1938, Cagney's *Swift* was featured in numerous Hollywood pirate movies and in more recent times has been available for charter and research. Between 1938 and 1948 Cagney owned tiny Collins Island, off the northwest tip of Balboa Island, leasing it to the Coast Guard during World War II.

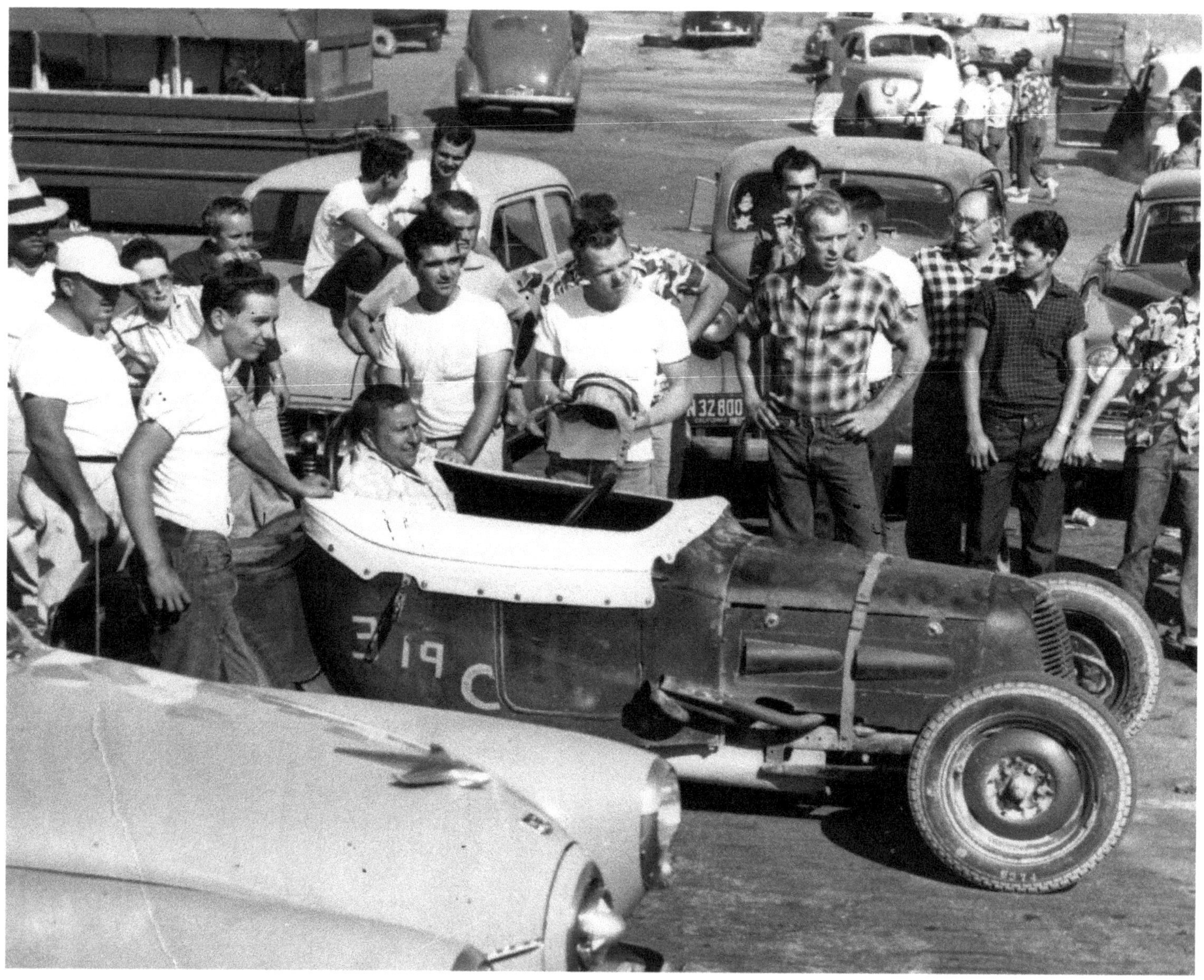

Between 1950 and 1959, drag races were held on an unused runway at Orange County Airport (now John Wayne Airport). Founded by C. J. "Pappy" Hart and Creighton Hunter, Santa Ana Drags was the first professional drag strip to charge admission and featured revolutionary, computerized speed clocks. The races were later moved to the Los Angeles County fairgrounds in Pomona. The man seated in the hot rod is possibly Creighton Hunter.

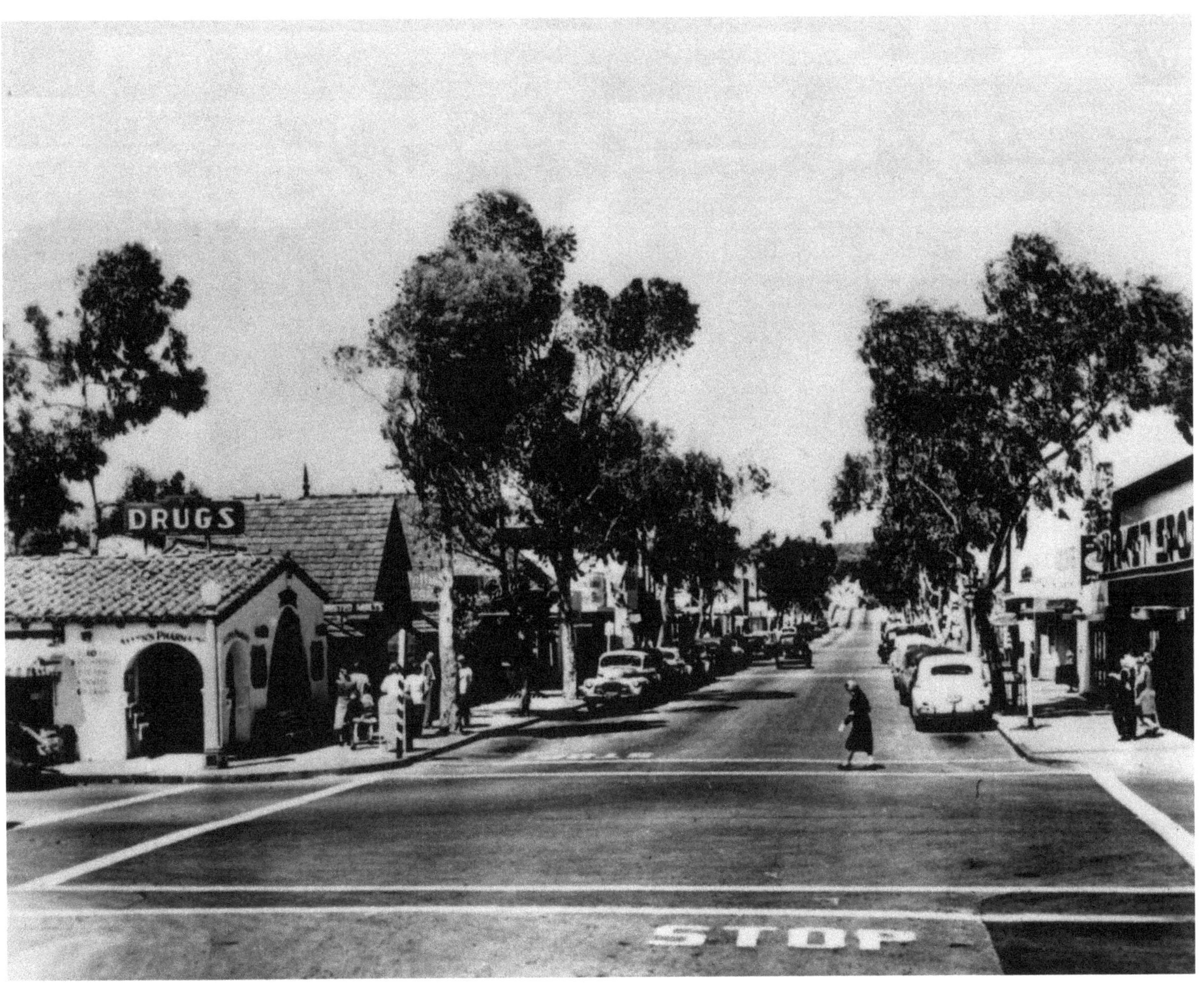

For several decades starting in the 1930s, tiny Balboa Island, shown here in the 1950s, was the site of an annual ritual known as "Bal Week." Every year during spring break, the usually sedate island's population soared as thousands of college students descended on it, sleeping dozens to a room and prompting thousands of arrests. The good times officially ended in 1966 when the Balboa Rendezvous burned to the ground.

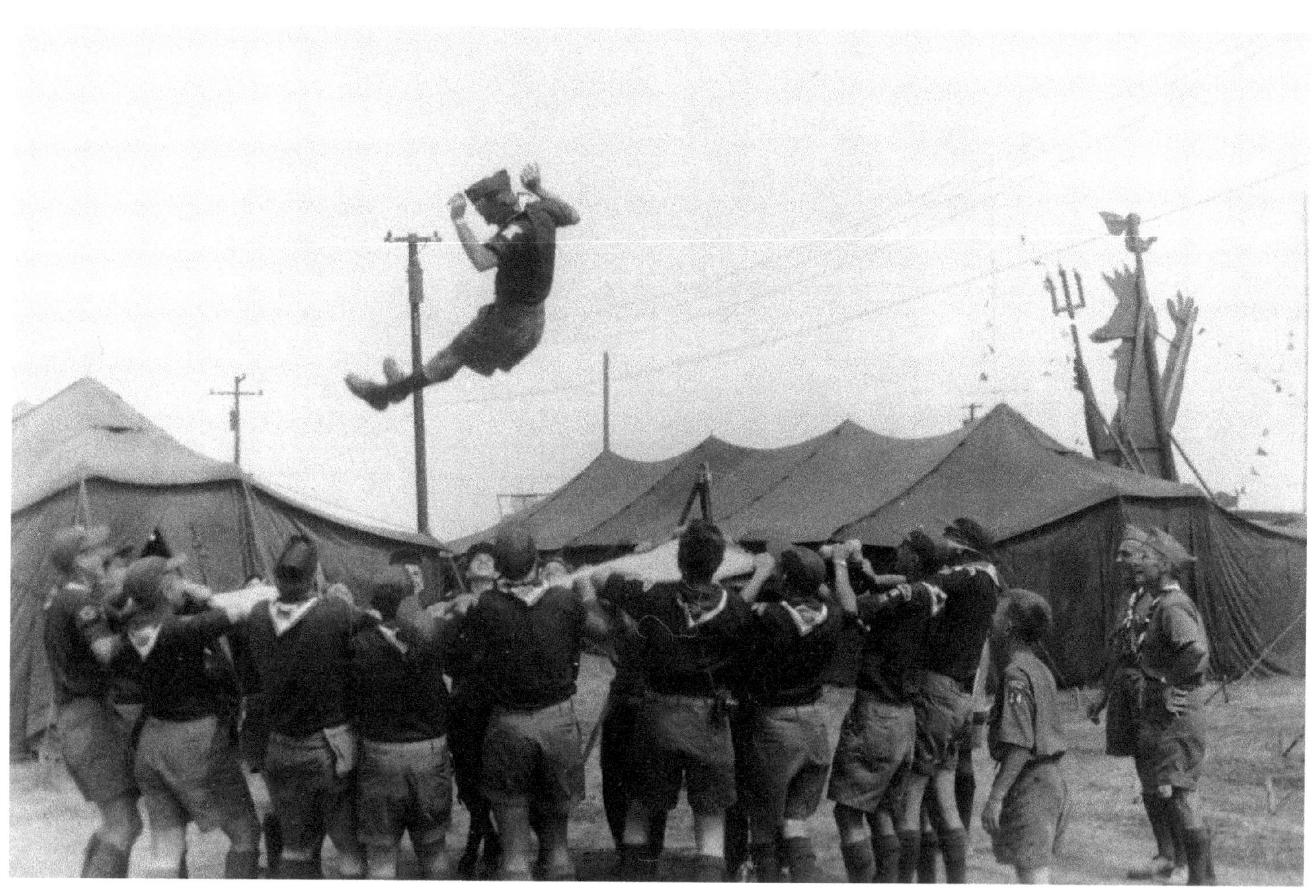

In 1953, 50,000 Boy Scouts from across the nation convened at the 3,000-acre Irvine Ranch in southern Orange County for the National Scout Jamboree, held every four years. The site was chosen from a field of 21 competing American venues. Shown here is the Jamboree blanket toss. The wooden sign at right is the reverse side of a King Neptune caricature welcoming the Scouts. A pelican perches on his head.

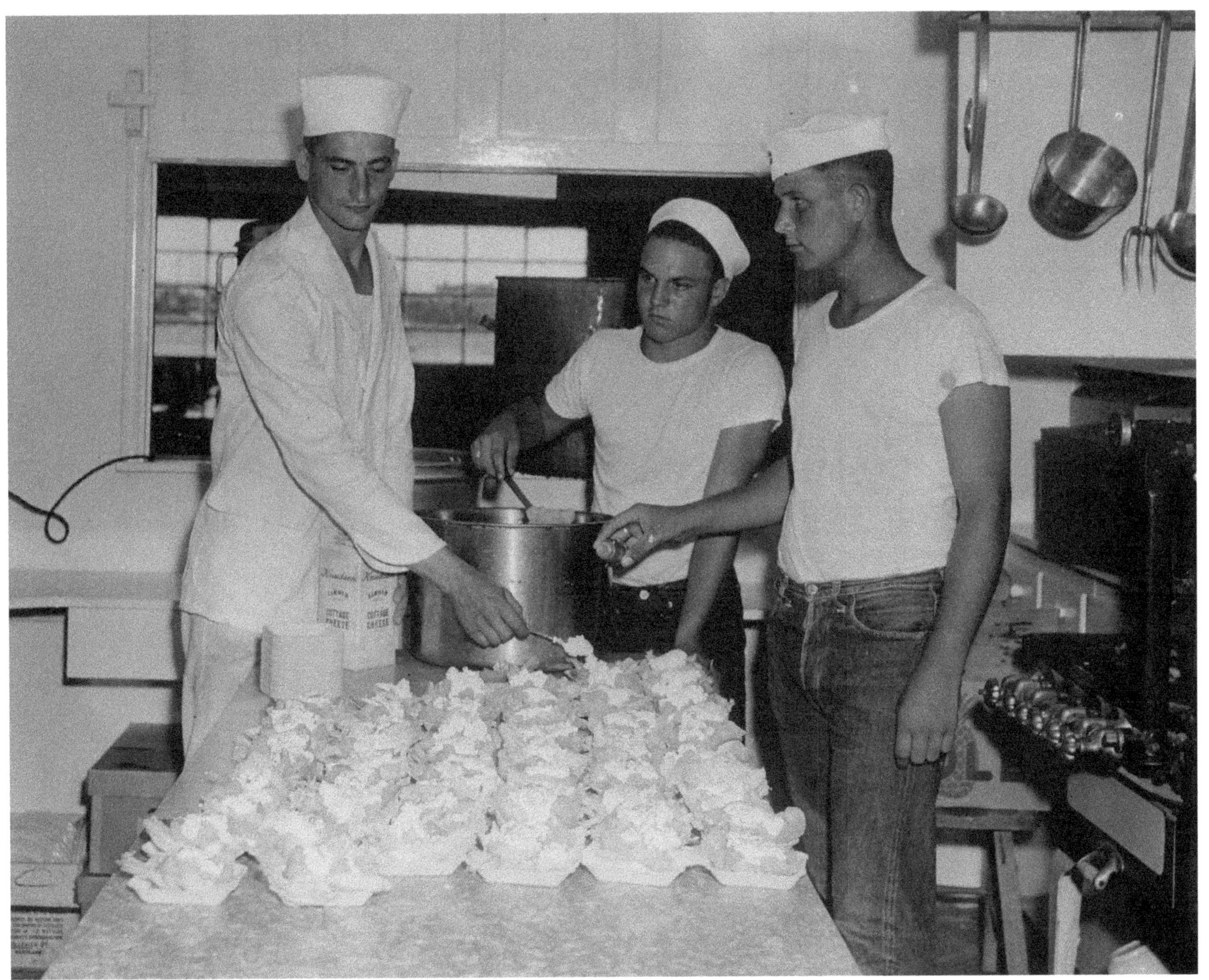

A full year of planning on the part of the National Boy Scout Council was required to ready transportation, sanitary facilities, and provisions for the Irvine Ranch Boy Scout Jamboree, which took place July 17-23. Kitchens at Newport Sea Base were pressed into service for preparation of the more than one million meals consumed that week by Scouts and troop leaders. Today Jamboree Road in Irvine commemorates the event.

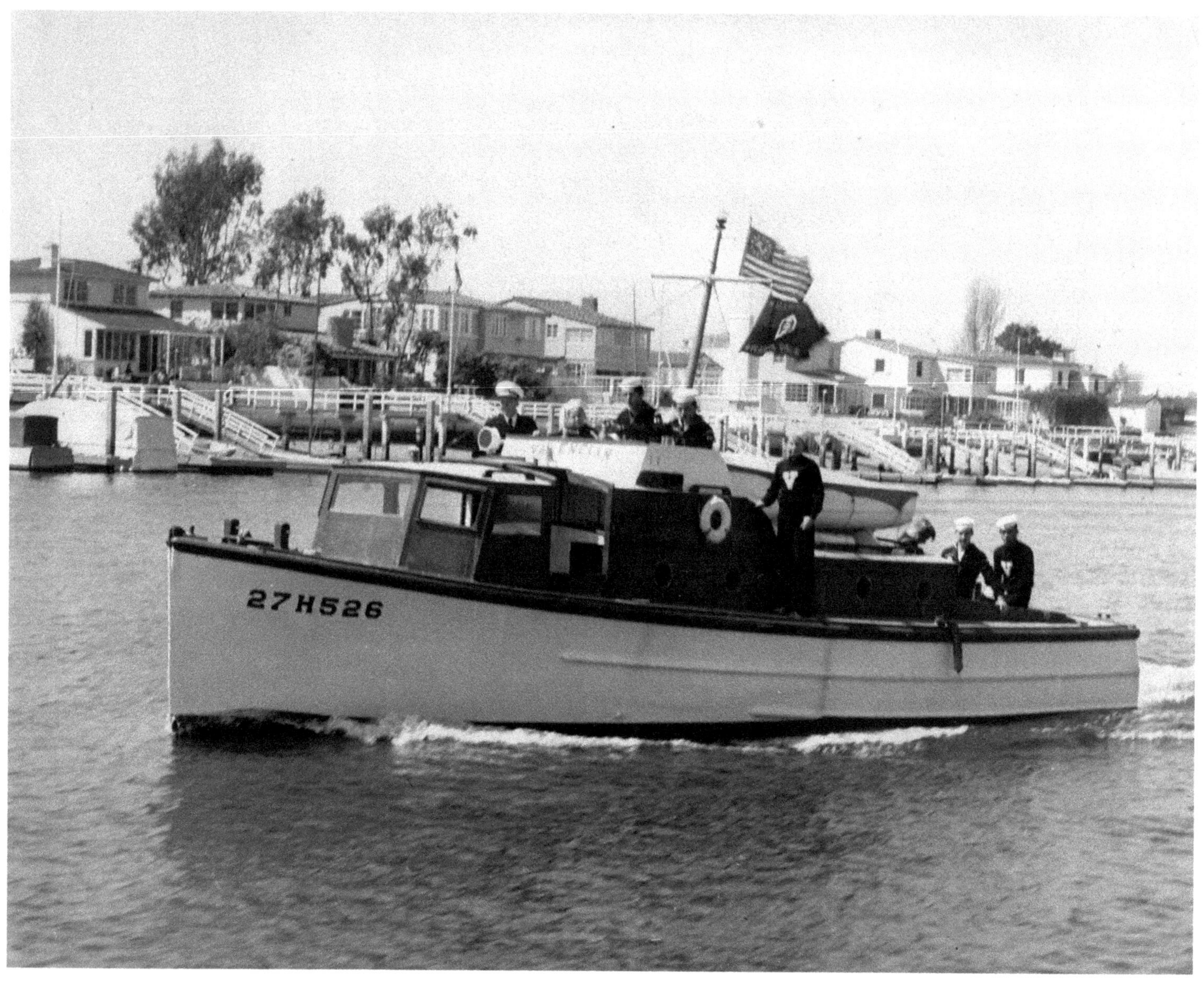

The Sea Scout program was started in 1912 to teach nautical skills to young people. The SSS *Valencian,* shown here in 1953, was operated by a teenage crew from Placentia. Skipper Hal Polly, a Placentia High School teacher, is on the boat at left. The *Valencian* was docked at Newport Beach Sea Base and participated with other Orange County Sea Scout boats in annual cruise convoys to destinations like the Channel Islands and San Francisco.

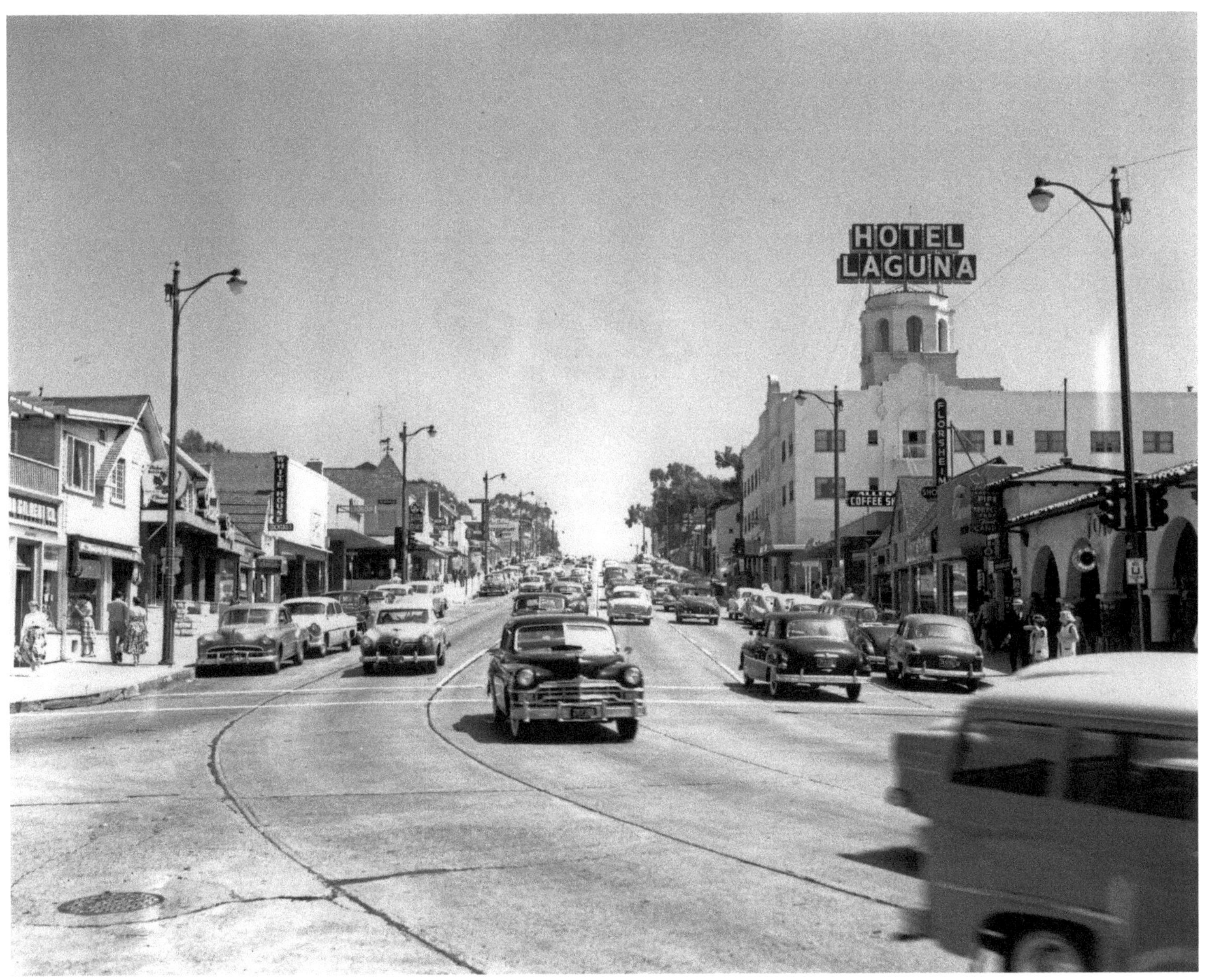

Laguna Beach's Yoch Hotel was condemned in 1928, and in its place rose Hotel Laguna, pictured here in 1954. The hotel was designed in the Mission Revival style popular at the time, with parapets, a bell tower, and an inner courtyard. Unfortunately it opened in the middle of the Depression, and at one point had only five registered guests. Luckily a celebrity clientele soon discovered the place, and Hotel Laguna is still in business today.

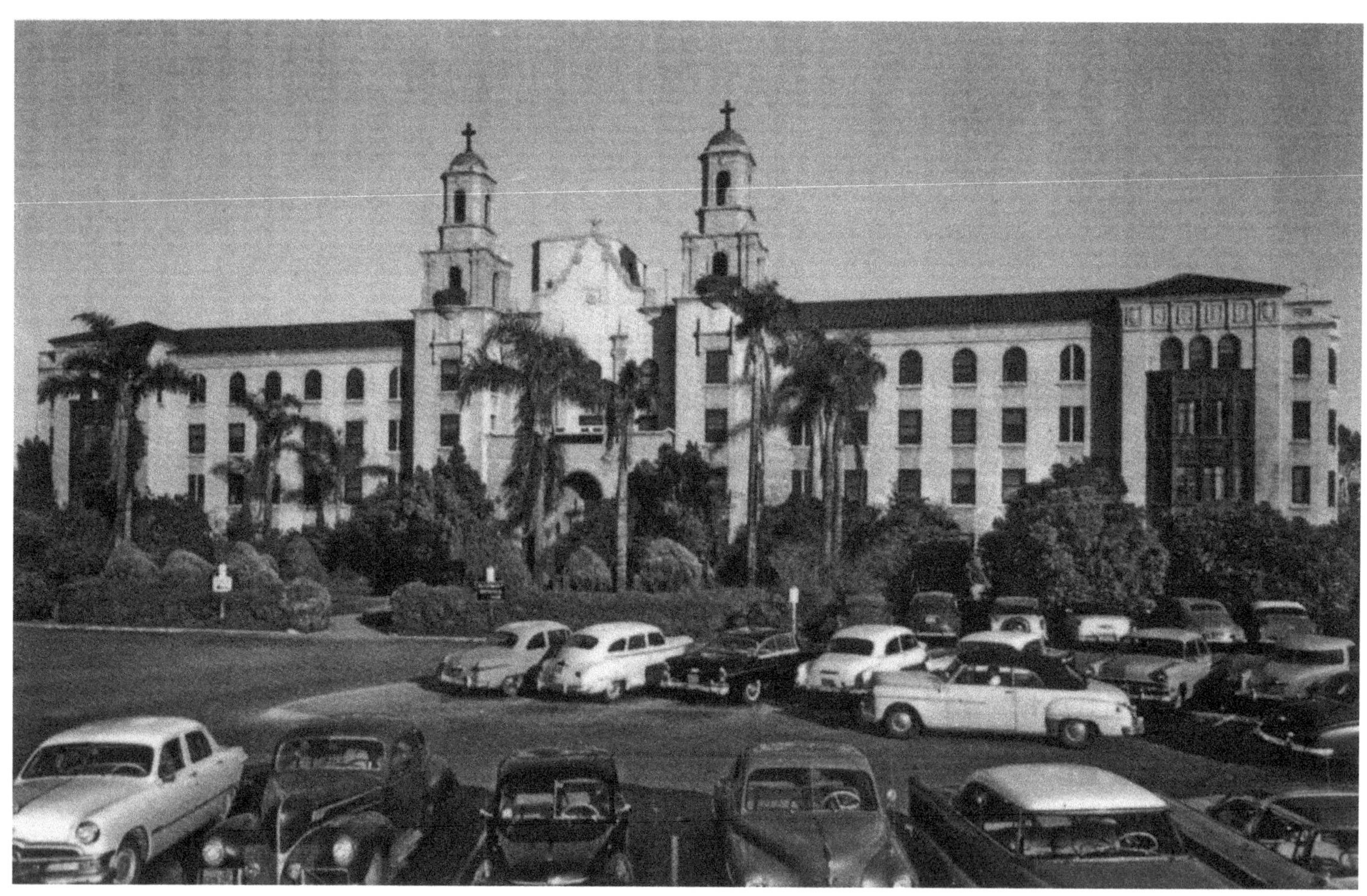

When St. Joseph's Hospital opened in the city of Orange in 1929, it was the largest and most modern hospital in Orange County. Over the years the facility has been on the cutting edge of new technologies, from developing breakthrough treatments for tuberculosis and alcoholism, to implanting the first pacemaker on the West Coast. Today St. Joseph's is part of a much larger complex that includes Children's Hospital of Orange County (CHOC).

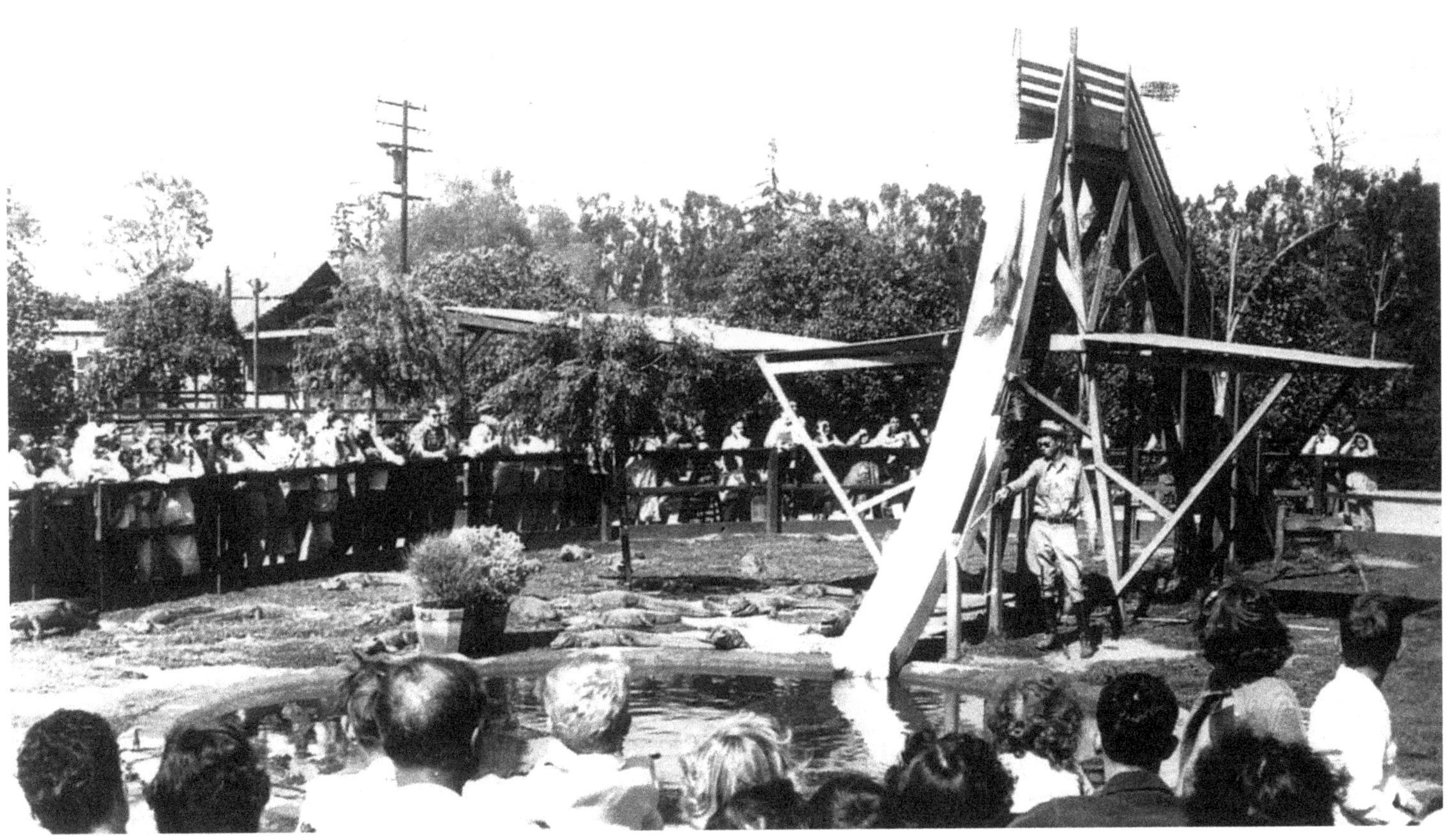

In the 1950s, '60s, and '70s, Buena Park hosted an assortment of unique tourist attractions, including the California Alligator Farm, which opened in 1954 directly across La Palma Avenue from Knott's Berry Farm. Here guests could feed an assortment of alligators and tortoises and even pose for pictures astride one of the giant reptiles. The Alligator Farm closed in 1983, and the site is currently an overflow parking lot for Knott's.

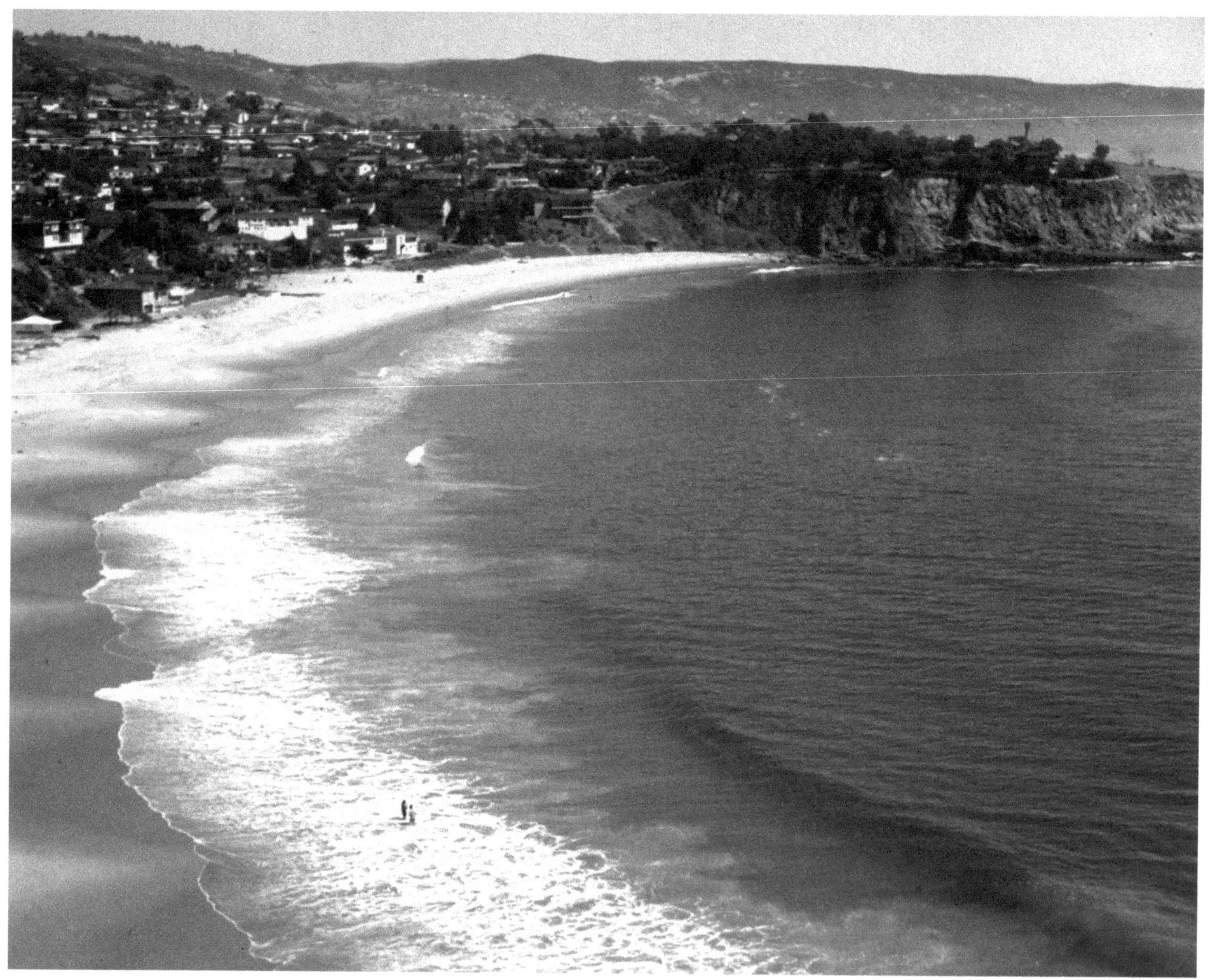

Two tiny beachgoers are dwarfed by the majestic natural wonders of Emerald Bay, shown here in 1956 as viewed looking south along the coast. Emerald Bay, not to be confused with Emerald Bay State Park near Lake Tahoe, or Emerald Bay Boy Scout Camp on Catalina Island, is an extremely exclusive coastal community just north of Laguna Beach where houses are currently selling in the $16-million range.

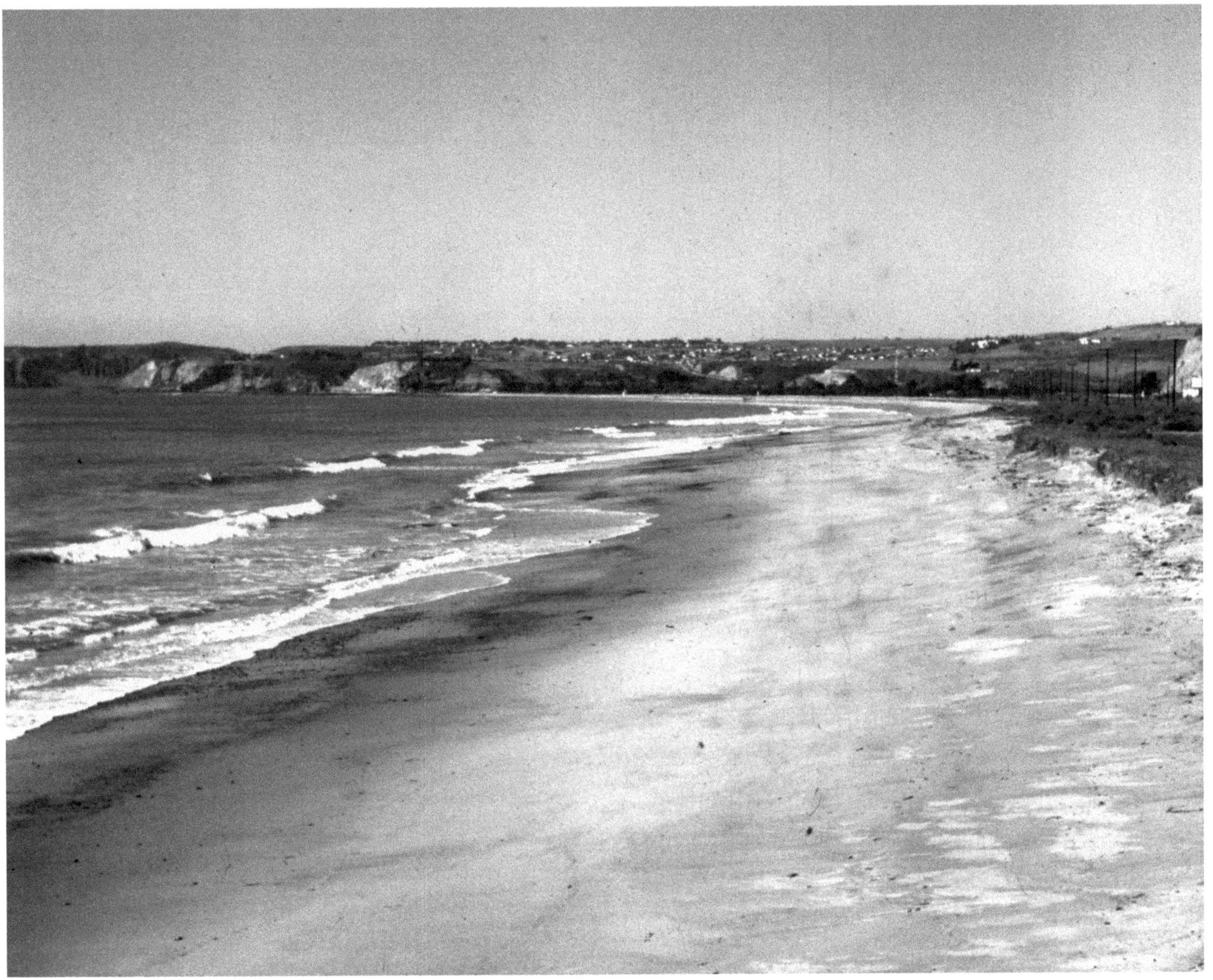

In 1928, Edward Doheny, Jr., scion of the fabulously wealthy Beverly Hills oil family, began developing the coastal community of Capistrano Beach along the high cliffs south of Laguna Beach. The following year Doheny was murdered at Greystone Mansion, allegedly by his emotionally unstable chauffeur, and the beach was donated to the state parks system. Shown here in 1956, it is today called Doheny State Beach in his honor and is popular with campers.

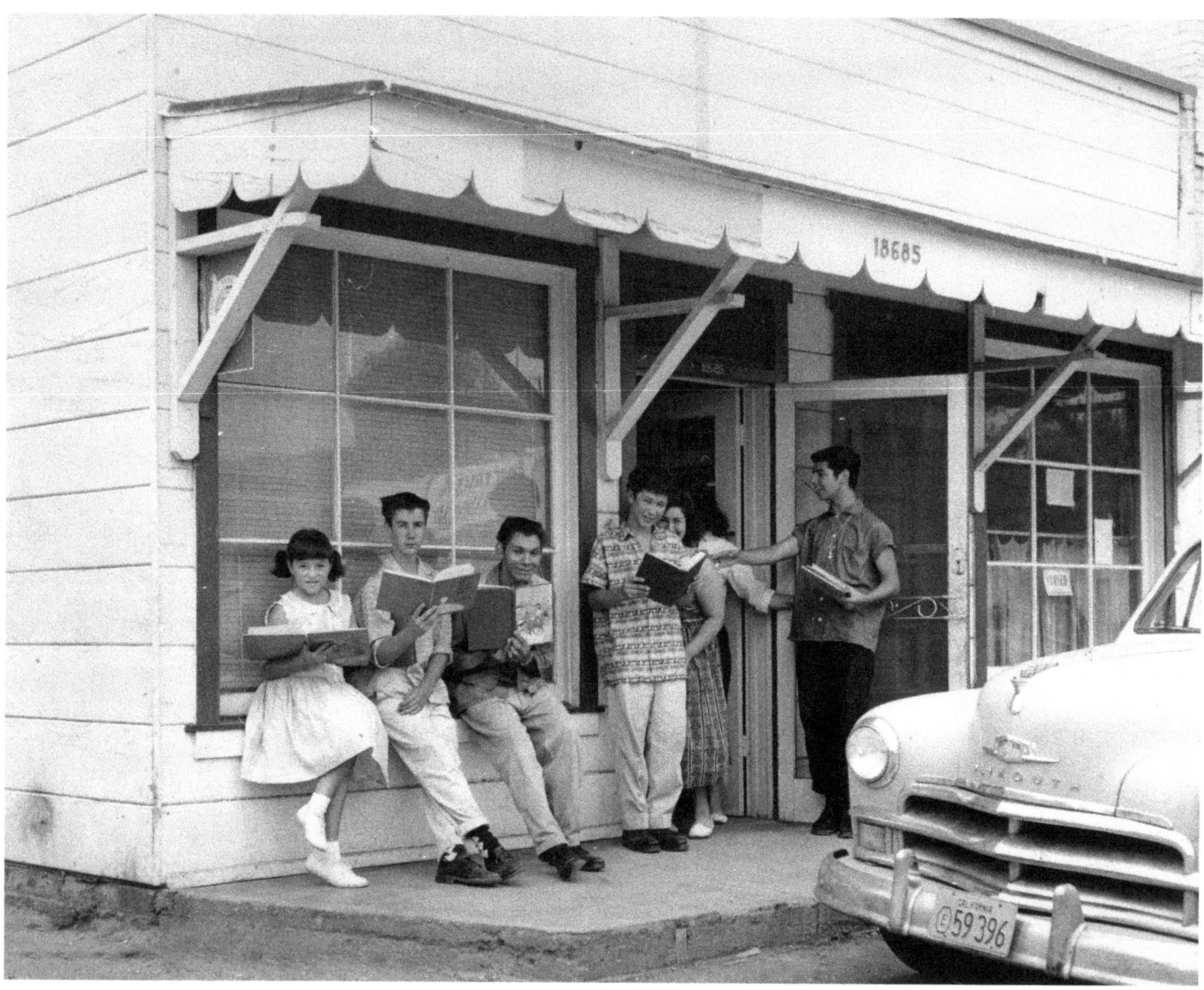

Before the El Modena city library opened in 1978, the literary needs of this largely Hispanic neighborhood in the city of Orange were met by a branch of the county library system that operated out of a storefront on Chapman Avenue next to Rice's Market, as shown here in 1957. Today the Orange County library system has 27 branches. Additionally, three city libraries serve the city of Orange.

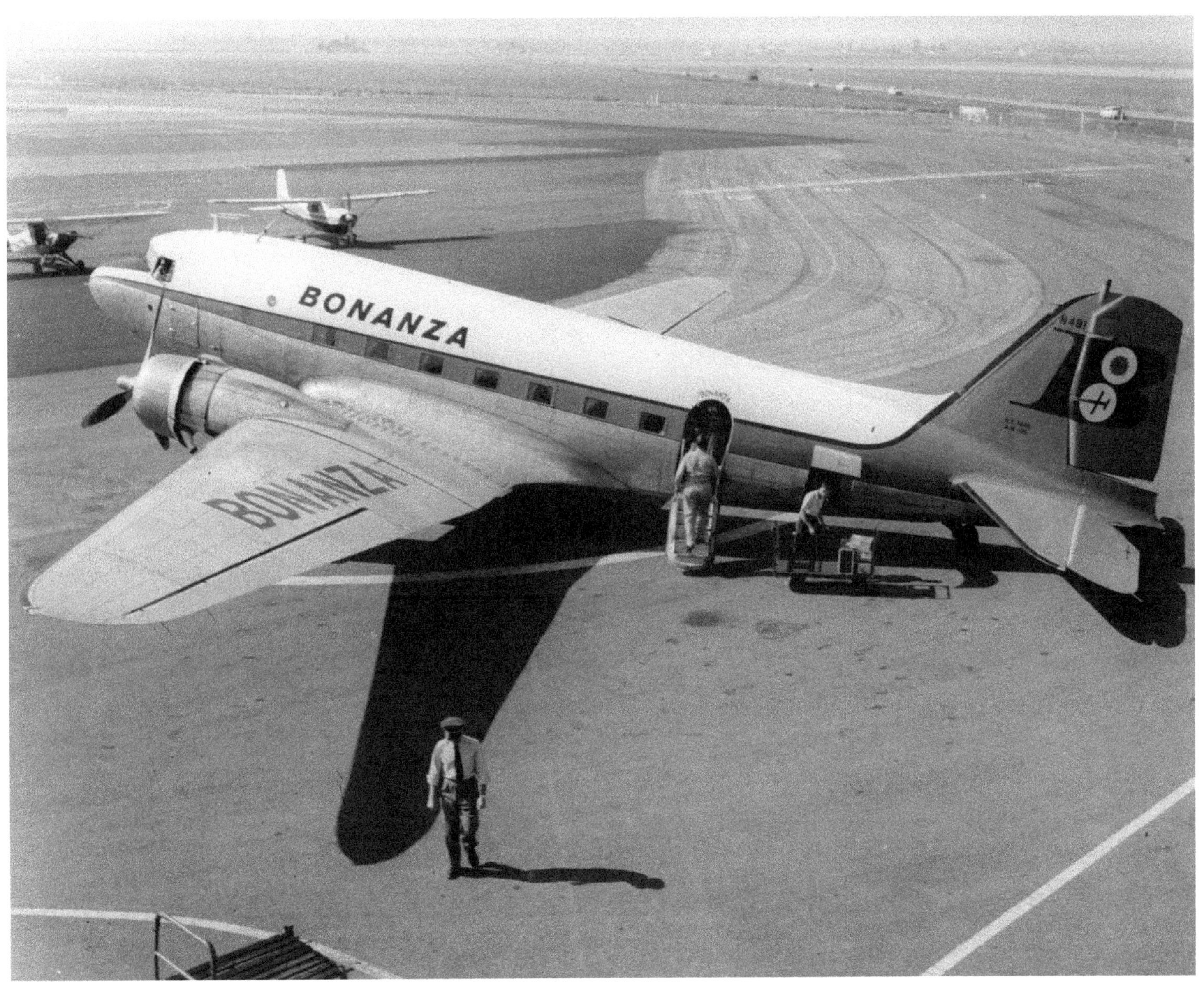

Las Vegas–based Bonanza Airlines, formed in 1946, ferried merchant marines from Southern California to the East Coast after World War II, and in 1952 launched the first scheduled airline service at Orange County Airport with a fleet of DC-3s, one of which is shown here in 1958. After two decades of operation, Bonanza merged with Pacific Airlines and West Coast Airlines in 1967 to form Air West.

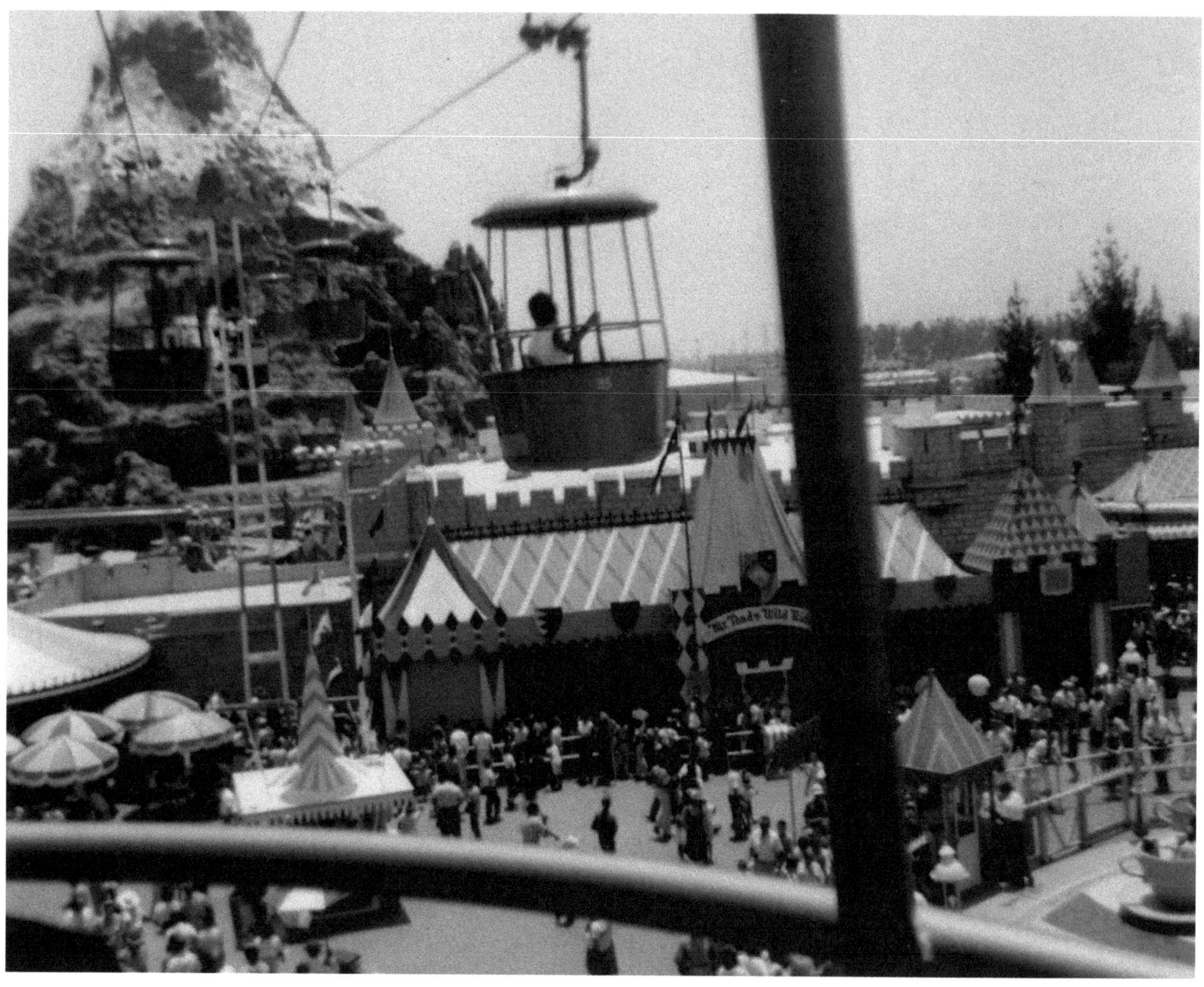

The mountain ranges ringing the greater Los Angeles area are snowcapped half the year, but Disneyland's Matterhorn is topped with Disney-imagineered snow 365 days a year. Rising improbably from the Anaheim flatlands in 1959, this 1/100-scale model of its namesake in the Swiss Alps has been an OC landmark to commuters on the 5 Freeway for five decades. The Matterhorn can be seen top-left in this 1959 photo.

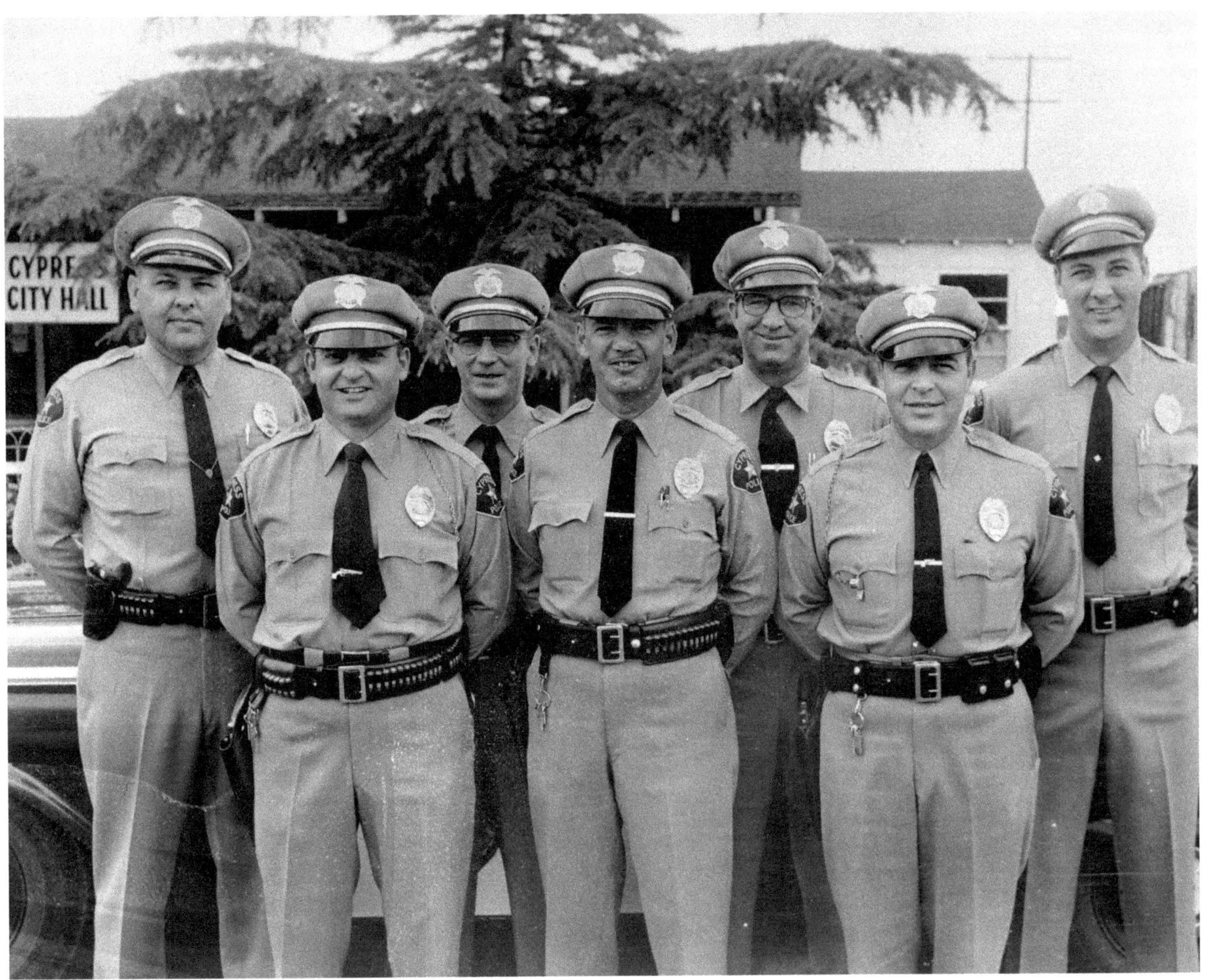

In a four-year period between 1953 and 1957, at the height of the postwar construction boom, eight Orange County towns incorporated to avoid annexation to neighboring Anaheim. Before Cypress voted to become a city in 1956, the community was known as Dairyland, with a population of 1,700 people and 100,000 cows. Needless to say, there are no longer any cows in Cypress. The city's recently formed police department is shown here in 1959.

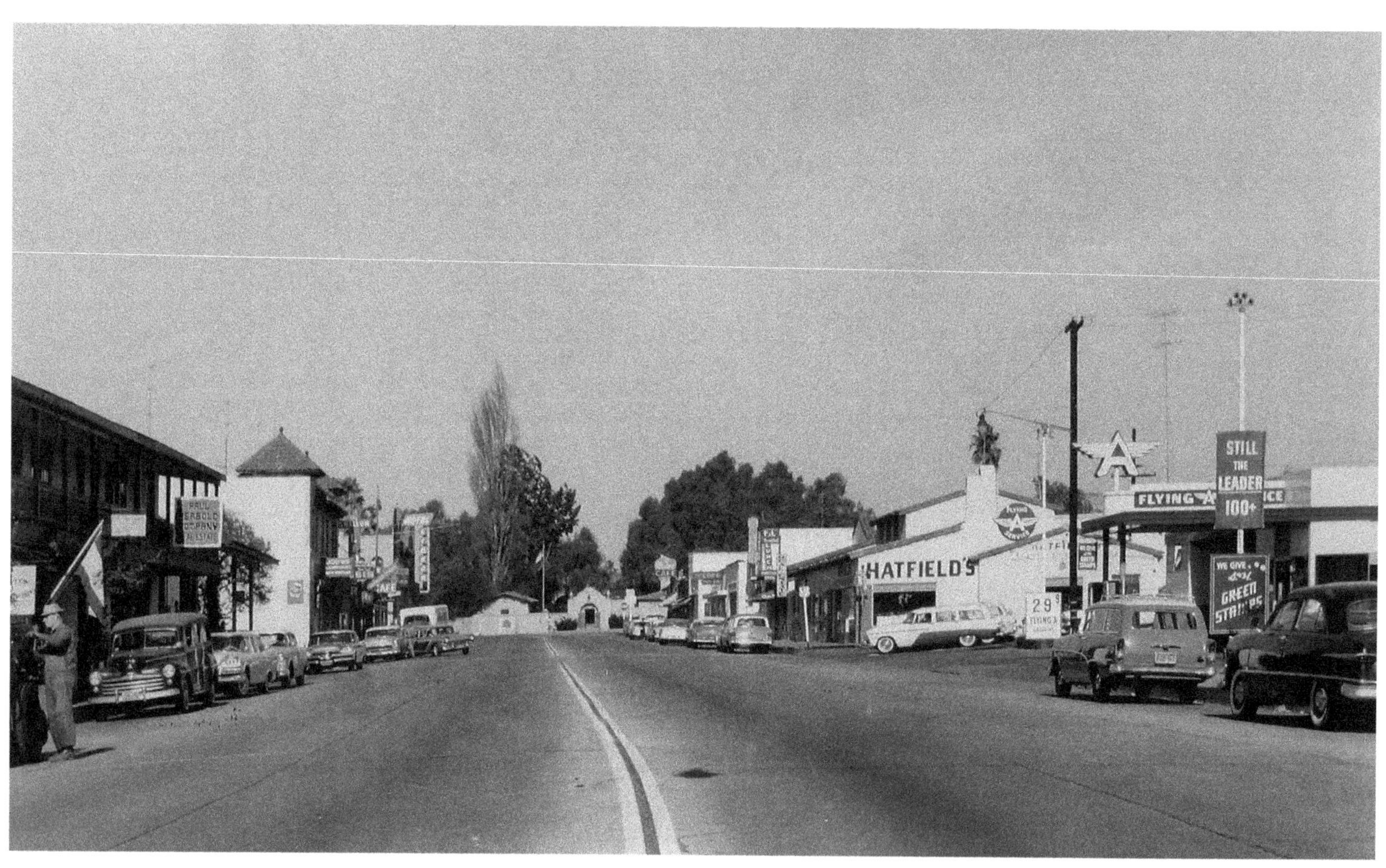

The city of San Juan Capistrano, shown here in 1959 (note the 29¢ gas!), developed around the mission, the entrance to which is visible at the end of the street. Each year the city marks the return of the swallows to the mission with Fiesta de las Golondrinas, a monthlong celebration featuring the nation's largest nonmotorized parade, performances by Aztec dancers and mariachi musicians, and a costumed ball celebrating the area's rich, multicultural history.

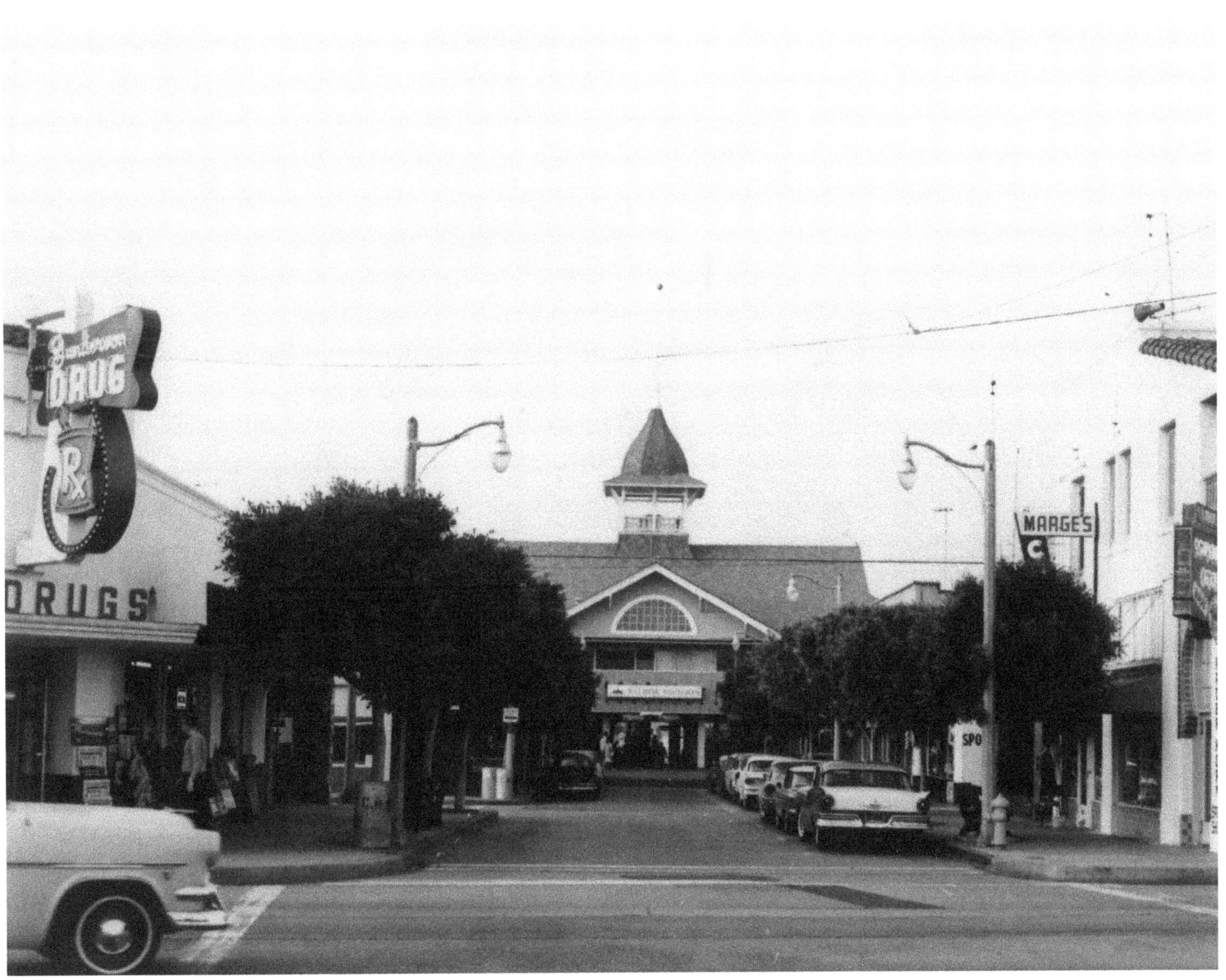

By the late 1940s, Balboa Pavilion was in danger of tumbling into the bay. Throughout the next few decades, the Newport landmark underwent a series of renovations by various owners who replaced deteriorating wood pilings with concrete, restored the interior to its original condition, and added 1,500 lights to the exterior. At the time of this 1960s photo, the Pavilion was home to the Newport Harbor Art Museum's collections.

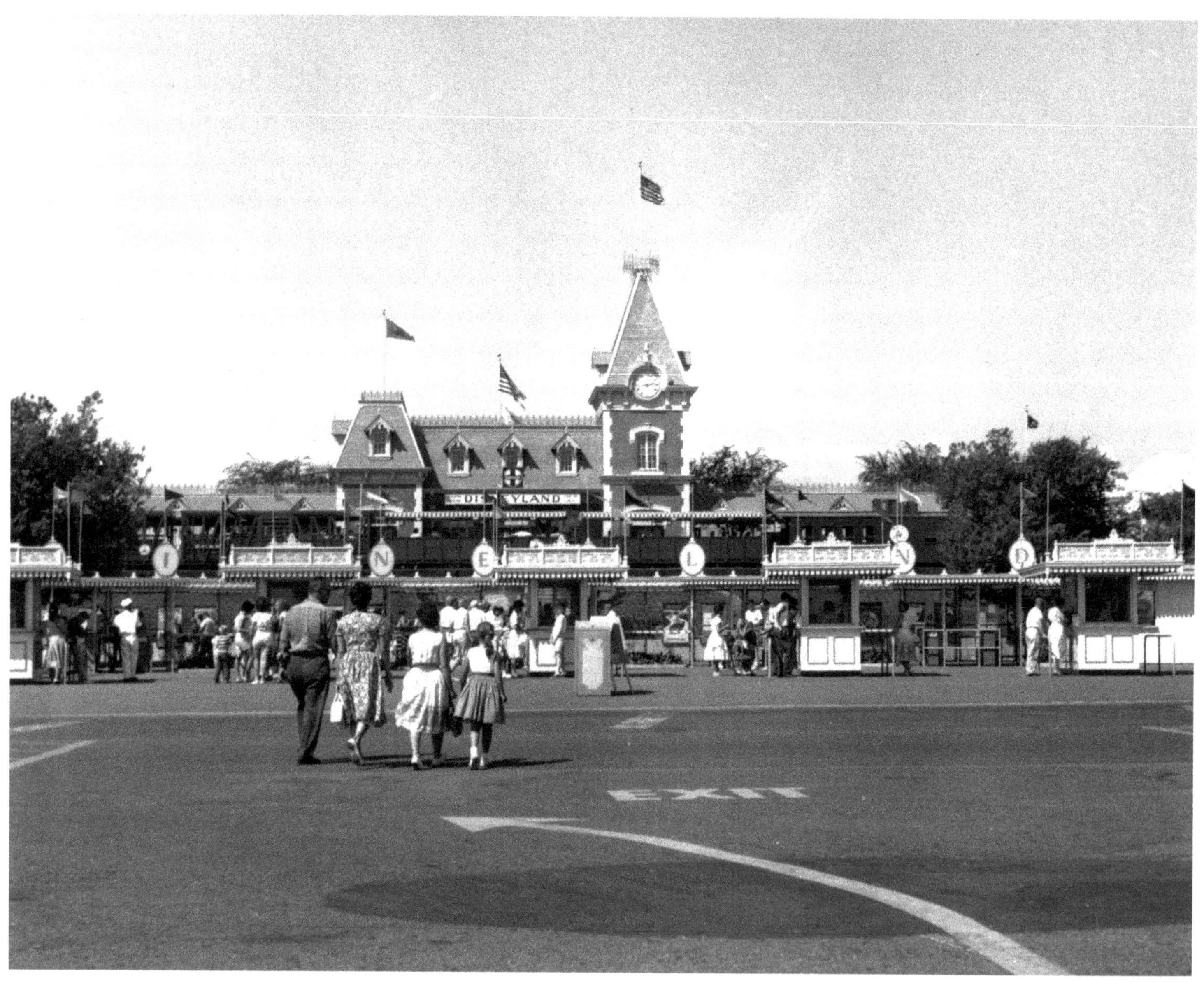

Disneyland opened in Anaheim in 1955 and, much to the surprise of its many detractors (including Walt's brother Ray), proved an immediate success, transforming the city around it and quickly becoming Anaheim's biggest employer. Shown here in 1960, Disneyland today attracts 13 million visitors annually and has grown to encompass Downtown Disneyland and also California Adventure, a separate theme park dedicated to California history.

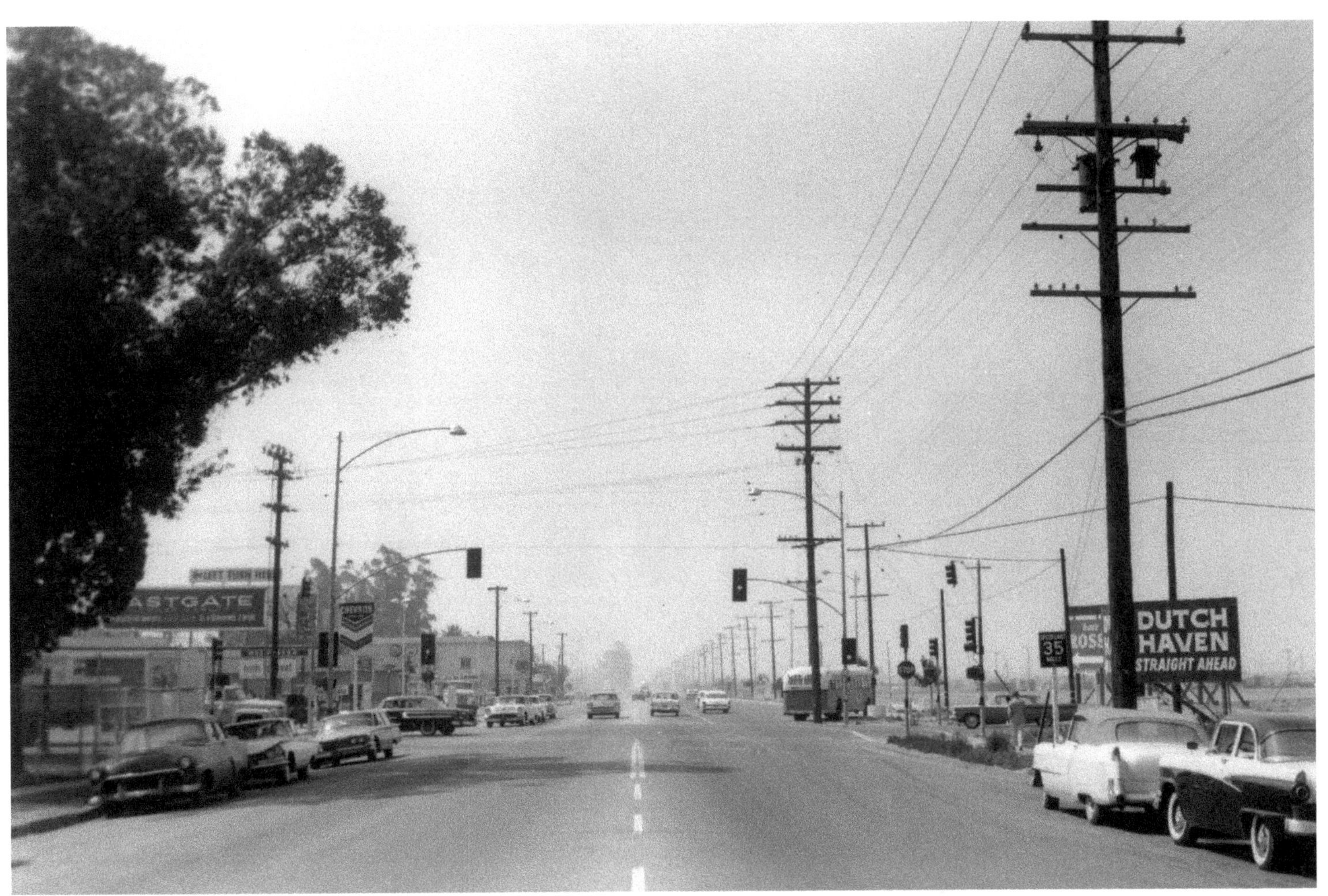

Postwar Orange County experienced unprecedented growth, with the population of some towns increasing an astounding nine or tenfold in the decade between 1950 and 1960. This 1960 photograph of a seemingly sleepy Los Alamitos, viewed down Katella Avenue, belies the reality of a frantic construction boom: billboards on both sides of the street advertise new housing tracts, including the walled community of Rossmoor.

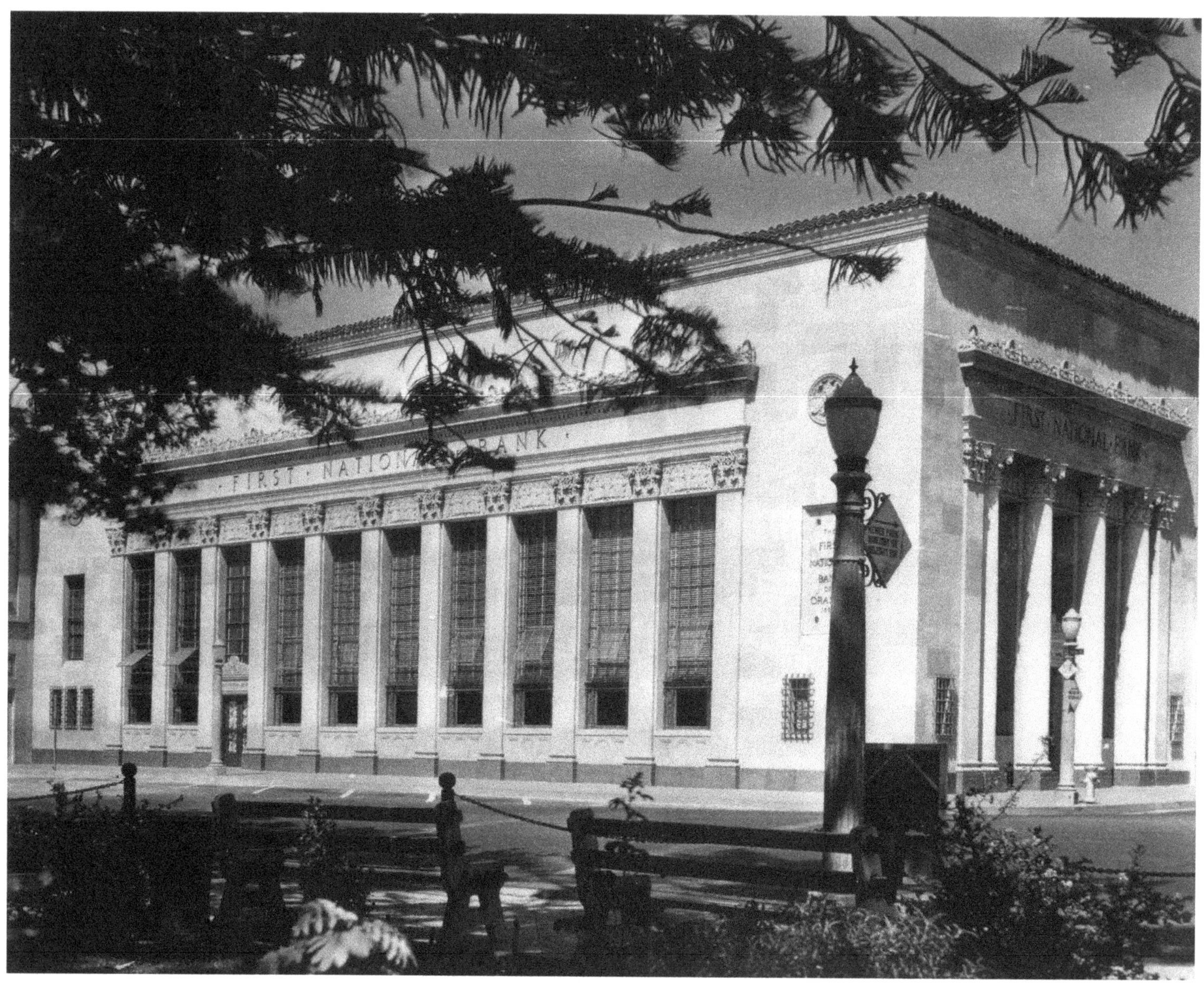

Located at 101 East Chapman, this imposing building continues to anchor the city of Orange's historic Plaza area and has changed little in nearly a century. Shown in the 1960s when it was still occupied by the First National Bank of Orange, it is currently home to a Wells Fargo and a Starbucks. Much of the original vaulted ceiling, composed of hand-carved, inlaid wood, is still visible inside.

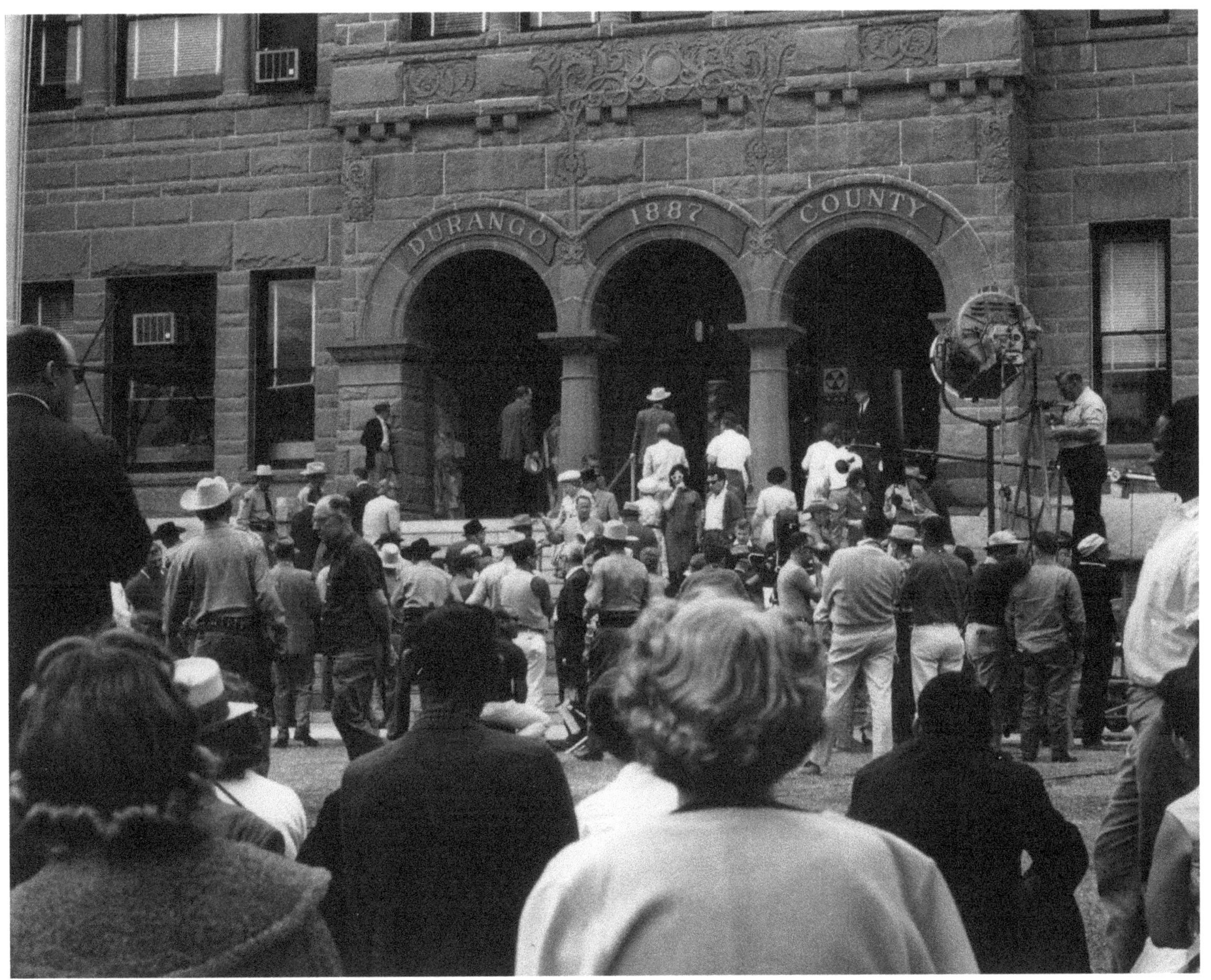

The Santa Ana County Courthouse has played host to many celebrities over the years. The 1915 D. W. Griffith silent film *The Flying Torpedo* and the 1978 miniseries *Studs Lonigan* are just two examples of the many Hollywood productions lensed in and around the photogenic site. Here the courthouse substitutes for "Durango County" ca. 1887 for a Western being filmed in the 1960s in front of a crowd of fans.

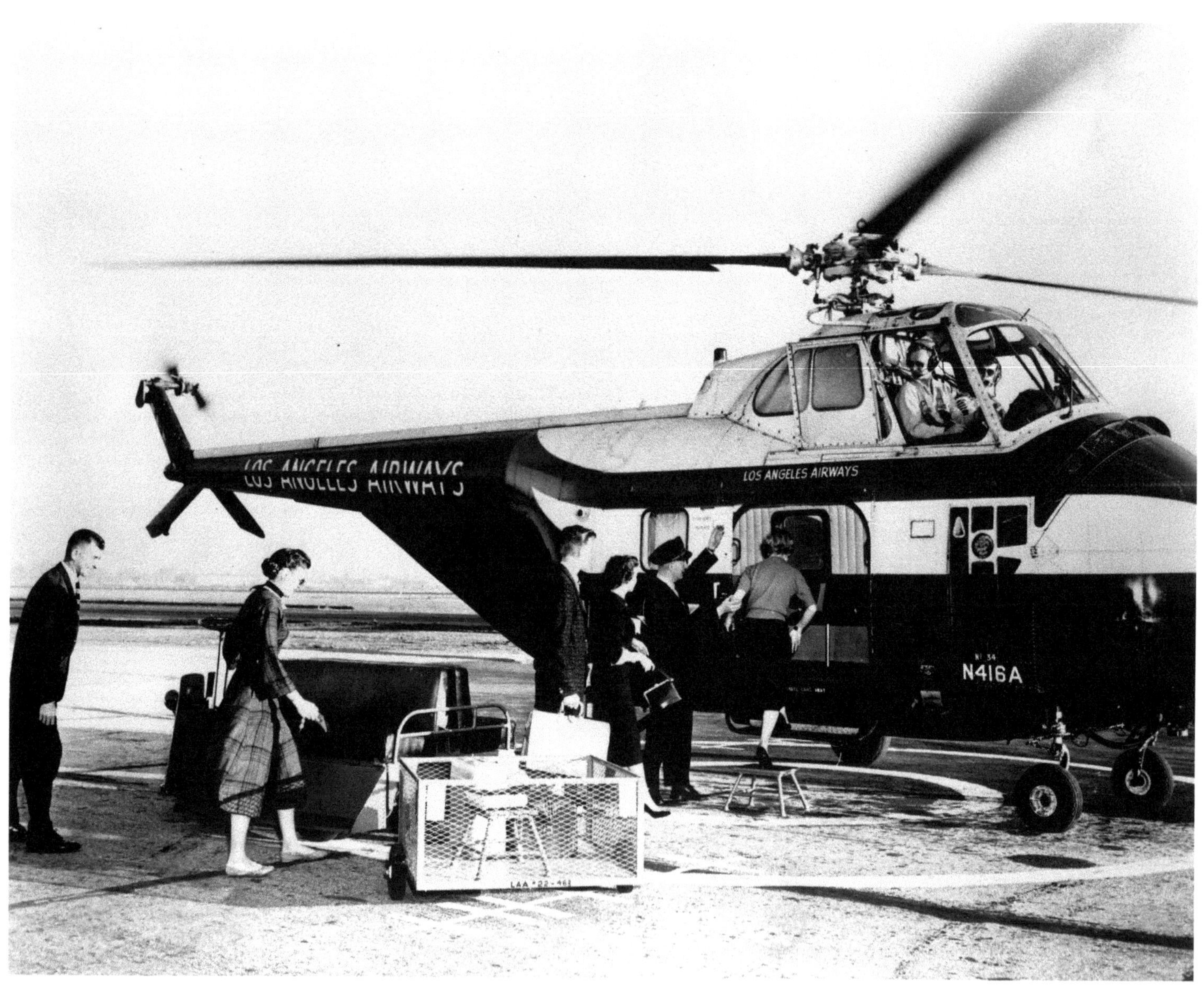

Between 1955 and 1968, Los Angeles Airways offered helicopter passenger service between Los Angeles International Airport and Disneyland. A 1963 *National Geographic* advertisement for United Airlines claimed, "You can step from a United jet, walk a few steps, and board a convenient flight to Disneyland and seventeen other points . . . what could be more convenient?" Service was discontinued after a 1968 crash killed eighteen.

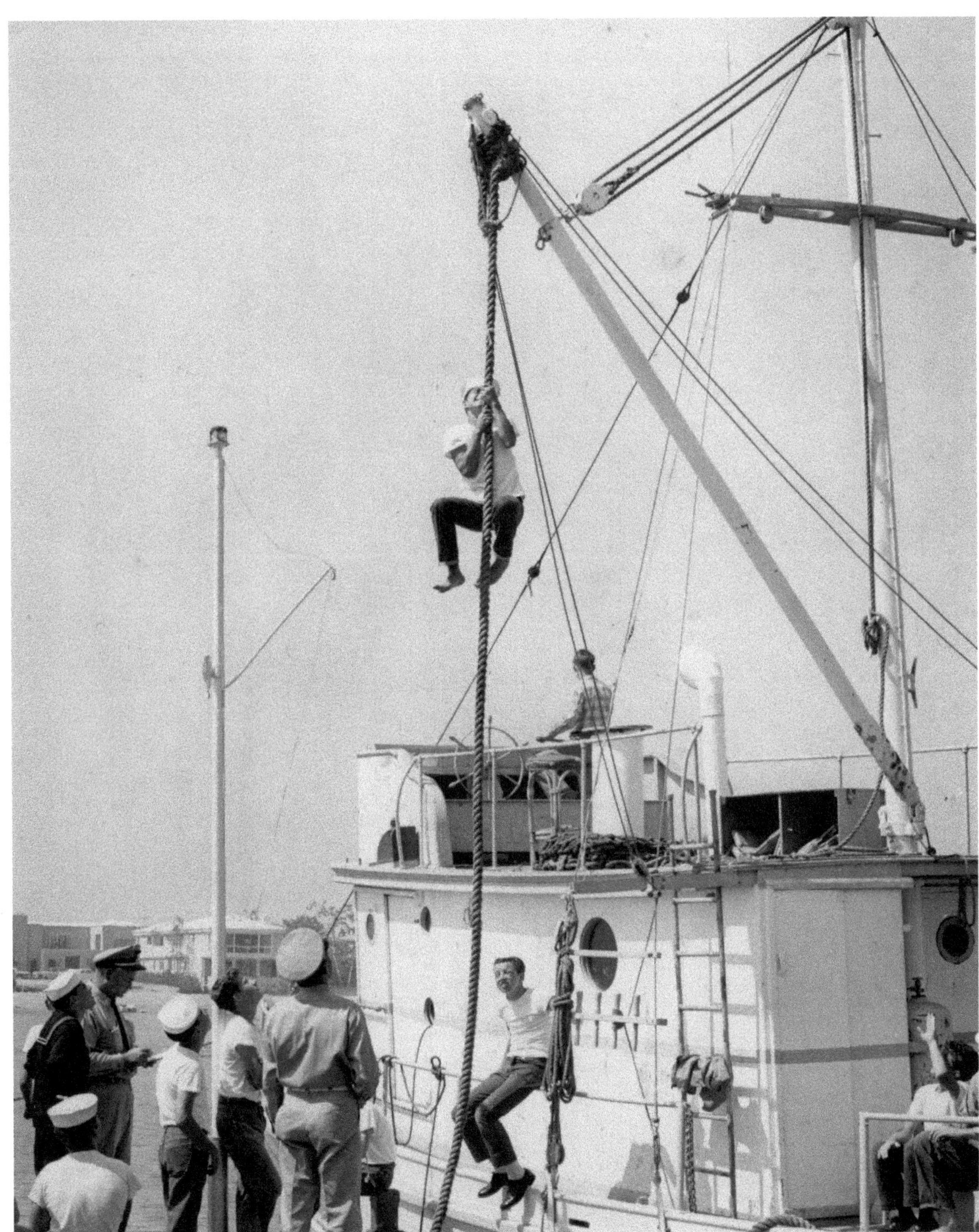

The Newport Sea Base, run by Boy Scouts of America, opened in 1937. Sea Scouts compete with those at other California Sea Scout bases in regattas that are composed of various tests of skill, like the Rope Climb, demonstrated by this agile Scout in 1961. Other regatta events include Ring Buoy, Heaving Line, Obstacle Course, and Marlin Spike. The sea base fleet includes kayaks, canoes, rowboats, and three-dozen sailboats.

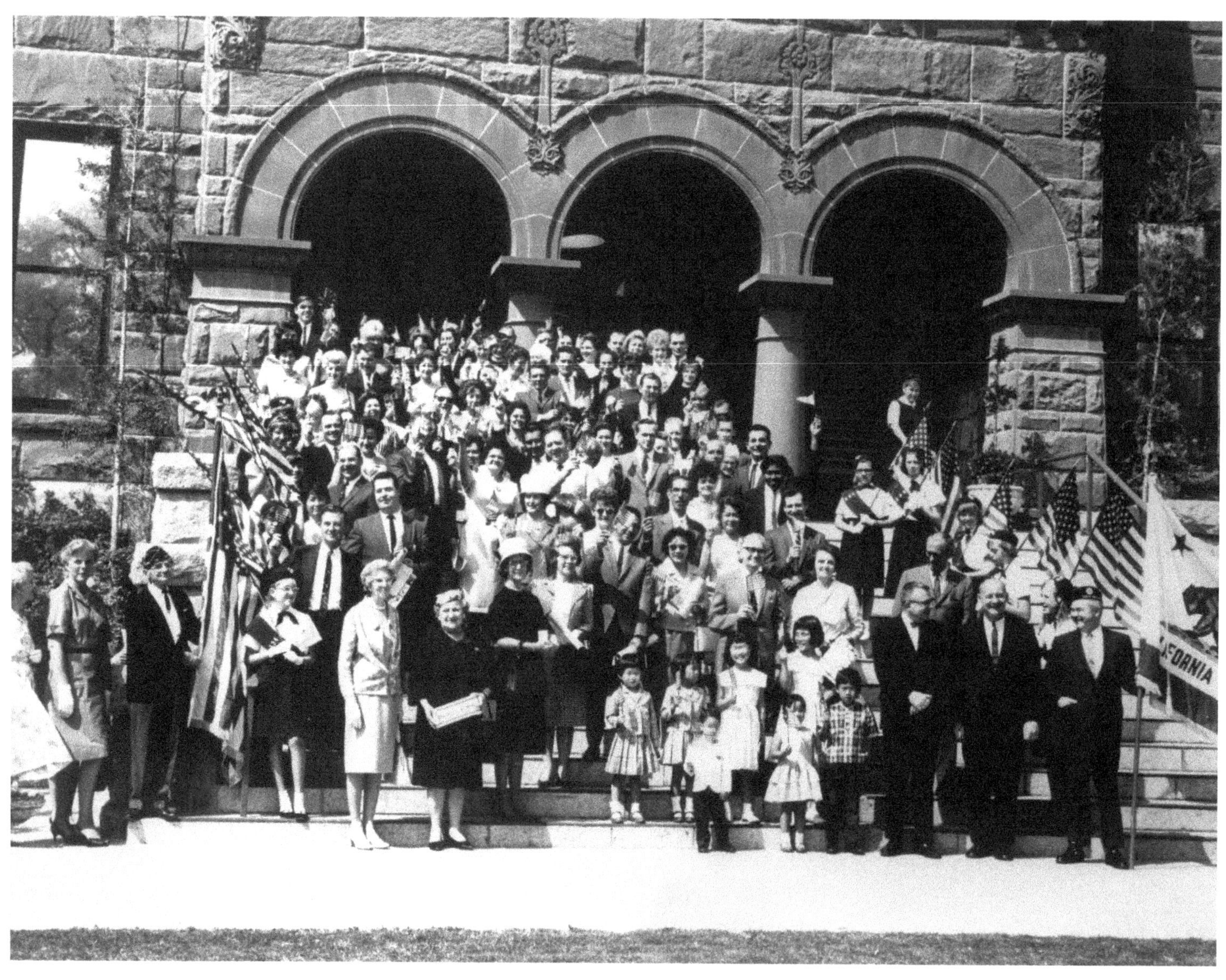

Listed on the National Register of Historic Places, the Old Orange County Courthouse, as it is now called, has served many functions over the years, including as a site for naturalization services. In this 1960s-era photo, newly minted American citizens wave U.S. flags and proudly display citizenship papers.

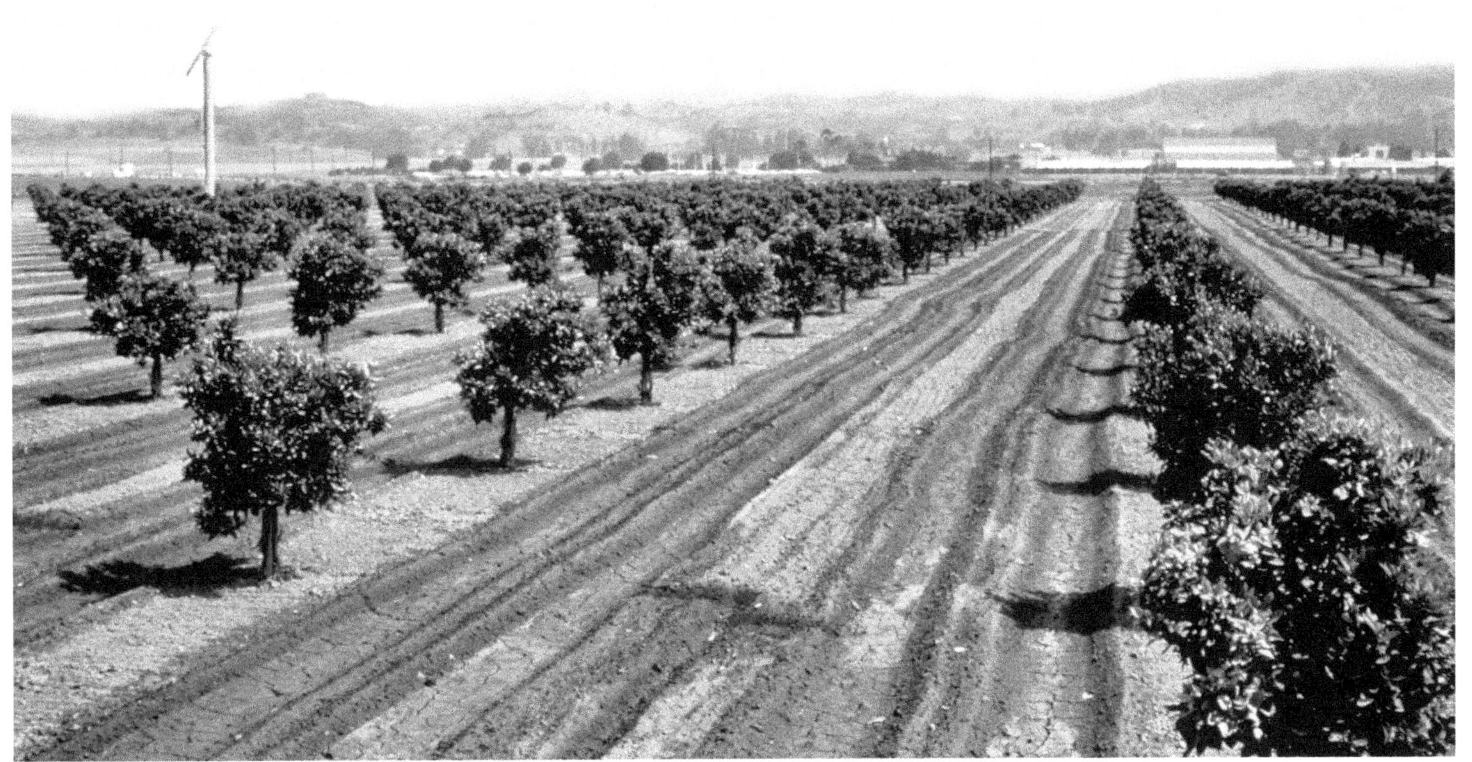

Contrary to popular conception, Orange County was not named for its most famous crop, which was still in its infancy when the new county split off from Los Angeles County in 1889. Citriculture peaked in the 1940s, with 68,000 acres planted in trees. By 1961, when this grove on Golden Avenue in Placentia was photographed, orange groves were being uprooted at a rapid rate to make way for housing tracts. Few remain today.

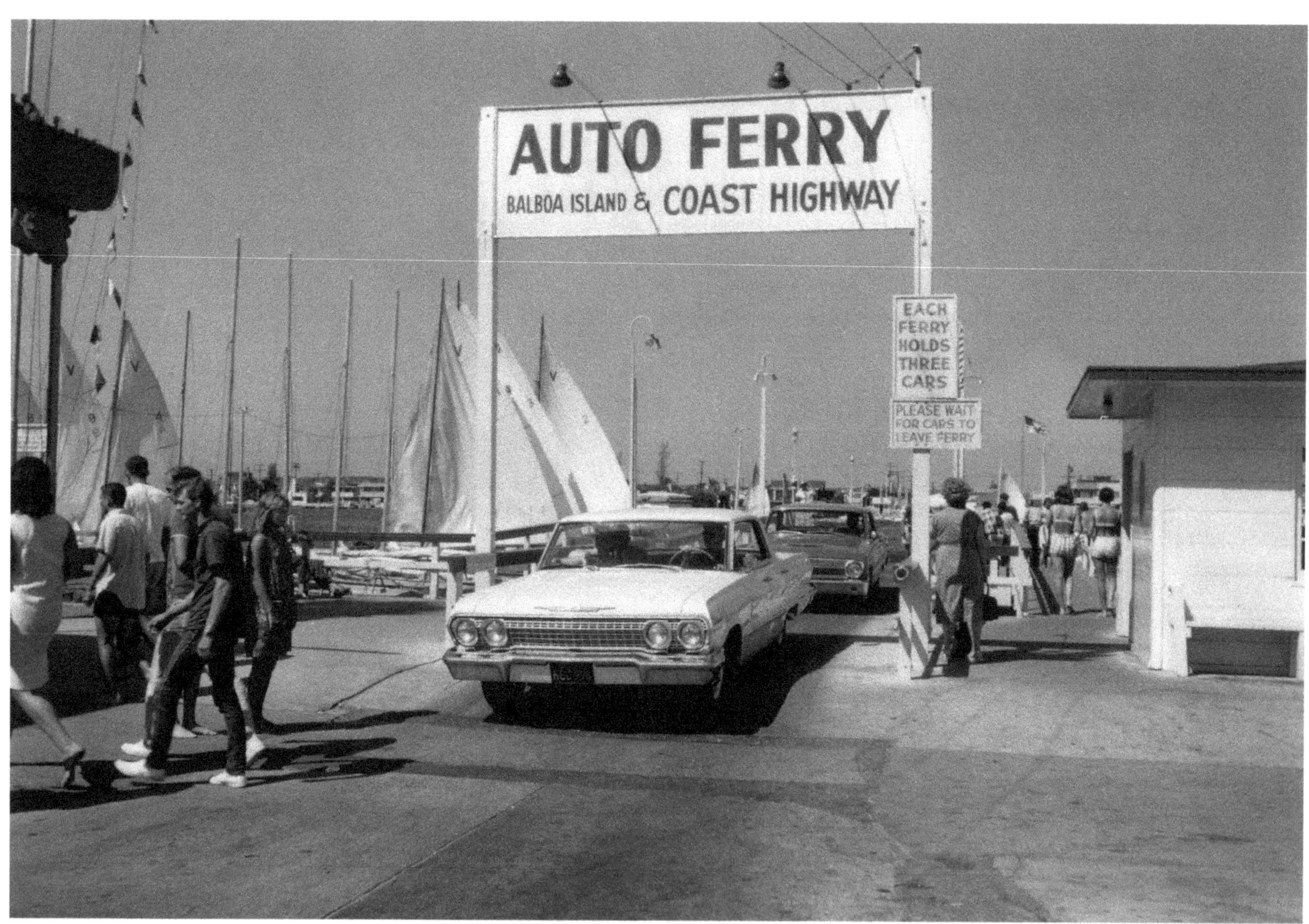

Owned and operated by the Beek family, the Balboa Island Ferry, shown here in 1963, has been in continuous service (except for minor shutdowns for repairs) since 1909. The fleet consists of three 64-foot boats that shuttle 2.5 million people a year between the island and the peninsula. Piloting the ferry is considered a plum summer job for local teenage boys. It doesn't pay much, but the bikini-viewing benefits are excellent.

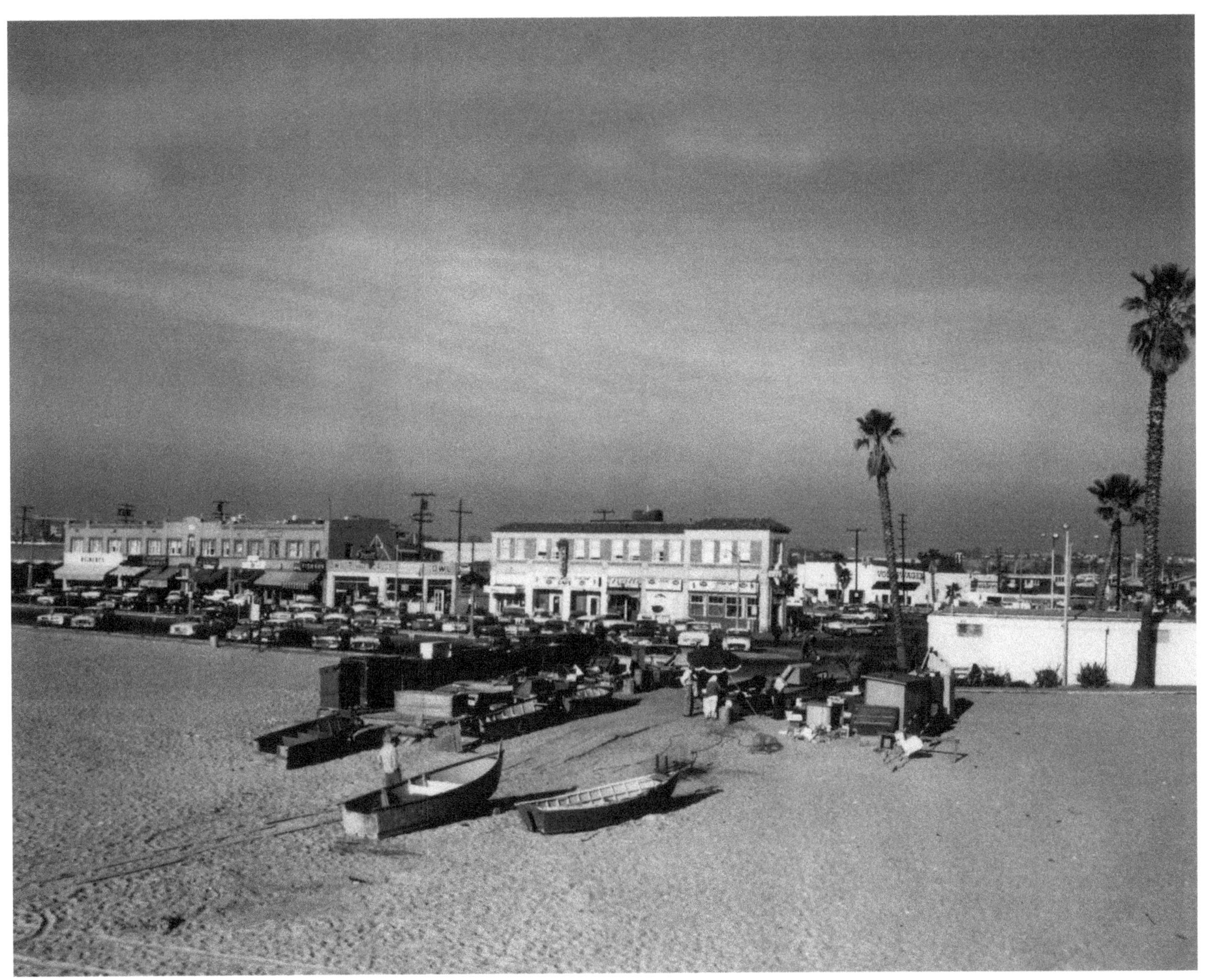

This shot of Newport Beach's famous dory fishermen was taken in December 1963. The Dory Fleet, the only one of its kind in the country, has operated from the base of Newport Pier for almost a century, and its boats are the only ones permitted to cast off from the beach. The Dory Fleet Market was dedicated as a historic landmark in 1969. Once 30-strong, the dorymen's numbers have dwindled to seven or eight and their future is uncertain.

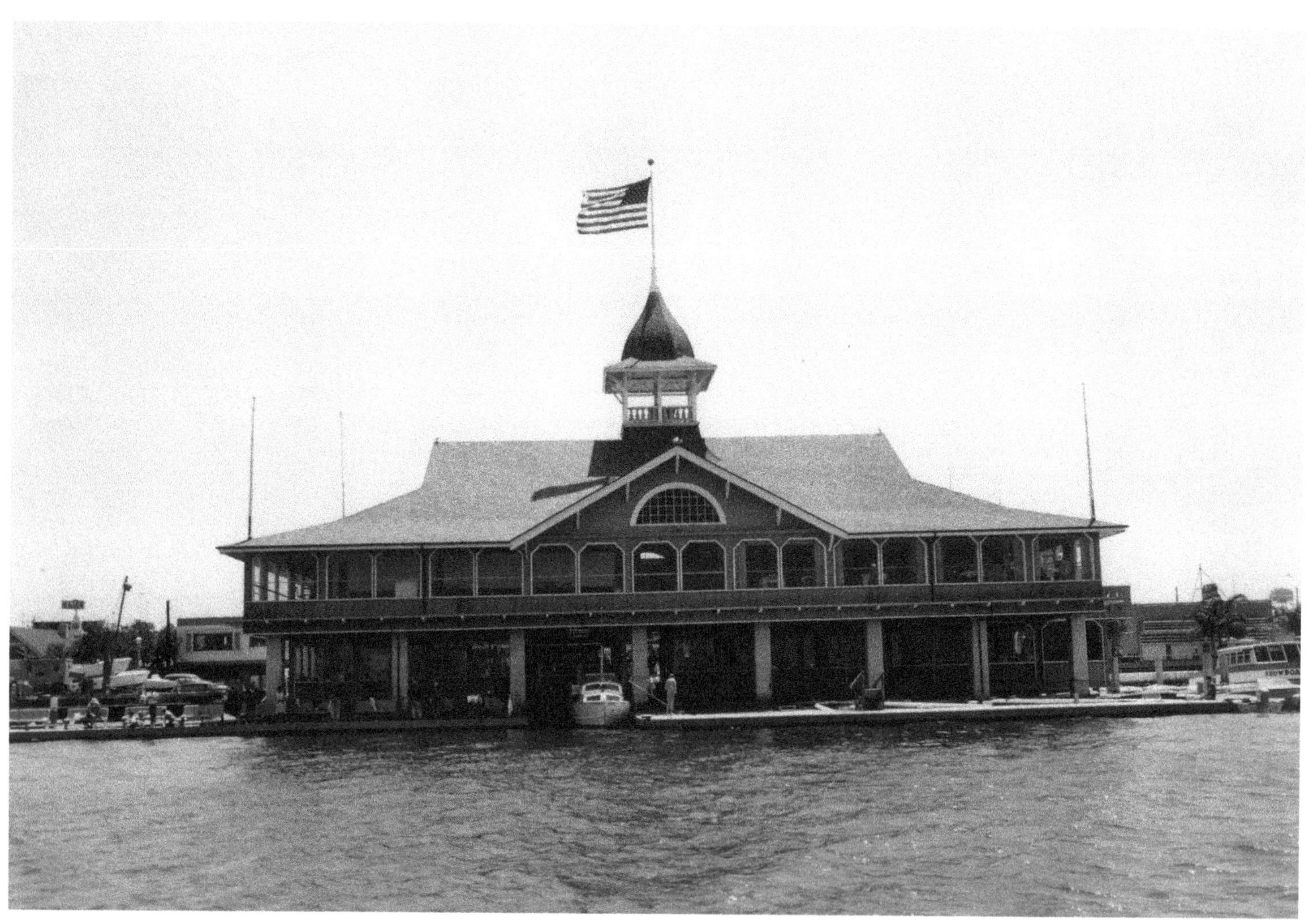

The Balboa Pavilion was designated a California Point of Historical Interest in 1981, in time for the celebration of Newport Beach's seventy-fifth anniversary. The Pavilion is the city's oldest building and most famous landmark, and one of the last surviving waterfront recreational pavilions in California. Known today for birdwatching and sportfishing, Balboa Pavilion is also the launching point for whale watching and Catalina Island excursions.

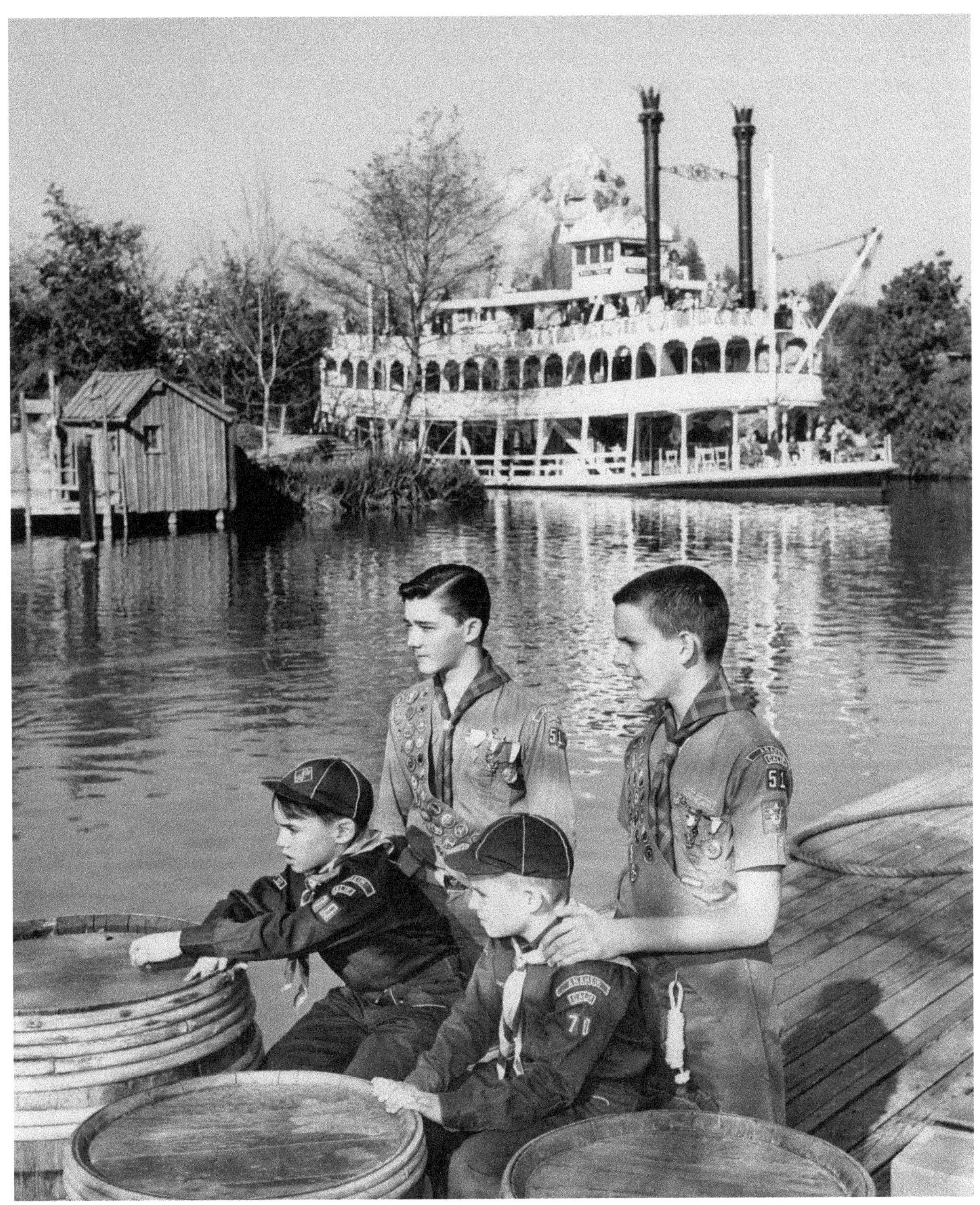

In this 1963 photograph, Anaheim Boy Scouts are participating in Scout Days at Disneyland. Walt Disney and the Boy Scouts of America had a long association. Disney was a Scout himself as a child and was later awarded the prestigious Silver Buffalo medal in 1946 for "contributing to the joy of youth in every land . . . and the elevation of their standards of good taste." Other awardees that day included General Dwight D. Eisenhower and Admiral Chester W. Nimitz.

Sleeping Beauty's Castle at Disneyland, shown here in 1965, was modeled in part on Germany's Neuschwanstein Castle. A crenellated confection of dusty rose and teal, the castle is 77 feet tall and has a working drawbridge that has only been raised twice—when the park opened in 1955 and when Fantasyland was rededicated in 1983. Each of the four Disney parks is laid out around a central castle, but each castle is unique.

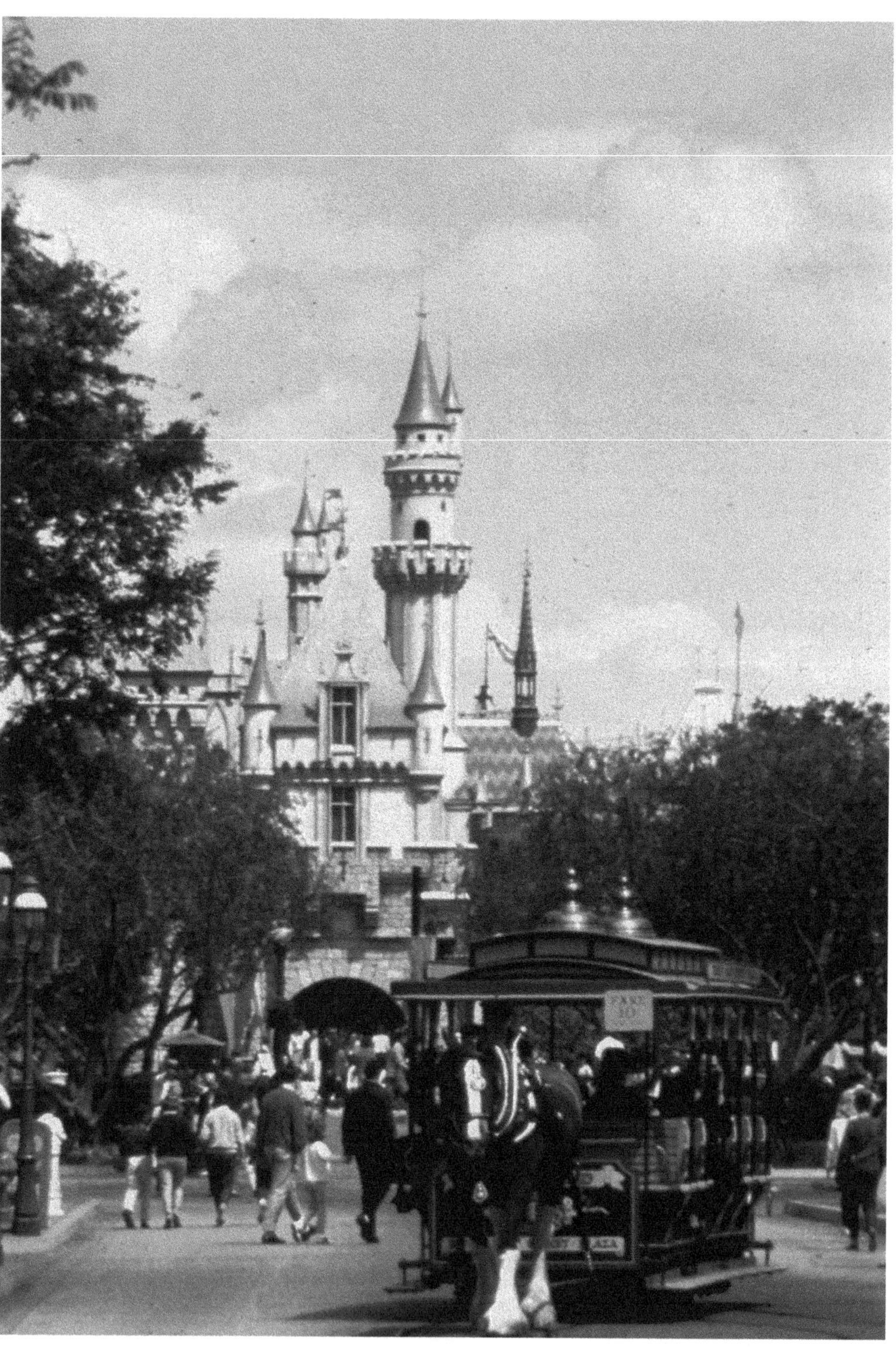

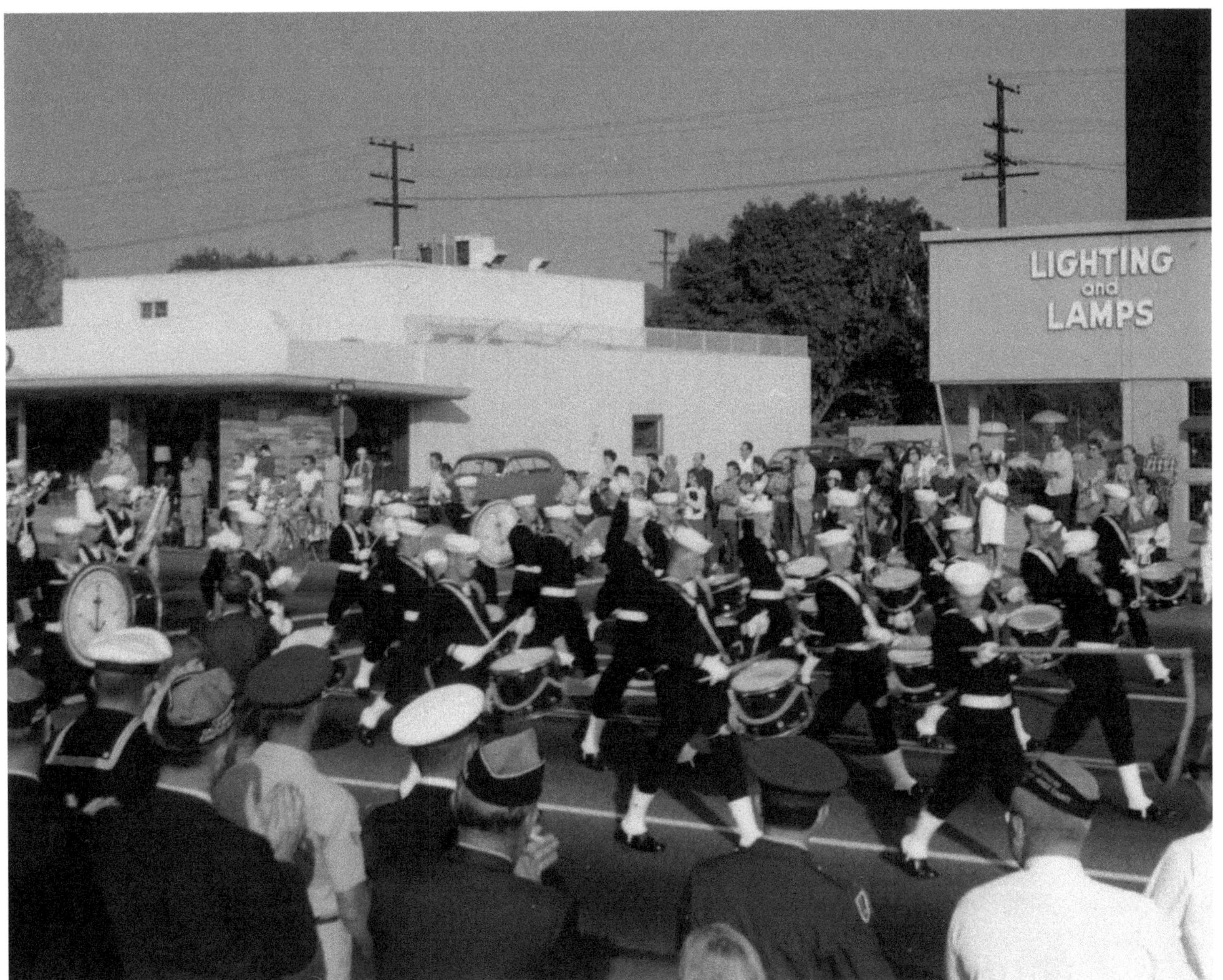

A spirited Navy band brings out the crowds for this 1967 Veteran's Day Parade on Main Street. Though the heyday of patriotic parades in Santa Ana has passed, local residents still turn out in droves to support community events such as historic home and garden tours and Artist Village open houses, and commemorate their multiracial heritage with celebrations like Chinese New Year at Bower's Museum and Mexican Cinco de Mayo at Centennial Regional Park.

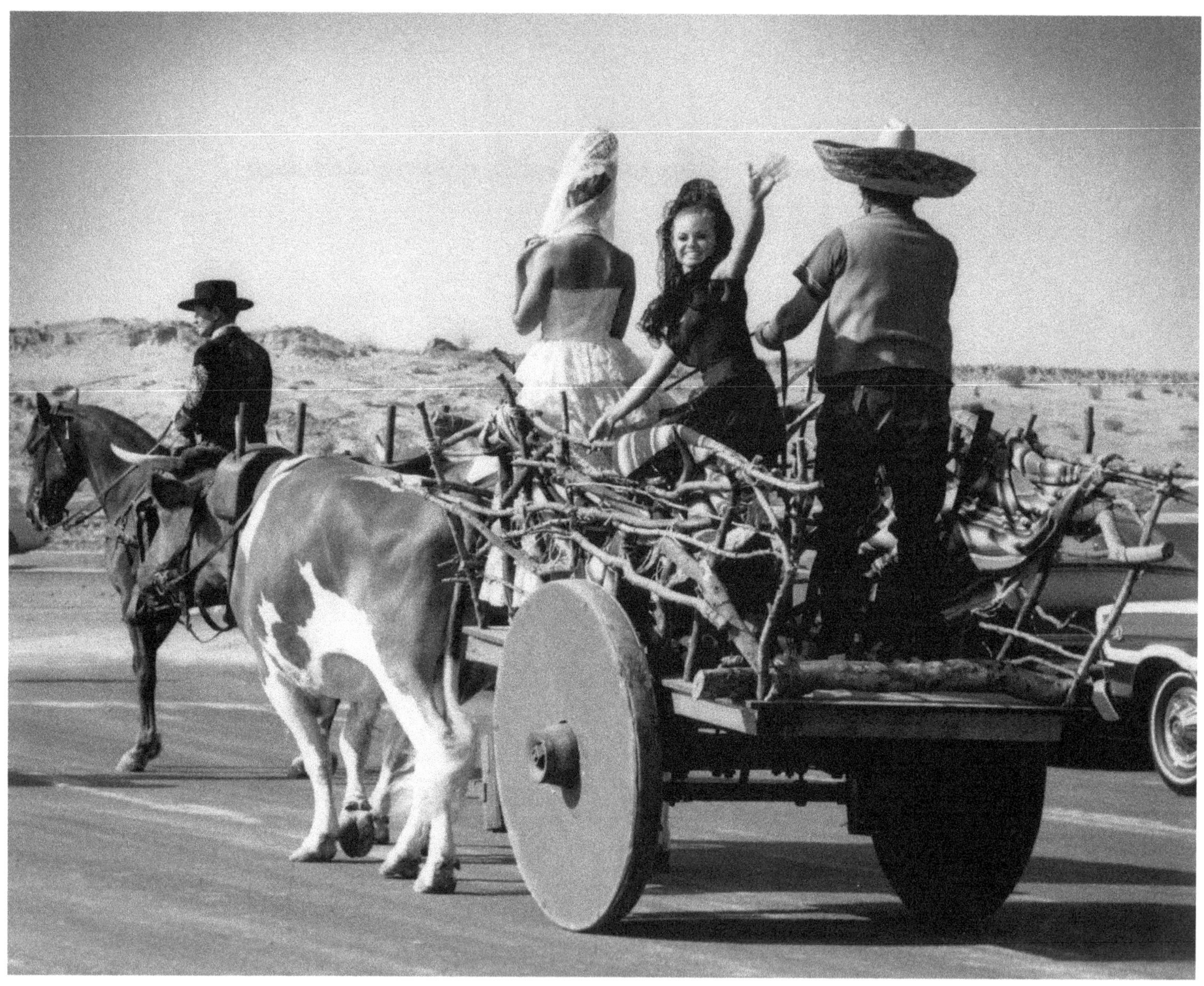

Two models dressed in costumes reminiscent of California's rancho period are shown here being pulled through the streets of Newport Beach in an ox-drawn *carretta* as part of a publicity stunt for the July 21, 1967, grand opening of the Newport Center. A business, shopping, and entertainment district featuring the upscale Fashion Island mall, Newport Center was built on the site of the 1953 Boy Scout Jamboree.

Notes on the Photographs

These notes, listed by page number, attempt to include all aspects known of the photographs. Each of the photographs is identified by the page number, photograph's title or description, photographer and collection, archive, and call or box number when applicable. Although every attempt was made to collect all available data, in some cases complete data was unavailable due to the age and condition of some of the photographs and records.

II **Newport Harbor**
Courtesy of OC Parks

VI **Beet Dump**
Courtesy of Orange County Archives

X **Santa Ana, Fourth Street**
Courtesy of Orange County Archives

2 **Mission San Juan Capistrano**
Courtesy of Orange County Archives

3 **Bank of Orange**
Courtesy of Orange County Archives

4 **McPherson Brothers Packinghouse**
Courtesy of Orange County Archives

5 **Buena Park Pacific Creamery Company**
First American Corporation

6 **W. C. Young and Company General Blacksmithing**
First American Corporation
FAC-SA4839

7 **C. E. French**
First American Corporation
FAC-SA2485

8 **City of Orange**
Courtesy of Orange County Archives

9 **The Rochester Hotel**
First American Corporation
FAC-OR1057

10 **Laguna Beach's Yoch Hotel**
Courtesy of Orange County Archives

11 **San Juan Hot Springs**
Courtesy of Orange County Archives

12 **Parade Participants**
First American Corporation
FAC-SA366

13 **Drill Team**
First American Corporation
FAC-SA4609

14 **McFadden Wharf**
Courtesy of Sherman Library

15 **Newport Beach Village**
Courtesy of Orange County Archives

16 **Horse Team Hauling Hay**
Courtesy of Orange County Archives

17 **Women Marching Down Fourth Street**
First American Corporation
FAC-SA480

18 **Talbott and Smith Shop**
Courtesy of Orange County Archives

20 **First County Offices**
Courtesy of Orange County Archives

22 **Auction at Talbert Ranch**
Courtesy of Orange County Archives

23 **Talbert Auction**
Courtesy of Orange County Archives

24 **Mountain View School**
Courtesy of Orange County Archives

25 **Buena Park Schoolhouse**
Courtesy of Orange County Archives

26 **Reis Residence**
Courtesy of Orange County Archives

27 **Joseph Young's Winery**
Courtesy of Orange County Archives

28 **Garden Grove School**
Courtesy of Orange County Archives

29 **First Christian Church**
Courtesy of Orange County Archives

30 **Boston and Narragansett Fishing Club**
First American Corporation
FAC-NB4846

31 **McFadden's Hardware On Fourth Street**
First American Corporation
FAC-SA139

32 **Downtown Anaheim**
Courtesy of Orange County Archives

33 **The "Tally Ho" Bus**
First American Corporation
FAC-SA396

34 **Commercial Building on Main Street**
Courtesy of Orange County Archives

35 **Railroad Crew**
Courtesy of Orange County Archives

36 **Hot Air Balloon**
First American Corporation
FAC-SA4172

37 **McFadden Wharf**
First American Corporation
FAC-NB5010

38 **Celery Fields Near Westminster**
First American Corporation

39 **Three Women Posing by Natural Rock Foundation**
First American Corporation
FAC-LB1670

40 **Apricot-Picking Camp**
Courtesy of Orange County Archives

41 **First National Bank Building**
Courtesy of Orange County Archives

42 **The John Martin Store**
Courtesy of Orange County Archives

43 **Courthouse Construction**
Courtesy of Orange County Archives

44 **Methodist Auditorium**
Courtesy of Orange County Archives

45 **Huntington Beach Tents**
Courtesy of Orange County Archives

46 **GAR Tent City Banner**
Courtesy of Orange County Archives

47 **Tent City Gathering**
Courtesy of Orange County Archives

48 **GAR at Huntington Beach**
Courtesy of Orange County Archives

49 **Huntington Beach News**
Courtesy of Orange County Archives

50 **J. E. Taylor Canning Company**
First American Corporation
FAC-SA2551

51 **Parade of Products**
First American Corporation
FAC-SA384

52 **WCTU Parade Float**
Courtesy of Orange County Archives

53 **Buena Park General Store**
First American Corporation

54 **Young Ladies on Bicycles**
Courtesy of Orange County Archives

55 **Balboa and Railcar**
Courtesy of Orange County Archives

56 **Downtown Orange**
Courtesy of Orange County Archives

57 **The Orange Dummy**
Courtesy of Orange County Archives

58 **The Orange Dummy**
First American Corporation
FAC-SA303

59 **Outing on Balboa**
First American Corporation
FAC-NB8432

60 **Couple in Surf**
Courtesy of Orange County Archives

61 **Chili Peppers**
Courtesy of Orange County Archives

62 **Parade of Products**
Courtesy of Orange County Archives

63 **Bird's-eye View of Santa Ana**
Courtesy of Orange County Archives

64 **Fourth and Main**
Courtesy of Orange County Archives

65 **John Sebastian's Confectionery and Fruit Store**
First American Corporation
FAC-SA6828

66 **Harvesting Sugar Beets**
Courtesy of Orange County Archives

67 **Drying Apricots**
Courtesy of Orange County Archives

68 **Birch Park**
Courtesy of Orange County Archives

69 **Vacationers and Day-trippers on Newport Beach**
First American Corporation
FAC-NB2262

70 **Street Fair at Night**
Courtesy of Orange County Archives

72 **En Route to Talbert Beet Dump**
Courtesy of Orange County Archives

73 **Men Modeling Latest Swim Togs**
First American Corporation
FAC-LB1795

74 **Frozen Fountain**
Courtesy of Orange County Archives

75 **Buena Park Southern Pacific Depot**
First American Corporation

76 **Picnic Grounds atop Victor Hugo Point**
First American Corporation
FAC-LB1540

77 **San Juan Capistrano Ruins**
Courtesy of Orange County Archives

78 **Campers on Newport Beach**
First American Corporation
FAC-NB4437

79 **Flood**
Courtesy of Orange County Archives

80 **World War I Bond Drive**
First American Corporation
FAC-OR8100

81 **First Cooking Class**
First American Corporation
FAC-SA581

82 **The Mission Woolen Manufacturing Company**
First American Corporation
FAC-SA2672

84 **South Glassell**
Courtesy of Orange County Archives

85 **Yorba Linda Garage and Blacksmith**
Courtesy of Orange County Archives

86 **Olinda**
Courtesy of Orange County Archives

87 **Laguna Beach**
First American Corporation
FAC-LB1879

88 **Downtown Brea**
First American Corporation

89 **Orange Plaza**
Courtesy of Orange County Archives

90 **Child at Plaza Fountain**
Courtesy of Orange County Archives

91 **Early Film Set on Laguna Beach**
Courtesy of Orange County Archives

92 **La Habra**
Courtesy of Orange County Archives

93 **Two Children Enjoying an Ice Cream Cone**
First American Corporation
FAC-NB5771

94 **Campers on Aliso Beach**
First American Corporation
FAC-LB1678

95 **Temporary Fireworks Store**
First American Corporation
FAC-LB-1521

96 **Talbert #1 Oil Rig**
Courtesy of Orange County Archives

97 **Cabrillo Ballroom**
First American Corporation

98 **Scouts Pulling Elks Float**
Courtesy of Orange County Archives

99 **Diver's Cove**
First American Corporation
FAC-LB1575

100 **Fourth and Ross**
Courtesy of Orange County Archives

101 **Bicycles**
First American Corporation
FAC-SA8782

102 **Fox West Coast Theater**
Courtesy of Orange County Archives

103 **Fox West Coast Theater at Night**
First American Corporation
FAC-SA8832

104 **Children Playing on Seesaw at Newport Beach**
First American Corporation
FAC-NB5219

105 **The Pavilion**
First American Corporation
FAC-NB9696

106 **Pacific Electric Red Car**
First American Corporation
FAC-SA2565

107 **Dana Point**
Courtesy of Orange County Archives

108 **Cabrillo Ballroom**
First American Corporation
FAC-LB1880

109 **Shop Clerk**
First American Corporation
FAC-SA2384

110 **Motorcyle Police Officer**
First American Corporation
FAC-SA8293

111 **Fourth Street in Santa Ana at Night**
First American Corporation
FAC-SA7768

112 **Brea Canyon**
Courtesy of Orange County Archives

113 **Huntington Beach Derricks**
Courtesy of Orange County Archives

114 **Capistrano Beach**
Courtesy of Orange County Archives

115 **Goodyear Blimp**
First American Corporation
FAC-NB11619

116 **Newport Beach Crowd**
First American Corporation
FAC-NB8424

117 Orange County Title Company
Courtesy of Orange County Archives

118 Santa Ana Breakfast Club
First American Corporation
FAC-SA2728

119 East Fourth Street
Courtesy of Orange County Archives

120 Dumping Booze
Courtesy of Orange County Archives

121 Pacific Coast Highway
First American Corporation
FAC-LB1623

122 Motorcycle Races
Courtesy of Orange County Archives

123 Motorcycle Races
Courtesy of Orange County Archives

124 The Arches
First American Corporation
FAC-NB989

125 Laguna Beach Police Officer
First American Corporation
FAC-LB1802

126 Earthquake Damage
Courtesy of Orange County Archives

127 Earthquake Damage
Courtesy of Orange County Archives

128 Haley Building Damage
Courtesy of Orange County Archives

129 Rossmore Hotel
Courtesy of Orange County Archives

130 Santa Ana Earthquake Damage
Courtesy of Orange County Archives

131 Midway City Volunteer Fire Fighters
Courtesy of Orange County Archives

132 Laguna Beach Coastline
Courtesy of Orange County Archives

133 Sailboats at Newport Beach
First American Corporation
FAC-NB2182

134 Newport's Dory Fleet
First American Corporation
FAC-NB5240

135 Bathhouses
First American Corporation
FAC-NB5338

136 February 1938 Flood
Courtesy of Orange County Archives

137 Anaheim During the Flood
Courtesy of Orange County Archives

138 Flooded Buena Park
Courtesy of Orange County Archives

139 President Franklin D. Roosevelt
First American Corporation
FAC-LB1829

140 Fun Zone on Balboa
Frst American Corporation
FAC-NB7503

141 Miss Santa Ana Endurance Flight
Courtesy of Orange County Archives

142 Laguna Beach View
Courtesy of Orange County Archives

143 View of Beach from Las Brisas Restaurant
First American Corporation
FAC-LB1854

144 Santa Ana Sign
Courtesy of Orange County Archives

145 Garden Grove Earthquake Damage
Courtesy of Orange County Archives

146 First National Bank of Orange
Courtesy of Orange County Archives

147 Sportland
First American Corporation
FAC-NB10807

148 Corona Del Mar
Courtesy of Orange County Archives

149 Flight of the Snowbirds
Courtesy of Orange County Archives

150 Storm Aftermath on Sunset Beach
Courtesy of Orange County Archives

151 Spurgeon Building
First American Corporation
FAC-SA2538

152 Corona Del Mar
First American Corporation
FAC-NB9722

153 Weatherly House of La Palma
Courtesy of Orange County Archives

154 Aerial View of Downtown Santa Ana
Courtesy of Orange County Archives

155 Marine Corps Air Station El Toro
Courtesy of Orange County Archives

156 Glassell Street
Courtesy of Orange County Archives

158 South Coast Boat Building Company
First American Corporation
FAC-NB8094

160 Laguna Beach During Christmas
Courtesy of Orange County Archives

161 Placentia Pioneer Valencia Growers Association
First American Corporation

162 Snow at Orange Union High School
Courtesy of Orange County Archives

163 Leo Carrillo
Courtesy of Orange County Archives

164 Corona Del Mar
Courtesy of Orange County Archives

165 Balboa Island Christmas Decorations
Courtesy of Orange County Archives

166 Ghost Town
Courtesy of Orange County Archives

167 Balboa Angling Club
First American Corporation
FAC-NB8015

168 Single-Engine Piper at Orange County Airport
Courtesy of Orange County Archives

169 James Cagney's Swift
Courtesy of Orange County Archives

170 Drag Races
Courtesy of Orange County Archives

171 Balboa Island
First American Corporation
FAC-NB8010

172 Jamboree Blanket Toss
Courtesy of Orange County Archives

173 Jamboree Sea Base Kitchen
Courtesy of Orange County Archives

174 SSS Valencian
Courtesy of Orange County Archives

175 Hotel Laguna
Courtesy of Orange County Archives

176 St. Joseph's Hospital
First American Corporation
FAC-OR10791

177 Alligator Farm
Courtesy of Orange County Archives

178 Emerald Bay
Courtesy of Orange County Archives

179 Doheny Beach
Courtesy of Orange County Archives

180 El Modena Branch Library
Courtesy of Orange County Archives

181 Bonanza Plane
Courtesy of Orange County Archives

182 Disneyland
Courtesy of Phil Brigandi

183 Cypress Police Department
First American Corporation

184 San Juan Capistrano
Courtesy of Orange County Archives

185 Balboa Pavilion
First American Corporation
FAC-NB3458

186 Disneyland Entrance
Courtesy of Orange County Archives

187 Los Alamitos on Katella Avenue
Courtesy of Orange County Archives

188 First National Bank of Orange
First American Corporation
FAC-OR2369

189 Santa Ana County Courthouse
First American Corporation
FAC-SA6499

190 Los Angeles Airways Helicopter Service
Courtesy of Orange County Archives

191 Newport Sea Base
Courtesy of Orange County Archives

192 Citizenship
Courtesy of Orange County Archives

193 Citrus Grove
Courtesy of Orange County Archives

194 Balboa Island Ferry
First American Corporation
FAC-NB6563

195 Dory Fishermen
First American Corporation
FAC-NB5704

196 Balboa Pavilion
First American Corporation
FAC-NB6486

197 Scout Days at Disneyland
Courtesy of Orange County Archives

198 Sleeping Beauty's Castle
Courtesy of Orange County Archives

199 Veteran's Day Parade
Courtesy of Orange County Archives

200 Two Models in an Ox-drawn Carretta
First American Corporation
FAC-NB4569

HISTORIC PHOTOS OF ORANGE COUNTY

Perpetual sunshine, palm trees, miles of unbroken beaches, yachts, cliff-top mansions, millionaires—these are the images of Orange County that come to mind for many people, and there is much truth in this depiction, for Orange County is a place of boundless natural wonders that attracts more than 25 million tourists a year.

However, the full story of Orange County is far more complex. It's a story of Juañeno Indians, conquistadors, Franciscan padres, rancheros, wildcatters, artists, and filmmakers. *Historic Photos of Orange County* offers some 200 images drawn from the county's fascinating past, from the mission ruins of San Juan Capistrano, to the turn-of-the-century celery fields of Westminster, to the eye-popping fantasia of a young Disneyland.

By East Coast standards, Orange County is a relative baby—just over a century old—and tiny compared to most California counties; but its population is second only to neighboring Los Angeles County and growing every day. This volume captures the story of Orange County's evolution from a sleepy backwater suburb of Los Angeles to an international tourist destination.

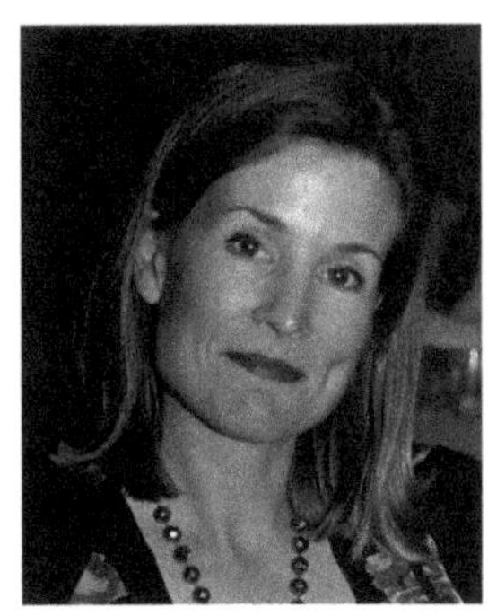

A 20-year resident of Orange County, Leslie Anne Stone received her master's degree in art history in 2007 from California State University, Long Beach. Stone developed an interest in local history while researching her thesis on the architecture of Buena Park's mid-century theme parks. She does volunteer work for the Buena Park Historical Society and the Earl Burns Miller Japanese Garden at CSULB. A member of Orange County Fine Arts, Stone is also an accomplished portrait artist and has been featured in numerous local publications and art shows.

WWW.TURNERPUBLISHING.COM

www.ingramcontent.com/pod-product-compliance
Lightning Source LLC
LaVergne TN
LVHW060606110826
845154LV00003B/43

9781684420292